Reforming Capital Income Taxation

Edited by Horst Siebert

Institut für Weltwirtschaft an der Universität Kiel

Routledge
Taylor & Francis Group
LONDON AND NEW YORK

First published 1990 by Westview Press

Published 2019 by Routledge
52 Vanderbilt Avenue, New York, NY 10017
2 Park Square, Milton Park, Abingdon, Oxon OX14 4RN

Routledge is an imprint of the Taylor & Francis Group, an informa business

CIP-Titelaufnahme der Deutschen Bibliothek

Reforming capital income taxation / Institut für Weltwirtschaft an der Universität Kiel. Ed. by Horst Siebert. - Tübingen : Mohr, 1990

NE: Siebert, Horst [Hrsg.]

ISBN 13: 978-0-367-28538-8 (hbk)
ISBN 13: 978-0-367-30084-5 (pbk)

Contents

III. The Harmonization Issue

IV. Restructuring Capital Income Taxation

Preface

In a world of highly integrated goods and capital markets, countries are linked not only by the cross-border transactions of private agents but also by their economic policies. The tax policy of one country affects economic activity and tax policies in other countries. With the world facing increased capital mobility and with the EC in the process of completing its Internal Market, capital income taxation in particular has to be reconsidered and analyzed in greater detail, theoretically as well as empirically. The impact of capital income taxation on capital flows, the need for tax harmonization and policy options for reforming the systems currently in existence represent important issues of economic policy in the industrialized countries. These are the topics addressed in this volume, which contains the papers of a conference held at the Institute of World Economics, 7-8 December 1989.

In the first paper of this volume, Giovannini surveys the theoretical issues that characterize the problem of reforming capital income taxes in an open economy. He describes the distortions to savings and investment induced by capital income taxes in the presence of international capital mobility. The imperfect integration of corporate income taxes and individual taxes, together with the imperfect application of the residence principle of taxation both at the individual and at the corporate level, generate distortions in the international allocation of capital. Giovannini outlines some alternative strategies for reform and discusses particularly the choice of the source principle versus the residence principle for taxing capital income.

Slemrod, in his paper, explores the tax incentives and disincentives to investment in an open economy framework allowing cross-border portfolio and direct investment. Slemrod uses his conceptual framework to analyze the impact of the 1986 US Tax Reform Act on direct investment from the US to Europe and vice versa.

Sinn contributes to the debate on the effects of the major direct and indirect taxes on international competitiveness. He studies the conditions necessary for the tax system to exhibit competitive neutrality in a model of international trade and capital movements. Competitive neutrality means that the tax system induces neither international capital movements nor the current account imbalances caused by these movements. Sinn concludes that it may well be the case that direct and indirect taxes counteract each other, so that a country with a high value-added tax rate needs a high capital income tax rate as well if it wants to maintain its international competitiveness.

Levich and Walter concentrate on the developments in the financial markets. Because of innovations during the recent years, communication costs and financial transaction costs are lower and capital mobility is higher than ever before. Using the concept of the net regulatory burden, the authors demonstrate the effects of taxes and non-tax regulations on the spatial allocation decisions of financial corporations, especially on the evolution of financial centers in Europe. They argue that it is becoming less feasible for a country to impose financial market regulations or taxes on capital market transactions if such regulations or taxes differ greatly from those of other major countries.

Schlesinger shows how the introduction and abolition of a withholding tax on interest income in the Federal Republic of Germany in 1989 influenced capital flows between Germany and other countries. The effects on the exchange rates and the interest rates are dealt with in some detail.

The topic of the paper by Gros is tax-evasion-motivated financial intermediation through offshore centers. Gros develops a model of costly tax evasion to evaluate the effects of (withholding) taxes on interest income from financial intermediation in offshore centers, on the interest rate differential between offshore and domestic markets, and on the total tax revenue that can be collected from interest income.

The subsequent four papers focus on the question of tax harmonization in the EC countries or the world on the whole. The paper by Frenkel, Razin and Symansky addresses itself to the global dynamic effects of VAT harmonization. Using dynamic simulations they analyze the consequences of revenue-neutral VAT harmonization in a two-country model of the world economy. They argue that the quantitative effects of VAT harmonization on key economic variables are very significant. As the effects are not spread evenly across income groups, generations and countries, different conflicts of interest can emerge. These conflicts might be solved by a transfer system in which those who gain from harmonization compensate the losers.

Razin and Sadka focus on the issues of international taxation that capital market integration brings up. They conclude that if countries are not able to effectively tax their residents on capital income earned abroad, tax competition leads to a full exemption from tax for the mobile factor capital. No gains relative to the competitive outcome can be obtained from capital income tax harmonization.

The paper by Tanzi and Bovenberg deals with the question of whether there is a need for ex ante harmonization of capital income taxes between EC countries or whether tax competition should be allowed. The authors point out that the answer depends to a large extent on political views, e.g., one's perspective of the adequate level of public expenditure and one's assessment of the working of the political process. They argue that some kind of concerted harmonization is needed. Otherwise the allocation of capital across countries would be inefficient; countries with high public expenditures might be forced to reduce these expenditures below the level preferred by their electorates. The view put forth by Tanzi and Bovenberg is contradicted by other participants. They hold that institutional competition, especially tax competition, between EC member countries does not lead to zero production of public goods. Tax competition would result in tax systems and expenditure levels that are more in line with the preferences of the citizens of the member countries and thus would increase economic welfare.

Cnossen discusses the principles that should govern the coordination of the taxes levied in the EC member states. He develops some arguments for tax diversity instead of tax uniformity. He points to the actual tax practices in federal countries such as the United States, Canada and Switzerland that show that subnational tax systems can differ widely from one another without being incompatible with the functioning of the domestic market.

Odling-Smee and Lawton provide an overview of the British tax system as it now stands, after the numerous reform measures taken in the course of the 1980s. These measures and the reasoning behind them (e.g., raising efficiency) are described in detail. The authors comment on the effects of tax reform on the economy, especially on the GNP growth and on the development of capital income as well as capital income tax receipts. Finally, they address the lessons which can be drawn from the UK experience.

Schneider's paper is essentially concerned with the German system of capital income taxation. He discusses how the German tax law affects entrepreneurial decisions concerning investment and finance and how it distorts market allocation processes.

Policy options for the Federal Republic of Germany are the focal point of the paper contributed by Boss. He advocates a revision of the German tax system towards a system that taxes consumption only instead of consumption as well as income and property. This might be achieved by a process of reducing taxes on capital income and business property while simultaneously cutting government expenditures, especially subsidies that impede economic efficiency and weaken competition.

The Institute is indebted to the participants of the conference for their contributions to a stimulating and sometimes heated discussion. We owe thanks to the Landeszentralbank Schleswig-Holstein for its hospitality. Alfred Boss and Vera Draack ensured that the conference was prepared and organized efficiently. Dietmar Gebert and Paul Kramer deserve acknowledgement for their editorial expertise. Finally, thanks are also due to Lisa Eckeberg for managing the more technical aspects of implementing our new publishing system, and to Nicole Petersohn and Kerstin Stark for the practical implementation.

Kiel, September 1990

Horst Siebert

I

Allocation and Taxation

Alberto Giovannini

Reforming Capital Income Taxation in the Open Economy: Theoretical Issues

1. Introduction

To a large extent, the international institutions of the postwar period have been shaped by economists. The international monetary system, the International Monetary Fund (IMF) and the World Bank, as well as the General Agreement on Tariffs and Trade (GATT), have all been inspired by mainstream economic liberalism. Economic thought has contributed especially to the field of trade negotiations. Few propositions have received wider professional support than that of the superiority of free trade, and at the same time few ideas have had more impact on the policies followed by scores of countries — despite the strong opposition by local pressure groups, and justifiably so.

Economists can offer another very substantial contribution in the area of taxation of capital income. This opportunity results from the historical evolution of tax laws and international capital markets.

During the era of the gold standard, international capital markets were relatively unincumbered. In the interwar period, on the other hand, they were subject to the most severe forms of restrictions. These restrictions were motivated in part by the inward-looking or beggar-thy-neighbor policies followed by many governments, and in part by the need for tax revenue. Precarious public finances and the military buildup led governments to limit the international mobility of capital, to facilitate its taxation, which in many countries came in the form of capital levies.[1] Indeed, controls on international capital flows became a necessary condition for insuring a stable base to capital levies.

At that time when confiscatory taxation and political persecutions went hand in hand, the modern "free financial centers" were born: Switzerland promulgated the *Federal Law Relating to Banks and Savings Banks* — the bank secrecy law — in November 1934, in order to protect German Jews from the attempts of Nazi agents

---

1 See Eichengreen [1989] and Giovannini [1988a]. In Italy, after 1938, transgressors of capital controls faced capital punishment.

to seize their assets. Years after, the Swiss law was copied by many countries, at a time when political persecutions were no more the issue.[2]

Unlike international trade restrictions, secrecy laws and capital controls have, to some extent, survived World War II and have characterized international capital markets in the last 40 years. The development of offshore markets was the typical outcome of an environment characterized by the coexistence of strict controls and the tolerance of tax and regulatory evasion through offshore centers. Additional relevant phenomena were the lack of cooperation among industrialized countries' governments in the field of tax enforcement, the generalized reliance on source taxation as the only form of taxation capable of insuring some revenue and the disastrous failure of individual countries' attempts at unilaterally increasing capital taxation (a good example of this is West Germany's recent experience in attempting to levy a withholding tax on interest).

The liberalization of European financial markets is likely to remove one of the two pillars of this postwar construction, and might, as a result, make it crumble: in the absence of capital controls the avoidance of taxes on capital income will be much easier. For this reason, the debate on possible reforms has recently been revived, even though European governments and the European Commission do not appear inclined to act quickly, perhaps because of the pervasiveness of the administrative and political constraints they face.

In this paper I survey the theoretical issues that characterize the problem of reforming capital income taxes in an open economy by collecting and discussing previous results of mine [Giovannini, 1988b; 1989], together with other current developments in the literature. I also try to highlight the important questions that are yet unanswered in the literature. Section 2 describes the distortions on savings and investment induced by capital income taxes in the presence of international capital mobility. Section 3 surveys the complications arising from the lack of integration of individual income and corporate income for tax purposes, with special reference to the laws currently enforced in Europe. Section 4 raises the question of the effects of taxes on international financial intermediation. Finally, Section 5 outlines alternative strategies for reform.

2. Savings-Investment Distortions

In the standard welfare analyses of capital income taxes in a closed economy [see, for example, Diamond, 1970], investment distortions equal savings distortions, since equilibrium in the goods markets requires the ex post equalization of savings and investment. This is not the case in the open economy, where savings and

---

2 See, for example, the secrecy laws in the Netherlands Antilles.

investment are equalized only over time (through the intertemporal budget constraint), but countries can engage in asset trade with the rest of the world. The analysis of the welfare effects of capital income taxes in the open economy thus becomes a comparison of savings taxation and investment taxation.

Indeed, the systems of capital income taxation currently in existence are a combination of two "pure" principles of taxation that reflect the distinction between savings and investment in an open economy: the *source* principle and the *residence* principle. According to the source principle, capital income is taxed only in the countries where it is produced: hence, foreign-source income is tax-exempt. By contrast, according to the residence principle, capital income is taxed by the country of residence of the investor: double taxation is avoided by granting credits against foreign taxes paid. Under the source principle, capital income is taxed at different rates in different countries, while under the residence principle, capital income is taxed at the same rate everywhere. In other words, in the first case, taxes provide incentives that affect decisions to allocate international investments; in the second case the location of investments does not affect taxes paid, i.e., international investment decisions are not distorted by taxes. According to the pure residence principle only savings are taxed, while according to the pure source principle *both* savings and investments are taxed. In the case where the investor has access to tax havens, the source principle exempts savings from taxes.

The welfare analysis of savings and investment distortions can be illustrated by considering separately the case of a small country facing a given world rate of interest, and the case of many countries whose joint actions affect the world rate of interest.

a. Small Country Case

The analysis of a small country makes use of the standard Fisherian graph portraying optimal savings and investment decisions, reported in Figures 1 and 2 [from Giovannini, 1988b]. There are two periods, and, in the first period, private agents allocate their endowment among consumption, and domestic and foreign investments. The foreign investment yields the fixed return $R^* = 1 + r^*$, while the domestic investment technology is represented by the bowed-out production-possibilities frontier. Production uses capital and labor. Since I intend to highlight the effects of *capital* income taxation, however, I assume that the supply of labor is fixed, so that the only nontrivial choices of the private agents in the economy are the savings and portfolio-allocation choices.

The government announces taxes in period 1, and proceeds to levy them in period 2, when they finance government spending. The latter enters the utility function of consumers. Once again, since I want to concentrate on the government choices among various forms of taxation of capital income, I assume that revenue from other taxes, and especially revenue from labor-income taxes, is subject to limitations. In particular, in the figures, labor cannot be taxed at a differential rate from capital.

Figure 1 — The Economic Effects of Source-Based Taxation

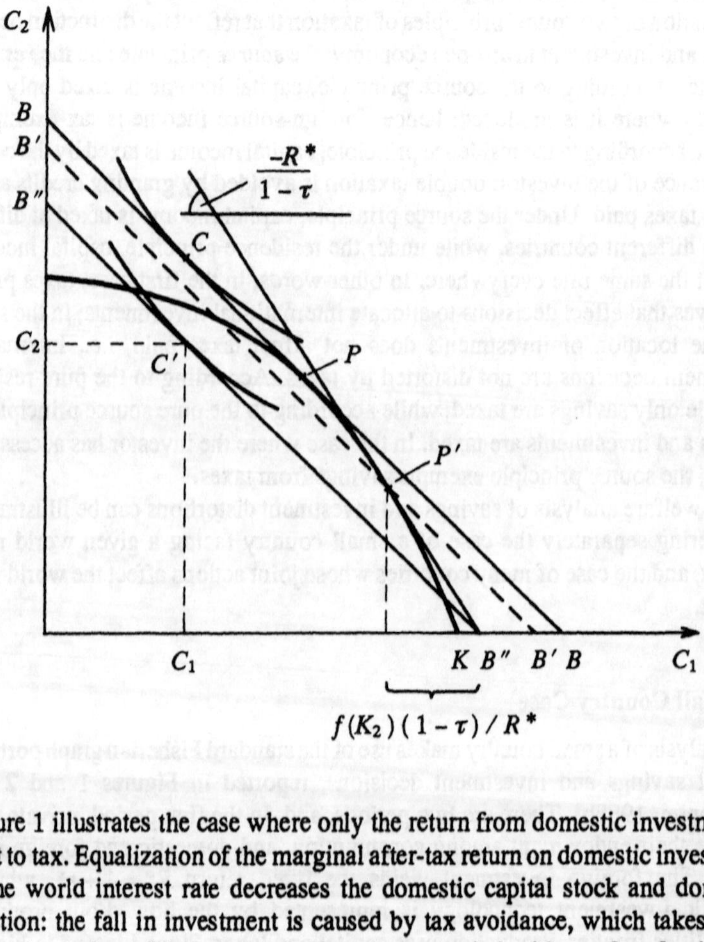

Figure 1 illustrates the case where only the return from domestic investment is subject to tax. Equalization of the marginal after-tax return on domestic investment with the world interest rate decreases the domestic capital stock and domestic production: the fall in investment is caused by tax avoidance, which takes place because domestic residents can substitute home capital with tax-free foreign securities. The production distortion originating from the tax, however, does not affect the marginal rate of substitution between present and future consumption, since the fall in domestic investment insures that the marginal return on savings is still R^*. The budget line shifts further down and to the left, from $B'B'$ to $B''B''$, since tax revenue is not rebated in a lump sum fashion to consumers, but is used to provide for utility-generating "infrastructures." At the consumption point C', the vertical distance between the lines $B'B'$ and $B''B''$ is equal to tax revenue and government spending. Consumption at time 2 is decreased accordingly for every level of investment.[3]

Figure 2 shows the case of savings taxes. The returns on domestic and foreign investment are taxed at the same rate. Investment and the domestic capital stock are unaffected by changes in the tax. Thus, international capital mobility now prevents capital income taxes from distorting the production side of the economy.[4] By contrast, the relevant rate of interest for savings is now the *after-tax* world interest rate. The line from B to B'' shows the consumption possibilities of domestic residents. At point B, first-period consumption equals the sum of the present discounted value (at world interest rates) of second-period output and the initial endowment K, second-period consumption equals zero, the revenue from taxation of domestic production offsets identically the tax rebates on foreign interest payments, and government spending is zero. The vertical distance between the line from B to B'' and the production point P is the revenue from taxation of domestic production. Equilibrium consumption, government spending, and the structure of tax revenues can be easily characterized as indicated in the figure. Line $B'B'$ shows the consumption possibilities of domestic residents before taxation of income from foreign assets. The vertical distance between BB and $B'B'$ is the revenue from the tax on domestic income, while the distance between the line from B to B'' and the $B'B'$ line is the revenue (or outlay) from foreign interest income (or payments).[5]

What are the welfare effects of the two forms of taxation? It can be shown that the relative welfare effects of savings and investment taxation depend, under the assumptions of this analysis, on the relative magnitude of the savings and investment distortions, which are proportional to the relative importance of intertemporal substitution in consumption and the substitution of domestic and foreign investment. A "consensus" view on the empirical magnitude of these parameters suggests that source taxation should be welfare-inferior to residence taxation.

The superiority of taxation of savings is generalized under the assumption that the government faces no constraints in the menu of taxes it can levy, even if all of the taxable commodities are elastically supplied. In that case, the well-known *production efficiency* theorem [Diamond, Mirrlees, 1971] implies that the optimal menu of taxes does not induce distortions between the domestic marginal rate of transformation of any two commodities and their world relative price; hence, the

---

3 If present and future consumptions refer to normal goods, an increase in τ increases savings, whereas savings decrease if future consumption is an inferior good. Since the no-arbitrage condition insures that the rate of return on savings is unchanged, savings are affected here exclusively by the income effect of the tax increase.

4 Notice that this would not happen in a closed economy; see, for example, Diamond [1970].

5 In the absence of international investment for tax avoidance, intertemporal substitutability in consumption tends to decrease savings, while the income effect — if C_1 and C_2 are normal goods — increases savings. Thus, the response of savings to an increase in the tax rate is ambiguous, because of conflicting income and substitution effects.

Figure 2 — The Economic Effects of Residence-Based Taxation

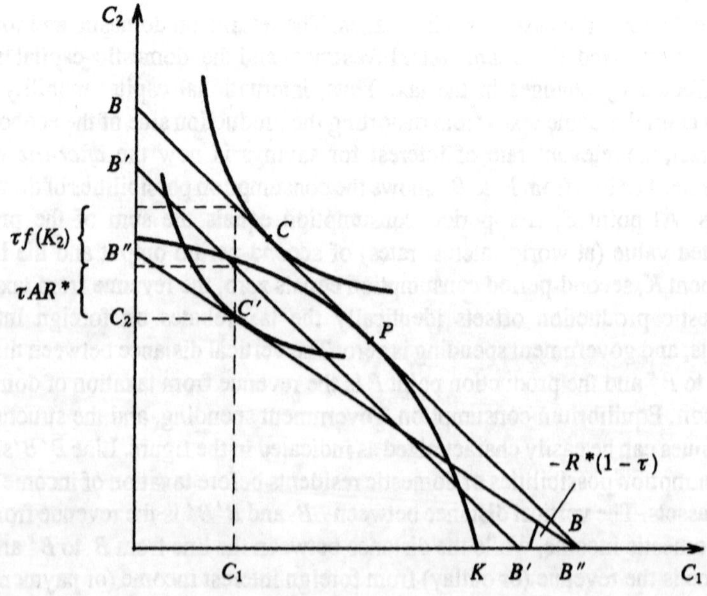

marginal productivity of domestic investment has to equal the world real rate of interest [Razin, Sadka, 1988; 1989].

b. World Equilibrium and Tax Competition

To highlight the externalities arising from tax-policy interactions, it is convenient to assume that a "world" economy is populated by many identical countries. The countries are too small to affect, on their own, the world rate of interest, although the world rate of interest is indeed determined by their interactions. The nature of the externalities generated by noncooperative tax setting is studied under two assumptions: that all countries set taxes on savings independently and that all countries set taxes on domestic investment income independently. The analysis, however, starts with the benchmark case of "tax coordination": a central planner sets taxes in all countries to maximize a weighted average of their welfare.

When the setting of capital income taxes is coordinated, the problem is to maximize a weighted average of individual countries' welfare, subject to the constraint that, in the aggregate, the current account is zero. Since countries are identical, this problem can be transformed into that of maximizing an individual (representative) country's welfare, under the condition of no borrowing and lending. Formally, the problem can be stated as follows:

$$[1] \quad \max_{\tau} U(C_1, C_2) + v(G),$$

subject to:

$$[2] \quad C_1 + K_2 = K$$

$$[3] \quad C_2 = f(K_2)(1-\tau)$$

$$[4] \quad G = \tau f(K_2)$$

$$[5] \quad U_1(C_1, C_2) = (1-\tau) f'(K_2) U_2(C_1, C_2).$$

The private sector's optimal decision rule (a constraint on the tax authority) is [5]. The subscripts of the utility function indicate the partial derivatives with respect to first- and second-period consumption, respectively.

The first-order conditions of problem [1]–[5] yield the following:

$$[6] \quad U_2(C_1, C_2) = [1 + \tau \frac{f'(K_2)}{f(K_2)} \frac{dK_2}{d\tau}] v'(G).$$

The expression in square brackets in [6] is less than 1, since an increase in the tax rate decreases first-period investment, thus increasing the gross rate of return of capital. If the supply of capital is fixed, the optimal level of government spending is chosen so that its marginal utility equals the marginal utility of consumption at time 2. With an elastic supply of investment, taxes are chosen so that the marginal utility of government spending at time 2 *exceeds* the marginal utility of consumption. Notice that the optimal (coordinated) taxation of capital is the same under both the *territorial* and *worldwide* taxation principle, since, in the aggregate, there is no international borrowing and lending.

I now turn to the optimal taxation problem solved by individual countries in a Cournot-Nash equilibrium when the territorial principle is followed. When individual authorities set taxes independently, they do not take into account that the outflow generated by their own tax increases is a positive externality in the rest of the area. Therefore, lowering domestic tax rates and hence attracting capital from the rest of the world are beggar-thy-neighbor policies. The problem is:

$$[7] \quad \max_{\tau} U(C_1, C_2) + v(G),$$

subject to:

[8] $C_1 + K_2 + A = K$

[9] $C_2 = f(K_2)(1-\tau) + A(1+r^*)$

[10] $G = \tau f(K_2)$

[11] $f'(K_2) = (1-\tau)(1+r^*)$

[12] $U_1(C_1, C_2) = (1+r^*)\,U_2(C_1, C_2)$.

Equation [8] shows that, in every country, initial resources are used to purchase domestic capital and foreign assets. From an individual country's perspective, the world rate of return is fixed at r^*. When only income from domestic sources is taxed, consumption plans are undistorted: international portfolio diversification insures that the after-tax rate of return on all assets equals the world rate of interest (see [12] and [11]). The first-order conditions for the problem [7]–[12] yield the following equation:

[13] $U_2(C_1, C_2) = [1 + \tau \dfrac{f'(K_2)}{f(K_2)} \dfrac{dK_2}{d\tau}]\,v'G$.

The difference between [13] and [6] is in the term $dK_2/d\tau$. In the Cournot-Nash equilibrium, this term is the perceived *outflow of capital* in response to a change in the tax rate: it is obtained by differentiating [11]. By contrast, in the cooperative equilibrium, $dK_2/d\tau$ is the decrease in the capital stock in response to a change in the after-tax rate of return to savings. The closer the function $f(K_2)$ is to being linear, the larger the perceived capital outflow in response to a change in the tax rate, and hence the lower the desired tax revenue. Indeed, the perceived decrease in savings can be arbitrarily large, as $f''(K_2)$ gets arbitrarily close to zero. By contrast, with smooth convex indifference curves, a linear production function does not give rise to an infinite response of savings to the tax rate in a closed economy. Hence, in a Cournot-Nash equilibrium with territorial taxation, the equilibrium tax revenue from capital income can be far below the optimal level. This is of course the phenomenon of *tax competition*.

Consider now the case where all countries, independently, apply the worldwide principle of taxation. The problem solved by individual countries is:

[14] $\max\limits_{\tau} U(C_1, C_2) + v(G)$,

subject to:

$$[15] \quad C_1 + K_2 + A = K$$

$$[16] \quad C_2 = [f(K_2) + A(1+r^*)](1-\tau)$$

$$[17] \quad G = \tau[f(K_2) + A(1+r^*)]$$

$$[18] \quad f'(K_2) = (1+r^*)$$

$$[19] \quad U_1(C_1, C_2) = (1+r^*)(1-\tau)U_2(C_1, C_2).$$

Notice that, from an individual country's perspective, changes in the tax rate do not affect investment, which is determined, through [18], by the world rate of interest. Hence, the change in savings in response to a change in the tax rate is reflected, from an individual government's perspective, in a change in foreign asset accumulation, A. The first-order conditions for the problem [14]–[19] yield the following:

$$[20] \quad U_2(C_1, C_2) = [1 + \frac{\tau(1+r^*)}{Y_2}\frac{dA}{d\tau}]\,v'(G),$$

where $Y_2 = f(K_2) + A(1+r^*)$ is the second-period GNP, and $dA/d\tau$ is, as I argued above, the response of savings to the rate of interest. This term can be positive or negative. Hence, when all countries follow the worldwide principle, the distortions from noncooperative tax policies can lead to either excessive or too little capital tax revenue. The size of this distortion depends on the size of the response of savings to the real rate of interest. In this case, countries set taxes on savings independently, believing that the marginal productivity of capital is given, and therefore believing that taxation only affects savings and foreign asset accumulation, but not investment.

Notice that, with a small interest-rate elasticity of savings, the externality from noncooperative tax setting is proportionately small when the worldwide principle is applied by all countries. Hence, in this case, too, the superiority of residence-based taxes is established if savings — relative to international investment allocation — are little responsive to the rate of interest.

3. The Role of Firms

The models discussed above do not make any distinction between individual investors and firms. In reality, many of the interesting effects of tax laws are those on the investment policies of firms, entities that are quite separate from individual investors. The separation between corporations and individual investors could be due, in part, to informational and agency problems, but is certainly also due to the features of tax laws in most industrial countries. Virtually no country's law allows for perfect integration between the income produced within the firm and the income of individual investors.[6]

Table 1, from Giovannini and Hines [1990], describes the tax treatment of corporate profits, dividend payments and capital gains in the 12 European countries (EC–12) and reports the system of integration of corporate and individual income for tax purposes: countries adopting the *classical* system tax investment income both at the firm level and at the level of the individual investor; countries adopting the *split rate* system tax distributed profits at a lower rate than undistributed profits; and finally, countries adopting the *imputation* system provide individuals with some credit for the taxes paid by the corporations they own. As the table shows, however, such credit is often partial and differs significantly across the EC–12. The table also shows that capital gains to individuals receive preferential treatment in virtually all countries.

The information in Table 1 is complemented by the treatment of foreign source income. Table 2, from Giovannini [1989], reports the method of taxation of foreign personal and corporate income in Europe. All countries, except France, and, to some extent, the Netherlands,[7] follow the worldwide (or residence) principle.[8] These rules reflect the intent to achieve a sort of "capital export neutrality," since, as we have seen before, the application of the worldwide principle is such that the geographical allocation of investment is unaffected by taxes.

Some of the countries that tax worldwide income allow exemptions of special kinds of foreign-source income. In Belgium, if a foreign corporation is a "permanent investment" of a domestic corporation, 95 percent of its dividend income is exempted from the Belgian tax.[9] In the Netherlands, dividends of companies that qualify for the "participation exemption" are exempted. These devices are generally designed to extend the provisions to avoid double taxation of group profits to foreign subsidiaries.

The application of the worldwide principle, however, is subject to two main exceptions. First of all, countries impose a *limitation* on foreign tax credits, which is usually equal to the domestic tax rate applied to foreign-source income. The limitation has two effects: (a) whenever investors accumulate excess tax credits

---

6 This is also due to the definition of corporate income for tax purposes.

7 Where only dividends can be exempted from domestic tax if they are produced by foreign investments qualifying for the "participation exemption."

8 The criteria for determining residence in the countries included in this study differ significantly, however.

9 This proportion is 90 percent if the Belgian parent company is a holding company.

Table 1 — The Integration of Corporate and Personal Taxes in EC Countries

Country	Corporate taxes	Taxation of dividends	Taxation of capital gains	Integration regime
Belgium	Basic rate 43%	na	na	Imputation
Denmark	50% (state income tax)	Marginal ind. rate	50% on short term gains	Imputation
France	42% on distrib. profits; 39% on undistrib. profits	Marginal rate less tax credits (=50% of cash div. received)	16% if gains > F 288,400 or shares held > 25 % firm capital	Imputation
Germany	36% on distrib. profits; 50% on undistrib. profits	Divs. grossed up; credit is granted on full 36% corpor. tax	Only long-term gains (> 6 mths.) untaxed	Split rate
Greece	35-46% depending on the nature of business	Divs. of < Dr 50,000 (per shareholding) or < Dr 200,000 (overall) not taxable	Not taxable	Imputation
Ireland	43% basic rate	Tax credit on div. (28/72nds of divs. received)	short term (< 1 yr) 60%	Imputation
Italy	Basic tax 36% plus 56.25% "excess" dividend distns.[a]	Divs. received grossed up by 56.25%; credit granted at 36%; also w/h tax 10%	Not taxable unless arising from spec. intent	Imputation
Luxembourg	Progressive schedule: 20 to 34%	W/h taxes on divs. credited	Taxed at ord. rate if < 6 mths.	Classical
Netherlands	35% basic rate	Fully taxed	Not taxable unless vendor has held "substantial interest"	Classical
Portugal	36.5% basic rate	Taxed at 25%	On shares held for more than 24 mths.: 10%	Split rate
Spain	Basic rate 35%; assumed w/h rate if profits distributed	Receipts grossed up and withhold. credited	Taxed as "irregular income"	Imputation
United Kingdom	35% basic rate	Receipts taxed at individual rate	Taxed at individual rate	Imputation

[a]Dividend distributions exceeding 64% of taxable income. — w/h = withholding.

Source: For corporate taxes, taxation of dividends, taxation of individual capital gains and the integration regime for Spain: Price Waterhouse [1989a; 1989b] (local income taxes are not included); for the other integration regimes: Alworth [1988].

Table 2 — Taxation of Foreign-Source Income

Country	Individual	Corporate	
	Taxation principle	Taxation principle	Credit/Deduction
Belgium	W	W	Deduction
Denmark	W	W	Credit
France	W	T[a]	Both[a,b]
West Germany	W	W	Both[b]
Greece	W	W	Credit
Ireland	W	W	Credit
Italy	W	W	Credit[c]
Luxembourg	W	W	Both[b]
Netherlands	W	W[d]	Exemption
Portugal	W	W	Credit
Spain	W	W	Credit
UK	W	W	Either

[a]In general, France does not allow any tax credits against foreign income taxes paid on the business income of foreign permanent establishments. However, the territorial principle applies only to the income of foreign permanent establishments. It does not apply to foreign-sourced dividends or interest, which are subject to French corporate tax when realized, and for which a foreign tax credit may offset French taxes. — [b]Taxes paid abroad in excess of the allowable credit are deductible as expenses. — [c]The taxpayer is entitled to a refund of the excess foreign tax credit. — [d]Resident corporations often receive proportionate relief for taxable income in other countries, granted by way of unilateral relief (see discussion of the "participation exemption"). — Note that W stands for "worldwide" and T for "territorial."

Source: Price Waterhouse [1989a; 1989b].

(foreign taxes paid exceed the credit limitation),[10] income from domestic and foreign investments is taxed at different rates (domestic and foreign investments end up being taxed at the domestic and foreign tax rates, respectively);[11] (b) whenever excess credits in some countries[12] can be offset against excess limitations in other countries, the allocation of foreign investments among high- and low-income-tax countries can also be distorted.

---

10 And whenever these credits cannot be offset against future or current taxes.

11 The calculation of tax credit limitations varies significantly across European countries. In Belgium, the foreign tax credit for "nonpermanent" investments is 15 percent. In Denmark, the limit is either 50 percent of the Danish income tax attributable to the net income of the foreign affiliate (in the case where the parent is jointly taxed with the subsidiary) or the equivalent of the Danish tax rate applied to foreign income (in the case where the parent is not jointly taxed with the subsidiary). In Germany, the tax credit is 36 percent of the foreign income. In Greece and Spain, the limitation is based on the domestic corporate tax rate. In Luxembourg, any foreign taxes in excess of the domestic rate are deductible as expenses.

12 In the United Kingdom, however, the tax credit limitations are based on averaging within countries, but not across countries [Alworth, 1988].

The second exception to the worldwide principle regards the timing of the determination of the domestic tax liabilities on foreign source income: in other words, a *peculiar definition of "income"* is adopted. In general, if foreign-source income is in the form of dividends, most countries require that domestic taxes be levied when the dividends are paid by the foreign subsidiary to the parent company, and not when the income is produced. Hence, the deferral of dividend payments amounts to a deferral of the payment of domestic taxes, while foreign corporate taxes are regularly paid as income is produced. The incentive to defer the payment of dividends is equal to the difference in the tax rates times the time-value of money.[13] Legislation against the systematic use of deferral is well developed only in the United States, and, to some extent, in West Germany (where special rules on the attribution of passive income were introduced in 1972) and the United Kingdom (where tax authorities may allocate a proportion of the undistributed profits of foreign subsidiaries of UK companies).[14] In France, the exemption of foreign-source income does not apply to income produced in tax havens.

The imperfect integration of corporate income taxes and individual taxes, together with the imperfect application of the worldwide principle, both at the individual and at the corporate level, generate distortions in the international allocation of capital even when the residence principle is adopted. In particular, to the extent that investment income is taxed both at the corporate and individual level, firms can carry out tax arbitrage for their stockholders by locating in low-income-tax countries and choosing the appropriate liability structure. Tax liabilities are further reducible by following dividend policies meant at exploiting the deferral of taxation of foreign income. In general, the relevant cost of capital for international firms is affected by the sum of the rules described above, as well as by the nationality of their shareholders. These tax effects on the cost of capital would determine both the size and the geographical distribution of investments.

4. Distortions in International Intermediation

A more radical view of the effects of capital income taxes in an open economy would contend that international capital markets offer such a wide array of opportunities to avoid taxes that differences in tax rules become hardly distortionary [see, for example, Gros, 1989]. Firms operate as intermediaries in tax-arbitrage schemes that are meant to eliminate the burden of taxes for their shareholders. Examples of

13 In addition, the tax deferral can become, in a sense, permanent if the timing of the dividend distribution can be matched with occurrence of excess tax credits from elsewhere. The deferral can also become permanent if the host-country tax rate falls in the future.

14 In places like the Netherlands, Belgium and Italy, there is no regulatory equivalent to the US Subpart-F rules.

these arbitrage schemes, the "conduit" companies located in low-withholding-tax countries, are a typical form of financial intermediaries offering tax-avoidance services.

The relevance of this view can only be assessed by thorough empirical work. One effect of capital income taxes stressed by this view is the geographical distortion of financial intermediation: financial centers tend to cluster in low-withholding-tax countries, and in countries offering strong bank secrecy laws and relatively looser prudential regulations. A challenging theoretical question is whether these geographical distortions have significant real costs. While in a frictionless world the physical location of intermediaries does not matter, a growing number of researchers are stressing the important role of banks and other intermediaries. For example, a very influential line of research in development economics, pioneered by Shaw and McKinnon, claims that a well-working financial intermediation industry is a necessary ingredient for supporting efficient investment decisions and economic growth. Recent developments in macroeconomics have revalued the role of financial intermediaries in environments characterized by imperfect information. These results suggest that the consequences of the geographical distortions of financial intermediation induced by taxes are far from being understood and that their welfare effects could be substantial.

An additional problem is raised by such tax-like rules as prudential regulation rules (capital asset ratios, limitations of exposure vis-à-vis individual counterparties, and so on). Internationally mobile financial intermediaries, together with the territorial nature of many of these prudential regulations, could induce phenomena like the undertaxation of capital income: that is, competitive deregulation. Competition among regulatory authorities might make the financial intermediation industry too vulnerable to risk.

5. Public Finance and the Limits of National Sovereignties

The brief survey of regimes of taxation of capital income in Europe suggests the following stylized picture:

—Countries rely on territorial taxation and withholding taxes in order to insure some tax revenue in the presence of high international capital mobility. In particular, the corporation tax is the typical territorial tax, and, in the presence of integration between corporate and individual income taxes, it works as a withholding tax on individual incomes. This situation has evolved partly because of the remarkable absence of cooperation among tax authorities in industrialized countries, mirrored by strategic use of bank secrecy laws to attract foreign tax evaders.

—The application of the worldwide principle at the firm and at the individual level is ineffective in the presence of deferral, tax-credit limitations, and imperfect integration of corporate and individual income taxes. This gives rise to distortions in the geographical allocation of investment.
—The increased integration of goods and assets markets increases the difficulties in administering a system that requires determining the territorial distribution of income produced by multinational corporations.

While it appears that the opportunities to improve on the current regime are plentiful, in order to determine which of the many available strategies is the most appropriate, it is necessary to settle an important theoretical issue: the definition of the limits of the sovereignty of individual countries. In particular, we need to determine whether countries should be allowed to tax the income produced within their territory by foreign residents, or whether the domain of individual countries' income taxes should only be the income of their own residents, produced both domestically and abroad.

If a country's right to tax income produced within its own territory is considered irrefutable, as Musgrave recently suggested,[15] then the strategy for improving the current system of capital income taxation requires harmonization of tax laws (including rates and bases) and a method of allocating income produced by multinationals to the different countries where they operate.

By contrast, if the domain of the income tax is only the income produced by domestic residents, then a possible strategy for reform includes the following:[16]

—Full integration of personal and corporate income taxes.
—Elimination of deferral and adoption of an appropriate definition of income.
—Exemption of income produced by foreign residents from taxes and therefore elimination of the tax credit limitation. This can be accomplished at the source, or with a system of tax clearing.
—Full exchange of information among tax authorities.

In Europe, the choice between these two broad alternatives will be in large part determined by the political constraints that individual governments face. This choice will be unavoidable after the completion of the internal market, and might well determine its success.

---

15 "The territorial concept of entitlement is *almost universally* recognized both at the national and subnational levels" [Musgrave, 1987, p. 198; emphasis added].

16 Giovannini and Hines [1990] show that a two-tier system of taxation — where the corporate tax is levied at a uniform rate at the corporation level, but is rebated in part to individual shareholders — would allow partial integration of personal and corporate taxes, as well as a simpler system of international tax clearing.

Bibliography

ALWORTH, Julian S., The Finance, Investment and Taxation Decisions of Multinationals. Oxford 1988.

DIAMOND, Peter A., "Incidence of an Interest Income Tax." Journal of Economic Theory, Vol. 2, 1970, pp. 211-224.

—, James MIRRLEES, "Optimal Taxation and Public Production I: Production Efficiency." The American Economic Review, Vol. 61, 1971, pp. 8-27.

EICHENGREEN, Barry, "The Capital Levy in Theory and Practice." Centre for Economic Policy Research (CEPR), Working Paper, No. 350, London 1989.

GIOVANNINI, Alberto [1988a], "Capital Controls and Public Finance." In: Francesco GIAVAZZI, Luigi SPAVENTA (Eds.), High Public Debt: The Italian Experience. Cambridge 1988, pp. 177-211.

— [1988b], International Capital Mobility and Tax Avoidance. Columbia University, New York 1988, mimeo.

—, "National Tax Systems vs. the European Capital Market." Economic Policy, Vol. 4, 1989, pp. 345-386.

—, James R. HINES, Jr., Capital Flight and Tax Competition: A Viable Solution to Both Problems? Columbia University, New York 1990, mimeo.

GROS, Daniel, Tax Evasion and Offshore Centres. Centre for European Policy Studies (CEPS), Brussels 1989, mimeo.

MUSGRAVE, Peggy, "Interjurisdictional Coordination of Taxes on Capital Income." In: Sijbren CNOSSEN (Ed.), Tax Coordination in the European Community. Amsterdam 1987, pp. 197-225.

PRICE WATERHOUSE [1989a], Corporate Taxes: A Worldwide Summary. New York 1989.

— [1989b], Individual Taxes: A Worldwide Summary. New York 1989.

RAZIN, Assaf, Efraim SADKA, Integration of the International Capital Markets: The Size of Government and Tax Coordination. Foerder Institute for Economic Research, Working Paper, No. 32-88, Tel Aviv University, December 1988.

—, —, "International Tax Competition and Gains from Tax Harmonization." National Bureau of Economic Research, Working Paper, No. 3152, Cambridge, Mass., October 1989.

Comment on Alberto Giovannini, "Reforming Capital Income Taxation in the Open Economy: Theoretical Issues"

Wolfgang Kitterer

When I received Giovannini's paper, I recognized that the telecopy was sent by the "Ministero del Tesoro," the Italian Treasury. This reminded me of a conversation I once had with an official from the German Ministry of Finance on European Tax Harmonization. He was of the opinion that his Italian colleagues were very creative in developing new ideas on the harmonization of taxes and norms and that his French colleagues were excellent in formulating the laws establishing these norms. But he was very concerned that the Germans might be the only ones to respectfully and thoroughly execute what has been thought, formulated and established elsewhere, whereas other nations might be very ingenious in evading the consequences of their own propositions.

With this psychological encumbrance to tax harmonization in mind while reading the paper by Giovannini, I was anxious to have the following three questions answered:

1) What is a capital income tax and how should capital be taxed in an open economy?
2) What are the major ideas for reforming capital income taxation and how do they relate to the reform of other taxes?
3) Is there a well-based theoretical counterargument either in favor of or against tax coordination or tax competition?

As to the first question, Giovannini's paper starts from an intertemporal production and consumption model and shows that the *source principle*, in which capital income is taxed in the country where the interest is produced, is welfare-inferior to the *residence principle*, in which capital income is taxed in the investor's country of residence. This result, though not necessarily the presentation of the model, is in line with common results in the literature. As Sinn [1987, p. 209] has shown, it is even valid in more complex tax settings where (i) different burdens are imposed on interest income, capital gains, retained and distributed profits, and where (ii) double taxation through the personal income tax and through the corporate tax is allowed, provided that there is financial optimization, true economic depreciation, no tax on the capital stock and international commodity taxation according to the destination principle.

But let me come back to a closer examination of one crucial assumption of the model presented in the paper. Contrary to the usual presentation of such models, the revenue from capital income taxation is not returned to consumers in a lump-sum transfer but is used to finance government spending that enters the utility function of consumers. As has been shown by Kotlikoff and Summers [1987, pp. 1072-1076], in the framework of the intertemporal life-cycle model, lump-sum compensation would alter the consumer's perceived after-tax price of future consumption and might lead to more or less steady-state savings, thus altering the steady-state capital stock. I wonder whether the author wants to make a point of avoiding intergenerational redistribution or whether he is a "Ricardian equivalist," denying any effects of explicit or implicit intergenerational redistribution. When considering the explicit formulation of the model in Section 2 of the paper, this does not seem to be the case. However, the conclusions concerning the investment tax no longer hold because the substitution effects of the tax increase must be added to the income effects.

In Giovannini's paper it is assumed that government expenditures provide for utility-generating "infrastuctures." Nothing is said about the effects of these public capital expenditures on the domestic production possibility curve in Figures 1 and 2. If the economy is on a dynamically efficient growth path, public investment moves the production set to the left along the budget line *BB* or away from the origin, depending upon the degree of substitutability or complementarity between public and private capital.[1] Additionally, public capital expenditures create a return that is appropriated either by the government or by the private sector. Though Arrow and Kurz [1970, p. 151] have demonstrated that the appropriability of return on government capital has no deleterious effects on intertemporal allocations, this is only true if the user-charges the government imposes in order to appropriate all or some part of the return to its capital can always be offset by appropriate changes in tax rates. I suppose, without being completely sure about it, that in this case the model presented in the paper might lead to a control problem because there is only one tax rate on capital income.

My deliberations so far should not be understood as a criticism of the basic approach presented in Giovannini's paper. On the contrary, the inclusion of government expenditures should help us to complete the reflections on world equilibrium and tax competition presented in Section 2, where it is shown that tax competition would be much stronger when the *source or territorial principle* of taxation is realized instead of the *residence or world-wide principle.* When the source or territorial principle is followed, lowering domestic tax rates immediately attracts capital from the rest of the world because each investor, at home and abroad, receives a higher net rate of return. Therefore, each country is interested in imposing

1 See Kitterer [1988, Figure 4], for the case of complete substitutability of private and public capital.

low domestic capital income tax rates and prefers high tax rates in the rest of the world. Thus, the noncooperative Cournot-Nash equilibrium might only be realized at a low level of tax revenue in the competing countries.

By contrast, in the case of the realization of the *residence or world-wide principle* of capital income taxation, lowering the tax rate has no immediate effect on the foreign investor's rate of return and therefore does not attract any capital from abroad. Only the higher net rate of return on domestic investment creates some additional savings that lead to a higher foreign asset accumulation. Therefore, the noncooperative Cournot-Nash equilibrium might be realized at a relatively high level of tax income and a low level of distortions.

In his paper Giovannini makes no clear-cut case for tax coordination or tax competition. At first glance, in order to avoid an extremely low level of tax revenue, the source principle seems to be the better candidate for tax harmonization. However, on the one hand, I do not see any a priori reason why a high level of taxation should be maintained by tax coordination. On the other hand, higher tax rates will only create large outflows of capital if government expenditures are less efficient than in other countries. Tax competition is therefore, in a larger sense, competition for more efficient government; thus, competition should not be jeopardized by political cartels crusading under the banner of tax harmonization.

I think that a substantial part of tax competition on the national, on the regional and on the local level should be conserved in order to establish efficient production and consumption. In summary, there seems to be no convincing theoretical argument for tax harmonization.

Bibliography

ARROW, Kenneth J., Mordecai KURZ, Public Investment, the Rate of Return, and Optimal Fiscal Policy. Baltimore 1970.

KITTERER, Wolfgang, "Der Einfluß der Alterssicherung auf die gesamtwirtschaftliche Kapitalbildung." Kredit und Kapital, Vol. 21, 1988, pp. 383-406.

KOTLIKOFF, Laurence, Lawrence SUMMERS, "Tax Incidence." In: Alan J. AUERBACH, Martin FELDSTEIN (Eds.), Handbook of Public Economics, Vol. II. Amsterdam 1987, pp. 1043-1092.

SINN, Hans-Werner, Capital Income Taxation and Resource Allocation. Amsterdam 1987.

Joel Slemrod

Tax Havens, Tax Bargains and Tax Addresses: The Effect of Taxation on the Spatial Allocation of Capital

1. Introduction

In the past decade, an enormous literature has arisen that attempts to estimate the effective tax rate on new investment. Calculation of the effective tax rate depends not only on the statutory rate of tax at the corporate and personal level, but also takes account of how accelerated tax depreciation schedules are, the rate of investment tax credit offered, and other features of the tax system. An outstanding example of this work is the volume produced by King and Fullerton [1984]. That volume first develops a theoretical framework for calculating the effective tax rate and then presents careful studies of the tax systems of four countries, the result of which is summary measures of the net impact of the tax system. One of the principal conclusions of this work (and of most other studies in the same tradition) is that the effective tax rate on new investment within any one country differs greatly across assets and type of financing. Concern with the potential inefficiencies that might arise from such a state of affairs was one of the important motivating factors behind the attempt by the US Tax Reform Act of 1986 to equalize the tax treatment of different kinds of capital investment. The King-Fullerton study also revealed large differences across countries in the effective tax rate on investment, but was unable to establish a significant relationship between a country's level of taxation and its level of new investment.

The King-Fullerton study, and most of the above-mentioned literature, assumed that each economy was completely closed. In particular, it was assumed that all funds for investment were provided by domestic residents and that all corporate investment was carried out by domestic corporations. This assumption has become less and less tenable in recent years as the volume of cross-border portfolio and direct investment has exploded. King and Fullerton themselves recognized the potential importance of abandoning the closed economy assumption, stating that "the intricacies of double tax agreements and of the accounting behavior of multinational companies introduce complexities that are better deferred to a separate study" [King, Fullerton, 1984, p. 8].

The purpose of this paper is to explore the issues involved in expanding a study of the tax disincentives to investment to an open economy perspective.[1] This requires an understanding of the interaction between the tax systems of the home and host countries for portfolio and direct investment, and the degree to which they are coordinated. The approach followed here is the reverse of the usual one adopted in an analytical paper. Whereas the typical analytical paper posits a set of assumptions and then derives the logical consequences of these assumptions, in this paper I examine the implications of alternative assumptions and modeling choices. I believe that, because the study of the effects of international tax systems is still in its infancy, it is appropriate to examine critically the foundation that is laid before proceeding to construct an edifice on an arbitrary and perhaps unstable base.

To pursue this goal, the paper is organized as follows. Section 2 briefly reviews the allocation of capital in a world of autarchic economies. Section 3 allows cross-border portfolio investments, and considers their implications for a model of capital allocation both in the absence and presence of tax evasion. In Section 4, foreign direct investment is introduced. Finally, Section 5 relates the conceptual framework to two policy issues of current importance to US-European economic relations: the impact of the US Tax Reform Act of 1986 and the European economic integration due in 1992.

2. A Closed Economy

Let r be the rate of interest on loans from individuals to users of capital, referred to as firms. The inflation rate is assumed to be zero, so that r is a real and nominal rate of interest. Individuals decide on how much wealth to hold depending on, among other things, the return they receive on their wealth after taxes. Let $W_i(r_i(1-t_i))$ be the relationship between the desired wealth of country i's residents and the after-tax rate of return in country i, where t_i summarizes the tax rate imposed by country i at the personal level on savings lent to firms. Let $K_i(r_i/(1-\tau_i))$ be the demand for capital by firms, where $r_i/(1-\tau_i)$ is the cost of capital and τ_i is the marginal effective rate of tax on investment.

In equilibrium, the level of capital and the interest rate will be determined by the requirement that $W_i = K_i$. In general, each country will have a different value of the capital stock (and capital stock normalized for population, etc.) and the interest rate, which will depend on the demand for wealth, supply of investment opportunities, and the tax system. Note that the property of the tax system that matters for the determination of the capital stock is $(1-t_i)(1-\tau_i)$. Also, note that it is immaterial

1 Other recent empirical studies that treat this issue are Bovenberg et al. [1990] and Crooks et al. [1989].

how the total tax burden $(t_i + \tau_i - t_i \tau_i)$ is divided between firm-level taxes and individual-level taxes.

More generally, K_i and W_i may depend on the quantity and nature of the services provided by the government, and on the structure of the rest of the tax system. For the purposes of this paper, these factors will be ignored. I will also assume that there are no tax implications to how the firm finances its capital investment. In particular, debt and equity finance are taxed alike. This assumption is maintained in order to avoid the troublesome questions of optimal corporate financial structure and the nature of equilibrium when different methods of finance have different tax implications. Because the focus of this paper is on capital allocation rather than capital accumulation, I will also assume that W'_i is zero for all countries (wealth of each country's residents is fixed). Furthermore, I will write the demand for capital, $K_i(r_i/(1-\tau_i))$, as the solution to $f_i = r_i/(1-\tau_i)$, where f_i is the marginal product of capital located in country i.

3. Allowing Cross-Border Portfolio Investments

a. The No-Evasion Case

Now I will proceed to generalize the model to allow the opportunity for wealth-owners to make portfolio investments in the securities of other countries. I will continue to assume that for each firm a controlling interest is retained by wealth-owners resident in the same country.

Consider a wealth-owner from country H (the "home" country). An investment in a domestic security yields an after-tax return of $r_H(1-t_H)$. What after-tax return is available from investment in the securities of other countries? The answer depends critically on the system for taxing cross-border transactions operated by both country H and country F (the country where the investment is located, i.e., the "foreign" country).

For portfolio investments, most home countries operate a "worldwide" system of taxation, so that income earned anywhere is subject to personal taxation at rate t_H. To avoid two levels of tax on the same income, these countries offer a credit against domestic taxes for taxes paid to foreign governments. This credit is limited to the domestic tax that would be due on the income, and does not apply to corporate taxes paid on the income.

All countries assert the right to levy taxes on income that is generated within their borders. A bilateral treaty network among developed countries sets the taxes (known as "withholding" taxes) that are levied on the cross-border flow of portfolio income. Let w_i be the rate of withholding tax imposed by country i on portfolio income leaving the country. In this case the rate of return earned by a resident of i on an investment in country j is $r_j(1 - \max(t_i, w_j))$. A resident of country j can earn $r_j(1 - t_j)$ at home or $r_i(1 - \max(t_j, w_i))$ on an investment in country i.

What will characterize the equilibrium in this world economy? First, allow the realistic assumption that countries' withholding tax rates lie below the lowest personal income tax rate. In this case $\max(t_i, w_j)$ is equal to t_i for any pair of countries i and j, and the effective personal tax rate is that of the home country regardless of where the investment is located. If all investments are viewed as perfect substitutes, then the only equilibrium will be one in which interest rates are equalized (at rate r) around the world. Note that the marginal product of capital will not be equalized worldwide, with $f_i = r/(1 - \tau_i)$, so that differing corporate-level taxes generate inefficiency in the world allocation of capital.

A few words about the implications of policy are in order here. First, in this model of the world it is always in a country's interest, if it can do so without retaliation, to increase its withholding tax at least to the minimum value of t in the world. By doing so, it collects more revenue but does not affect the real allocation of resources, because any additional taxes paid to its government are offset by foreign tax credits paid by the home governments of investors. Alternatively, offering a tax subsidy to foreign portfolio owners only costs the home country revenue if the subsidy reduces the investor's foreign tax credit received dollar for dollar.

In this model it certainly does matter whether taxes are imposed at the firm level or the individual level. Firm level taxes reduce the equilibrium domestic capital stock, because $f_i = r/(1 - \tau_i)$, but do not reduce the after-tax rate of return earned by domestic savers. Individual level taxes affect the after-tax rate of return earned by domestic savers (equal to $r(1 - t_i)$), but not the amount of capital located in the country.

b. Tax Evasion

The model discussed above forecasts that all countries would want to increase their withholding taxes (at least to the minimum value of other countries' individual tax rates), and implies that it is the bilateral treaty network that restrains these rates in a negotiation process of dividing the tax revenue among countries. This prediction contrasts sharply with recent policy trends, which have seen the US and other countries eliminate their withholding taxes on interest income.

I believe that our reasoning has been led astray by the implicit assumption that all wealth-owners comply with their home country's tax laws and pay tax on portfolio income, be it foreign-source or domestic-source. In fact, there is a widespread perception that much of foreign-source portfolio income, and a good deal of domestic-source portfolio income, is not reported to the home country's tax authorities.

To test the implications of introducing evasion into the model, first assume that no country can collect tax on its own residents' foreign-source income, but that taxes on interest paid within the country, including withholding taxes on foreigners, are collectible. In this case a resident of country i can earn $r_i(1-t_i)$ on an investment in his own country but can earn $r_j(1-w_j)$ on an investment in any other country j. Then if $(1-t_i)/(1-w_i) \neq (1-w_j)/(1-t_j)$ for any pair of countries i and j, there exist no values of r_i and r_j for which both countries' wealth-owners are indifferent between home and foreign investment. If withholding taxes are less than domestic taxes on interest in both countries, then at least one country's wealth-owners will find that foreign investment dominates home country investment.

The character of equilibrium in the presence of evasion depends on several assumptions. If the alternative investments are perfect substitutes, then it matters whether it is possible to have negative holdings of an asset (borrowing) and, if so, whether the tax consequences are symmetric to positive holdings. Specifically, can an investor borrow in his home country and receive tax rebates (due to the deductibility from taxable income of interest payments) at the rate t_i? Can interest be deducted even if no interest receipts are reported (because it is unreported foreign-source income)? If the answer to these questions is yes, the model as it stands suggests the presence of unlimited tax arbitrage gains made at the expense of treasuries, as investors receive interest deductions that exceed withholding taxes paid. The arbitrage may be limited by the graduated nature of income tax systems, which implies that the t_i values are endogenous and would eventually (with sufficient interest deductions) be driven low enough so that equilibrium is achieved where $(1-t_i)/(1-w_i) = (1-w_j)/(1-t_j)$, for each pair of countries.

If interest payments are not deductible in the absence of interest receipts, the equilibrium is likely to be characterized by investors being at corner solutions to their portfolio choice problems, with some or all countries' investors holding all their wealth in foreign assets and no wealth in domestic assets, and perhaps some countries' investors being indifferent between domestic and foreign assets. The details of the equilibrium will depend on the pattern of wealth-holdings and opportunities for investment across countries as well as on the tax rates.[2]

Note that in this equilibrium interest rates will, in general, differ across countries. The policy implications are also quite different than in the model with no evasion. Increasing the withholding tax can, in some situations, increase the country's rate of interest and, by increasing the cost of capital, decrease its capital stock. Similarly, increasing the tax on interest income may also, unless domestic wealth-owners hold only foreign assets, increase the domestic interest rate. In essence, the world is characterized by only source-based taxes, but where the tax rate imposed can depend on the citizenship of the investor.

---

2 This kind of equilibrium is elaborated in Slemrod [1988].

This model's prediction that, for many countries, all wealth will be invested abroad is not consistent with the observed phenomenon that most wealth of all countries is invested in domestic assets. The failure of the model to match observed behavior may be due to any of several assumptions maintained up to this point.

First, investors may have a preference for domestic assets, so that they are willing to hold these assets in their portfolios even if their after-tax rate of return is dominated by foreign assets. Recognizing that the return to capital income is uncertain and that individuals are risk averse reduces the tendency of the model to predict specialization in the international pattern of asset ownership. If the return to capital income is uncertain, all investors are likely to diversify their portfolios and to own both domestic and foreign assets.[3] As long as the real returns of owning foreign and domestic assets are not perfectly correlated, diversification permits investors to reduce risk without sacrificing expected return. Returns may be imperfectly correlated because of country-specific business cycles or exogenous shocks.

One logical question to ask of a portfolio model is whether it can generate the empirical fact that wealth-owners tend to specialize in assets denominated in the domestic currency. Exchange rate risk, in the absence of purchasing power parity, will cause optimal portfolios to differ across residents of countries with different currencies.[4] It can be shown, however, that each resident should hold the security that is the best hedge against his own country's inflation — probably a short-term nominal instrument, such as treasury bills — and should also hold a diversified portfolio of the other assets that is common to all residents [Adler, Dumas, 1983]. This proposition implies that if there were no transaction costs and everyone had the same information, the exchange rate risk might not be sufficient to induce as much specialization in domestic assets as is actually observed.

The political risk of expropriation or default varies according to the residence of the wealth-owner and could cause wealth-owners to favor investments in their own country's assets. A well-specified model of political risk should recognize that if behavioral responses to the threat of expropriation are ignored, the losses from expropriation exactly offset the gains. In essence, the threat of expropriation or

3 Introducing risk aversion and capital income uncertainty does not preclude the possibility that unconstrained optimal portfolios will contain negative holdings of some assets.

4 Note that if purchasing power parity held at all times (that is, if countries' relative price indexes were exactly in line with exchange rates), exchange rate risk would not be a reason for the portfolios held by different countries' residents to be different, because all countries' investors would view the real return of a given security identically. For example, an American holding a yen-denominated bond would suffer a loss if the yen depreciated against the dollar and if the two countries' relative price levels remained unchanged. With purchasing power parity, this depreciation would be accompanied by an increase in the Japanese price level (in which case a Japanese holder of the bond would suffer an identical real loss), by a decrease in the US price level (in which case neither owner would suffer a real loss), or by some combination of the two price effects. In all cases both investors would be affected identically.

default on externally held debt is that such risk is a random tax assessed only on nonresidents. This factor is clearly more important for North-South investments than for investments in developed countries.

How evasion is modeled is also critical to the model. Above I assumed that no investor pays tax to his home country on foreign-source income, but all taxpayers pay tax to the host country (i.e., home country residents pay t_i and foreigners pay w_i to country i). In fact, some individuals evade tax on domestic-source capital income, while others remit tax to their home government due on foreign-source income. Moreover, governments can impose withholding taxes that apply to domestic residents' investment in domestic assets. These levies are more easily collectible than income taxes that rely on self-assessment.

No one has formalized a model of international financial equilibrium which simultaneously allows for home asset preference and the presence of individuals with heterogeneous propensities to evade taxes, and I have neither the time nor space to attempt such a modeling effort here. Nevertheless, it may be valuable to sketch out what such a model would look like.

Each country's wealth-owners are divided into several types. Some, who tend to be low-wealth individuals for whom the transaction costs of foreign investment are prohibitive, invest only in domestic assets and pay t_H in tax to the home government, denoted by H. They are honest and myopic. Others are willing to evade taxes to different degrees. Some diversify their portfolio between domestic and foreign assets, depending on the relative after-tax returns. They pay taxes on domestic assets, so receive a return of $r_H(1 - t_H)$ on domestic investment, but pay no home country tax on foreign investment—only withholding taxes to foreign governments — so that the typical return on foreign investment is $r_F(1 - w_F)$, where r_F is the foreign interest rate and w_F is the withholding tax rate imposed on foreigners by the host government. Each country also has some wealth owned by individuals who make diversified portfolio decisions but pay only withholding taxes and no personal income tax to their home country on any investment, foreign or domestic. They thus compare the after-tax return on home investment, $r_H(1 - v_H)$, where v_H is the withholding tax on domestic investment, to $r_F(1 - w_F)$. Finally, a large and growing amount of wealth is controlled by tax-exempt institutions, who diversify but legally owe no tax to their home government, although they may have to pay withholding taxes to foreign governments. They compare r_H to $r_F(1 - w_F)$.

In this case an increase in any of the tax instruments available to a government (t, w, or v) will reduce the demand for domestic capital and tend to increase interest rates. An increase in t will cause the second group (who diversify but evade tax on foreign-source income) to move wealth abroad; an increase in v will cause the third group (who diversify but pay only withholding taxes) to more wealth abroad; and an increase in w will cause foreigners, including foreign tax-exempt institutions, to reduce their demand for the taxing country's assets.

c. Tax Havens

Up to this point, I have continued to assume that withholding taxes cannot be avoided. But now even this assumption must be abandoned because of the existence of tax haven countries.

Tax haven countries permit the operation of untaxed financial intermediaries within their borders. Cross-border financial intermediation is potentially highly profitable because of the lack of coordination of countries' tax systems. The country hosting the financial intermediaries can set license fees to tax away some of the intermediaries' profits. If there is free entry into the club of tax haven countries, competitive pressure will keep these fees low.

The Netherlands Antilles provides a classic example of how tax havens work. Before 1984 the United States imposed a withholding tax on interest paid to foreigners. Many US-based firms arranged to do their borrowing through a subsidiary based in the Netherlands Antilles, which levied no withholding tax. The funds were then relent to the US parent. According to the US treaty with the Netherlands Antilles, no withholding tax was levied on interest payments from the US to the Netherlands Antilles. Thus, by this route withholding taxes were avoided (but not "evaded," a term which connotes illegality).

This sort of avoidance through treaty "shopping" could have been shut off if the US had not excused via treaty withholding taxes on any payments of interest outside of the country. In any event, the US abolished its withholding tax in 1984, thus eliminating the need to borrow through Netherlands Antilles' subsidiaries.

Even in the absence of withholding taxes imposed on foreigners, tax havens are attractive to investors who are evading home country taxation, either of the self-assessed or withholding variety. For these types of wealth-owners, only the host-country tax rate matters, and an intermediary can offer a lower pretax rate of return in return for low taxation. The most striking recent example of this is the response to the imposition of a domestic withholding tax by West Germany. There was a substantial flight of assets to financial intermediaries (many of which were branches of German banks) based in Luxembourg, which had no withholding taxes and offered assets that were near-perfect substitutes for assets in Germany.

4. Foreign Direct Investment

In this section, the model is generalized to allow firms operating in one country to be owned by foreign wealth-owners. This is of interest because, in general, the home country system of taxing the income from cross-border investment changes when the investment is considered to yield a controlling interest in the operations of the business.[5] It is also of interest because of the rapidly growing importance of foreign direct investment and multinational businesses.

There are two different systems for taxing the income from foreign direct investment. Under a "territorial" system, used by France and the Netherlands, the foreign-source income of resident corporations is exempt from home country taxation. Under a "worldwide" system of taxation, used by Japan, the US, and the UK, foreign-source income is subject to home country taxation, but income and withholding taxes are credited, subject to limitation, against taxes due to the home country. (In some situations, what is nominally a worldwide system is converted by treaty — which exempts foreign-source income from home country taxation — into a territorial system. This is the case for West German investment in the US). The earnings of foreign subsidiaries are treated as (foreign-source) income of the parent company only upon repatriation of the earnings, so that any home country tax liability may be deferred to the extent that earnings are retained by the foreign subsidiary firms.

There is a broad consensus among economists that foreign investment is best understood from an industrial organization perspective. Dunning [1985] has argued that foreign direct investment by firms of country *A* in country *B* is more likely if *A*'s firms (1) possess ownership-specific advantages relative to *B*'s firms in sourcing markets, (2) find it profitable to use these advantages themselves rather than lease them to *B*'s firms, and (3) find it profitable to utilize their ownership-specific advantages in *B* rather than *A*. For present purposes, I will simplify the exposition by assuming that incorporated in each country there is a multinational enterprise which has a unique fixed factor (e.g., a patented technology, brand loyalty, etc.) which the multinational prefers not to license to other firms, but rather to exploit directly by setting up wholly owned subsidiaries throughout the world. Ownership-shares in these multinationals can be purchased by residents of all countries, subject to the preferences for home assets discussed above. Thus, the portfolio problem of wealth-owners must be expanded to include not only shares in purely domestic firms (and tax-haven financial intermediaries) in each country but also shares in all countries' multinationals. In addition, each multinational must decide on the profit-maximizing location of its production facilities. For this decision the tax system of both the potential host country and the home country of the multinational interact in a complicated way to determine the tax consequences of alternative locations.

---

5 The dividing line for tax purposes between a portfolio investment and a controlling, or direct, investment varies across countries.

a. Tax Bargains

Suppose that a country wishes to use its tax system to encourage investment located within its borders (i.e., it wishes to become a "tax bargain") and that its chosen method is to maintain its statutory corporate tax rate but also to increase its rate of investment tax credit. How effective will this strategy be? First of all, it will increase the attractiveness of domestic investment to multinationals from countries operating territorial systems. For multinationals residing in countries using a worldwide tax system, whether this strategy will be effective depends on two things. If the multinationals are in an excess limitation position (where the average rate of tax to foreign governments is less than the tax on foreign-source income due to the home government), the incentive is dampened by the fact that reduced taxes paid to the host country are to some extent offset by reduced foreign tax credits received from the home country. Multinationals from these countries will thus not be able to take full advantage of the tax bargain being offered. This latter effect does not apply if the home country of the multinational has a "tax sparing" treaty agreement with the host country, under which a fixed level of foreign tax credits can be claimed by the multinational regardless of the level of taxes actually paid to the host government.

If the investment tax credit is also available to purely domestic firms, then it would also be an incentive to this type of investment. But we might expect the investment decisions of multinationals to be more sensitive to changes in taxation than purely domestic firms, because for multinationals the investment decision is more a locational decision than a capital deepening decision.

Lowering the statutory corporate rate as an investment incentive creates a slightly different set of incentives. A reduced statutory rate gives multinationals operating in the country an increased incentive to shift income (in an accounting, rather than a real, sense) into the country. Thus, an equivalent investment incentive may be accompanied by less reduction in tax revenues than would an investment tax credit.[6] For this reason, a country offering a "tax bargain" via a low rate takes on the flavor of a "tax haven," because it benefits from the cross-border movement of taxable income rather than from the cross-border movement of real resources. For domestic multinationals in countries using a worldwide tax system, a rate cut is likely to be less effective in increasing domestically located investment because investment tax credits (and accelerated depreciation) are typically limited to only domestically located assets, while rate cuts apply to worldwide income.

---

6 On the other hand, an investment tax credit can increase the incentive to invest without conferring, as a rate cut does, windfall tax benefits to the owners of existing capital.

b. Tax Addresses

Up to this point, I have treated as exogenous the assignment of multinationals to their country of incorporation. In fact, the domicile of a corporation generally has tax consequences for the shareowners, holding constant the real activities of the firm. To the extent that corporations can choose where to incorporate, there will be tax effects at work at this margin, too. The most prominent examples of countries that currently take advantage of this flexibility are Liberia and Panama, which offer resident firms favorable regulatory as well as tax treatment.

In most countries, liquidation and subsequent reincorporation in another country incur a significant one-time tax liability that is large enough to offset the present value of tax benefits resulting from being incorporated at a more attractive tax address. However, over time, existing corporations at favorable tax addresses will be able to outbid corporations at relatively unfavorable tax addresses for control of other firms (i.e., their unique fixed factors). Furthermore, new corporations will, other things being equal, be attracted to incorporation at favorable tax addresses.[7] The policy issues relating to tax addresses have not been given much attention. Why, for example, should the US care if its third largest automobile company became a Japanese corporation, as long as its real operations were unchanged? Certainly, there may be consequences for the division of tax revenues between the US and Japan, but the more profound issues of control are likely to dominate policymakers' attention.

5. Current Tax Policy Issues Affecting US-European Capital Flows

In this final section I try to relate the conceptual discussion above to some issues of current policy interest to US-European economic relations. I focus primarily on the impact of the US Tax Reform Act of 1986 (TRA86), and then discuss briefly the European economic integration due in 1992.

---

7 Many of the issues raised by tax havens, tax bargains, and tax addresses apply to labor as well as capital. Individuals may be induced by low tax rates (relative to services offered) to move their true country of residence, thus taking advantage of a tax bargain. Alternatively, they may be induced to establish a nominal place of residence, a tax address. The classic example of this is Björn Borg's Monaco tax address. Tax havens are less of an issue for labor because the source of the income is less slippery (usually taken to be where the individual is located when the work is carried out).

a. The Tax Reform Act of 1986 and the Changed Incentives for Foreign Direct Investment from the US to Europe[8]

The two most significant aspects of TRA86 for FDI from the US to Europe were the reduction in the statutory corporate rate from 46 to 34 percent and the resulting increase in the number of firms in an excess credit situation, and the change in the rules governing the sourcing of income and the allocation of interest expenses between domestic- and foreign-source income.

The Reduced Statutory Corporate Tax Rate

The single most important aspect of TRA86 for FDI was the reduction in the statutory rate of corporate income tax from 46 to 34 percent. Many of the repercussions of the new law follow this change.

To see this, a brief digression on the impact of TRA86 on domestic investment is required. It is well known that the net effect of the tax system on the incentive to invest depends not only on the statutory rate but also on, among other things, the schedule of depreciation allowances, the rate and scope of investment tax credits, the source of financing, and the rate of inflation. TRA86 eliminated the investment tax credits that had previously applied to equipment and machinery, and provided generally less generous depreciation allowances, both of which tended to offset the tax rate reduction. Most analysts concluded that the net effect of these provisions was to slightly increase the effective corporate-level tax on new domestic investment, an important *alternative* to FDI.

An analysis of how these same changes affected the effective tax rate on FDI must proceed quite differently because, with certain exceptions, foreign-source income of foreign subsidiaries enters the parent's tax base only to the extent that dividends are repatriated. There is thus no calculation of foreign-source taxable income from which depreciation allowances are deducted and against which investment tax credits can be offset. The tax base is simply dividends received minus allocable deductions, grossed up by the average rate of foreign taxation (calculated using an earnings and profits measure of taxable income, which is not sensitive to legislated changes in the tax depreciation schedules used for domestically located assets, investment credits, etc.). To this base is applied the corporate statutory tax rate.

Thus, the corporate tax changes of TRA86 reduced the statutory rate from 46 to 34 percent but did not broaden the tax base, resulting in an unambiguous reduction in the tax rate on income from FDI. Assuming that the taxes imposed by the foreign

---

8 This section is based on Slemrod [1990].

governments remained unchanged,[9] it follows that the amount of additional taxation imposed by the US upon repatriation would either stay the same or decline. It would stay at zero for multinationals whose average[10] tax rate paid to foreign governments exceeds 46 percent. Any multinational subject to an average tax rate by foreign governments between 34 and 46 percent had formerly been paying taxes upon repatriation, but under the new rate would no longer be liable for any additional taxes. For firms paying less than the 34 percent average tax rate to foreign governments, the tax due upon repatriation would fall substantially, although not to zero.[11]

Another important implication of the reduction of the US statutory rate from 46 to 34 percent is that a much higher fraction of US multinationals are likely to be in an excess credit situation.[12] For a firm in excess credit status, every additional dollar paid in tax to a foreign government generates a foreign tax credit that cannot be used immediately, and has some value to the multinational only if the firm is in an excess limitation position either in the next five years (the carryforward limit) or had been in an excess limitation position in the previous two years (the carryback limit). Thus, a US multinational in an excess credit position is likely to be much more sensitive to differences in foreign effective tax rates than a firm in an excess limitation situation.[13] This increases the relative attractiveness of investment in a low-tax foreign country such as Ireland compared to a high-tax country such as West Germany.

---

9 Since the passage of TRA86, several European countries have enacted tax reforms which share some of the corporate rate-reducing, base-broadening aspects of TRA86. To the extent that TRA86 *caused* these reforms (or increased their likelihood), the host country's effective tax rate was influenced by the US tax reform. The analysis that follows holds the foreign tax system constant.

10 The average tax rate is subject to a degree of control by the multinational via its repatriation policy. By repatriating income primarily from high-tax countries, the average tax rate on its foreign-source income is high and less likely to attract additional US tax liability.

11 Hartman [1985] has argued that, regardless of the excess credit status of the US parent, the level of repatriation tax is irrelevant for the incentive to undertake FDI financed by earnings of the foreign subsidiary. This is because the repatriation tax reduces equally both the return to investment and the opportunity cost of investment (reduced dividends). This argument would not apply to the infusion of new equity capital from the parent. See Jun [1989] for a critique of this view.

12 Grubert and Mutti [1987] quote US Treasury estimates that the fraction of manufacturing multinationals (weighted by worldwide income) in excess credit will increase from 20 to 69 percent. Goodspeed and Frisch [1989], using updated corporate tax return information, estimate that the fraction of foreign-source income subject to excess credits will rise from 50 to 78 percent, and from 32 to 82 percent in manufacturing. These calculations, however, consider only the change in statutory rate and do not consider changes in the allocation rules or the separate baskets discussed below. In addition, neither analysis considers changes, perhaps induced by the US reform, in other countries' tax rates.

13 Of course, Hartman's argument implies that only the host-country's tax rate matters for investment financed by retained earnings, even for firms in an excess limitation position, so that no post-TRA86 increased sensitivity to host-country tax rates should be observed.

Is there any evidence of a post-TRA86 shift toward US multinationals' investment in low-tax foreign countries? Table 1 assembles some evidence to assess this question. European countries are divided into groups based on their effective tax rates on investment as calculated by Crooks et al. [1989]. It shows that the growth rate of capital expenditures in low-tax countries (Belgium, Ireland, and Luxembourg) is notably higher than in high-tax countries (Denmark, France, West Germany, Greece, Italy, the Netherlands, Portugal, and Spain).

Table 1 — Capital Expenditures by Majority-Owned Foreign Affiliates of US Corporations, by Low-Tax and High-Tax Countries in Europe, 1984-1989 (mill. US$)

	1984	1985	1986	1987	1988	1989	Increase (%) 1985-89
Low-tax[a]	767	778	1054	1160	1417	1672	114.9
High-tax[b]	7283	7602	8836	8561	10142	11405	50.0

[a]High-tax countries: Denmark, France, West Germany, Greece, Italy, the Netherlands, Portugal, Spain. — [b]Low-tax European countries: Belgium, Ireland, Luxembourg.

Source: US Department of Commerce [various issues].

New Source Rules

A firm in excess credit status can reduce the present value of its tax burden to the extent that it can increase the limit on foreign tax credits. For US tax purposes, this increases the importance of the rules determining the source of worldwide income. Holding worldwide income constant, if a dollar of income is shifted from domestic-source to foreign-source, it increases the limitation by one dollar and allows 34 cents more of foreign taxes to be credited immediately against US tax liability. Only to the extent that foreign governments enforce the same source rules will there be an offsetting increase in foreign tax liability.

One existing source rule that becomes more important applies to production for export. According to current regulations, between forty and fifty percent of the income from domestic US production of export goods can effectively be allocated to foreign-source income. For a multinational in an excess credit position, this has the effect of reducing the effective tax rate on domestic investment for export by as much as a half. Thus, if a contemplated FDI is to produce goods for sale outside the US, the alternative of domestic US production has become tax favored for those firms which have shifted into excess credit status, in spite of the base broadening aspects of TRA86. This reasoning does not, though, apply to FDI designed to reexport to the US, because the alternative of domestic production for internal consumption does not benefit from the export source rule.

Interest expenses must be allocated to either US or foreign-source income. The general rule is to allocate on the basis of the book value of assets, so that interest expenses deductible from foreign-source income are equal to total interest payments multiplied by the fraction of worldwide assets represented by assets expected to generate foreign-source income. Although TRA86 did not significantly alter this allocation formula, it did add a "one-taxpayer" rule, under which corporations that are members of an affiliated group are consolidated for the purpose of allocating interest expenses between US and foreign sources.[14] In the absence of this rule, a multinational could load its debt into a US subsidiary with no foreign-source income and have the interest expense be allocated to US-source income, thus maximizing foreign-source income and the limitation on foreign tax credits. With the one-taxpayer rule, a fraction of these interest payments has to be allocated to foreign-source income regardless of the legal structure of the multinational.

For multinationals in excess credit position that are forced to reallocate interest payments, this provision increases the average cost of capital of domestic or foreign investment to the extent that debt finance is used. It also increases the marginal cost of foreign investment, because foreign investment increases the amount of interest payments that must be allocated abroad, which decreases foreign-source income and therefore the amount of foreign taxes that are immediately creditable. This provision is obviously most important for multinationals with a high debt-to-capital ratio.

The net effect of these, and several other, tax changes on the overall incentive of US multinationals to invest in Europe is difficult to discern. Netting the tax increases on foreign-source income (due primarily to the new interest allocation rules and separate "baskets" for the foreign tax credit limitation) against the reduction in US tax on foreign corporate income due to the statutory rate reduction, Grubert and Mutti [1987] calculated a slight decline in overall taxation. No similar calculation has been made specifically for Europe. If, though, on the whole, Europe is a high-tax area, then the argument discussed above might suggest a decline in the attractiveness of Europe as an investment locale. Offsetting this are the prospect of a unified European market after 1992 and the fear of increased protectionism at the same time. Judging by survey evidence on planned capital expenditures, the increase in US foreign investment is broadly distributed across geographical areas. The overall increase between 1985 and 1989 is, however, higher for Europe and Japan (49.4 and 47.6 percent respectively) than it is for Canada (19.1 percent) and developing countries (15.7 percent).

---

14 The one-taxpayer rule had already effectively applied to the allocation of expenses on research and development.

b. The Tax Reform Act of 1986 and the Changed Incentives for Foreign Direct Investment from Europe to the US

Foreign corporations and foreign-controlled US corporations that are engaged in a trade or business in the US are subject to taxation according to rules that are roughly comparable to those that apply to US corporations. Thus, the reduction of the statutory rate, elimination of the investment tax credit, and changes in depreciation schedules apply directly to these foreign-controlled businesses.

TRA86 did introduce a new branch profits tax, which imposes a 30 percent tax (often reduced by treaty) on the repatriated profits and certain interest payments of a US branch of a foreign corporation. This tax, which affects primarily financial institutions, was designed to equalize the tax treatment of foreign corporations operating through a US branch and those operating through a wholly owned domestic subsidiary.

The conclusion of many observers that TRA86 increased the effective rate of taxation on new corporate investment dominated the forecasts about inward FDI made by those few brave souls who offered a prediction before the actual impact could be discerned. Both Grubert and Mutti [1987] and Sinn [1988] based their conclusions that inward FDI would fall on this aspect of TRA86.

In fact, foreign direct investment into the US has surged since the passage of TRA86. Inward FDI totalled $46.9 bill. in 1987 and $58.4 bill. in 1988, compared to an average of only $20.9 bill. in the 1980-86 period. This post-TRA86 surge is corroborated by the data on investment outlays for US business enterprises acquired or established by foreign direct investors.

After observing the surge of inward FDI to the US immediately after the passage of TRA86, Scholes and Wolfson [1989] offered the ingenious argument that the increase in the effective tax rate on domestically located capital was a key element in the sharp increase of inward FDI. Their argument begins (as does the argument of Grubert-Mutti and Sinn) with the presumption that TRA86 increased the effective rate of taxation on domestically located capital. Now consider a foreign firm resident in a country that taxes on the basis of worldwide income and offers a tax credit for income taxes paid to foreign governments. If the US average tax rate is below the foreign statutory rate and the benefits of deferral are ignored, the total effective tax rate on a US investment is unchanged by the increase in the US effective tax rate. To put it another way, the increased US taxation is offset by the increased credits offered by the foreign government. If the total effective tax rate faced by foreigners stays unchanged, while the tax rate faced by US investors increases, then then *relative* tax rate of foreigners declines, causing a shift in ownership of US-located assets to foreign corporations. Because multinationals from foreign countries were previously not able to take advantage of the US position as a tax bargain, when the bargain is discontinued these multinationals are more likely to be attracted to investment in the US. Thus, the counterintuitive prediction of this analysis is that increases in US corporate taxation will *increase* foreign ownership of US-located capital. The Scholes-Wolfson hypothesis bears further discussion because of its startling predictions, its ability to apparently explain some of the post-TRA86 data (discussed below), and because it offers a convenient organizing focus for thinking about the effect of US tax law on inward FDI.

The analysis rests on two assumptions which are subject to some qualification. First, of the six principal countries exporting capital to the US, only two (Japan and the UK) operate a worldwide system with foreign tax credit. France and the Netherlands operate a territorial system, so that the foreign-source income of their resident multinationals is untaxed by the home country. Although Canada and West Germany in theory have a worldwide system, by treaty with the US, repatriated dividends bear no further taxation. For multinationals in these four countries, the effective tax rate on FDI in the US is no different than for US companies, so that the analysis does not apply. Japan and the UK have, however, accounted for slightly more than half of the six countries' FDI in the US in the past several years. Nevertheless, the assumption that the investing country operates a worldwide system of taxation does not apply universally. Furthermore, even for Japan and the UK, the tax rate on FDI in the US remains the same only to the extent that the multinationals are in an excess limitation position and are repatriating income that is subject to additional taxation in the home country.

Second, the Scholes-Wolfson hypothesis says that an increase in US corporate taxation reduces the *relative* tax burden on foreign-owned investment, but certainly does not imply a decline in the absolute level of taxation. Thus, the hypothesis suggests a change in the ownership pattern of existing capital, but is consistent with a decline in the rate of increase of foreign-owned capital due to the heavier absolute tax burden imposed by TRA86.

Table 2 breaks down inward FDI to the US by country of origin. Shown are the flow of FDI as well as outlays for acquisition or establishment by nonbank US affiliates of foreign corporations. For the former, investments are classified by the country of the foreign parent. For the latter, investments are classified by the country of "ultimate beneficial owner," who is that person, proceeding up a US affiliate's ownership chain, beginning with and including the foreign parent, that is not owned more than 50 percent by another person.

Although most investing countries participated in the post-TRA86 surge in investment, the increase was dominated by investment from Japan and the UK. These two countries account for about three-quarters of the 1985-88 increase in FDI

Table 2 — FDI and Outlays for Acquisition or Establishment of a US Business Enterprise by Country of Origin, 1983-1988 (mill. US$)

	1983	1984	1985	1986	1987	1988
			Foreign direct investment inflows			
France	201	774	30	1017	2471	962
West Germany	1007	1291	2292	1982	3150	2306
Japan	1653	4374	3794	7268	7504	17838
Netherlands	2778	3520	2776	4374	8293	4766
United Kingdom	3727	6882	4665	10827	22444	18774
Total	11946	25359	19022	34091	46894	58435
			Outlays for acquisition or establishment of a US business enterprise			
France	295	330	754	2491	2044	3753
West Germany	584	685	2270	1351	4664	1375
Japan	392	1806	1152	5416	7006	14166
Netherlands	492	562	771	4700	391	1937
United Kingdom	2366	3714	6732	8572	15142	21520
Total	8091	15197	23106	39177	40310	65019

Source: US Department of Commerce [various issues].

and outlays by foreigners for acquisition or establishment of US business enterprises.[15]

The recent predominance of FDI from Japan and the UK is consistent with the Scholes-Wolfson hypothesis, because they are the two countries that effectively operate a worldwide tax system with a foreign tax credit, and therefore may be relatively less affected by increases in the US tax burden on investment. To some extent, the large rate of increase of FDI from Japan and the UK may simply reflect the worldwide increase in FDI from these countries. Worldwide FDI from the UK (measured in pounds sterling) did increase by 149 percent between 1984 and 1988, but this large growth rate is still below the rate of increase in FDI located in the US. Worldwide FDI from Japan (measured in US dollars) doubled between 1986 and 1988, though the share going to the US did increase over this period.

c. European Integration in 1992

The European integration scheduled for 1992 would reduce or, in some cases, eliminate existing barriers to the cross-border flow of goods and factors within the

---

15 The increase in UK activity would appear even larger if the measure of FDI was the change in a country's FDI position, which differs from capital inflows by including valuation adjustments that arise, for example, due to the transfer in ownership of a FDI from one owner to another. Such a transfer took place in 1988, when a large holding in Shell Oil was transferred from a Dutch holding company to the British parent.

community. Apparently integration will not increase barriers to the flow of goods between countries within the community and countries outside the community.

Discussion of the integration has inevitably led to consideration of the need to harmonize European tax systems. Up to this point, most of the discussion has focused on the harmonization of value-added taxes. There is, though, a widespread recognition that any reduction in barriers to trade will impart more significance to differences across countries in their systems of taxing capital income. In the past, access to the French market might have been obtained only (or, at least, most cheaply) through production within France, so that the relative tax consequences of locating production in France versus Spain was not of critical importance. If no important barriers exist, relatively low taxation of multinationals' foreign-source income may become of decisive importance in locating productive activity there.

Thus, the prospect of European integration compounds, rather than offsets, the implications of the US Tax Reform Act of 1986. Both increase the economic importance of tax differences in the taxation of foreign direct investment. This implies an increase in the effectiveness of attracting investment by lowering tax rates on foreigners and an increase in the cost of not meeting the tax incentives of neighboring countries.

Bibliography

ADLER, Michael, Bernard DUMAS, "International Portfolio Choice and Corporation Finance: A Synthesis." Journal of Finance, Vol. 38, 1983, pp. 925-984.

AULT, Hugh J., David BRADFORD, "Taxing International Income: An Analysis of the U.S. System and its Economic Premises." In: Assaf RAZIN, Joel SLEMROD (Eds.), Taxation in the Global Economy. University of Chicago Press, NBER, Chicago 1990, pp. 11-46.

BOVENBERG, A. Lans, Krister ANDERSSON, Kenji ARAMAKI, Sheetal K. CHAND, "Tax Incentives and International Capital Flows: The Case of the United States and Japan." In: Assaf RAZIN, Joel SLEMROD (Eds.), Taxation in the Global Economy. University of Chicago Press, NBER, Chicago 1990, pp. 283-324.

CROOKS, Ed, Michael DEVEREUX, Mark PEARSON, Charles WOOLEY, "Transnational Tax Rates and Incentives to Invest." Institute for Fiscal Studies, London, March 1989, unpublished manuscript.

DUNNING, John (Ed.), Multinational Enterprises, Economic Structure and International Competitiveness. Clichester 1985.

GOODSPEED, Timothy J., Daniel J. FRISCH, "U.S. Tax Policy and the Overseas Activities of U.S. Multinational Corporations: A Quantitative Assessment." July 1989, unpublished manuscript.

GRUBERT, Harry, John MUTTI, "The Impact of the Tax Reform Act of 1986 on Trade and Capital Flows." In: US DEPARTMENT OF THE TREASURY, OFFICE OF TAX ANALYSIS, Compendium of Tax Research 1987. Washington 1987.

HARTMAN, David E., "Tax Policy and Foreign Direct Investment." Journal of Public Economics, Vol. 26, 1985, pp. 107-121.

JUN, Joosung, What is the Marginal Source of Funds for Foreign Investment? National Bureau of Economic Research, Working Papers, 3064, Cambridge, Mass., August 1989.

KING, Mervyn, Don FULLERTON (Eds.), The Taxation of Income from Capital. Chicago 1984.

SCHOLES, Myron, Mark A. WOLFSON, The Effect of Changes in Tax Laws on Corporate Reorganization Activity. Stanford Business School, Stanford, Calif., April 1989, unpublished manuscript.

SINN, Hans-Werner, "U.S. Tax Reform 1981 and 1986: Impact on International Capital Markets and Capital Flows." National Tax Journal, Vol. 41, 1988, pp. 327-340.

SLEMROD, Joel, "Effect of Taxation with International Capital Mobility." In: Henry AARON, Harvey GALPER, Joseph A. PECHMAN (Eds.), Uneasy Compromise: Problems of a Hybrid Income-Consumption Tax. The Brookings Institution, Washington 1988, pp. 115-148.

—, "The Impact of the Tax Reform Act of 1986 on Foreign Direct Investment to and from the United States." In: Joel SLEMROD (Ed.), Do Taxes Matter?: The Impact of the Tax Reform Act of 1986. Cambridge, Mass., 1990.

US DEPARTMENT OF COMMERCE, BUREAU OF ECONOMIC ANALYSIS, Survey of Current Business. Washington, various issues.

Comment on Joel Slemrod, "Tax Havens, Tax Bargains and Tax Addresses: The Effect of Taxation on the Spatial Allocation of Capital"

Julian S. Alworth

The potential effect of government policies (especially tax policy) on the allocation of capital across countries can be considered for analytical as well as practical purposes under two separate headings:

(1) Does the tax treatment of savings and investment in one country favour the production of goods and services by firms in that country relative to the production of firms located elsewhere (i.e. is investment in France, for example, subsidised relative to investment in Germany, or are French companies more "competitive" because of tax advantages)?

(2) Are companies encouraged by tax and other fiscal provisions to locate their production facilities in one country rather than another? In other words, do multinationals have an incentive to shift their production facilities from their "home country" (assuming this can be identified) to other countries, and, amongst other countries, are there any which actively encourage inward investment?

Until very recently the instinctive reaction of economists in examining the first question was to compare average tax burdens across countries or, in more sophisticated approaches, to simulate "cost-of-capital based" marginal effective tax wedges. The computation of these wedges has proven very sensitive to the assumptions concerning financial behaviour. Moreover, with wide deviations in exchange rates from "fundamentals", it has been difficult to assess the extent to which differences in effective tax rates have affected competitiveness. Owing to measurement problems, tax burdens on multinationals have generally eluded empirical research, so that the instinctive reaction by economists in answering the second question has been to join the banner of (worldwide) "capital export" or (territorial) "capital import" as objective criteria against which to judge highly stylised descriptions of existing tax systems. Indeed, this approach has been taken further, and a number of mathematically more or less elegant expressions have been derived to establish the appropriate deviations from the desired level of capital export and import neutrality.

Remark: The views expressed in this commentary are personal and do not necessarily reflect those of the BIS.

Slemrod's paper and other recent work which it cites represent a welcome break from this tradition. The fundamental contributions of the "new" as distinct from the "old" approach are, firstly, greater attention to the role of international financial markets in intermediating funds across countries and, secondly, a more careful examination of the interplay of various tax provisions with the financial and investment decisions of multinationals. Since I sympathise with this approach, the remainder of my comments will be addressed to examining some of the specific propositions put forward by Slemrod and to suggesting some further issues which may deserve attention.

The central question addressed in the first half of Slemrod's paper can be phrased as: "What is the role of capital markets (and their changing character) in attenuating or accentuating the inefficiencies arising from tax differentials across countries?" Slemrod adopts a "matrix approach" to discussing the issue. The matrix comprises returns on cross-border instruments, with the individual cells of the array indicating the return net of tax for funds flowing from one country to another. An additional facet of this analysis would allow for various types of investors and borrowers in each country.

Taking this approach to world capital flows leads to some interesting propositions. The most important conclusion is that the potential for arbitrage between lenders in different countries may limit the actual incidence of taxes and lead to perverse two-way capital flows or even to the absence of an overall "capital market equilibrium" for the world as a whole. Investment bankers, accountants and lawyers organise international borrowing and lending programmes on the basis of similar considerations every day. Indeed, one of the factors which has contributed to the success of one of the most popular new financial instruments, the longer-term interest and currency swap, is the possibility of circumventing withholding taxes in various countries.

However, the natural outcome of pushing this reasoning to its logical conclusion is, on the one hand, a multiplicity of pre- and post-tax interest rates with a very wide degree of variation and, on the other, a high degree of financial specialisation with segmentation of borrowers and lenders in an international version of the "clientele effect". This outcome is somewhat unsatisfactory because such segmentation is rarely observed in practice. Moreover, resident investors dominate the financial markets of most countries without being favoured, in many cases, from a tax standpoint in comparison with foreign investors.

There are four possible ways out of this quandary. The first is to assume that the world behaves according to a "Miller equilibrium". The conditions for such an equilibrium are, unfortunately, rarely verified in practice. The second is to assume that legal and regulatory constraints limit the extent to which cross-country, tax-driven specialised capital flows are possible. The third is to assume that risk premia limit the capacity of individual borrowers to exploit arbitrage opportunities in full (foreign exchange risks but also credit risk come immediately to mind). The fourth is that arbitrage actually takes place in a somewhat different fashion from that apparently considered by Slemrod, namely through tax-paying institutional intermediaries in the markets.

Banks (and possibly some large corporate entities with a continuing presence in the financial markets) act as marginal investors by "washing out" or arbitraging differences in taxes across countries. For example, they may help to transform heavily taxed interest income into more lightly taxed capital gains. In view of these factors, the "matrix approach" appears somewhat inappropriate as a description of the manner in which taxes affect the functioning of the international financial markets.

There are two related issues which I think do not receive enough attention in Slemrod's paper. The first concerns the role of financial intermediaries such as pension funds and insurance companies benefiting from a particular tax and regulatory status. At present these institutions account for a very large share of international capital flows. To the extent that they may not be able to reclaim withholding tax, such investors may be as sensitive as "tax evaders" to taxes deductible at source. The second issue is the role of foreign exchange gains and losses. International investments are often motivated by currency diversification considerations, and it is not very clear whether many countries' foreign gains and losses are considered explicitly by the tax legislation.

As regards the tax treatment of direct investment, it is a merit of Slemrod's paper that the most important issues are discussed concisely and in a tractable manner. I wish to add only two remarks.

The financial behaviour of multinationals has an important bearing on discussions of tax coordination and harmonisation, since multinationals have the ability to internalise differences in financing costs across countries, particularly those arising from tax distortions. This can be done in several ways, the simplest of which is to shift the source of financing from one country to another; the more complex schemes involve exploiting the leeway left open by "transfer pricing" rules. The incentives for such behaviour are provided by the differences in tax provisions across countries and the existence of a provision for deferral of domestic taxes on foreign profits (or in some instances the exemption of foreign earnings from domestic taxes). One upshot is that since tax authorities have been reluctant to scrap deferral but at the same time have not been keen to see domestically taxable income funnelled off to tax havens or low-tax countries, a number of anti-avoidance provisions have been introduced in many countries along the lines of the US "Subpart F" provisions. The net effect of this is the continuous leap-frogging of tax authorities closing up loopholes and accountants structuring new devices to avoid tax, and in the process the tax code has become increasingly complex. In Europe tax planning efforts by multinationals are likely to be stepped up after 1992. In order to prevent Europe from becoming the playground of smart tax accountants and an edifice of complicated anti-avoidance provisions from being built up as a result, some serious thinking on tax harmonisation or tax coordination will be needed. A concept such as "tax competition" appears particularly unhelpful in guiding tax reform in this domain.

Another aspect that deserves greater attention is the manner in which taxation affects the decision between expanding existing capacity, setting up new companies ("greenfield investments") or taking over existing firms. One of the striking features of the surge of direct investment in the United States since 1987 is the large volume of foreign acquisitions of existing US assets, particularly takeovers by UK entities of existing US companies.

The US tax reform in 1986 resulted in an increase in marginal tax rates on new investment and a decrease in average tax rates, in other words, a decline in marginal q and an increase in average q, i.e. there was a shift in incentive from the acquisition of "new" assets to that of "old" assets. As far as US companies are concerned, a number of other tax advantages to takeover activity were repealed in 1986. This was not the case for foreign firms investing in the United States. It would be interesting to examine whether the composition of foreign investments in the United States — particularly the takeover activity of UK companies — may have been influenced by tax considerations.

Hans-Werner Sinn

Can Direct and Indirect Taxes Be Added for International Comparisons of Competitiveness?

1. The Problem

The current world economy seems to be going through a phase of increased tax competition. Corporate and personal income tax rates are being reduced in many countries, and there is growing concern that countries which retain high tax rates will suffer because of increased mobility of goods and production factors. European countries in particular are anxious not to lose their competitiveness due to tax-induced capital flight and distortions of trade flows when the barriers fall in 1993.

The public debate on the issue of how taxation affects competitiveness is intense, but confused. Even the most fundamental economic insights seem unlikely to survive in the debate between nonexperts.

An obvious sign of confusion is the popular belief that a policy that makes a country attractive for internationally mobile capital will simultaneously improve this country's competitiveness in international trade. Of course, with flexible exchange rates, this cannot be true, since the capital import equals the current account deficit. The investors' attempt to import capital will be successful only to the extent that it leads to a revaluation and thereby to a deterioration of the current account. The confusion is shared by countries that take pride in being world export champions without realizing that they could equally well regard themselves as capital flight champions. Economists have warned of such types of irrationality.[1]

A somewhat more subtle, but no less common, mistake in the public policy debate is the focus on measures of aggregate tax burden. It is frequently argued that international comparisons of company tax burdens can reveal meaningful informa-

---

1 It has been argued by Summers [1986], Masson and Knight [1986], and Sinn [1984b; 1985] that the investment incentives introduced in the United States in 1981 have hurt that country's competitiveness and favored Europe's by causing the dollar to appreciate. It is true that capital imports require a positive trade balance *in the future* to pay for the debt service. However, this long-run effect may not be very relevant for political decisions. With a 2.5 percent rate of return to capital, it takes 40 years for the debt service to offset the influence on the trade balance of any given flow of capital imports, and in a growing economy where this flow rises at a constant rate, the required time period can be much longer. It seems unlikely that most of those who advocate capital imports to improve a country's competitiveness have the debt service effect in mind.

tion about the influence of tax on competitiveness. Research institutes, political parties, and government publication offices use such comparisons to support their contentions.

Every serious public finance economist is aware, however, how dubious such comparisons are, for he knows that a tax burden as such cannot reveal much about the incentive effects of taxation. What matters is how the tax burden reacts to a change in private choice variables, the size of the burden itself is less important. Some taxes are less distortionary than others, and some have perverse incentive effects. Lump sum taxes are neutral because the revenue they generate is not at all responsive to changes in private behavior, and taxes can be designed whose revenue declines when the activity being taxed increases. With efficient capital markets, the mere size of the tax burden is meaningless for company behavior since the separation theorem excludes all income effects. Only substitution effects matter.

Apart from these general observations, however, the particular knowledge about the effects of the major direct and indirect taxes on international competitiveness is rather limited. It is not at all clear to what extent it makes sense to lump these taxes together for the purpose of international comparisons of competitiveness.

This paper offers some basic insights into the problem by studying conditions for the tax system to exhibit *competitive neutrality* in a conventional model of international trade and capital movements. The taxes studied are an ideal value-added tax and an income tax with alternative depreciation provisions. Much emphasis is placed on the analysis of alternative combinations of origin, destination, residence, and source principles. The conditions under which the effects of direct and indirect taxes on competitiveness are additive and those under which they are not additive will be distinguished. Interestingly enough, there are a number of combinations under which at least one of the taxes is neutral in the sense that it does not affect a country's competitiveness, and there are two combinations under which a somewhat paradoxical "subtractive neutrality" prevails.

Subtractive neutrality means that direct and indirect taxes have countervailing effects on a country's competitiveness, so that, if they are to be taken together at all, the respective tax burdens should be subtracted rather than added for meaningful international tax comparisons. It goes without saying that the subtraction is not meant in a strict mathematical sense. It just means that an increase in one domestic tax requires an *increase* in the other to maintain a country's competitiveness. By way of contrast, the more conventional idea of *additive neutrality* means that, to preserve neutrality, the increase in one tax must be compensated by a *decrease* in the other.

Competitive neutrality cannot necessarily be identified with economic efficiency. For the purposes of this paper, it simply means that the tax system neither induces international capital movements nor the current account imbalances caused by these movements. Competitiveness is a concept that captures what politicians may have in mind when they use this term, but, apart from that, it has little normative content. Indeed, there are many reasons why an extended period of capital imports and reduced competitiveness may be in a country's interest. Even if this is the case, however, it is useful to know the conditions for neutrality, for without them it is difficult to design the tax system in a way that brings about the desired deviation from neutrality.

The question of competitive neutrality of tax systems is by no means new. In Europe, in particular, it is well-known and has frequently been discussed. The interest dates back to the early sixties when France and Germany argued about the appropriate tax treatment of cross-border trade flows. The countries disagreed about the necessity of border adjustments for indirect taxation. France, which had high indirect, but low direct, taxes favored the destination principle to protect its own industry against cheap German imports. Germany, on the other hand, favored the origin principle, arguing that the high German direct taxes would compensate for its low indirect taxes. Germany maintained that it would be unfair to burden its exports to France with both the high German direct taxes and the high French indirect ones. As is well known, France won the case and the destination principle, with appropriate border adjustments, was implemented.

To clarify the question and presumably to defend the German position, the German Iron and Steel Industry Group ordered a number of scientific reports which were published and intensively discussed in the scientific community.[2] Most experts who were consulted implicitly shared the additive neutrality view. They argued that both direct and indirect taxes enter firms' marginal cost schedules and must therefore affect commodity prices and international competitiveness in similar ways. Only one expert, Herbert Timm, rejected the idea of additive neutrality. In his view, direct business taxes resemble rent taxes that cannot be shifted. He agreed with the French position that a border tax adjustment for indirect taxes would bring about tax neutrality and he strongly rejected the idea of additive neutrality.[3]

The problems discussed nearly 30 years ago have become topical again in Europe because the destination principle will be difficult to maintain without border controls. The old claim of the Neumark Committee [1963] that only the origin principle is technically feasible in a fully integrated European market will probably prove to be true after 1992, since a good alternative to the current system of border tax adjustments has not yet been designed. With unhindered cross-border shopping, and direct consumer purchases via mail orders, or with the aid of a rapidly growing

---

2 Overviews and extensions of these reports can be found in Andel [1965] and Sievert [1964]. See also the summary of the subsequent literature given by Höhn [1980] and the papers edited by Shoup [1967].

3 The Iron and Steel Industry Group prevented Timm's report from being published.

carrying industry, the origin principle will be operative even though the destination principle continues to be prescribed by the tax laws.[4]

The solutions reached in the earlier literature are less topical, though, than the problems analyzed. The previous discussion clarified many aspects of the problem, but did not anticipate the results of the current research. It did not pay much attention to international capital movements, did not discuss the role of depreciation allowances, and neglected intersectoral distortions resulting from the fact that the value-added tax is a tax on consumption, but not on investment.[5] Taking up these issues, the present analysis tries to shed new light on the old problem. It identifies the conditions under which one or the other opinion could possibly be true, and it develops the case of subtractive neutrality, which, 30 years ago, would have raised eyebrows even more than today.

In Section 2 of the paper, a formal framework of the discussion is specified and a definition for tax neutrality is given. Section 3 discusses the role of taxation in determining market equilibria. Section 4 analyzes the borderline cases between additive and subtractive neutrality where at least one of the taxes has a lump sum characteristic and thus does not affect a country's competitiveness. Section 5 discusses the conditions for additive and subtractive neutrality, and Section 6 offers a conclusion.

2. A Framework for a Comparison

As a framework for a comparison of tax effects on a country's competitiveness, the conventional two country, two commodity, two factor Heckscher-Ohlin model is used, whereby, however, capital movements are allowed. In the absence of taxation, the model predicts equal factor prices and thus the possibility of capital movements is unimportant. As capital earns the same rate of return everywhere when there is no perfect specialization, international capital flows are indeterminate. Even if capital moves, the rates of return it can earn in the two countries will not be affected. Because of the Rybczynski effect, an increase in one country's capital stock will simply be absorbed by a growth in the capital-intensive sector at the expense of the labor-intensive sector, with no change in either sector's own capital intensity.

Suppose, however, distortionary taxes are introduced that drive wedges between the national rates of return to capital, either directly by taxing these rates of return or indirectly by taxing the commodity flows and changing factor demands. Under these circumstances, very large capital movements will take place, large enough to

---

4 For a criticism of the proposals of the European Commission, see Sinn [1989].

5 The same is true of the more recent discussions of the origin and destination principles by Whalley [1979; 1981] and Berglas [1981].

drive at least one of the countries into perfect specialization. An interior equilibrium where both countries produce both commodities is impossible with distortionary taxation, for, in the Heckscher-Ohlin model, there is a horizontal demand curve for capital when both commodities are produced.[6]

To be sure, the neglect of fixed factors of production in the Heckscher-Ohlin model overstates the tax distortions. However, the main focus of this paper is not on the size of distortions, but on the *conditions for tax neutrality*. The very fact of its sensitivity to tax differentials makes the Heckscher-Ohlin model ideally suited for this task. Following the definition given in the introduction, the tax systems of the two countries are said to be neutral with regard to international competitiveness if, despite taxation, no reallocation of the given world capital stock is induced and both countries continue to produce both commodities.

It is true that, in addition to changing the allocation of the world capital stock, taxation can also affect a country's competitiveness by changing its flow of savings. For example, a tax cut that stimulates domestic savings may induce capital exports and thus improve a country's competitiveness via a devaluation. However, the present paper neglects this possibility. Apart from the fact that a reallocation of a capital stock is capable of generating larger capital movements than a reallocation of its increments, the concentration on the neutrality conditions for stock adjustments is legitimated by the Rybczynski effect. It will take many years before a change in savings generates a change in the stock of capital large enough to drive a country into perfect specialization, and until this happens, the change in savings can neither induce international capital movements nor affect a country's competitiveness. Of course, these aspects of the model cannot be applied literally to an existing economy, but they clarify why international stock adjustments may be the dominant channel through which tax reforms affect a country's competitiveness.

Let France *(F)* and Germany *(G)* be the two countries considered and assume that the commodities produced and traded are a homogeneous investment good *(I)* and a homogeneous consumption good *(C)*. As usual, the countries have identical technological knowledge. Production of sector *i* in country *j* is determined by the linearly homogeneous, well-behaved function $f_i(K_i^j, L_i^j)$; $j = F, G$; $i = C, I$; the arguments of which are capital *(K)* and labor *(L)*. Capital and output are fully mobile, labor is only mobile within each country. The aggregate stocks of labor and capital are exogenously given: $K = K_C^F + K_I^F + K_C^G + K_I^G = const.$, $L^F = L_C^F + L_I^F = const.$, $L^G = L_C^G + L_I^G = const.$ All prices are expressed in terms of money or gold and assumed to be constant over time because the economies have settled to a stationary equilibrium. The producer prices of the four outputs are denoted by P_i^j; $j = F, G$; $i = C, I$; and the marginal pretax rates of return to capital in the four sectors are given by

6 This is a well-known phenomenon in the theory of foreign trade. See Kemp [1969, Ch. 9].

[1] $R_i^j = (\partial f_i / \partial K_i^j)(P_i^j / P_I^j); j = F, G; i = C, I.$

Accordingly,

[2] $W_i^j = (\partial f_i / \partial L_i^j)(P_i^j / P_I^j); j = F, G; i = C, I$

defines the sector-specific marginal value products of labor in terms of the respective national investment good.

Assuming a competitive equilibrium and equal tax treatments of all sectors within an economy, there will be a unique pretax return to capital in each country:

[3] $R^j = R_C^j = R_I^j$ for $j = F, G$

and a unique marginal value product of labor:

[4] $W^j = W_C^j = W_I^j$ for $j = F, G.$

Since no labor taxes are considered in the present paper, the latter can be identified with the respective national real wage rates. By way of contrast, capital income taxation implies that R^j is not necessarily equal to country j's national pretax rate of interest; the separate variable r^j, $j = F, G$ is therefore reserved for this rate.

The crucial relationship in the model is the relationship between the commodity and factor prices. Because of the linear homogeneity assumption, it follows from [1]–[4] that the factor price ratio R^j/W^j uniquely determines the absolute level of the domestic pretax rate of return to capital, $R^j = \partial f_I / \partial K_I^j, j = F, G$, and the producer price of consumption goods in terms of investment goods (or rate of commodity transformation): $P_C^j / P_I^j = (\partial f_I / \partial L_I^j)/(\partial f_C / \partial L_C^j) = (\partial f_I / \partial K_I^j)/(\partial f_C / \partial K_C^j), j = F, G$. If it is assumed that the sectors exhibit different and non-reversing capital intensities: $k_I^j > k_C^j$ or $k_I^j < k_C^j$ for all $R^j/W^j, k_i^j = K_i^j / L_i^j; j = F, G; i = C, I$, then the relationship between the pretax rate of return to capital, R^j, and the producer price of consumption goods in terms of investment goods, P_C^j / P_I^j is monotone and unique, independent of the national factor endowments. This is the well-known Stolper-Samuelson result.

Figure 1 illustrates the case where $k_I^j > k_C^j$ for all possible factor price ratios. The two heavy lines in the right part of the diagram are marginal product curves which depict the relationships between the sectoral factor intensities and the pretax of return to capital, and the heavy line in the left part shows the relationship between the latter and the producer price of consumption goods in terms of investment goods. The higher this price, the more consumption goods are produced and the lower is the rate of return to capital, which is the more abundant factor of production in the consumption goods industry. If, alternatively, $k_C^j > k_I^j$ for all R^j/W^j is assumed, then there is a positive relationship between R^j and P_C^j/P_I^j: a higher relative price of consumption goods and a higher output in the consumption goods industry in this case imply a higher relative scarcity of, and hence a higher rate of return to, capital. To summarize,

$$[5] \quad \frac{\partial R^j}{\partial (P_C^j/P_I^j)} \begin{Bmatrix} < \\ = \\ > \end{Bmatrix} 0 \Leftrightarrow k_I^j \begin{Bmatrix} > \\ = \\ < \end{Bmatrix} k_C^j \,;\, j = F, G.$$

Figure 1 — The Producer Price of Consumption Goods and the Pretax Rate of Return to Capital ($k_I^j > k_C^j$ for all R^j/W^j)

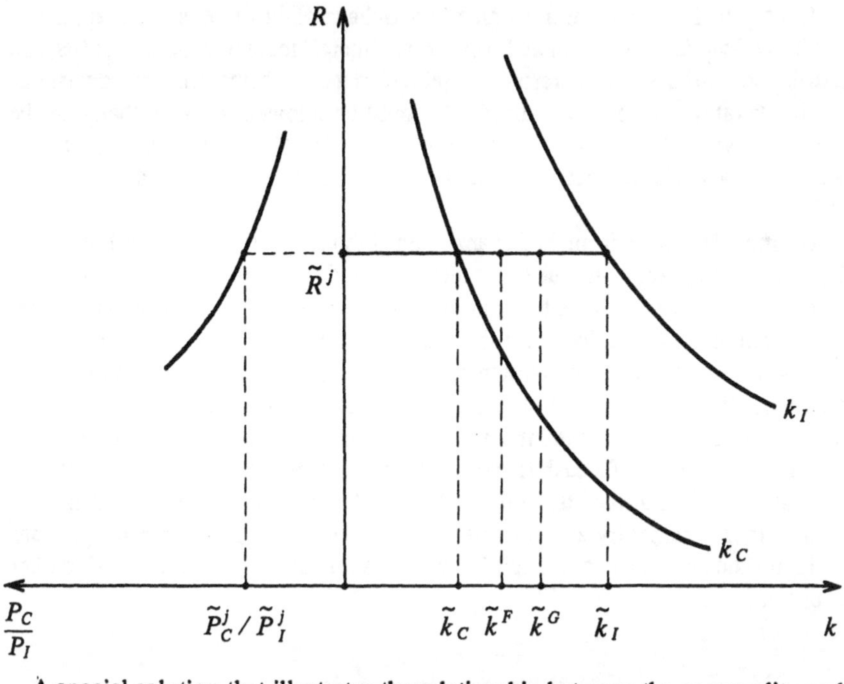

A special solution that illustrates the relationship between the commodity and factor prices is indicated by tildes in Figure 1. The solution makes it clear that a given set of factor and commodity prices uniquely determines the sectoral capital intensities, but not the average capital intensities, k^G and k^F, in the two countries. Any reallocation of the world capital stock, K, is compatible with the solution as long as $k_C \le k^j \le k_I$, $j = F, G$.

3. The Role of Taxation

In the absence of taxation, trade equalizes the commodity price ratios, $P_C^F/P_I^F = P_C^G/P_I^G$, and the Heckscher-Ohlin mechanism described equalizes the rates of return to capital: $R^F = R^G$. The latter equality does not result from free capital movements, but it harmonizes perfectly well with such movements.

Taxes drive wedges between the commodity and factor prices and can thus severely distort this equilibrium.[7] This paper considers value-added and capital income taxes. It is assumed that the rates of these taxes are uniform within a country, but not necessarily between countries.

The value-added tax is of the European type. It is a tax on consumption which exempts investment goods. Let τ^F and τ^G be the French and German tax rates.

The capital income tax is a variant of the Schanz-Haig-Simons tax. It applies to all kinds of capital incomes including personal interest income, retained profits, and distributed profits, and is therefore neutral with regard to firms' financial decisions. Double taxation of corporate dividends could be allowed without changing the results, provided that debt and retained profits are sufficient to satisfy the firms' need for funds. The respective national capital income tax rates are denoted by t^F and t^G.

The model deviates from the Schanz-Haig-Simons requirements by allowing tax depreciation to differ from true economic depreciation. Actual deviations from true economic depreciation have been so dramatic in recent years that this important aspect should not be neglected. It is assumed that country j allows the proportion α^j of gross investment to be written off immediately, while the proportion $1 - \alpha^j$ is written off gradually over time, in strict proportion with true economic depreciation. With $\alpha^j = 0$, the capital income tax is a pure Schanz-Haig-Simons tax; with $\alpha^j = 1$, it is a variant of a cash flow tax where debt interest remains deductible.

Apart from the national tax codes, it is important to specify the tax treatment of cross-border commodity and interest income flows. Four taxation principles are distinguished and checked for their implications for commodity and capital market equilibria.

a. Commodity Market Equilibrium

As investment commodities are untaxed, it can invariably be assumed that trade equates their prices:

[6] $\quad P_I^F = P_I^G$ (all systems).

---

7 This paper neglects distortions that may arise from international differences in the production of public goods, an aspect emphasized by Möller [1968].

However, for consumption goods two alternatives will be considered. Under the destination principle, which is currently in use in Europe, and is also recommended by the GATT, French consumers are indifferent between domestic and foreign goods when $P_c^F(1+\tau^F) = P_c^G(1+\tau^F)$, and German consumers are indifferent when $P_c^F(1+\tau^G) = P_c^G(1+\tau^G)$. Obviously, the tax rates cancel out, and there is an equilibrium in consumption goods markets if the national producer prices are equated:

[7] $P_c^F = P_c^G$ (destination principle).

By way of contrast, under the origin principle, which in all likelihood will characterize post-1992 Europe, consumers from both countries are indifferent between French and German consumption goods when the tax inclusive prices are equal:

[8] $P_c^F(1+\tau^F) = P_c^G(1+\tau^G)$ (origin principle).

b. Capital Market Equilibrium

Unlike the equilibrium in the commodity market, equilibrium in the capital market is characterized by two types of equation. The first describes a single firm's optimal investment strategy.

With true economic depreciation, the Johansson-Samuelson theorem would ensure that firms invest up to the point where the pretax of return to capital, R^j (from [3]), is equated with the national market rate of interest, r^j, $j = F, G$. There is a partial analytic investment neutrality, since the income tax burdens the returns from real investment in the same way as the returns from a financial capital market investment do. If an immediate write-off of real investment expenses were allowed, firms would equate their pretax rate of return to the net of the tax market rate of interest, $R^j = (1-t^j)r^j$. In general, the firms' optimal investment condition is[8]

[9] $R^j = (1-\alpha^j t^j)r^j;\ j = F, G,$

where α is the depreciation parameter introduced above ($0 \leq \alpha^j \leq 1$).

The second equation relates the national interest rates via international arbitrage.[9] Under the residence principle for interest income taxation, which is postu-

8 For a derivation of this formula from an explicit intertemporal optimization model of the firm, see Sinn [1987].

9 Discussions of the implications of residence and source principles for international capital movements can be found in Mutti and Grubert [1985], Slemrod [1988], and Sinn [1984a; 1984b].

lated in the OECD Model Double Taxation Convention of 1977 and legally installed by most countries, interest income is taxed in the investor's home country. The German investor is therefore indifferent between French and German investment if $r^F(1-t^G) = r^G(1-t^G)$, and the French investor is indifferent if $r^F(1-t^F) = r^G(1-t^F)$. Obviously, the terms in brackets cancel out, and a capital market equilibrium prevails if

$$[10] \quad r^F = r^G \qquad \text{(residence principle).}$$

As in the absence of taxation, arbitrage equates the pretax interest rates across the borders.

The alternative to the residence principle is the source principle. This principle is technically easier to implement, but, as the German failure to introduce such a tax in 1989 showed, it induces strong international capital movements. Under the source principle, investors are indifferent between French and German assets if the interest rates, net of the national capital income taxes, are the same:

$$[11] \quad r^F(1-t^F) = r^G(1-t^G) \qquad \text{(source principle).}$$

Different assumptions on depreciation allowances, different principles for cross-border interest income and commodity flows, and different assumptions on the capital intensities of the consumption and investment goods industries yield a considerable variety of tax worlds. The alternatives are summarized in Table 1, which serves as a guideline for the subsequent discussion of neutral tax policies.

4. Robust Neutrality

The discussion of neutral tax policies begins with what may be called "robust neutrality." *Robust neutrality* means that a country can freely choose a tax rate without affecting its international competitiveness. The capital income tax can exhibit robust neutrality, the value-added tax can have it, and they may both have it together. Robust neutrality is the borderline case between additive and subtractive neutrality as defined in the introduction.

From [6], [7], [9], and [10] it is obvious that the combination of the destination principle, true economic depreciation ($\alpha = 0$), and the residence principle will ensure robust neutrality for both taxes. As in the laissez-faire case, producer prices of consumption goods in terms of investment goods are the same in both countries:

$$[12] \quad P_C^F / P_I^F = P_C^G / P_I^G ,$$

Table 1 — Neutrality Conditions

<table>
<tr><td colspan="2" rowspan="2">Commodity taxation
Taxation of interest income</td><td rowspan="2">Destination principle</td><td colspan="2">Origin principle</td></tr>
<tr><td>$k_I > k_C$</td><td>$k_C > k_I$</td></tr>
<tr><td rowspan="2">Source principle</td><td>$\alpha < 1$</td><td>τ: robust neutr.; harmonize α and t</td><td>subtractive neutrality</td><td>addititve neutrality</td></tr>
<tr><td>$\alpha = 1$</td><td rowspan="2">τ, t: robust neutrality</td><td colspan="2" rowspan="2">t: robust neutr.; harmonize τ</td></tr>
<tr><td rowspan="2">Residence principle</td><td>$\alpha = 0$</td></tr>
<tr><td>$\alpha > 0$</td><td>τ: robust neutr.; harmonize $\alpha \cdot t$</td><td>additive neutrality</td><td>subtractive neutrality</td></tr>
</table>

and pretax rates of return to capital are also the same:

$$[13] \quad R^F = R^G.$$

Clearly, it remains possible that both countries produce both goods. Note that [12] and [13] are not only neutrality but also efficiency conditions. They ensure that, given their aggregate factor endowments, the two countries operate on their joint efficiency frontier. The next section will analyze neutrality conditions which do not coincide with efficiency conditions.

The case considered is represented in the third box in the first column of Table 1. It can be seen as the ideal legal combination recommended by the GATT, the OECD Model Double Taxation Convention and the Schanz-Haig-Simons income definition. Interestingly enough, even this case strongly contradicts the view that aggregate tax burden comparisons matter for a country's international competitiveness. Contrary to that view, each country is able to choose its capital income tax and value-added tax rates freely without changing its competitiveness.

An equally robust neutrality case is described by the second box in the first column of Table 1. When the destination principle is maintained, but the source principle and immediate depreciation ($\alpha = 1$) are chosen, then [12] and [13] will again be true. The latter equation follows from equation [9], with $\alpha = 1$, and from [11]. Equation [9] says that firms invest up to the point where their pretax rate of return to capital equals the net of tax market rate of interest, and [11] says that international arbitrage equates the national interest rates, net of the respective national tax rates. This tax world was analyzed by Sinn [1987, Ch. 11] and recommended as a feasible alternative to the theoretical idea of true income taxation, which was rejected as theoretically unattractive and practically not feasible.[10]

It should perhaps be noted that the assumption of an immediate write-off, which characterizes the present case, is not as remote as it might seem at first sight. In fact, it characterizes almost perfectly the situation in the Reagan era in the United States. Official estimates by the Office of Tax Analysis in the Treasury Department confirmed that, in the period from 1981 to 1986, the United States had investment incentives that resembled and even exceeded an immediate write-off.[11] Mind, though, that the United States and its trading partners continued to apply the residence principle. As can be seen from [9] and [10], this policy constellation was strongly nonneutral, creating incentives for capital imports that, in the Heckscher-Ohlin model of Section 2, would have wiped out capital-intensive sectors in the rest of the world and/or labor-intensive sectors in the US.[12]

To avoid these consequences of accelerated tax depreciation without sacrificing the destination and residence principles, it would have been necessary to harmonize the capital income tax rates and depreciation allowances across countries in a way that equated the national values for the term αt. This can be seen from [9] and [10], which show how the pretax rates of return to capital are related in a capital market equilibrium:

[14] $R^F/(1-\alpha^F t^F) = R^G/(1-\alpha^G t^G)$ (residence principle).

Obviously $R^F = R^G$ if, and only if, $\alpha^F t^F = \alpha^G t^G$.

The property of robust neutrality applies only partially under these circumstances; it is maintained for the value-added tax, but not for the capital income tax.

10 The main reasons for recommending the alternative tax system were its administrative advantages and its intertemporal neutrality properties.

11 See US Department of the Treasury [1984, pp. 106, 107, and 112]. See also Gravelle [1982] and Fullerton et al. [1987, p. 144, Table 5.4].

12 An analysis of the 1981 US tax reform in a Heckscher-Ohlin model is provided in Sinn [1984b, pp. 568-572]. See Krause-Junk [1988] for a welfare analysis of accelerated depreciation in an open economy.

Nevertheless, it remains true that a simple summation of the national tax burdens reveals almost nothing about the influence of taxes on international competitiveness. The case is illustrated by the last box in the first column of Table 1.

A related case is the first box in this column, where the source principle applies, but immediate depreciation is not allowed. Again, the destination principle ensures robust neutrality for the value-added tax. However, to equate the national pretax rates of return to capital, it is not sufficient to harmonize the αt. Equations [9] and [11] imply that

$$[15] \quad R^F[(1-t^F)/(1-\alpha^F t^F)] = R^G[(1-t^G)/(1-\alpha^G t^G)] \quad \text{(source principle)}.$$

This shows that for $R^F = R^G$ it is necessary to harmonize both the tax rates and the depreciation allowances.

Consider now a replacement of the destination principle with the origin principle, the policy advocated by the German iron and steel industry. Regardless of whether the residence principle and true economic depreciation ($\alpha = 0$) or the source principle and free depreciation ($\alpha = 1$) prevail, it will remain true that the equilibrium in the international capital market is characterized by $R^F = R^G$. Direct taxation continues to enjoy robust neutrality. However, as shown by [6] and [8], only a harmonization of the national value-added tax rates can prevent a distortion by ensuring that $P_C^G/P_I^G = P_C^F/P_I^F$. In the table, these are the second and third boxes in the second and third columns.

When the French value-added tax rate exceeds the German rate ($\tau^F > \tau^G$), as in the historical case, it follows from [6] and [8] that the German producer price of consumption goods in terms of investment goods exceeds its French counterpart: $P_C^G/P_I^G > P_C^F/P_I^F$. Because of the Stolper-Samuelson result [5], this demands a wedge between the pretax rates of return to capital even though a wedge is excluded in the assumed system of direct taxation. Perfect specialization and a dramatic change in international competitiveness result regardless of whether the overall tax burden imposed on French and German firms is the same. This provides strong support for the French position that the origin principle would be nonneutral without a harmonization of value-added tax rates.

It is frequently argued that different value-added tax rates are harmless even with the origin principle, since mere exchange rate adjustments are sufficient to neutralize the tax rate differences.[13] In the case of France and Germany, for example, a revaluation of the German currency is expected to fully compensate for the lower value-added tax rate. This view certainly cannot be confirmed with the model used in this paper, even though it is a model of pure exchange that implicitly assumes full exchange rate flexibility. The fallacy of the exchange rate argument is

[13] The argument dates back to the Tinbergen Committee [1953], which referred to a uniform indirect tax, not a value-added tax.

that it neglects the fact that even an ideal value-added tax of the European type is not a uniform tax on all commodities: it is a pure consumption tax that exempts investment goods. It is impossible for exchange rate adjustments to compensate for tax-induced changes in relative prices. The revaluation of the German currency (or the inflation) that will probably occur after 1992, when direct consumer purchases enforce the origin principle in Europe, will undoubtedly hurt the German investment goods industry. There will be a reallocation of productive factors from this industry to the German consumption goods industry, and the French investment goods will gain at the expense of the French consumption goods industry.[14]

5. Additive and Subtractive Neutrality

The model offers a number of options for preventing excessive international capital movements which would eliminate the German investment goods industry and/or the French consumption goods industry. When the origin principle, with non-harmonized value-added tax rates, applies, only one option is left. It is necessary to deviate from neutrality in the taxation of cross-border interest income flows to create a tax distortion in capital markets that just compensates for the tax distortion in goods markets. Via sectoral shifts, the distortion in goods markets translates into a gap between the national pretax rates of return to capital, $R^F - R^G$. The distortion in the capital market must therefore be designed in a way that makes this gap compatible with a capital market equilibrium.

The required compensating distortion in the capital market can, in principle, be achieved either by not combining the source principle with instantaneous depreciation or by not combining the residence principle with true economic depreciation, and its direction depends on which sector is more capital intensive. There are thus four possible cases. They are represented by the first and fourth boxes in the third and fourth columns of Table 1.

Suppose first that the investment goods industry is more capital intensive than the consumption goods industry: $k_I^j > k_C^j$ for $j = F, G$, and all relevant factor price ratios. In this case, it follows from [5] that the commodity price distortion $P_C^G/P_I^G > P_C^F/P_I^F$ which [6] and [8] imply for the case of a comparatively low German value-added tax rate ($\tau^G < \tau^F$) results in an excess of the French pretax return to capital over the German return: $R^F > R^G$. Other things being equal, the high-tax country attracts the capital. To compensate for this attraction, a comparatively high source tax on French interest income ($t^F > t^G$) and/or more restrictive depreciation allowances than in Germany ($\alpha^F < \alpha^G$) are required. Equation [15]

14 This criticism of the exchange rate argument is also made in Sinn [1989].

shows that both measures make a capital market equilibrium with $R^F > R^G$ possible and prevent the countries from being driven into perfect specialization.

This paradoxical case is an example of what in the introduction was called subtractive neutrality. The country with the higher value-added tax needs a higher capital income tax to maintain its competitiveness. The result turns the conventional additive neutrality view upside down.

Other, even more paradoxical, options for preventing the high French value-added tax from attracting capital from Germany exist under the residence principle. As with the source principle, it remains true that comparatively restrictive depreciation allowances in Germany will do the job. However, with given and identical accelerated depreciation allowances in the two countries ($\alpha^G = \alpha^F > 0$), it would also be possible to keep the capital in Germany by implementing comparatively *higher* capital income tax rates. Equation [14], the capital market equilibrium condition for the residence principle, shows this very clearly: when $\alpha^F = \alpha^G$, an equilibrium with $R^F > R^G$ can occur if, and only if, $t^G > t^F$. The mechanism operating here is the by now well-known *taxation paradox* [see Sinn, 1987, Ch. 5.4.3]. Its essence is that, with accelerated depreciation and the residence principle, an increase in the national tax rate punishes real domestic investment less than financial investment abroad. Investors have therefore an incentive to invest in the country with the higher capital income tax rate, and this incentive may just compensate for the higher pretax return that lures the capital from abroad.

The result of all this is, as is indicated in the last box in the second column of Table 1, additive neutrality. A country with a high value-added tax needs a low capital income tax to maintain its international competitiveness, and vice versa. A conventional belief is confirmed. It must be stressed, however, that in this case the conventional belief is right for the wrong reason. It is not true that a high value-added tax rate deters the capital and that a low capital income tax rate is needed to attract it again. On the contrary, in the case considered, a *low* value-added tax deters the capital, and a high capital income tax rate is needed to attract it. The conventional belief is confirmed because two paradoxes offset one another.

Fortunately, there is a case where the conventional view is confirmed. It is represented by the first box in the third column of Table 1. If the consumption goods sector is more capital intensive than the investment goods sector, then the country with the lower value-added tax rate can offer a higher pretax rate of return to capital. Formally, if $k_C^j > k_I^j$ for $j = F, G$ and all relevant factor price ratios, and if $\tau^G < \tau^F$, then it follows from [5], [6], and [8] that $P_C^G / P_I^G > P_C^F / P_I^F$ and $R^G > R^F$. Under the source principle without immediate write off ($\alpha < 1$), it is possible to compensate for this and to stop the drive towards perfect specialization that otherwise would occur by accompanying the low value-added tax rate with a high capital income tax rate and/or restrictive depreciation allowances. This is obvious by again inspecting [15]. The case considered should be the one which those who focus on aggregate tax burden comparisons have in mind. At last, there is a combination where they are right for the right reason. There are no paradoxes and additive neutrality prevails.

Unfortunately, there is insufficient empirical evidence to ultimately decide which of the two sectors is the more capital intensive. In two-sector models of economic growth with Keynesian savings functions, it is usually necessary to assume that the consumption goods sector is more capital intensive because otherwise the growth path would not be stable [see Shinkai, 1960; Uzawa, 1962]. However, there is no good reason for applying the correspondence principle across theoretical models, let alone for using Keynesian stability conditions to predict the outcome of neoclassical allocation models. More intriguing evidence comes from a study on Germany by Wallenwein [1986]. This study confirms the assumption that the consumption goods sector is more capital intensive, although no attempt is made to explain the empirical significance of the results that are offered. An earlier study by Sutton [1976] finds the evidence in favor of the stability case less convincing.

Should the consumption goods sector really turn out to be more capital intensive than the capital goods sector, then the application of the source principle for the taxation of cross-border interest income flows will ensure that the conventional additive neutrality view does have its merits. It must not be forgotten though that the source principle is just a theoretical possibility. As mentioned earlier, the residence principle is the most widely used among OECD countries. Moreover, accelerated depreciation is the relevant assumption for most countries. Under these circumstances, the taxation paradox applies and is not counterbalanced by the value-added tax paradox studied above. A low value-added tax rate expands the capital-intensive sector and attracts capital imports. To compensate for this attraction and to prevent the countries from being driven into perfect specialization, the capital income tax rate must also be low. This case is represented by the last box in the last column in Table 1. Again, the tax system exhibits the property of subtractive neutrality. Perhaps this will be the most plausible case of all in post-1992 Europe.

6. Concluding Remarks

The preceding analysis is a study in the effects of taxation on international competitiveness, with particular emphasis placed on neutrality conditions. Focusing on ideal versions of the value-added tax and ideal versions of a capital income tax, it demonstrates the general invalidity of the common claim that the tax influence on a country's competitiveness can be assessed by measuring the aggregate company tax burden. Various conditions for "robust neutrality" and "subtractive neutrality" were isolated, under which the conventional claim is completely unjustified. The conclusion is that it may well be the case that direct and indirect taxes counteract each other, so that a country that has a high value-added tax rate needs a high capital income tax rate as well if it wants to preserve its international competitiveness.

The analysis was confined to two single model taxes, albeit with a variety of modifications. More institutional detail can, and should, be introduced at a later stage. For example, it would be useful to allow for diverging tax rates on interest income and retained profits, to introduce capital gains taxation, and to consider alternative indirect taxes and subsidies. However, the basic interaction possibilities between indirect and direct taxation that were pointed out in this paper, including the effects operating through changes in sectoral structures and pretax factor prices, are likely to survive.

The paper is neither a normative nor an empirical study. It is an attempt to develop a systematic framework for international tax comparisons and policy recommendations, and it makes predictions about the effects of alternative tax systems on international competitiveness. Hopefully, this framework will prove useful for further applied work, including that of research institutes which specialize in the field of world economics.

Bibliography

ANDEL, Norbert, "Zur Diskussion 'Ursprungs-' versus 'Bestimmungslandprinzip'." Finanzarchiv, N.F., Vol. 24, 1965, pp. 115-125.

BERGLAS, Eitan, "Harmonization of Commodity Taxes. Destination, Origin and Restricted Origin Principles." Journal of Public Economics, Vol. 16, 1981, pp. 377-387.

FULLERTON, Don, R. GILETTE, James MACKIE, "Investment Allocation and Growth Under the Tax Reform Act of 1986." In: OFFICE OF TAX ANALYSIS (Ed.), Compendium of Tax Research 1987. Washington 1987.

GRAVELLE, Jane G., "Effects of the 1981 Depreciation Revisions on the Taxation of Income from Business Capital." National Tax Journal, Vol. 35, 1982, pp. 1-20.

HÖHN, Monika, Zur Diskussion 'Mehrwertsteuer versus Körperschaftssteuer.' Bochum 1980.

KEMP, Murray C., The Pure Theory of International Trade and Investment. Englewood Cliffs 1969.

KRAUSE-JUNK, Gerold, "Außenwirtschaftliche Konsequenzen beschleunigter Abschreibung." Finanzarchiv, N.F., Vol. 46, 1988, pp. 252-267.

MASSON, Paul R., Malcolm KNIGHT, "The International Transmission of Fiscal Policies in Major Industrial Countries." IMF Staff Papers, Vol. 33, 1986, pp. 387-438.

MÖLLER, Hans, "Ursprungs- und Bestimmungslandprinzip. Ein Beitrag zur Lehre von den Steuerwirkungen auf die internationalen Wirtschaftsbeziehungen unter Berücksichtigung des Gemeinsamen Marktes." Finanzarchiv, N.F., Vol. 27, 1968, pp. 385-458.

MUTTI, John, Harry GRUBERT, "The Taxation of Capital Income in an Open Economy: The Importance of Resident-Nonresident Tax Treatment." Journal of Public Economics, Vol. 27, 1985, pp. 291-309.

NEUMARK COMMITTEE, Report of the Fiscal and Financial Committee. International Bureau of Fiscal Documentation, The EEC Reports on Tax Harmonization, Amsterdam 1963.

ORGANIZATION FOR ECONOMIC COOPERATION AND DEVELOPMENT (OECD), Model Double Taxation Convention on Income and on Capital. Report of the OECD Committee on Fiscal Affairs. Paris 1977.

SHINKAI, Yoichi, "On Equilibrium Growth of Capital and Labor." International Economic Review, Vol. 1, 1960, pp. 107-111.

SHOUP, Carl S. (Ed.), Fiscal Harmonization in Common Markets, Vol. 1. New York 1967.

SIEVERT, Olaf, Außenwirtschaftliche Probleme steuerlicher Ausgleichsmaßnahmen für den internationalen Handel. Köln 1964.

SINN, Hans-Werner [1984a], "Systeme der Kapitaleinkommensbesteuerung. Ein allokationstheoretischer Vergleich." In: Dieter BÖS, Manfred ROSE, Christian SEIDL (Hrsg.), Beiträge zur neueren Steuertheorie. Berlin 1984, pp. 209-238.

— [1984b], "Die Bedeutung des Accelerated Cost Recovery System für den internationalen Kapitalverkehr." Kyklos, Vol. 37, 1984, pp. 542-576.

—, "Why Taxes Matter: Reagan's Accelerated Cost Recovery System and the U.S. Trade Deficit." Economic Policy, Vol. 1, 1985, pp. 239-250.

—, Capital Income Taxation and Resource Allocation. Amsterdam 1987.

—, "Tax Harmonization and Tax Competition in Europe." European Economic Review, Papers & Proceedings, Vol. 34, 1990, pp. 489-504.

SLEMROD, Joel, "Effect of Taxation with International Capital Mobility." In: Henry J. AARON, Harvey GALPER, Joseph PECHMAN (Eds.), Uneasy Compromise. Problems of a Hybrid Income-Consumption Tax. Washington 1988.

SUMMERS, Lawrence H., Tax Policy and International Competitiveness. Harvard Institute of Economic Research, Discussion Paper, 1256, Cambridge, Mass., 1986.

SUTTON, John, "The Relative Factor Intensities of Investment and Consumer-Goods Industries: A Note." Econometrica, Vol. 44, 1976, pp. 819-821.

TINBERGEN COMMITTEE, Report on Problems Raised by the Different Turnover Tax Systems Applied within the Common Market. Luxembourg 1953.

US DEPARTMENT OF THE TREASURY, Tax Reforms for Fairness, Simplicity, and Economic Growth. Washington 1984.

UZAWA, Hirofumi, "On a Two-Sector Model of Economic Growth." Review of Economic Studies, Vol. 29, 1962, pp. 40-47.

WALLENWEIN, Erich, Die Bedeutung der Kapitalintensitätshypothese im neoklassischen Zwei-Sektoren Modell und ihre empirische Überprüfung. Frankfurt am Main 1986.

WHALLEY, John, "Uniform Domestic Taxes, Trade Distortions, and Economic Integration." Journal of Public Economics, Vol. 11, 1979, pp. 213-221.

—, "Border Adjustments and Tax Harmonization: Comment on Berglas." Journal of Public Economics, Vol. 16, 1981, pp. 389-390.

Comment on Hans-Werner Sinn, "Can Direct and Indirect Taxes be Added for International Comparisons of Competitiveness?"

Christian Seidl

As is usually the case with Sinn's papers, I am in agreement with most of his findings, I enjoyed reading his interesting analysis and, once again, I learned a lot from his insights. I admire outrightly the beautiful taxonomy of his model world, which provides us with a decided clue to the appropriate combination of commodity taxation and taxation of capital income needed to attain neutrality of the tax system.

The analysis seems to be rather clear-cut whenever the destination principle applies for commodity taxation. In that case, no need for tax harmonization arises when the destination principle for commodity taxation is combined either with the source principle for capital income taxation and immediate depreciation (i.e., $\alpha = 1$) or with the residence principle for capital income taxation and economic depreciation (i.e., $\alpha = 0$). Different depreciation rules require harmonization of α and t under the source principle and harmonization of αt under the residence principle in order to attain robust neutrality of the respective tax systems.

It seems that we may well assume that this analysis carries over by and large to the real world, provided that we are allowed to make two assumptions: first, that business profits are sufficiently high to realize the tax credits resulting from accelerated depreciation in the very same period in which the capital investment is made; and second, that domestic preferential treatment of depreciation is confined to residents of the respective country. Though we can expect some discrimination against newly founded firms, we are certainly allowed to accept this part of Sinn's model taxonomy as a good working hypothesis about the neutrality properties of tax systems when the source principle applies to capital income taxation. It is less convincing under the residence principle for capital income taxation.

Yet this analysis, however well known its general results are, commands little contemporary interest, as the European Community is about to adopt the origin principle for commodity taxation anyway. But the Sinn paper allows for this case, too. Because of the imminent significance of this case in the face of the European coalescence, we have to take a closer look at it.

When the source principle for capital income taxation and immediate depreciation apply, or when the residence principle for capital income taxation and economic depreciation apply, Sinn makes a case for *harmonization* of the VAT rates. Otherwise, neutrality of taxation would be violated. In particular, Sinn rejects the exchange rate argument, which has been employed for a long time to convince us that the *invoice method* applied to goods that are exported or imported by firms can coexist with the *origin principle* for the VAT applied to goods that are exported or imported by direct consumer purchases. In essence, the exchange rate argument contends that exchange rate adjustments of the respective currencies will restore the same marginal rates of transformation in the production sector that exist under the destination principle.

In the present paper, Sinn touches only shortly on the exchange rate argument, but he elaborated on this argument in his Invited Paper on "Tax Harmonization and Tax Competition in Europe" delivered to the Fourth Annual Meeting of the European Economic Association in Augsburg in September 1989. While sharing Sinn's objection to the exchange rate argument, I think that there is a flaw in his reasoning that also overshadows the analysis of the origin principle combined with the cases of $0 < \alpha < 1$ in the model taxonomy of his present paper.

Sinn treats goods as if they had an inherent property of being either investment goods or consumer goods, where investment goods are VAT-exempt and consumer goods are subject to a VAT. But under the VAT regulations, the characteristic of a good is determined by the buyer of a good. When the buyer is a firm, the good is treated for VAT purposes as an intermediate[1] good or as an investment good. If the buyer is a consumer, it is treated as a consumer good. For instance, a particular car is treated as a consumer good when sold to a household, as an intermediate good when sold to an automobile dealer, and as an investment good when sold to a taxi-driver. This requires that we not denote goods as consumer goods or investment goods, but classify them according to whether the buyer happens to be a firm or a household. I shall demonstrate the problem for the case involving two countries, say France and Germany.

Let P denote the producer prices and τ the VAT rates in France and in Germany, respectively. By assuming perfect competition and employing the invoice method, for goods imported or exported by firms, we have

$$[1] \quad P_i^{fG} = P_i^{fF}.$$

For the case of direct consumer imports or for goods bought from mail-order firms, we have

$$[2] \quad P_i^{cG}(1+\tau_G) = P_i^{cF}(1+\tau_F).$$

Suppose $\tau_G < \tau_F$. Immediately after a switch from the destination principle to the origin principle, we then have

1 Notice that this category of goods is neglected altogether in the Sinn analysis.

[3] $P_i^{fG}(1+\tau_G) < P_i^{fF}(1+\tau_F)$.

But as the exchange rate responds, we have

[4] $[(1+\tau_F)/(1+\tau_G)]P_i^{fG}(1+\tau_G) = P_i^{fF}(1+\tau_F)$,

such that

[5] $P_i^{cG}/P_i^{cF} = (1+\tau_F)/(1+\tau_G)$.

Therefore, the adaptation in the exchange rate [5] equilibrates [3], but simultaneously brings [1] into disequilibrium, as we have

[6] $P_i^{fG}(1+\tau_f)/(1+\tau_G) > P_i^{fF}$.

This means that adaptations in the exchange rate cannot simultaneously accomplish [1] and [2] as long as we have goods which are traded according to the invoice method. Yet investment goods and intermediate goods will be traded following the invoice method anyway, as the tax credit would be lost otherwise. The inequality [6] therefore shows that exchange rate adaptations would discriminate against Germany *both* for *investment* goods and for *intermediate* goods.

Allocative efficiency can therefore be preserved either under the origin method for perfect tax harmonization, i.e., for $\tau_G = \tau_F$, or by combining the origin method with tax credits calculated according to the tax rates of the importing country. The latter means that immediately after its introduction

[7] $P_i^{fG} < P_i^{fF}(1+\tau_F)/(1+\tau_G)$ and $P_i^{fF} > P_i^{fG}(1+\tau_G)/(1+\tau_F)$.

But the adaptation of the exchange rate as shown in [5] again restores the condition of allocative efficiency [1]. Tax credits calculated according to the tax rates of the importing country are therefore also able to reconcile [1] and [2], but contrary to the perfect tax harmonization condition, this would be accomplished by way of adaptations in the exchange rate, which cannot be dispensed with in such a case.

Formally, this method is equivalent to the subtraction method addressed in Section V of Sinn's Augsburg paper. However, Sinn neglects to mention that this approach can accomplish allocative efficiency only when there is a concomitant exchange rate adjustment.[2]

This approach obviously requires that France subsidize the imports of German investment goods and German intermediate goods, whereas Germany must be

---

2 Notice that there is no explicit term for the exchange rate adjustment in Sinn's analysis.

allowed to tax the imports of French investment goods and French intermediate goods. I doubt that something like that would carry the day in the contemporary European Community.

Notice that even when tax rates are perfectly harmonized (and more so under other regulations), a clearing house is required whenever large imbalances of foreign trade happen to persist. The adoption of the origin principle would shift the VAT revenue to the countries with large export surpluses, contrary to the destination principle, which assigns the higher VAT revenue to countries with import surpluses. I am sure that the Ministers of Finance would demand a compensation for this effect.

This analysis shows that under the origin principle for the VAT we can accomplish tax neutrality, both for the source principle and immediate depreciation, and for the residence principle and economic depreciation for capital income taxation, either under perfect harmonization of the VAT rates or under the subtraction method supplemented by an adequate adjustment of the rates of exchange. Contrary to his Augsburg paper, Sinn did not mention this second viable method in the present paper.

Four cases in Sinn's table of neutrality conditions remain to be discussed. They arise under the origin principle for the VAT and for depreciation policies characterized by $0 < \alpha < 1$ for the taxation of capital income. For these cases, Sinn makes the remarkable suggestion that violations of neutrality through commodity taxation due to the adoption of the origin principle should be compensated for by an appropriate policy of capital income taxation with respect to tax rates and depreciation rules. But, alas, the appropriate policy of capital income taxation happens to differ fundamentally (subtractive versus additive neutrality) depending on the relative capital intensity of production in the consumer goods industry and in the investment goods industry, respectively.

This is certainly an impressive result in a model world with only two goods, which, moreover, happen to be treated homogeneously under a VAT system. However, results derived from this model must not be applied to the real world without prior close reflection upon policy recommendations. In the real VAT world, goods do not in general possess the property of being consumer goods or investment goods (or intermediary goods) a priori. Moreover, even if this were the case, different consumer goods could be produced with largely varying capital intensities of production, some of which might have greater capital intensity than some investment goods. Intermediate goods (though neglected by Sinn) contribute to a still greater confusion. I think that the Sinn analysis, if it is to be useful for applied tax policy at all, must be recast in terms of a multisectoral model allowing for different capital intensities in production and based on empirical data for the economies involved.[3] In the present case, policy recommendations based on mere theoretical speculation can be grossly misleading because the prevailing conditions require more careful and more comprehensive analyses. Sinn's model is certainly an important first step in the right direction, but I am afraid that in its present form it could even be dangerous as a guideline for applied tax policy in the coalescing European Community.

There is also another disturbing trait in Sinn's analysis. While the source principle of capital income taxation confines accelerated depreciation benefits only to capital that is actually invested in the respective country, it is not clear why the residence principle should exclude residents of country *G* from accelerated depreciation benefits in country *F*, or vice versa. The residence principle can hardly be confined, as Sinn's analysis suggests, to mere interest income from given credits.

Let us assume that all barriers to entry are removed within the European Community. When $t_F > t_G$, we obviously have

$$[8] \quad [r_G/(1-\alpha_G t_G)](1-t_F) < [r_G/(1-\alpha_G t_F)](1-t_F).$$

Given this situation, what could induce a Frenchman to buy German bonds (left side) instead of German equity (right side)?

Alternatively, we have

$$[9] \quad [r_F/(1-\alpha_F t_G)](1-t_G) < [r_F/(1-\alpha_F t_F)](1-t_G).$$

In this case, what could induce a German investor to buy French equity (left side) instead of French bonds (right side)?

These inequalities contrast with Sinn's characterization of the residence principle as expounded in [14] of his paper. Contrary to Sinn, I think that nonharmonized rate structures for the income tax will matter in the European Community when barriers to entry are removed. The inequalities [8] and [9] show that citizens of high-tax countries will chose to invest in equity, whereas residents of low-tax countries will prefer to invest in bonds. This will certainly have repercussions for the equity structure of firms. The French will be tempted to acquire more firm shares and the Germans will become the creditors.

In the real world, however, this would not occur because capital income largely escapes taxation. But when tax loopholes are effectively closed, this problem may well arise.

---

3 I suspect, however, that there is no solution for such general models. The Sinn model has two policy instruments (i.e., two tax rates) for two goods markets. More than two goods will certainly require an equivalent number of instruments.

Let me close with a final comment. Concerning the income tax, Sinn's results hold only when there is *no mobility* on the part of capital and labor. Otherwise, the owners of capital and labor services will simply change their country of residence. It is hard to imagine why people should chose a high-tax country as their residence instead of a low-tax country. Problems of this kind are indeed addressed and analyzed in Section VIII of Sinn's Augsburg paper, in which he even goes as far as to deny people the right to change their nationality after they have reached a certain age. Though I believe that his fears expressed in the Augsburg paper under the heading "Tiebout and the Death of the Insurance State" are somewhat exaggerated because the thrust of the *equivalence principle* of the social security system is largely neglected, I have the impression that such problems are assumed away in the Kiel paper. Should regional mobility really turn out to be a threat to European tax and redistribution systems, it can hardly be disregarded in any closely related analysis.

II

Taxation and Capital Flows

Richard M. Levich
Ingo Walter

Tax-Driven Regulatory Drag: European Financial Centers in the 1990s

1. Introduction

The competitive dynamics of financial markets over the past quarter century has been affected by three powerful forces: product innovation, process innovation and technological change [see Levich, 1988]. *Product innovation* encompasses several dimensions: new financial products (e.g., caps, futures, options, swaps) along with the ability to replicate certain products by bundling existing products (synthetic securities) or to highlight only a single financial attribute by unbundling an existing product. *Process innovation* encompasses contract design (e.g., cash settlement futures contracts), methods of settlement and trading (e.g., the Chicago Mercantile Exchange link with the Singapore International Monetary Exchange, or the London Stock Exchange's system of automated stock price quotations (SEAQ)), methods for efficient margin calculation, methods of contract pricing (e.g., the Black-Scholes option-pricing model and the delta-hedging technique for risk management), and passive or index-based portfolio investment techniques, along with a range of other innovations. *Technological change*, primarily in telecommunications and information processing, has greatly facilitated the drive to create and broaden the market for such product and process innovations.

The growth of automated trading systems provides an appropriate example. In December 1989, the London International Financial Futures Exchange (LIFFE) inaugurated the Automated Pit Trading (APT) system to simulate electronically the dynamics of an open-outcry market. Beginning with Euromark futures contracts and being capable of processing about 100 transactions per second, the APT system is intended to extend the trading day and make LIFFE accessible to a much wider range of international users. Besides actual trading, the APT system can receive and route orders, clear transactions, handle order-processing, and monitor compliance. In many ways it is similar to another system (Aurora), under development by the

Remark : The views expressed in this paper are those of the authors and do not necessarily reflect the views of any of the affiliated institutions. The authors accept responsibility for any errors that remain.

Chicago Board of Trade. Meanwhile, the Chicago Mercantile Exchange is completing work on Globex — an order-matching system which will list the products of various exchanges around the world when the floors of those exchanges are closed.

The end result of these forces is that communications costs and financial transaction costs are lower and capital mobility higher than at any time in living memory. Both financial firms and the users of financial services can access a broad range of location choices, including an array of foreign or offshore operations. This is certainly true at the wholesale end of the industry, and it is becoming more true at the retail end as well through the origination and distribution of asset-backed securities and through unit trusts or mutual funds. Under such conditions, we will argue that it is becoming less feasible for a state or a nation to impose financial market regulations or costs that stand very far apart from world norms.

The overall cost of financial regulation and taxation of capital market activities — which we define as the net regulatory burden (NRB) — will become increasingly important as EC financial liberalization is implemented in 1990, as the 1992-related initiatives in the real sector take hold, and as governments increasingly recognize the real costs of inefficient domestic financial markets. The magnitude and dispersion of these NRBs across countries will be influenced as well by rapid growth in institutionalized savings throughout Europe, particularly funded pension programs, that will of necessity be far more performance-oriented than individual savers have been in the past.

In Section 2 of the paper, we outline the conceptual reasoning underlying the competitive dynamics of financial markets in an open economy. In particular, we review how competitive forces affect both users and suppliers of financial services, as well as how they affect regulators. In Section 3, we consider securities taxation in Europe, specifically taxation bearing directly on the investor and taxation bearing on primary- and secondary-market transactions. We assess the incidence of tax rates across the EC countries and Switzerland and conclude that tax-related costs imposed on securities activities in Germany and Switzerland have generally been high relative to competitive financial centers. These costs have constituted a regulatory "drag" for both of these countries that may have inflicted significant and possibly long-lasting damage on their role as competitive locations for securities and other financial transactions. This is an important conclusion given the heightened level of global financial competition, but especially as Europe faces still fewer restrictions on capital mobility in the 1990s. Section 4 concludes with a review and outlook for the future.

2. Dynamics of Financial Market Regulation in an Open Economy

a. Financial Market Participants and Competitive Behavior

In order to analyze the dynamic effects of regulation on financial markets (and vice versa), it is convenient to consider three sets of market participants: (1) individuals and institutions that demand financial services, (2) firms that supply financial services, and (3) regulatory bodies that set the rules and monitor various aspects of financial transactions. Since around the turn of the century, a complex set of regulations has evolved to circumscribe the activities on both the demand and supply sides of financial transactions. These regulations can entail both costs and benefits for users as well as suppliers of financial services.

Looking first at the demand side, we see that individuals benefit to the extent that regulations act to reduce the negative externalities associated with a fully competitive banking and financial system, or to the extent that regulations provide a subsidy to the consumer of financial services. Financial markets are often characterized by imperfect information, which is of particular interest to the small investor, who gains to the extent that regulators produce increased information. However, regulations that restrict the menu of financial products, raise transaction costs, or otherwise reduce financial efficiency or mobility also reduce individual welfare.

Considering next institutions that supply financial services, we note that a given regulatory regime bestows both benefits and costs on individual financial-services firms. Regulations that (1) assure the stability and orderliness of the financial system over time and promote public confidence in financial institutions, (2) restrict entry into the industry and monitor anti-competitive pricing arrangements, (3) provide ancillary services — such as deposit insurance or wire transfers — at below private cost and other transaction-cost-savings measures, all benefit private firms. Regulations may also result in revenue losses from (1) foregone interest on required reserves, (2) foregone earnings on high capital requirements, (3) cost of regulatory information and compliance, and (4) foregone revenues from limitations on geographic activity or product offerings, as well as explicit charges. The difference between these costs and benefits defines the NRB placed upon private firms.[1]

In an individual, closed economy with a lone regulatory body, competition would spark a dynamic interplay between demanders and suppliers of financial services, much as in any market situation. Users of financial services would vote with their

1 Note that because some regulations may not generate revenues and some regulations entail externalities, the value of the net regulatory benefits received by firms need not equal the net regulatory costs collected by the regulatory authorities.

feet, seeking similar or superior services if justified by cost and risk considerations. Private firms would seek to reduce their NRB and increase their profitability. If they could do so at low cost, financial firms would actively seek product innovations and new venues that (legally) avoid cumbersome regulations.

However, the familiar story of competitive equilibrium must be extended in two directions: first, to include the case of multiple and sometimes overlapping domestic regulatory bodies, and second, to the case of many countries with many suppliers of financial services and many regulatory bodies.

A single economy may have multiple regulatory bodies at the national level, complemented by a host of other regulatory groups at the state and local levels in countries organized politically along federal lines. In the case of the United States, at the federal level financial activities could fall under the domain of the Federal Reserve Board, the Comptroller on the Currency, the Securities and Exchange Commission, and the Commodity Futures Trading Commission, to name only the major regulatory agencies. Each of the fifty States has its own regulatory bodies to deal with banking and insurance. Every city and municipality has an agency responsible for local income taxes, real estate taxes, transfer taxes, stamp duties, and so on, all of which affect the NRB falling on financial institutions. In practice, the situation is complicated still further by ambiguity regarding the definition of a "bank," a "security," an "exchange," and so forth — which may blur the categorization of a financial service as well as raise questions about which regulatory agency holds jurisdiction.

In a provocative article, Kane [1987] has argued that regulation itself may be thought of in a market context. Via a political process, regulatory bodies may be established along geographic, product, or functional lines. These regulators then compete with one another to extend the reach of their regulatory domains. Domestic financial firms understand this competition, which widens their scope for reducing the NRB, and for enhancing their market share or profitability. In this game-theoretic setting, domestic regulators are likely to respond to private initiatives with *re*regulations in an effort to recover part of their lost regulatory domain.

In the open, international economy with many governments and many regulatory authorities, we find a still more fertile ground for firms to reduce their NRB. National regulatory authorities may compete among themselves on the basis of the NRB to preserve or reclaim their regulatory domain. Again, private firms benefit from such international competition, especially if financial innovation and technological change allow them to operate successfully at a distance from their home bases. Users of financial services also benefit to the extent that competition forces financial firms to pass-through to them the lower NRB. An important question (discussed below) is whether society as a whole gains or loses as a result of the lower world-wide NRB brought about by regulatory competition.

b. Competition among Regulators and Contestable Markets

Compliance with regulations in onshore financial markets creates opportunities to develop a parallel, offshore market for the delivery of similar services. Barriers must exist to keep all activity from migrating offshore. In this case, political risk and minimum transaction size temper the flow of deposits and investments offshore, while size and credit quality perform a similar role for borrowers. In addition to the narrow provision of bank deposits and loans, offshore markets can be used to replicate a variety of nonbank, financial instruments (e.g., long-term forward contracts, short-term commercial paper, long-term bonds, Eurocurrency interest rate futures, and the like), many of which may also be regulated by onshore financial authorities. Consequently, offshore markets raise a general competitive threat to the activities of onshore financial services.

The rise of offshore markets underscores the fact that market participants face a range of alternatives for executing transactions in any of several financial centers. Consequently, if domestic regulators desire to have the transactions conducted within their respective financial centers — driven by the regulators' desire to maintain an adequate level of prudential regulation, to sustain their revenues from the taxation of financial services, to support employment and output in the financial services industry and linked economic sectors, or simply to maximize their regulatory domain — the regulatory requirements cannot be set arbitrarily.

Indeed, as Kane has argued, domestic financial regulations are determined competitively and endogenously after taking into account regulations (both present and prospective) in other financial centers. The essence of his analysis is that the market for suppliers of financial regulation is highly competitive. As such, the movement to liberalize regulations affecting financial institutions is not the result of a sudden outpouring of laissez-faire behavior, but rather the result of an endogenous process as national regulators vie for market shares. The market for financial regulation is contestable in the sense that other national regulatory bodies offer (or threaten to offer) rules that may be more favorable than those of the domestic regulator. This actual or threatened competition serves to constrain the actions of financial regulators and tax authorities.

This view results in what has been referred to as a "regulatory dialectic" — a dynamic interaction between the regulator and the regulated, where there is continuous action and reaction by all parties. The players in this game-theoretic setting may behave aggressively or defensively. To the extent that the parties behave adaptively, even if underlying factors (such as communications technology and the level of financial transactions) remain constant, it is likely to require considerable time for an equilibrium regulatory structure to emerge.

In a changing environment, players will adapt with varying speed and degrees of freedom. Kane [1987, p. 115] summarizes the "average adaptive efficiencies" of various players as follows:

—Less-regulated players move faster and more freely than more tightly regulated ones.
—Private players move faster and more freely than governmental ones.
—Regulated players move faster and more freely than regulators.
—International regulatory bodies move more slowly and less freely than all other players.

Given this ordering of adaptive efficiencies, we expect that the lag between a regulation and its avoidance is on average shorter than the lag between avoidance and *re*regulation. The lag in reregulation may be shorter for industry-based, self-regulatory groups than for governments. It may be longest when international regulatory efforts are involved. Appreciation of this likelihood seems to have affected the style of tax and regulatory harmonization that the EC has adopted.[2]

c. Net Regulatory Burden and Structural Arbitrage

Private firms thus monitor their NRB and transfer activities into another regulatory regime when, ceteris paribus, their NRB can be reduced. In a perfect capital market with no entry or exit costs, no transaction costs, no barriers between countries, and no sovereign risk, we would predict that all banking and securities activities would migrate to the country with the lowest NRB, inclusive of taxes. In the real world, a variety of imperfections exist that permit some dispersion of the NRB across countries. For example, when transaction costs and information costs are positive, firms will need to be located in those countries where they intend to sell financial services. Nevertheless, this dispersion among NRBs cannot be too great, otherwise private firms will have an incentive to relocate their activities. Entry and exit costs, currency conversion costs, and distance-related delivery costs, plus uncertainties surrounding these costs and other control measures, act as effective barriers to completing NRB equalization across countries. Technological change that has markedly lowered communications and information processing costs, combined with the rapid growth of international financial transactions, has cut the gap in the NRB needed to induce arbitrage.

In a similar fashion, regulators have also become more willing to compete on the basis of the NRB. The regulator must insure that his regulatory revenues (when combined with supplementary budgetary support that comes willingly from in-

[2] A basic objective of the 1992 plan is to provide a common core of regulation that is shared by all EC countries and that is intended to safeguard certain fundamental public goods dealing with the safety and solvency of the financial system, as well as to set minimum standards for investor, depositor and consumer protection. The principle of mutual recognition leaves scope for accommodating differences in regulation across countries. Rather than to "straight-jacket" regulation across the EC, this feature allows for competition and dynamic adjustment [see Levich, 1989].

formed taxpayers) are sufficient to produce a given set of regulatory services. If this condition is not met, the regulatory burden is not sustainable, and reregulation will force it back into line. However, if the regulator is generating more than enough revenues to cover his costs, he needs to be concerned that private firms will migrate to lower NRB regions unless the associated transaction costs and information costs exceed the tax savings and/or regulatory savings. In this case, the regulator could either lower his NRB or impose taxes and controls to stop the migration of financial activity.

Since taxes and controls are easily avoided, the policymaker is likely to alter his NRB. The question is therefore: "What is the long-run, sustainable equilibrium value of the net regulatory burden (NRB*)?"

A somewhat separate, but related, question involves social welfare and whether a reduction in the NRB that shifts the fiscal burden from financial market participants to other segments of society serves general welfare optimization goals. Our point is simply that, as any factor of production or economic activity gains mobility, it becomes increasingly difficult to subject it to tax. Of necessity, the fiscal burden will be redistributed onto less mobile factors or activities.

d. Implications for Regulatory Coordination[3]

Even within a single economy, the optimal design of financial regulation is a complex matter. Continuing to think of regulation as a net tax from the perspective of financial market participants, the issue we wish to consider is whether a government will necessarily be able to collect a tax that is considered by those taxed as "excessive."

Regulations impose costs that, in part, will be transferred to clients. Costly regulations create incentives for financial firms to innovate in order to reduce their costs and capture a larger market share. Money market mutual funds and off-balance-sheet financing techniques are two well-known domestic examples that exist in a number of countries. The greater the regulatory costs, the greater the incentive is to innovate or to avoid the domestic financial system. In the United States, for example, the 1,200 mile shift of Citibank's credit card operations from New York to South Dakota (in part, to escape New York's usury ceilings) illustrates this kind of mobility within federal states. The limiting case might be found in a country experiencing hyperinflation, in which case residents may shift into commodities as the medium of exchange or avoid domestic financial institutions altogether.

In the international setting, the scope for governments to collect excessive regulatory taxes is reduced because there is greater competition among national

3 This section draws heavily on Levich and Walter [1988].

regulatory environments. Each domestic financial center faces competition from foreign and offshore financial centers. As transactions costs and information costs decline, the cost of using an offshore financial center declines as well. The development of offshore currency and bond markets in the 1960s represents a case in which borrowers and lenders found that they could carry out the requisite market transactions more efficiently and with sufficient safety by operating offshore — in a parallel market. Capital flight from LDCs is an extreme example of residents escaping the local inflationary tax or fleeing from low or highly variable real rates of return. While the capital flight example appears extreme, Michael Dooley has argued that under some definitions the shift by Americans of $250 bill. from domestic to Eurocurrency accounts in 1980-82 could equally be interpreted as capital flight [Dooley, 1987].

In the past, policymakers have often set financial regulations as if no international feedback effects would occur. The obvious point is that in today's world, communications costs are low and capital mobility is high, so that it is becoming less feasible for a state or a nation to impose a NRB that stands too far apart from world norms. In the 1970s and 1980s, US and European financial institutions moved a large part of their operations offshore, suggesting that they judged the cost of domestic financial regulations to be excessive. If we assume that transaction costs, information costs and communication costs continue to decline, would it follow that the NRB* on financial institutions is zero — i.e., that a financial institution would migrate rather than pay any positive regulatory tax?

In our judgement, a long-run equilibrium can be maintained with a *positive* NRB. Financial transactions involve uncertainty — about the monetary unit of account, about the creditworthiness of the financial institutions and other counterparties, and about the political stability of the financial center. Financial institutions ought to value their access to lender of last resort facilities, the opportunity to be headquartered in a stable political climate, and the like. Indeed, we observe that those markets which are largely unregulated, with a NRB approaching zero, such as the Eurocurrency markets, have not in fact completely dominated financial transactions subject to location-shifting. If financial institutions find it in their interest to pay some regulatory tax, the economic question then concerns the sustainable magnitude of this tax.

It is evident that the NRB will be an important determinant of the location of financial activities in the Europe of the 1990s. Competition between London, Luxembourg, Zürich, Paris, Frankfurt and Amsterdam in particular has intensified, and there is active debate regarding future concentration or dispersion of financial transactions based on market depth, liquidity, efficiency, client location, and other factors. The conventional wisdom is that the size, openness of markets, trading activity, sophistication of institutional investors, quality of research, transaction services, and innovative thinking that have traditionally characterized London will be subject to challenge in specific areas by various continental financial centers, with significant implications for local employment and other real-sector considerations.

The volume of transactions potentially subject to differentials in NRB is impressive. Table 1 shows new issues of debt and equity securities exceeding $1 trill. in the United States, Europe and Japan in 1987. While no consistent data exist on trading in fixed-income securities in the various domestic and offshore markets, Table 2 indicates trading volume in equities in various countries as a percentage of global trading activity. These figures show the sharp decline of the US market share from over 60 percent in 1982 to only 25 percent in 1988, and a similar sharp decline in Switzerland. Japan's share of world trading volume more than doubled from 16 to 42 percent, while Germany and Taiwan each gained five percentage points.

Table 1 — Volume of Capital Market Financing by Regional Corporations in Their Respective Regional Markets, 1987[a] (proceeds in bill. US$ at average exchange rates in 1987)

	Financial	Nonfinanical	Total
United States			
Equities	25.3	28.1	53.4
Bonds	143.2	220.1	363.3
Total	168.5	248.2	416.7
Europe			
Equities	13.8	75.8	89.6
Bonds	170.1	31.5	201.6
Total	183.9	107.3	291.2
Japan			
Equities	14.0	28.5	42.5
Bonds	227.9	103.1	331.0
Total	241.9	131.6	373.5
World			
Equities	53.1	132.4	185.5
Bonds	541.2	354.7	895.9
Total	594.3	487.1	1,081.4

[a]Equities are total gross shares sold through public distributions, including privatization issues. Bonds include private placements where reported. Capital market issues by domestic firms outside of their home regions are excluded, e.g., US corporate issues of Eurobonds. However, the totals include European corporate issues of Euro and foreign issues estimated at $35.7 bill. in 1987. Data for Japan include discount notes issued by banks, many of which can be considered short term.

Source: OECD [1988], based on data supplied by central banking authorities.

Table 2 — Percentage of Global Trading Volume in Equities Attributable to Individual Countries, 1982-1988

	1982	1983	1984	1985	1986	1987	1988
Australia	0.55	0.72	0.38	0.46	0.43	1.01	0.72
Austria	0.01	0.01	0.01	0.04	0.04	0.03	0.04
Belgium	0.21	0.21	0.20	0.18	0.21	0.19	0.20
Canada	1.56	1.90	1.52	1.85	0.63	1.34	1.04
Denmark	0.01	0.02	0.01	0.01	0.02	0.03	0.10
Finland	0.01	0.02	0.03	0.03	0.06	0.10	0.13
France	1.04	0.98	0.78	1.05	1.91	1.73	1.41
West Germany	1.81	3.02	2.64	4.58	4.75	8.36	6.54
Hong Kong	0.00	0.00	0.00	0.00	0.48	0.80	0.44
Italy	0.30	0.30	0.30	0.70	1.41	0.57	0.59
Ireland	0.06	0.07	0.08	0.04	0.07	0.11	0.09
Japan	15.98	17.88	21.13	18.89	30.03	30.76	41.73
Korea	0.29	0.18	0.28	0.24	0.34	0.44	1.49
Luxembourg	0.00	0.00	0.00	0.00	0.00	0.00	0.01
Malaysia	0.15	0.26	0.18	0.14	0.04	0.07	0.05
Mexico	0.09	0.07	0.15	0.20	0.18	0.29	0.14
Netherlands	1.11	1.64	1.86	1.94	1.90	1.40	1.16
New Zealand	0.00	0.00	0.05	0.05	0.08	0.05	0.02
Norway	0.02	0.07	0.20	0.21	0.11	0.16	0.09
Singapore	0.26	0.43	0.28	0.16	0.12	0.08	0.12
South Africa	0.23	0.28	0.19	0.15	0.09	0.10	0.06
Spain	0.13	0.07	0.13	0.17	0.39	0.53	0.39
Sweden	0.51	0.77	0.63	0.55	0.63	0.35	0.35
Switzerland	5.96	5.11	4.86	5.24	3.95	3.79	3.64
Taiwan	0.00	0.00	0.60	0.28	0.58	1.49	5.16
Turkey	0.00	0.00	0.00	0.00	0.00	0.00	0.00
United Kingdom	7.12	6.60	7.27	7.69	8.37	11.23	8.90
United States	62.58	59.38	56.24	55.14	43.18	34.99	25.39
Europe	18.30	18.88	19.01	22.43	23.81	28.58	23.64
Pazific Basin	17.24	19.48	22.90	20.23	32.10	34.70	49.72
World ex UK	92.88	93.40	92.73	92.31	91.63	88.77	91.10
World ex US	37.42	40.62	43.76	44.86	56.82	65.01	74.61
World ex Japan	84.02	82.12	78.87	81.11	69.97	69.24	58.27
World	100.00	100.00	100.00	100.00	100.00	100.00	100.00

Source: Goldmann, Sachs & Co. [1989].

3. Securities Taxation in Europe

Taxation of investment income and securities transactions may well represent a significant component of the NRB with respect to the evolution of financial systems in an international, competitive environment. This issue comes to the surface especially when other (non-tax) distortions of competitive conditions are eliminated, as is true in the European context with respect to the EC 1992 initiatives. Differences in securities taxation among financial centers can involve (1) levies placed on financial assets themselves, (2) interest and dividend income, (3) capital gains and losses, and (4) securities transfer (stamp) taxes. In the European environment, where Luxembourg has often been considered the logical tax base for securities activity, taxation differences will certainly affect where securities transactions are executed and settled, where securities are issued and held, and where investment funds are managed. We focus our attention first on investment income taxation and then turn our attention to transfer taxes.

a. Investment Income Taxation

Tax rates applied to investment income have differed widely among EC member countries. In 1988, for example, France applied up to 45 percent in personal income tax on interest receipts and a 25 percent withholding tax on dividend income, while Luxembourg imposed a 15 percent resident tax on stock dividends and no taxes at all on bond and bank interest receipts. Withholding tax rates for 1988 on dividend and interest income applied to nonresidents in each EC member country are given in Table 3.

Table 3 — Base Withholding Tax Rates for Most Nonresident Individual Bank-Account Holders, 1988 (percent)

	Dividends	Bond income	Savings interest
Luxembourg	0[a]	0	0
Netherlands	25	0	0
Portugal	12	12	15
Belgium	25[b]	25[b]	25[b]
Denmark	30	0	0
France	25	0	0
Ireland	0	0[c]	0
Spain	20	0	20
Britain	0	25	0
Greece	42-53	0	0
West Germany	25	10[d]	10[d]
Italy	32.4	12.5	30

[a]Except on dividends of Luxembourg corporations, usually 5 percent. — [b]Exempt under certain circumstances. — [c]Government intends to introduce 10 percent withholding tax. — [d]As of January 1, 1989. Abolished as of July 1, 1989.

Source: European tax authorities, as reported in the European Wall Street Journal of February 15, 1989.

Investment income taxation becomes particularly important in the light of the liberalization of European transactions in mutual funds. The EC directive governing the operation and sale of mutual funds — Undertakings for the Collective Investment of Transferable Securities (UCITS) — was the first set of business conduct rules on investments to go into effect. The UCITS directive, which came into force on October 1, 1989 after 15 years of negotiation, specifies general rules for the kinds of investments that are appropriate for mutual funds and how they should be sold. The regulatory requirements for fund management and certification are left to the home country of the firm, while specific rules for adequacy of disclosure and selling practices are left to the respective host countries.

Consequently, funds duly established and monitored in any EC member country, such as Luxembourg — and that are in compliance with UCITS — can be sold Community-wide to investors in local markets, and promoted and advertised through local selling networks and direct mail, as long as the selling requirements applicable in each country are met. This includes high-performance "synthetic" funds, based on futures and options, not permitted in some financial centers, such as London. Under UCITS, 90 percent of assets must be invested in publicly traded companies, no more than 5 percent of the outstanding stock of any company may be owned, and there are limits on investment funds' borrowing rights. Real estate funds, commodity funds and money market funds are excluded.

In the light of free intra-EC capital mobility and the UCITS initiative, a decision on narrowing or eliminating intra-EC differentials in the taxation of capital earnings has been of great interest to such high-tax countries as Denmark and France, which have vigorously advocated full harmonization of national taxes on interest, including imposition of a common withholding tax. The United Kingdom has just as vigorously resisted direct tax harmonization on the grounds that it would represent a step in the direction of monetary unification and fiscal integration, and was probably unnecessary in preventing serious tax evasion [The Banker, "Future Perfect?" November 1988]. The UK has also resisted threats to the Eurobond market, where bearer securities offer potentially tax-free income to investors.

The withholding tax issue has also been related to the sensitive question of financial confidentiality, where both Luxembourg and Switzerland have high stakes, although serious controversy surrounding common policies on financial oversight in the OECD has suggested limited progress could be made in this area as well [Walter, 1989a, Ch. 10].

In February 1989, the European Commission formally proposed a minimum 15 percent withholding tax (administered at source) on interest income of investments (bonds and bank deposits) by Community residents in other EC countries. Eurosecurities and non-EC residents were exempted from the withholding tax proposal. Also exempted were savings accounts of young people and small savers who were already exempt from taxation in a number of EC countries, although member states would be free to impose withholding taxes above the 15 percent floor. Governments could exempt interest income subject to withholding at source from declaration for tax purposes. Also exempted were countries that already apply equal or higher withholding taxes on interest income. Additional aspects of the proposal concerned cooperation in enforcement and exchange of information among EC fiscal authorities. Dividends were omitted from the proposals because they are generally less heavily taxed by EC member countries and because national income tax systems were thought to capture this type of income relatively effectively.[4]

Supporters of abolishing investment income tax differences within the EC argued that tax harmonization was essential if a common capital market was not to lead to widespread tax evasion after the final removal of intra-EC capital restrictions on July 1, 1990. The effort was led by France, together with Belgium, Italy and Spain. All four countries argued that the absence of tax harmonization would weaken their currencies in relation to those of other EC members. All four have tax collection systems that are relatively weak in other respects.

Opponents, mainly the United Kingdom and Luxembourg as well as the Netherlands, argued that tax harmonization is both unnecessary and harmful to the functioning of efficient capital markets, and that substantial investments would subsequently flow out of the EC, especially to Switzerland and Caribbean tax havens. Indeed, they argued that the proposal failed to recognize that Europe is part of a global capital market and that EC securities returns might have to be raised to levels that provide equivalent after-tax returns in order to prevent capital outflows from becoming a serious problem. The United Kingdom was also concerned about the special role of the Isle of Man and the Channel Islands (which are "semi-detached" from the EC) and their treatment in the withholding tax initiative.

Any single EC country has the power to veto the EC withholding tax initiative. In this case, attention focused on the United Kingdom and Luxembourg. According to Jacques Delors, President of the EC Commission, "If Luxembourg does not agree, it will have to choose between that and its European calling. Everyone has to make sacrifices and concessions for each other."[5] Nevertheless, in a subsequent meeting of EC finance ministers every country other than France raised specific objections to the plan — ranging from British and Luxembourgian objections in principle to German objections to the proposed 15 percent rate, which was felt to be excessive, as well as to be a threat to banking confidentiality.

---

4 See Steven Greenhouse, "Withholding Tax Plan on Investment is Likely in Europe," New York Times, February 11, 1989; see also David Buchan and Tim Dickson, "Commission Tax Proposal Meets Hostile Reception," Financial Times, February 2, 1989; The Economist, "Europe's Withholding Tax: Fizzling Out," February 11, 1989; and David Buchan, "Plans for EC Minimum Savings Tax Get Rough Ministerial Ride," Finanical Times, February 14, 1989.

5 As quoted in: New York Times, "Plan to End European Havens," February 6, 1989.

After two years of intense debate on the issue, the 15 percent EC withholding tax proposal collapsed in mid-1989 as the Germans withdrew their support of the Commission's initiative and joined the opposition. Nevertheless, there was little doubt that the proposal for a uniform tax on capital income and closer cooperation between EC tax authorities would eventually be revived — although harmonization of withholding tax rates and collection methods remained constrained by the possibility of capital flight to low-tax environments outside the EC.

In 1988, Germany unilaterally introduced a 10 percent withholding tax on interest and dividend income in what became an embarrassing demonstration that such taxes can provoke immediate and massive capital flight. Overall, Bundesbank estimates show a total long-term capital outflow of $42.8 bill. during 1988, while the 10 percent withholding tax was being discussed. An estimated $10.7 bill. of German investment funds flowed into the Luxembourg bond market following the announcement that the tax was to be effective January 1, 1989. Investor reactions to the German tax bid up the price of Euro-DM issues and depressed yields to the point where in early 1989 it was cheaper for PepsiCo to borrow in DM than it was for the German federal government to do so on the domestic market. The German authorities were subsequently induced to allow "coupon washing" — i.e., to permit investors to sell bonds immediately prior to the interest payment date and buy them back immediately afterward in order to escape the tax — by shifting the coupon payments to tax-exempt investors.[6] On April 27, the German authorities announced that the withholding tax would be abolished on July 1, 1989.

Two financial centers (Luxembourg and Switzerland) are particularly sensitive to the issue of investment income taxation in terms of its impact on their competitive positioning in financial services [for a more detailed discussion, see Walter, 1989b]. We review their cases in more detail.

Luxembourg has for many years focused on building up investment funds and private banking business as a way of further developing the financial services industry. This industry, which employed 8 percent of the work force and accounted for 20 percent of the GNP in 1988, is based on strict secrecy, low costs, central location, multilingual capabilities, professional funds management, regulatory stability and favorable tax environment. As of 1989, Luxembourg had some 160 registered banks (compared with 37 in 1970 and 143 at the end of 1988) and over 660 approved mutual funds and unit trusts (compared with 75 in 1981), half of which are approved to market their services throughout the EC. UCITS investment funds are not subject to any income tax, and are only subject to a registration tax of LFr 50,000 plus an annual fiscal charge of 0.06 percent of the net assets invested. Luxembourg is an attractive base for UCITS also because tax treatment of investment companies is based only on the underlying securities and funds may be

6 The Banker, "Papering Over the Euro-Cracks," November 1988; see also Stephen Fidler, "Swiss Gain Most from Securities Euro-Tax," Financial Times, February 4, 1989.

open-ended, as is the case on the Channel Islands. There is no withholding tax on fund distributions and no value-added tax on gold transactions. Luxembourg's drawbacks include high labor costs, and concerns over the adequacy of the operations infrastructure and financial supervision. Suspicions of money laundering using Luxembourgian financial institutions were countered in 1989 with strict legislation that includes significant criminal penalties. The Luxembourgian view is that taxation is a matter for the country of residence of the asset-holder, and the authorities will not respond to enforcement requests except in criminal cases.

Switzerland levies withholding taxes, payable on interest and dividend income, set at a high 35 percent level. However, this exerts virtually no drag on Swiss financial markets since the withholding tax is waived for foreign bond issues and fiduciary account holders. Switzerland thus remains a withholding-tax-free environment for the bulk of international business transactions and could have benefitted from the attempt to impose a uniform 15 percent withholding tax throughout the EC. The defeat of the proposal confirmed that neither the London-based Euromarket nor Luxembourg's European financial center would in fact be taxed out of existence and driven to Switzerland.

b. Securities Transfer Taxes

As deregulation and competitive forces push their way through Europe against the backdrop of the 1992 reforms and an increasingly performance-oriented market for investments, movement towards linking national markets into a common, intra-European securities market can be expected [Walter, Smith, 1989]. This will increase the sensitivity of securities activities to even small intercountry NRB differences in the form of transactions taxes.

In the absence of a high NRB through such taxes, London has already begun to function as an intra-European trading center. In French stocks, for example, London secondary market trading in 1988 accounted for the equivalent of about 20 percent of the daily volume on the Paris Bourse.[7] In this respect, London has several advantages in addition to the absence of transaction taxes. It is the home not only of the Euromarket (Eurocurrency deposits, Euroloans, Euronotes, Eurocommercial paper, and Eurobonds) and many large, globalized institutional investors, but also of the SEAQ system and a related (but different) system, international SEAQ, which is a system for the trading of equity shares attractive to international investors.

Efforts by French and Dutch securities firms to become part of the SEAQ system have met strong resistance from London. There is every reason to believe, however, that the system will ultimately be expanded further to include the principal stocks from all of the major European financial centers. Many of these stocks are already

7 The Economist, "Boursemanship," October 8, 1988.

traded on the international SEAQ. Incorporating brokers/dealers from other countries into the system would not be technically difficult. For many European stocks (and virtually all international bonds), the market linkages are already in place. The technology and the know-how for a major market expansion exists, has been debugged, and is relatively easy to install.

If markets are to be made abroad in the internationally popular stocks of a country, it seems reasonable for that country to take steps to recapture a substantial proportion of the trade in its stocks. Expanding an existing intra-European SEAQ system to include national market makers not only in the stocks that the foreigners want to buy, but also in the foreign stocks that national investors wish to purchase, would seem a practical way to begin the process of forming an active pan-European equity market.

The United Kingdom, for its part, has tried to hang on to its historic role as the wholesale financial center for Europe and the home of the offshore markets in its time zone. After twenty-five years of activity, the London-based Euromarket continues to be the single most important market for new issues and secondary market trading of fixed income securities. Its creation and rapid growth was in large part driven by NRB-related considerations, both US and European. But in the process, it has become by far the most technically developed market in Europe. The United Kingdom levies a stamp tax of 0.5 percent on most domestic equity trades, but none on trades in foreign-registered securities.

In equities as in debt securities, a necessary condition in a recapture-scenario by the continental European financial centers is the creation of a level playing field with respect to securities transfer taxes, which are levied by neither London nor Luxembourg, yet have been applied by all four of the remaining principal financial centers: Germany, Switzerland, the Netherlands and France. Whether the abolition of securities transfer taxes will be sufficient to enable a recapture of business is problematic, given the head start enjoyed by London and Luxembourg.

France. The emergence of Paris, formerly one of the most regulated financial markets in Europe, as an international financial center is a notable additional pressure on other European financial centers to reduce the fiscal drag on their markets. France has made significant efforts to increase its attractiveness, including liberalization of exchange controls, opening-up the Paris Bourse, major investments in market-making and efficient securities settlement, privatizations in the financial sector, new markets for options and futures — with some 168 foreign-based banks (second only to London and New York) — and a clear aim to be the premier financial center on the continent. Among the shortcomings has been the view, particularly by foreign-based players, that insider transactions remain a serious obstacle along with the existence of a stamp duty on securities transactions.

The Netherlands. Amsterdam has likewise promoted itself as a significant financial center for the 1990s by encouraging deregulation and innovation in local debt and equity markets as well as its European Options Exchange. By leveraging off traditional skills in investment management and developing an efficient infrastructure, Amsterdam is attempting to overcome its relatively small domestic financial sector.

Securities transactions in the Netherlands have been taxed at a rate of 0.12 percent, with a cap of Fl 1,200 per transaction in place since 1987 — a rate that is relatively low by European standards and that has not raised more than Fl 100 mill. annually. In late 1989, it was announced by the Finance Ministry that the tax would be scrapped on January 1, 1990.[8]

The Federal Republic of Germany. German stamp taxes are of two types: (1) those imposed on primary equity issues and (2) those imposed on secondary market transfers of equity and debt securities. Payment of tax is evidenced by the affixing of a stamp to the document of transfer. Registering authorities and notaries are under legal obligation to report whether or not the appropriate stamp is affixed.

Taxes on primary equity issues in Germany range from 0.5 to 1 percent, with the lower rate applicable to issues where the equity is impaired or where certain types of corporate reorganizations are involved [Deloitte et al., 1982]. Secondary market or "exchange turnover" stamp taxes are imposed on the acquisition of any security including stocks, debentures, other types of bonds, and rights issues. Rates are 0.25 percent on equity shares, 0.20 percent on bonds and 0.10 percent on government debentures (see footnote 9). Interdealer, interbroker and some interbank transactions are exempt from the tax.

The German government has been under strong criticism for maintaining its stamp tax structure, which has allegedly resulted in the Federal Republic becoming a large importer of financial services from London. Consequently, the government committed to abolishing stamp taxes by 1993 in the interest of stimulating the domestic financial sector, particularly in the context of the EC 1992 initiatives. However, it was reluctant to do so quickly, since stamp taxes contributed almost DM 1 bill. annually to the Federal Treasury in 1988. On October 31, 1989, bowing to financial community pressure and reacting to a severe price slide on the German stock exchanges (which exceeded the severity of the decline in New York two weeks earlier), the Economics Minister announced that on January 1, 1991 — two years earlier than originally planned — stamp taxes on both primary and secondary market transactions will be abolished. It was hoped that Germany could recapture much of the trading in shares that had reportedly migrated to London's international SEAQ system, as well as the trading in bonds that had migrated to the DM-denominated sector of the Eurobond market.[9]

---

8 Laura Raun, "Dutch Stamp Duty to be Scrapped Next Year," Financial Times, November 5, 1989.

9 Financial Times, "Germans in Early Move to Abolish Stock Exchange Turnover Tax," January 1, 1989.

Such a revision would still leave Germany as a relatively high NRB country in the international competitive context, however. Personal and corporate taxes would remain high, and trade taxes would raise the incidence of corporate taxation to the 55-60 percent range. While this would affect all German corporations, its incidence on financial firms operating in Germany might well have a significant impact on the future role of Frankfurt as a financial center.

Switzerland. The Swiss bond capital market has traditionally been the largest in continental Europe, driven in part by an international investor penchant for discretion. The banking industry in Switzerland accounted for some 10 percent of the GNP in 1988, contributed over SFr 7 bill. in tax revenues, and employed about 4 percent of the work force. Some 117 foreign banks operated in Switzerland in 1988. Like the other domestic markets within the EC, it has traditionally been dominated by large financial institutions — three universal banks — particularly with respect to new issues of securities. The Swiss Cartel Commission proposed in 1989 that ad hoc underwriting syndicates be allowed, and that the single syndicate for government issues — together with fixed brokerage and foreign exchange commissions, and restrictions on private placements of securities — be abolished.

The Swiss stamp tax structure involves transaction taxes payable on securities purchases and sales [Swiss Bank Cooperation, 1987; Coopers & Lydbrand, 1986]. The stamp tax was first imposed in 1918, and subsequently revised several times — as in 1974 and again in 1978. Notwithstanding the name, payment is not evidenced by "stamping" of documents. For purposes of tax liability, foreign branches of Swiss banks are considered to be separate entities, legally distinct from their Swiss parents, and therefore not subject to stamp taxes on their transactions abroad. The incidence of taxation is the same for both bearer and registered securities.

Stamp taxes affect Swiss capital market transactions in two principal areas: (1) primary equity issues and (2) secondary market transfers of equity and debt securities.

With respect to domestic primary equity issues, the rate (payable on the greater of the transaction face value or the transaction amount) is 3 percent on issues of new shares, dividend certificates and participation rights certificates, 1 percent on participation rights associated with merger and acquisition (M&A) transactions and 0.9 percent on investment fund rights issues. Stamp taxes on new issues of debt securities in the Swiss market are 0.315 percent payable by borrowers and 0.3 percent payable by investors.

With respect to secondary market transfers of equity and debt securities, the rates in general are 0.15 percent on transfers of domestic market securities and 0.3 percent on transfers of foreign securities. For money market securities of less than 3 months maturity, however, the rates are 0.1 percent and 0.2 percent for domestic and foreign securities, respectively. The secondary market tax affects all transactions in stocks, bonds, investment fund units, bills of exchange, participations and subparticipations and money market instruments, regardless of how the transaction occurs — on the floor of an organized exchange, through a broker or dealer, or by direct private sale. Liability for the tax on secondary market trades is split evenly between the buyer and the seller. Stamp duties are also levied on payment of insurance premiums.

The Swiss stamp tax has tended to force offshore all capital market transactions that can be undertaken abroad with incremental costs that are less than the applicable tax on the domestic transaction. This has led to the absence of a viable Swiss money market, and has represented a serious drag on the national stock and bond markets, in particular the development of an active secondary securities market of international stature. Swiss banks have been increasing their share placement and secondary market trading in London in order to avoid the tax — with shares ultimately lodged in Swiss accounts — while certain new issues and swap-driven transactions have likewise migrated to London.

In an apparent effort to create an active money market, the Swiss government has relaxed its application of stamp tax to certain short-term transactions. So-called "paperless commercial paper" programs have been developed to avoid the tax, with government acquiescence. The Swiss federal government itself has used such an approach since 1979 to avoid the stamp tax. However, the approach was not used commercially until 1988. Then, in a succession of transactions beginning in mid-1988 and led by Crédit Suisse and the Swiss Bank Corporation, offshore paperless commercial paper programs were arranged for Unilever, Fiat, the Beecham Group, the Export Development Corporation of Canada, and the World Bank. The facilities were apparently structured to use only book-entries to avoid stamp tax liability.

The stamp tax law has thus been seriously bent, with the tacit understanding of the authorities, to begin to accommodate the development of a Swiss international money market. The market now appears to be established for non-Swiss companies (withholding taxes making it prohibitively expensive for domestic corporations) although it remains exceedingly small by international standards.[10]

In order to partially compensate for the tax-induced regulatory drag, the Swiss National Bank has ruled that all Swiss franc denominated bond issues should be lead-managed by banks domiciled in Switzerland. The presumption is that this rule, too, will go once the stamp duty on securities transactions is abolished, resulting in both a reduction in transaction costs and an increase in competition for new securities issues as foreign-based players compete for deals.

A fundamental reform of the stamp duty has been very actively debated in Switzerland. In view of the fiscal role of the tax as a significant source of revenues,

---

10 Money Report: "Fiat Unit Sets SFR Paperless Borrowing Scheme," June 3, 1989; "Beecham Group Signs for Paperless Programme," June 1, 1989; "World Bank Launches New Swiss Franc Instrument," September 2, 1988.

contributing approximately SFr 2.2 bill. annually to the Treasury, the government has been reluctant to abolish it, or has said that revenue losses from any repeal of the tax should be fully compensated from unspecified new taxes on financial services activities. This position appeared to be in conformity with the views of a sizable domestic constituency opposed to awarding "gifts" to Swiss banks, which are perceived to be both financially profitable and politically powerful. Indeed, as opposed to eliminating or seriously modifying the stamp tax, the Swiss Finance Minister proposed in 1988 that other countries adopt similar taxes in order to cut their budget deficits.

For their part, bankers have argued persuasively that the tax seriously impedes the competitiveness of the Swiss market in international finance, forcing them to move securities operations offshore, and having adverse effects on Swiss employment and other macrovariables. An array of studies documenting the relative decline of Zürich as a financial center seems to confirm their arguments [Swiss Bankers Association, 1988].

In October 1988, the Swiss Bankers Association issued a report formally calling for the abolishment of the stamp tax, together with various stock market reforms and an easing of capital adequacy requirements. In effect representing a compromise solution worked out jointly with the Swiss tax authorities, the proposals specifically recommended the elimination of the stamp tax on money market transactions (paper up to one year maturity), on any securities held purely for trading purposes, on trading of foreign securities between foreign clients, and on new issues of Eurobonds. To compensate partially for the loss of tax revenue, the proposals included an issue tax on new domestic debt securities and cash bonds (Kassenobligationen) as well as on insurance premiums, although the net revenue loss would still amount to some SFr 450 mill.

Presumably in order to accelerate the debate, in late 1988, Robert Studer, chairman of Union Bank of Switzerland, issued an ultimatum in a presentation addressed to the Swiss finance minister, that the bank's underwriting of Swiss franc bonds would be moved to London within a year if the stamp tax was not abolished.[11] Soon thereafter, it was determined that over 80 percent of Swiss financial respondents in an opinion poll took the view that stamp taxes should be revoked or significantly modified.[12]

In September 1989, the lower chamber of the Swiss federal parliament voted by a large majority for a rapid revision of the stamp tax in order to relieve the burden on the competitiveness of Swiss banks and the international financial role of Switzerland. The upper chamber of parliament voted 33 to 5 in December 1989 to cut the stamp tax, having defeated a plan to compensate for an estimated SFr 350

[11] Stephen Fidler, "Europe Falls Behind in the Securities Race," Financial Times, January 25, 1989.

[12] Tony Shale, "A Litany of Woes," Euromoney, December 1988.

mill. in lost revenues through compensatory levies on life insurance premiums and Swiss fiduciary accounts — thereby shifting the tax incidence to activities that are presumably less sensitive to the NRB. Both actions delinked the stamp tax revisions from a broader overhaul of the Swiss tax structure as a matter of competitive urgency. However, the Social Democratic Party threatened to put the entire issue to a referendum, which would make any material change unlikely to occur before 1993.

Table 4 summarizes, for a variety of sample transactions, the differences in the NRB represented by securities transfer taxes in various European financial centers, as well as in New York, Singapore and Tokyo. In particular, the debilitating nature of the Swiss stamp tax becomes evident.

Table 4 — Securities Transfer Taxes in Major Financial Centers on Domestic and Foreign Transactions (percent)

Transaction type	ZRH	FRA	LON	LUX	NYC	TYO	SIN
Purchase of local debt[a]	0.75	0	0	0	0	0	0
Purchase of local equity[b]	0.75	0	5	0	0	0	2
Purchase of locally traded foreign debt[a]	1.50	0	0	0	0	0	0
Purchase of locally traded foreign equity[b]	1.50	0	5	0	0	0	3
Foreign resident makes local purchase of US debt traded in New York[c]	1.50	0	0	0	0	0	0
Foreign resident makes local purchase of US equity traded in New York[d]	1.50	0	5[e]	0	0	0	0
Foreign resident sells via local bank debt traded in London[f]	1.50	0	0	0	0	0	0
Foreign resident sells via local bank equity traded in London[g]	1.50	0	0	0	0	5.5[e]	0

[a]Purchase tax in Frankfurt: 1.25 percent if foreign client has account with a German bank. Securities sales in Tokyo subject to 0.3 percent tax. — [b]Purchase tax in Frankfurt: 1.25 percent if foreign client has account with a German bank. London: No tax on equity sales. Tokyo: Equity sales subject to 5.5 percent tax. — [c]Tokyo: Maximum tax on sale 0.3 percent. New York purchase assumed direct. — [d]London: No tax on equity sales. Tokyo: Equity sales subject to 5.5 percent tax. New York purchase assumed direct. — [e]Maximum rate. — [f]Tokyo: Maximum tax on sale 0.3 percent. London sale assumed direct. — [g]Tokyo: Equity purchases not subject to tax. London sale assumed direct.

Source: Swiss Bankers Association [1988].

4. Summary and Conclusions

In the context of the EC-1992 initiatives, the banking centers of Europe are caught in a vigorous struggle for market-shares in primary- and secondary-market financial transactions that are likely to grow rapidly in volume. Amsterdam, for example, has positioned itself as the "financial gateway to continental Europe." Frankfurt is seeking ways to rationalize Germany's fragmented system of eight regional stock exchanges, restructure its poorly developed markets for fixed-income securities, and overcome the entrenched interests of the universal banks. Paris has pushed through the liberalization of currency controls, the introduction of derivative markets, and the stock exchange reform. Zürich is grappling with the increased institutionalization of investments and long-standing limits to financial competition, as well as the far-reaching consequences of EC harmonization for Switzerland. Luxembourg is consolidating its role as a private banking and investment center to replace its traditional position in Eurosyndications, and is keeping a wary eye on the harmonizers in Brussels.

In each of the continental financial centers there are powerful, entrenched interests, and differences of view between the government and the financial services industry that may yet limit the competitive challenge to London, even as there are open questions as to the location of the policymaking and operational arms of a future EC central bank.

The free flow of capital throughout the EC should eventually lead toward a single, integrated European capital market rather than back to the traditional, fragmented collection of separate national markets [for an elaboration, see Walter and Smith, 1989]. Institutional investors will operate within Europe as a whole, seeking the most attractive opportunities. Both borrowers and bankers will tap into the common pool of funds to build a market in various real and synthetic securities that suit their needs.

In this context, we assume that access to the Euromarket will continue to be free and unregulated. The NRB in the national markets may well remain greater than in the Euromarket, especially if initiatives for EC withholding taxes on investment income are eventually carried through. Given a choice, most market participants will prefer an unregulated market to a regulated one, particularly if both can be accessed simultaneously. Retail investors, still representing the major part of the Euromarket, will prefer to remain beyond the view of tax collectors or other authorities that they have always sought to avoid.

Much more likely than the decline and collapse of the Euromarket as a consequence of the EC-1992 initiatives is therefore the emergence of a new intra-European, integrated financial marketplace that is built upon and encompasses both the various EC domestic markets and the London-based Euromarket. In such an integrated financial market, issues aimed at national investors can also be sold to Euro-investors at the same time. Larger, regional issues normally targeted at the Euromarket should come to be marketable in national markets as well, once common prospectus requirements, issuing procedures and withholding tax matters have been harmonized. In time, the distinctions between national markets and the

Euromarkets will fade, and nonnational investment banks will compete, on a performance basis and in other dimensions, for the business of national companies. A substantially unified capital market that draws from all parts of Europe, from the national markets as well as from the Euromarkets, will be the most efficient way to marshal capital resources.

In this context, tax-related regulatory drag that takes the form of differences in the NRB between European banking centers can be assumed to have increasingly thin tolerances and will be subject to rapid convergence in the period immediately ahead. The Euromarkets will provide an anchor against which the maximum feasible NRB in each center may diverge without committing financial hara-kiri. Logically, such tolerances should ultimately approach those found interregionally in the United States.

Bibliography

COOPERS & LYBRAND, The Swiss Federal Stamp Duties Act. New York 1986.

DELOITTE, HASKINS, SELLS, Taxation in Germany. New York 1982.

DOOLEY, Michael, "Comment." In: D. LESSARD, J. WILLIAMSON (Eds.), Capital Flight and Third World Debt. Institute for International Economics, Washington 1987, pp. 79-81.

GOLDMAN, SACHS & CO., Anatomy of World Markets. New York 1989.

KANE, Edward J., "Competitive Financial Reregulation: An International Perspective." In: Richard PORTES, Alexander SWOBODA (Eds.), Threats to International Financial Stability. London 1987, pp. 111-450.

LEVICH, Richard M., "Financial Innovation in International Financial Markets." In: Martin FELDSTEIN (Ed.), The United States in the World Economy. Chicago 1988, pp. 215-570.

—, "The Euromarkets After 1992." In: Jean DERMINE (Ed.), European Banking in the 1990s. London 1990, pp. 373-990.

—, Ingo WALTER, "The Regulation of Global Financial Markets." In: Thierry NOYELLE (Ed.), New York's Financial Markets. Boulder, Colo., 1988, pp. 71-74.

ORGANIZATION FOR ECONOMIC COOPERATION AND DEVELOPMENT (OECD), Financial Statistics Monthly: Domestic Markets. Paris, October 1988.

SWISS BANK CORPORATION, Taxation in Switzerland. Basel 1987.

SWISS BANKERS ASSOCIATION, Bericht der Arbeitsgruppe "Finanzplatz Schweiz" betreffend Revision des Stempelgesetzes. Basel 1988.

WALTER, Ingo [1989a], Secret Money. 2nd Edition, London 1989.

— [1989b], The Secret Money Market. New York 1989.

—, Roy C. SMITH, Investment Banking in Europe: Restructuring for the 1990s. Oxford 1989.

Comment on Richard M. Levich and Ingo Walter, "Tax-Driven Regulatory Drag: European Financial Centers in the 1990s"

Harmen Lehment

The paper provides an excellent account of the effects which taxes and non-tax regulations have on the spatial allocation decisions of financial corporations, and especially on the evolution of financial centers in Europe. The paper clearly shows that regulations, including taxation, have become an important and even decisive factor in determining the locational decisions of financial corporations in Europe, as well as on a worldwide scale. Competition among European financial centers has increased substantially in recent years due to technological progress in international banking, larger volumes of funds and the increased importance of institutional investors.

A major issue dealt with in the paper concerns the dynamic interplay between private actors in the financial markets and the regulating authorities, a concept that in recent years has been stressed particularly by Edward Kane. Private actors seeking to avoid existing regulations, e.g., by moving to other financial centers, put continuous pressure on the authorities to rethink and actually change existing regulations. The competition among various financial markets which we can observe today thereby forces the authorities to reregulate or — more simply — to deregulate or remove existing taxes. Since I fully agree with the thrust of the paper, I would like to limit my comments to some complementary remarks, drawing to some extent on recent experience in Germany.

One interesting aspect in my view is the process by which reregulation is brought about. It often looks as if the response by the regulators to changes in financial competitiveness is quite ad hoc, both with respect to the measures taken and the timing of these measures. One recent example is the announcement to remove the German stamp-tax (Börsenumsatzsteuer) by the end of 1990. This announcement resulted mainly from the combined effect of the sudden fiscal leeway resulting from unexpectedly high general tax revenues and the mini-crash of October 1989, which caused policymakers to take actions that could support confidence in financial markets. The announcement was not the outcome of a conscious optimization procedure weighting the costs of abolishing of the stamp-tax (i.e., the immediate loss in revenue) against the benefits from the induced increase in domestic financial activity. One reason for the ad hoc behavior of the regulating authorities is to be seen in the lack of quantitative studies on the relationship between regulations and economic activity. A comparison of regulations and taxes among financial centers, e.g., by using the concept of the net regulatory burden, may provide a basis for assessments on the direction of shifts from one center to another. For the regulator, however, this information is not usually sufficient. In considering a removal of existing taxes or non-tax regulations, the policymaker will also be interested in the quantitative effects of such a measure: how much additional employment, income and induced tax revenues could be expected from a lowering of the regulatory burden? It will certainly make a difference whether a regulation affects mainly bookkeeping, such as the opening of a Cayman Island book, with people remaining in the same offices, or whether it implies an actual shift of jobs to foreign financial centers, especially London and Luxembourg. Here, I think we are facing a very interesting agenda for research. An important part of such research would consist of cross-country studies and, in particular, a careful quantitative evaluation of the recent reregulation attempts that have been made in various countries, including EC-member states.

Another German experience to which I would like to refer concerns the reduction of minimum reserves by the Bundesbank in spring 1986. One of the major aims of this reduction was to strengthen the international competitiveness of domestic banks. It is interesting to observe that despite this step, Euro-market DM-deposits of German non-banks did not decline, but rather continued to increase both in absolute terms and in relative terms. One explanation for this phenomenon can be seen in the segmentation among financial actors between private households on the one hand, which respond only little to interest-rate differentials in domestic and offshore locations, and institutional investors on the other hand, which are very sensitive to such interest differentials. For the institutional investors, the reduction of minimum reserve rates may just not have been sufficient to shift their deposits back to domestic banks. With the remaining minimum reserve rate of about 5 percent for time deposits in Germany and a current market interest rate of approximately 8 percent, Luxembourg banks can offer approximately 40 basis points more than domestic German banks can — which means there is a strong incentive for institutional investors to stay in the offshore market and to shift even more deposits to that market. One lesson that can be derived from this experience, therefore, is that for a profound strengthening of domestic financial markets it may not be sufficient to merely reduce competitive disadvantages. With the presence and increasing importance of institutional investors, competitiveness is only likely to be visibly improved if disadvantages are removed completely, e.g., via the payment of market interest on minimum reserve holdings.

Helmut Schlesinger

Capital Outflow and Taxation — The Case of the Federal Republic of Germany

1. Introduction

In Germany trends on the financial markets were recently overshadowed for 18 months by a taxation decision the macroeconomic implications of which were initially underestimated in many quarters. This happened in spite of warnings, including one from the Bundesbank. I am referring to the decision in autumn 1987 to introduce the so-called "Quellensteuer", a withholding tax of 10 per cent on domestic interest income, at the start of 1989 — a decision which was reversed in the spring of the same year, as we all know, on account of the effects it had produced. The introduction of a tax at source on interest income was justified largely in terms of the tax system: mainly by arguing that more tax equity could be attained in this way. However, as can be seen from the effects, quite clear effects, which subsequently occurred, more tax equity in this area can only be bought at an economic "price", and this price can be fairly high.[1] For when taxing investment income and assets, one has to take into consideration that capital is a production factor with particularly high international mobility, and this means that national changes in tax legislation have to take account of avoidance behaviour to a much greater extent than changes in other areas. But before I discuss the special lessons which Germany has learned from the temporary levy of a tax at source on interest income, I would like to discuss in somewhat more detail the basic conflict of goals under which all tax regulations affecting investment income are to be subsumed.

2. Should Investment Income Be Taxed at All?

The question of whether and to what extent investment income should be taxed at all has been one of the most controversial problems in taxation and economic theory

---

1 Regarding the problems posed by a general withholding tax on investment income, see: Schlesinger, Helmut, "Zur Besteuerung von Kapitalerträgen" (Taxation of Investment Income). In: Dieter Cansier, Dietmar Kath (Eds.), Öffentliche Finanzen, Kredit und Kapital. Festschrift für Werner Ehrlicher. Berlin 1985, p. 237.

for a long time now. All regulations which are drawn up with respect to this question move between two poles: tax equity on the one hand and economic policy targets on the other. From the macroeconomic point of view, one can demand of a "rational" taxation system that it at least does not favour current consumption over capital formation. There are structural economic problems to be solved. Above all, they include unemployment, the abolition of subsidies for enterprises and the increase in the number of pensioners relative to the size of the labour force that is expected to occur at the start of the next century. These problems would make it appropriate not to place a bonus on borrowing for consumption purposes, but on the contrary, to give tax concessions to capital formation. The theoretical solutions suggested for the treatment of investment income and savings are admittedly manyfold and varied: they range from the concept of a comprehensive income tax to the taxation of consumption only.

One argument against a comprehensive income tax, which also extends to interest income, was put forward by John Stuart Mill 140 years ago: he argued that it would lead to double taxation of savings, as the interest income usually stems from income that has already been taxed. But naturally, interest is income which as such has not been taxed before. However, there is a certain element of truth to his argument, from the economic point of view: taxing interest income makes saving for the future more expensive relative to current consumption, and this constitutes an excess burden for savers. For a given market interest rate, savers receive a smaller premium for temporarily refraining from consumption. As a consequence of the lower net interest yield, it is then less worthwhile to save (unless the tax on the interest can be passed on to the borrower — a case, however, which gives rise to lower real investment). Hence, given a comprehensive income tax which also taxes interest income, there may be an intertemporal misallocation of economic resources: less capital formation, more consumption and a weakening of growth. Pigou drew attention to this economic "price" of taxing interest income some sixty years ago. Keeping investment free from income tax is a position which has always had its proponents in the last few decades.

The other extreme of pure consumption taxation — in the form of either an indirect levy or a personal expenditure tax — also has grave disadvantages. First, it could strengthen the flight into the underground economy because, given a smaller tax base than in the case of a comprehensive income tax, higher tax rates would be necessary to yield the same revenue. Secondly, an expenditure tax would probably be perceived as being unjust because it would not fit into the ability-to-pay concept.

Theoretically, the ability to pay taxes is generally measured by the periodic increase in the individual's capacity to command economic resources, i.e. (since Schanz's time) by all accretions to wealth, given by personal consumption plus the increase in net worth during a given period. Taxation defined as "equitable" according to this norm would, as is well known, boil down to the concept of a comprehensive income tax — i.e. an income tax which, to be exact, would have to be much broader-based than it is in our current tax system. In addition to interest and dividends, it would also have to consider capital gains. Further, if such a comprehensive income tax were to be applied, an imputed rental for owner-occupied housing would also have to be taxed. Such imputed income is not taxed either in Germany (since 1987) or in other major countries. And what is also left out of consideration is the interest yield from pension claims, not only on life and private pension insurance funds, but also on employers and the social security funds.[2]

It is already evident that even income tax in its current form is still a long way from the norms of tax equity. Stronger effective taxation of de jure taxable interest income alone would not change this basic state of affairs very much. However, it would have disadvantageous consequences for capital formation, and thus growth. The taxation of net worth itself (e.g. the assessment of real property as opposed to financial assets) is anything but convincing, quite apart from the question of whether it is reasonable to levy a net worth tax in addition to an income tax. Besides, there are a number of further taxes which can hardly be incorporated into a "rational" taxation system: I am thinking here, for example, of capital transfer taxes, the abolition of which has been under discussion for a long time and is now being planned for the years 1991 and 1992. In actual fact, the problem of tax equity in our current tax system appears practically insoluble. The tax system consists of the more or less uncoordinated coexistence of many direct and indirect individual levies. I shall be dealing in the course of my later comments with some special aspects of this problem, specifically as regards the taxation of investment income and of total capital. First, however, I shall say something about the effects in Germany of the temporary levying of a withholding tax on interest income.

3. Effects of the Temporary Withholding Tax on Interest Income

Those responsible for making tax policy had been considering introducing a general withholding tax on interest income in Germany since the start of the eighties. The

---

2 Particularly if one visualises what equivalent in terms of capital the claims on the statutory pension insurance funds represent from the point of view of the insured, it becomes clear that the high shares of interest included, so to speak, in the pensions are tax-free. If, instead of the present pay-as-you-go system, the funding principle were used, at an interest rate equal to the rate of wage increase, a capital stock of DM 6.5 trill. would have to be formed in order to finance current pension claims, according to calculations by the Association of German Pension Insurance Funds. The cash value of these claims would thus be three times as high as the total interest-bearing financial assets of households in the Federal Republic of Germany. This should not be interpreted to mean that taxation of the interest share in the pensions is being proposed, but it does mean that the concentration of the debate on the interest income from financial assets is too one-sided.

reason was to be found less in the wish to improve the tax system than in the wish to generate additional tax revenue. In looking for ways of consolidating what was at the time the very precarious state of government budgets, the last SPD-FDP coalition government was tempted in 1981-82 to open up what was, at first sight, a not inconsiderable revenue potential by introducing a withholding tax on interest income. On the other hand, warnings were issued already at that time, not least by the Bundesbank, that investors would take actions in order to avoid the stronger taxation of interest income, which would be disadvantageous in macroeconomic terms.

Plans to tax interest income at source were not pursued any further at that time, probably inter alia with an eye to the particularly difficult monetary policy situation at the beginning of the eighties: surpluses on external capital transactions were required to finance a high current account deficit. A further reason was that a similar tax in Austria, which had been introduced at the start of 1984, led to a weakening of the government and the governing party in that country. The new Federal Government in Bonn then abolished, in the course of 1984, a tax policy relic dating back to a period when it had been a question of fending off capital inflows into Germany. I am referring to the so-called "coupon tax", which had been introduced in 1965 under what were then still fixed exchange rates, and which had subjected interest income from domestic bonds held by non-residents to tax at source, at the rate of 25 per cent. The removal of this tax confirmed that taxes of this nature have a considerable influence on capital flows and interest rates.

For years, incidentally, the new government coalition decisively rejected a stronger taxation of domestic interest income. Thus, in 1986, in a report prepared in cooperation with the Bundesbank for the Audit Committee of the Deutsche Bundestag, the Federal Ministry of Finance was still drawing attention to the considerable macroeconomic risks posed by a tax at source on interest income. The report also corrected the exaggerated fiscal expectations entertained in some quarters as regards the introduction of a withholding tax. All the greater was the public surprise in autumn 1987 when the governing coalition decided to finance revenue foregone as a result of the tax reform of 1990 inter alia by levying a withholding tax of 10 per cent on interest income in Germany as from the start of 1989.

The mere announcement of this measure set off considerable reactions on the financial markets. Thus, on the very day of the announcement — October 9, 1987 (ten days before Black Monday and seven days before Secretary Baker's attack on the Bundesbank for raising its tender rates by 0.2 percentage points) — there was on the bond markets a downright selling wave of domestic debtors' paper which would in future be subject to the withholding tax. Consequently, yields — especially those on federal bonds — rose by 0.2 percentage points and more. This rapid interest rate effect could basically have been expected, because the abolition of the "coupon tax" three years before had triggered interest rate reactions going the opposite way immediately after the decision to abolish the tax had been announced. The single market which had been in existence for DM-issues from that time now split into two sub-markets again with differing conditions: a market for domestic paper subject to the withholding tax and a market for foreign DM-bonds not subject to the tax. Correspondingly, the interest rate pattern changed: top-drawer domestic addresses such as the Federal Government now had to offer a quarter to a half percentage point more interest than did non-resident addresses. It was possible to calculate that, after some time, the withholding tax would have caused capital market conditions for the public authorities to deteriorate by almost as much as the sum total of the additional revenue expected from the tax. In other words, the fiscal burden on the capital lenders was largely passed on to the capital borrowers.

In actual fact, the adverse effects of the withholding tax were more than merely fiscal. The readiness on the part of investors to undertake long-term investment on the domestic markets fell rapidly. After a long phase of dynamic growth, the capital market in Germany was faced with a severe setback in 1988. Thus, the revenue from the sale of domestic bonds shrank by almost two-thirds last year. At only DM 35 bill., it contrasted with a magnitude of almost DM 90 bill. in 1987. This was due to the fact that, first, foreign investors were withdrawing from the market and, secondly, domestic non-banks were hardly buying any bonds subject to the withholding tax.

It was mainly foreign capital markets that profited from this change in investment behaviour after the announcement of the withholding tax. To a growing extent, they attracted savings from Germany. Thus, domestic funds of approximately DM 70 bill. net went into foreign bonds last year (this figure includes the shares in foreign investment funds). This was over twice as much as in 1987. Interest focused particularly on foreign currency bonds. The strong demand for this paper naturally had non-tax motives, too, for major investment currencies were offering much higher yields than DM-bonds. Investors did not assess the currency risks associated with these attractive yields as being very serious, not least because the D-Mark also depreciated as a result of the withholding tax. The foreign DM-bond market segment also experienced a revival in 1988, along with investment in foreign currencies. German residents preferred this paper, even though it was providing somewhat lower interest than was obtainable for domestic bonds.

It would be a gross oversimplification to say that capital exports from Germany in 1988, at a record level of DM 120 bill. net, were due to reactions to the withholding tax. After all, the current account was running a surplus and capital exports were thus the order of the day anyway. But the size of the long-term capital exports, at a level of DM 85 bill. net (almost four times as high as in 1987), and the normalisation of capital transactions after the Federal Government decided in April 1989 to repeal the withholding tax by midyear are proof of the strong influence the tax exerted. Since that time, foreign securities investments in Germany have been holding the upper hand again and, in the case of DM-issues, the market split between domestic and foreign paper caused by the tax has shrunk again.

The D-Mark's exchange rate trend fits this picture, too: from the start of 1988 to the end of March 1989, the external value of the D-Mark fell by 5 per cent against the average of the currencies of 18 key industrial countries, and in real terms — i.e. after accumulated price differences are taken into consideration — it actually went down even more strongly. This depreciation of the D-Mark also influenced the terms of trade negatively and to this extent generated a "welfare loss", or the loss of a prospective gain in affluence for Germany. Since April, there have been first signs of a normalisation, as the depreciation trend of the D-Mark has not continued and has in fact recently corrected itself somewhat. Admittedly, many factors have played a role here: higher interest rates in Germany as a consequence of the Bundesbank's policy, the interest rate fall in the USA and a further increase in the competitiveness of the German economy, which, at constant exchange rates, can be seen particularly vis-à-vis the EC countries.

I would mention in passing that the withholding tax also put a temporary strain on the Bundesbank's monetary policy, for the reduced readiness to invest in long-term financial assets led to a bigger increase in liquid monetary holdings. There were a number of investors who were so confused by the announcement of the withholding tax that, for a time, they behaved in an economically irrational manner and invested their savings more in (non-interest-bearing) banknotes or those savings accounts which were not subject to the withholding tax, but promised only a low yield. The increased tendency to hold cash (+15 per cent in the last year) makes it clear how easy it is to antagonise the population with unexpected data changes in the monetary area, an area which many do not understand. Money, paper money, is created on the basis of trust. One cannot stress this fact too often; there is not any room for experiments with new ideas.

4. Tax Distortions between Financial and Real Assets

Summarising the lessons which Germany has learned from the withholding tax on interest income, one comes to the retrospective conclusion that it did considerable damage to the German capital market, damage which, with few exceptions, was repaired by its abolition. On the other hand, the step towards more tax equity which had been intended in the form of the withholding tax was a relatively modest one. This could be seen already in the choice of the tax rate (a rate in the sense of a prior tax) of 10 per cent. Even in association with the partial amnesty offered under the law for retroactive declarations of investment income, this rate, which was still far below the floor rate for income tax, would probably have made only a small minority of taxpayers be more honest in their tax declarations than before, i.e. would have made them declare their interest income more fully. It is true that, according to provisional information up to the middle of this year, about 500,000 declarations had been lodged by taxpayers, freeing them from retroactive prosecution for the years 1986-87, but the interest amount declared, at about DM 1 bill. for the two-year period mentioned, was small. While the goal of greater tax equity was hardly better fulfilled in this way, particularly as regards higher income earners, the withholding tax gave rise to unfairness in the case of savers whose interest earnings were definitely exempt from income tax but who neglected to have themselves exempted from the new form of income tax by obtaining a certificate from the tax authorities. Pensioners in particular have a broad scope for tax-free interest income, on account of the de facto non-taxation of social security pensions.

All these experiences show that a withholding tax on investment income, given freedom of movement for capital and big differences in national tax regimes, is not a procedure to be recommended if one wants to promote tax equity without incurring macroeconomic disadvantages. I would imagine that the question of tax equity can be assessed here only in one further connection. Some questions may shed some light on the matter: if taxpayers fully declare their interest income and financial assets, is it not the case that they can then be worse off than recipients or owners of other types of income and assets? In the current tax system, for example, the real investment income from the use of one's own home or an owner-occupied apartment has been completely tax-free for some years now. It is of no less importance that the principle of nominal value does not permit offsetting the loss of the real value of financial assets through inflation against interest income, although it is evident today that the nominal interest rate and thus the tax base rise with the inflation rate.[3] And the interest accumulation occurring in life insurance contracts as well as in private and public pension claims remains out of consideration (when pension claims are reduced, admittedly, there is also unsystematic taxation). I am not suggesting changing all this, I only think that one should not try to enforce equity for interest income only.

There are also considerable differences in the tax treatment of assets in the context of net worth and inheritance tax, where, as is well known, financial assets are much more heavily taxed than real property estimated at out-of-date values. The Advisory Council at the Federal Ministry of Finance, in its study on assessed valuation published at the beginning of this year, commented that "there is hardly any other area in the German tax system which features bigger discrepancies in the

3 The Federal Constitutional Court thus ruled in 1978 that, when taxing interest income, the principle of nominal value is to be maintained. Admittedly, it qualified its judgement at that time with the proviso that "a significant change in the value of money could lead to a disruption of the tax legislation framework".

basis of assessment".[4] As the tax on real estate in Germany is still largely geared to the situation 25 years ago, its tax base often represents only a fraction of the current market value. An investigation by the Federal Ministry of Finance, based on about 50,000 real estate transactions in 1986, shows that the average assessed value for vacant building plots corresponded to only about a fifth of the purchase price (provided that the purchase price was not even higher than the recorded one!). As many years of experience show, the prospects of bringing about a more realistic valuation of real estate are dim. If, however, the current preferential tax treatment of real estate cannot be reduced for political reasons, then there would be strong arguments in favour of avoiding too much of a bias in taxing financial assets and income. For example, I would comment here that the value of households' financial assets is currently a good DM 2 trill. — assets which, where they exceed the allowable deductions, are subject to net worth and inheritance tax. The value of owner-occupied housing at current prices is also estimated to be DM 2 trill. net, but — as already mentioned — it is tax-privileged because real estate is assessed for tax purposes using out-of-date values (and this gives rise to a number of misallocations).[5]

5. Conclusions

I have certainly not exhausted the subject of illogical taxation of investment income and capital, as differentiated by financial and real assets. For example, I have not dealt with the taxation of private capital gains (which are tax-free after 6 months for equities, 2 years for real estate), nor have I dealt with the question of how one transforms interest income into tax-free capital gains, on the one hand, or the limited scope for households to deduct debt interest, on the other hand, etc. The introduction of a withholding tax on interest income in Germany showed at any rate that taxpayers' willingness on this particular point to make their contribution to tax equity had been overestimated. The negative macroeconomic consequences make this clear.

I do not feel qualified to present a theoretically coherent taxation concept in this area. I believe that the legislature can, and indeed must, proceed on a pragmatic basis here. In aggregate terms, intertemporal allocation considerations in particular

4 Wissenschaftlicher Beirat beim Bundesministerium der Finanzen, "Die Einheitsbewertung in der Bundesrepublik Deutschland — Mängel und Alternativen". In: Schriftenreihe des Bundesministeriums der Finanzen, Heft 41, Bonn 1985, p. 1.

5 It is true that in formal terms, and because of the "consumer goods solution" for housing which has been in force since 1987, no more write-downs *as such* can be offset against income tax. In actual fact, however, given the allowance for special expenses in place of the § 7b EStG provision, the preferential tax treatment of housing to date has been strengthened.

would seem to indicate that savings should be taxed sparingly. The complete taxation of investment income would, after all, disadvantage saving for the future against current consumption and thus, in the final analysis, hinder a solution to structural economic and growth problems. Particularly as regards the growing difficulties with which the old age social security scheme is faced in the long term as a result of demographic trends, and this in spite of the inflow of ethnic Germans from Eastern Europe and immigrants from the GDR, it would seem appropriate to promote private saving and in this way facilitate private saving for old age as a supplement to the provision offered by the state. (Indeed, the tax-free accumulation of claims on life insurance funds is playing a growing role relative to other forms of private saving.) I am not thinking here of the reintroduction of saving premiums, but in my opinion, the allowable deductions for investment income and assets should be assessed as generously as possible. For example, the saver's allowable deduction for income tax, which was recently doubled in the Federal Republic of Germany and now amounts to DM 600 for single persons and DM 1,200 for married couples, is still well below the level of tax-free investment income in France. The basic allowance of DM 70,000 which has been applied for net worth tax since 1974 also appears, in comparison with other countries, to be in need of adjustment: most countries do not levy a net worth tax at all. Some dispensations are necessary here, too, to alleviate what is de facto double taxation of investment income.

The approach I have described, of moving towards stronger tax relief for investment income, may at first sight appear to contradict the principle of greater tax equity. But this principle is definitely not contradicted by the need to ensure that financial assets and the income they generate do not receive worse tax treatment than other forms of private asset formation. In the final analysis, and in view of the ongoing liberalisation of capital transactions in the EC, it is a question of creating favourable local conditions for that particularly mobile factor, capital.

Comment on Helmut Schlesinger, "Capital Outflow and Taxation — The Case of the Federal Republic of Germany"

Manfred Neumann

The paper is concerned with both efficiency and equity considerations of taxing capital income. Equity played a prominent role in the debate about taxation of capital income and particularly in the case of the withholding tax on interest income in Germany. Since equity is an elusive concept of an ideal state practically impossible to attain, Schlesinger proposes to minimize discrimination against income from financial assets. This is of course no more than a minimal requirement. Yet, given the difficulties in defining equity, it appears to be a practical proposition that will command widespread agreement.

The paper then focuses on the withholding tax on interest income introduced in Germany in 1987, and subsequently abolished, largely because it turned out that it aroused extreme public resentment, to say the least. The paper deals extensively with the unfavorable effects of this episode and makes a fervent case against a withholding tax, and thus kills an already deceased tax, probably in order to prevent any resurrection attempts. Although I agree with the basic message, I have some doubts regarding the exact figures for the changes in capital outflows attributed by Schlesinger to the withholding tax. It might be noted that net capital exports from Germany first arose in 1982 and then gradually increased. Even in 1989, i.e., after the repeal of the withholding tax, the surplus in the balance on current account, and for that matter net capital outflow, will probably attain a new record height.

Nevertheless, I think the case of the withholding tax is a good example with which to document the detrimental effects on investment in the home economy which are engendered by income taxation. These effects, in my judgement, far outweigh any improvement in equity which may arise from income taxation. Certainly, a substantial part of net capital outflows from Germany can be attributed not only to the withholding tax on interest income but also, and more generally, to an unfavorable tax treatment of profits from domestic investment, as compared to other competing countries. In the game of tax competition, Germany's position has deteriorated relatively.

It should not be overlooked, however, that capital outflows also arose for other reasons as well. Among these the high level of labor costs and regulations in the labor market have played an important role. Since labor costs are lower in other European countries, a substantial amount of capital is flowing to those countries.

Given the discrepancy between the profitability of investment at home and abroad in recent years, net capital exports can, thus, to a considerable extent, be attributed to this fact. On the other hand, net capital exports and the accompanying surplus in the balance on current account arise simultaneously. Whereas the shortfall in the profitability of domestic investment against foreign assets has caused an increase in net capital exports, the improvement in the trade balance can also be attributed to additional causes of its own. The real exchange rate for the D-Mark has declined within the European Currency System in the more recent past because a realignment of exchange rates met with the opposition of some countries, notably France. For this reason, the German trade balance has improved, which has entailed an additional increase in net capital exports.

Finally, I should mention that the withholding tax has been justified on the grounds that other EC countries also levy such a tax. The French government, in particular, at one time made the liberalization of intra-European capital flows contingent on a harmonization of tax rates for capital income and the introduction of a withholding tax throughout Europe. I think that such reasoning is fallacious, at least as far as the withholding tax is concerned. Capital income, as any income, is subject to income taxation in all countries of the European Community. A withholding tax is merely a way of collecting tax revenues. Unless a withholding tax is levied on income that would otherwise illegally evade taxation, the introduction, or the removal, of a withholding tax does not affect the tax burden at all. To what extent tax evasion obtains is a matter of dispute and may also differ, as among the various European countries. I submit that the tremendous effects on capital flows which Schlesinger suggests are attributable to the introduction of the withholding tax in Germany could only have arisen if tax evasion is of overriding importance in the case of income from financial assets. If tax evasion is more limited, the effects of the withholding tax on capital flow can be expected to be less important.

Daniel Gros

Tax Evasion and Offshore Centres

1. Introduction

In most models of the taxation of capital, financial intermediation does not play a role. It is usually simply assumed that firms obtain savings directly from private households and that the return to capital can be observed and taxed in the country where the capital is physically located. (See, for example, the contributions by Giovannini as well as Razin and Sadka in this volume.) Alternatively, it is also sometimes assumed that investment can be financed via intermediaries located offshore, i.e. outside the reach of the domestic tax authorities. In the first case, it is possible to tax the return to capital effectively, although this might create undesirable distortions. In the second case, it is totally impossible to tax capital, attempting to do so would cause all financing to migrate offshore, without yielding any real effects.

This paper departs from this 0–1 choice by assuming that financial intermediation offshore is possible but also that it is subject to costs, so that some, although not all, financing of investment migrates offshore in response to a domestic tax on capital income. This paper develops therefore a simple analytical model of *costly* tax evasion to evaluate the effects of (withholding) taxes on: (1) interest income from the volume of financial intermediation in offshore centres; (2) the interest rate differential between offshore and domestic markets; and (3) the total tax revenue that can be collected from interest income. The model is based on the assumption that there are costs for households to switch their asset holdings to an offshore centre and that there are also costs for corporations to switch their borrowings to the offshore market. An essential element of the model is that these costs differ across households and firms.

In the presence of these switching costs, not all financial activity will emigrate to the offshore centre even if there is a positive tax on the interest income from domestic bonds, since, for some households and firms, the costs of going to the offshore centre outweigh the advantages of the tax free environment. Capital controls can be considered to increase the switching costs; the model can therefore

Remark : I wish to thank Paul de Grauwe and Chris Boyd for comments on an earlier draft. Conference participants, especially Joel Slemrod, Alberto Giovannini and Julian Alworth provided valuable criticism and discussions.

also be used to analyze the consequences of the abolition of capital controls in the presence of differences in the taxation of interest income.

A first result of this simple model is that the offshore/domestic interest rate differential induced by a domestic tax is a fraction of the tax rate. The magnitude of this fraction is determined by the *relative* switching costs in the corporate and the household sectors. The scale of financial activity displaced to the offshore centre is, however, a function of the *sum* of the two switching cost parameters.

The simple linear structure of the model yields analytical solutions for the revenue the domestic government can obtain from the taxation of interest income. There exists a Laffer curve for the tax revenue from the taxation of interest income: the revenue maximizing tax rate is below 50 per cent and the maximum tax revenue that can be collected is below 25 per cent of total interest income.

Finally, the model can be used to analyze tax competition between the domestic government and the authorities of the offshore centre. It suggests that tax competition with an offshore centre does not necessarily lead to zero tax rates.

The current debate about the need for harmonization of the fiscal treatment of savings following the capital market liberalization in the EC that is scheduled for July 1990 provides a policy issue for which this model can be useful. The framework of this paper confirms the idea that capital market liberalization will make it more difficult to tax interest income, but it also implies that capital market liberalization does not necessarily eliminate the possibility of taxing domestic savings. A further result is that offshore centres, like Luxemburg, would oppose an *equalization* of withholding taxes, but should not be against any taxation of cross-border interest payments.

Germany's recent experience with the 10 per cent withholding tax introduced in January 1989 (and abolished in July 1989) provides an interesting example that can be used to test some of the implications of the model. The behaviour of the interest differential between Euro-DM and domestic German bonds seems to confirm one prediction of the model, namely, that the (proportional shift in the) interest rate differential should be a fraction of the tax rate.

The organization of the paper is as follows: Section 2 presents the model of switching costs for households and the corporate sector. Section 3 analyzes, based on the assumption that taxes in the offshore centre are zero, the implications of the imposition by the home country government of a tax for interest rate differentials, offshore financial activity and government revenue. Section 4 analyzes tax competition between the offshore centre and the home country government in a Nash setting. Section 5 points out some of the limitations of the analysis and suggests topics for further research.

2. The Model

There are only three simple building blocks to this model, the ***first building block*** of which is given by the household sector, which represents the only source of savings. All households save the same amount and can hold their savings only in the form of (one-period) bonds.[1] All households also face the same domestic interest rate, i, and pay the same proportional tax on their interest income, τ, which is deducted at the source and cannot be evaded. The last assumption corresponds to reality in those countries that have a withholding tax on interest payments on bonds that releases savers from declaring interest to the tax authorities, as, for example, in Italy (where the rate is 12.5 per cent). The net return on domestic bonds for all households is therefore equal to $(1 - \tau)\, i$. The only alternative to holding domestic bonds is to hold withholding-tax-exempt international bonds, henceforth called Eurobonds, that have been issued in an offshore centre.

An offshore centre is defined here as a place where withholding-tax-exempt Eurobonds can be issued that allow households to evade taxes on interest income. The offshore centre might therefore be a country like Luxemburg, or it might be really "offshore", like the Channel Islands for UK residents. To avoid complications regarding the currency of denomination of the bonds, it is simply assumed that bonds in domestic currency can be issued in the offshore centre, which is true for most offshore centres. Although, in reality, Euromarket activity tends to concentrate in a few centres for most European countries, the entire rest of the world is really an offshore centre, since most industralized countries do not levy withholding taxes (or provide information to foreign tax authorities) on the interest income of nonresidents.

Although Eurobonds are withholding tax free, domestic residents are required to declare the interest they earn on these bonds, which is then taxed as ordinary income. Failure to report this income constitutes tax evasion and carries potentially important penalties. The only way for residents to maximize the probability of escaping detection is to go personally to the offshore centre and to transfer their investment in a manner that cannot be traced, i.e. by using cash. Belgian and Dutch residents seem to do this on a large scale in Luxemburg. Such an operation involves costs in the form of direct travel expenses and value of the time lost.

Moreover, even when this method is used, the probability of detection is never equal to zero; by not reporting the interest income, residents therefore face a low probability of a potentially large penalty. The evaluation of this potential cost depends not only on the expected value of the penalty (i.e. the value of the penalty

---

1 Stock shares are not considered here because they are subject in most countries to high withholding taxes which ensure an effective taxation of dividends. The results would not be affected if a certain proportion of savings (and investments) were to be financed with shares.

times the probability of being caught), but also on the degree of risk aversion, since this aspect introduces an important stochastic element.

The crucial element of the model is that the costs that arise in connection with tax evasion through investment in Eurobonds are assumed to differ across households. Different households face different costs because the distance to the offshore centre will, in general, differ, because the opportunity cost of going to the offshore centre differs and also because the degree of risk aversion might differ across households.[2] The assumption that there are different costs in evading taxes is made operational by assuming that there is a continuous and uniform distribution of households, which can be indexed by the real number j, with j in the interval [0, 1], such that the cost of switching to a Eurobond investment is equal to $\theta_h j$, where θ_h is a positive constant. This constant indicates the maximum switching cost, that of the household with index 1, and also the degree to which this cost rises from one household to the next. Although there is always one household (with index 0) with zero switching costs, the parameter θ_h will be referred to generically as "the" switching cost.

Another source of differences in switching costs across households might be differences in "civic conscience". Some households might not take advantage of opportunities to evade taxes because they want to be able to feel like good citizens. The importance of this noneconomic cost is difficult to evaluate. However, it is alleged that in some countries, tax systems that rely on the honesty of the taxpayers work well because of this reason.

The analysis of the effects of capital control can be incorporated into this framework by assuming that capital controls increase the cost for domestic residents of investing in Eurobonds through an offshore centre. For example, in Italy in the early 1980s, exports of banknotes were forbidden and bank transfers by individuals were legally almost impossible. Anecdotal evidence and evidence from interest rate differentials suggest that capital controls were never completely effective in impeding flows to offshore markets. However, they did impose some additional costs on residents trying to export capital, since the penalties were stiff and the remaining channels were not without risk.

Given the interest rate on Eurobonds, henceforth called the offshore interest rate, (and assuming that households do not declare the interest income from Eurobonds) the equilibrium is determined by the household that is indifferent between keeping its domestic bonds and evading taxes through an investment in Eurobonds. This household, whose position in terms of switching cost is indicated by c_h, can be determined by the condition that the return on the two alternatives has to be equal:

[1] $$(1-\tau)i = i^* - \theta_h c_h,$$

2 This point was suggested to me by Paul de Grauwe.

where i^* denotes the Euro or offshore interest rate.

All households with switching costs lower than household c_h invest in Eurobonds; all other housholds hold domestic bonds. Given that the distribution, j, of switching costs has been normalized to lie in the interval [0, 1] and given that all households have the same investment, the index c_h indicates immediately the proportion of total savings that emigrate to the offshore centre.

The stock/flow problem is eliminated by assuming that the switching cost applies over the same time period as the interest rate. This assumption can be justified in at least two ways: first, one could imagine that the switching cost applies only to the transfer (the flow), in which case households would make one initial decision and the switching cost would be the flow equivalent of the initial cost. Second, one could imagine that households can hold their bonds only for one period; after that, they need them to make transactions, and the switching cost therefore has to be sustained each period.

The *second building block* derives from a similar assumption for firms that need to issue bonds to finance their investment projects.[3] The issuance of bonds is organized by intermediaries (perhaps banks) that have no costs. Assuming costs for intermediaries would not change the nature of the model, but would introduce considerable complications in the computations without changing the nature of the results. The interest rate at which firms can obtain loans in the domestic market is therefore equal to i. All firms have projects and therefore funding needs of the same size which they could fund at the interest rate i on the domestic market or at the interest rate i^* on the offshore market. However, in order to be able to raise funds on the offshore market, firms have to sustain additional costs. These switching costs for firms vary across firms in the same manner as they vary across households. There is a continuous and uniform distribution of firms, which can be indexed by the real number k, where k lies again in the interval [0, 1], such that the switching cost for firms is equal to $\theta_f k$.

This difference in switching costs for firms can be motivated by the differences in international exposure different firms have. Firms in the domestic non-tradeables sector would have a higher switching cost since they would not be known to the offshore market. Firms that engage in international trade, or simply large firms, might already be known in the offshore market and would therefore not have to spend resources to make themselves known. The empirical basis for this assumption is, again, the observation that even with open capital markets not all domestic firms chose to use offshore centres to finance their investments. If some firms choose not to do this, they must be facing costs, although these costs might be difficult to specify.

---

3 See footnote 1 above for the reason why financing in equity is not considered.

The experience of the US, which had a withholding tax on interest payments of foreign residents until 1984, confirm this point.[4] US corporations could avoid this withholding tax by going through the Netherlands Antilles, which apparently involved some costs, since, after the abolition of the withholding tax, total issues of international bonds by US corporations increased considerably.

Capital controls can again be considered to increase the cost for corporations to raise capital abroad, i.e. capital controls would increase the switching cost for firms.

Offshore bond markets are free of any restrictions, whereas some national bond markets have issue calendars or other regulations, such as disclosure requirements that increase the cost of using the national bonds market relative to the Euromarket.[5] This can be incorporated in the model by assuming that the switching cost is equal to $\theta_f c_f - \alpha$. The constant α represents, then, the net cost of the regulations concerning the domestic bond market. This additional assumption is not essential for most results of the model. As can be easily verified, setting α equal to zero in the results below would not change their nature.

Although it will be shown below that the cost imposed by domestic regulations, as incorporated by the term α, and income taxes have equivalent effects on the Eurodomestic interest rate differential, the legal position of households and firms is quite different. The corporate sector can legally *avoid* the cost, α, of domestic regulations, whereas households *evade* taxes and act outside the law.

Given the continous and uniform distribution of firms and given the two interest rates, there will be a firm that is indifferent between going to the offshore market and staying in the domestic market. This firm is indicated by c_f, and the condition for this firm to be indifferent between the two modes of financing is

$$[2] \quad i^* + \theta_f c_f - \alpha = i \, .$$

Similarly, as for households, c_f indicates the proportion of total investment that is financed via the offshore markets.

The *third building block* derives from the assumption that only domestic households and domestic firms use the domestic capital market.[6] Scaling the number of households so that each household saves enough for one firm (or, equivalently, so that the density of savings and investment projects along j and k is the same) implies immediately that $(1 - c_f) = (1 - c_h)$ and therefore

---

4 See Papke [1989] for further details about the US experience.

5 This assumption incorporates the differences in the net regulatory burden (NRB) described by Levich in this volume.

6 Foreign savers would not be interested in buying taxable domestic bonds anyway. Foreign firms would not be able to issue debt on the domestic market since they are better known at home, and big foreign firms would prefer the Euromarket to the domestic market.

$$[3] \quad c_f = c_h = c\,.$$

Since it is assumed that bonds are the only way to save, this assumption is equivalent to setting savings equal to investments and therefore to a balanced current account. The main justification for this assumption is that the place where financial intermediation takes place should have, at most, a second-order effect on the real economy and thus on overall savings and investment.[7] Therefore, the variable c indicates henceforth the total amount of offshore activity (as a proportion of total domestic savings or investments).

Government revenue from the taxation of savings, indicated by t, can be collected only from interest payments on domestic bonds. It is therefore given by

$$[4] \quad t = \tau(1 - c)\,i\,.$$

The reason for the government to levy taxes is not further analyzed here. It would be sufficient to assume that the government needs revenues to provide a public good; this is done in Giovannini's and Razin and Sadka's contributions to this volume.

3. The Determinants of Interest Rates, Offshore Activity and Tax Revenue

Using the equilibrium condition [3] in equations [1] and [2], the model developed so far consists of three (linear) equations that can determine the three variables of interest; namely, the amount of offshore financial activity, c, the Euro/domestic interest rate differential, $i - i^*$, and the tax revenue of the domestic government, t. These three "endogenous" variables are determined by the parameters of the model, which are the tax rate, τ, and the switching costs, θ_f and θ_h. This leaves one interest rate undetermined, but the purpose of this model is not to build a theory of the level of interest rates. For the purpose of this discussion, it is therefore sufficient to arbitrarily fix the level of interest rates by fixing either i or i^*. It turns out to be more convenient to fix the domestic interest rate, i. The assumption retained is therefore that i is exogenous. This assumption can be easily defended if the domestic currency floats; the home government can then determine the domestic interest rate through its monetary policy.

---

7 Germany's experience with the 10 per cent withholding tax is compatible with this assumption, since there were apparently massive capital flows, but the current account did not change at all. See also Schlesinger's contribution to this volume.

Eliminating c from [1] and [2] yields immediately a solution for the interest rate differential in relative terms:

$$[5] \quad (i - i^*)/i = [\tau - (\alpha\theta_h/\theta_f i)]/[1 + (\theta_h/\theta_f)].$$

In the absence of a competitive advantage of the offshore centre in terms of regulatory restrictions, i.e. if $\alpha = 0$, the offshore interest rate always has to be below the domestic interest rate, otherwise domestic firms would never use the offshore market. Conversely, in the absence of a tax on interest income on domestic bonds, i.e. if $\tau = 0$, the offshore interest rate would have to exceed the domestic interest rate to induce households to go to the offshore centre. Before the introduction of the 10 per cent withholding tax in Germany in January 1989, interest rates on Euro-DM bonds were indeed somewhat higher than interest rates on comparable domestic issues.

This solution also implies that the change in the relative interest rate differential that is caused by the introduction of a tax is equal to a fraction of the tax rate applied to interest payments on domestic deposits. The value of that fraction depends only on the *relative* switching costs, and not on their absolute sizes.[8]

A further implication of this result is that a partial capital market liberalization for the corporate sector (as done by France in early 1989) which reduces the relative switching cost of the corporate sector should also reduce the interest rate differential. Conversely, a partial liberalization for households, while maintaining strict controls on the corporate sector, would bring the relative interest rate differential close to the tax rate.

The amount of financial activity that emigrates to the offshore centre can also be easily computed by eliminating the offshore interest rate, i^*, from [1] and [2]. This yields c as a function of the regulatory cost advantage, α, the tax rate, τ, and the domestic interest rate:

$$[6] \quad c = (\tau i + \alpha)/(\theta_f + \theta_h).$$

The product τi stands for the effective tax on domestic bonds. This result shows that the amount of offshore activity is a function of the *sum* of the two switching cost parameters, in contrast to the offshore/domestic interest rate differential, which is only a function of the *ratio* of these parameters. A reduction in both parameters due to generalized capital market liberalization would therefore always increase offshore activity, but could make the interest rate differential go either way.

---

8 The switching costs can also be regarded as the slopes of the demand for and supply of funds. The result [5] can therefore be interpreted to mean that what matters are the relative slopes of demand and supply.

Given the "leakage" provided by the offshore markets, the model also exhibits a Laffer curve type relationship between the tax rate, θ, and total tax revenue, t. Using [6] in the definition of the tax revenue, [4] yields

$$[7] \quad t = i\tau[1 - (i\tau + \alpha)/(\theta_f + \theta_h)].$$

Given the totally inelastic supply of savings, the government could raise the tax rate to over 100 per cent and it would still collect a substantial revenue if the switching costs were high enough. To eliminate this possibility, it is necessary to impose a restriction on these parameters which guarantees that at a 100 per cent tax rate, revenue cannot be positive. It is apparent from [7] that this can be obtained by imposing: $\theta_f + \theta_h - \alpha < i$. In economic terms, this condition implies that even those households and firms with the highest switching costs will go to the offshore centre as taxes are raised towards 100 per cent.

Inspection of [7] shows that it is quadratic and implies a Laffer curve for the tax revenue. For a given tax rate, the revenue is an increasing function of the switching cost parameters. Capital liberalization therefore leads to a loss of tax revenue.

The revenue maximizing tax rate can be calculated by setting the derivative of the right-hand side of this equation with respect to τ equal to zero:

$$[8] \quad dt/d\tau = i[1 - (2i\tau + \alpha)/(\theta_f + \theta_h)] = 0.$$

The revenue maximizing tax rate is therefore equal to

$$[9] \quad \tau_{max} = (\theta_f + \theta_h - \alpha)/2i.$$

As intuition would suggest, the revenue maximizing tax rate is an increasing function of the two switching cost parameters, since these indicate to what extent the domestic capital market can be considered captive. The revenue maximizing tax rate is a decreasing function of the domestic interest rate, since the effective tax rate is the product of the interest rate and the tax rate. The restriction on the size of the switching costs mentioned above implies that t_{max} has to be below 50 per cent.

Substituting the solution [9] back into the expression for tax revenue yields the maximum revenue the government can obtain

$$[10] \quad t_{max} = (i/4)[(\theta_f + \theta_h - \alpha)/(\theta_f + \theta_h)][(\theta_f + \theta_h - \alpha)/i],$$

which collapses to $(\theta_f + \theta_h)/4$ if α goes to zero.

Again, as suggested by intuition, the maximum revenue is an increasing function of the two switching cost parameters. Using again the restriction on the switching cost parameters, it can be shown that for $\alpha = 0$ the limit on tax revenue for the government is equal to one fourth of the total potential interest revenue of households (i.e. one fourth of the interest paid if all financial intermediation took place domestically). This can also easily be shown by considering that at the maximum revenue more than one half of savings has emigrated and that the revenue maximizing rate is below 50 per cent. The same holds true if α is positive; in this case, the maximum revenue is smaller than one fourth of the interest payments on domestic bonds at a zero domestic tax rate.

The switching costs the private sector sustains by going to the offshore centre (only for households is the direct motive tax evasion) are a net loss to society. The total costs sustained by the private sector have to be calculated by integrating across households and firms since each household and firm has a different cost. Denoting this evasion cost by e the result for households is

$$[11] \quad e_h = \int_0^{c_h} s\,\theta_h\,ds = \theta_h c_h^2 / 2 .$$

Firms are attracted to the offshore centre because of the lower regulatory costs and the lower interest rate. The costs they sustain to profit from these two advantages of the offshore centre can be calculated in a completely analogous manner. Using the solution for c in equation [6], the total evasion cost sustained by firms and households can then be written as

$$[12] \quad e = (i\tau + \alpha)^2 / [2(\theta_f + \theta_h)] .$$

Inspection of this expression reveals that the total evasion and avoidance cost (for firms) increases with the square of the total tax on financial activity, i.e. the sum of $i\tau$ and α. This result corresponds to the usual triangles that appear in graphical analyses of welfare losses from taxation. Since, in reality, governments impose many different taxes that all incite to evasion or avoidance activity, it is more useful to consider the tax revenue per unit of welfare loss in terms of evasion costs. Dividing [7] by [12] and rearranging yields:

$$[13] \quad t/e = [i\tau(\theta_f + \theta_h - (i\tau + \alpha))] / [(i\tau + \alpha)^2] .$$

Setting α equal to zero, which implies that the offshore centre exists only because of tax evasion, leads immediately to the result that the tax revenue per unit of evasion cost also decreases with the tax rate.

4. Tax Competition

This section considers the interests of the offshore centre as well. The offshore centre can gain from the financial activity on its territory only if it taxes the activity, since in this model financial intermediation is costless. Although some offshore centres do not impose any direct taxes, they still gain from the financial activity they attract because they can tax the revenue that is created by financial intermediation, which in reality does involve the use of some resources. Most offshore centres, however, impose some taxes, usually at a low rate.[9]

If the offshore centre also imposes a tax on the interest on the bonds issued in its territory, the condition for the marginal household that is indifferent between investing in domestic bonds or Eurobonds becomes:

$$[14] \quad i^{*}(1 - \tau^{*}) - \theta_{h} c = i(1 - \tau),$$

where τ^{*} denotes the tax imposed by the offshore centre. The choice of the domestic firms is not affected directly by this additional tax. The solution for the interest rate differential can therefore be calculated by combining [2] and [14], which yields after several transformations:

$$[15] \quad (i - i^{*}) = [i(\tau - \tau^{*}) - (\alpha\theta_{h} / \theta_{f})] / [1 + (\theta_{h} / \theta_{f}) - \tau^{*}].$$

As one would expect, an interest rate differential (apart from the one created by the regulatory cost advantage, α) arises only if there is a positive differential in the tax rates. (The case $\tau < \tau^{*}$ does not make sense and is not further considered.) The amount of offshore activity is also a function of the tax differential, as can be shown by further manipulation of these equations:

$$[16] \quad c = [i(\tau - \tau^{*}) + (1 - \tau^{*})\alpha] / [\theta_{h} + \theta_{f}(1 - \tau^{*})].$$

The home country tax revenue is obviously affected by any tax imposed by the offshore centre. By simply inserting [16] into [4], the solution for the home country tax revenue becomes

$$[17] \quad t = i\tau\{1 - [i(\tau - \tau^{*}) + (1 - \tau^{*})\alpha] / [\theta_{h} + \theta_{f}(1 - \tau^{*})]\}.$$

It is not immediately apparent from this expression, but it can be shown that an inrease in the tax of the offshore centre, τ^{*}, always increases home country tax revenue. Under the Nash assumption that the home country takes the foreign tax as

9 These taxes can at times be implicit. For example, in Luxemburg foreign banks are required to have a certain presence even if it is not necessary from a strictly technical point of view.

given, the revenue maximizing tax rate can be calculated by setting the derivative of the right-hand side of this expression with respect to τ equal to zero. Simplifying yields

$$[18] \quad \tau_{max} = (\theta_f + \theta_h - \alpha) / 2i + (\tau^* (i + \alpha - \theta_f)) / 2i .$$

Given the restriction on the size of the switching cost parameters $(\theta_f + \theta_h - \alpha < i)$, it follows that $i + \alpha - \theta_f$ has to be positive and therefore that the revenue maximizing domestic tax rate is an increasing function of the offshore tax rate. The extent to which this is the case depends on the relative magnitudes of the domestic interest rate and the switching cost for firms. Although this result might appear obvious, it becomes less obvious if one considers that the tax rate that maximizes revenue is determined by the point where the elasticity of tax revenue is equal to one. Although an increase in the offshore rate always increases the revenue for the home country, the effect of such an increase in offshore taxation on the elasticity of the revenue (with respect to the home country's tax rate) is not clear a priori. It is apparent that with $\tau^* = 0$ equation [18] collapses to equation [9], which gives the revenue maximizing tax rate if the offshore centre does not impose a tax.

The tax revenue of the offshore centre is given by: $t^* = i^* c\tau^*$. Since the offshore interest rate is determined by the tax rates, it is necessary to rewrite this as $t^* = i(i^*/i)c\tau^*$ and then to use [15] in order to obtain the offshore tax revenue in terms of the parameters of the model:

$$[19] \quad t^* = \tau^* \frac{[\theta_f (1 - \tau) + \theta_h (1 + (\alpha/i))] [i (\tau - \tau^*) + (1 - \tau^*) \alpha]}{[\theta_h + \theta_f (1 - \tau^*)]^2} .$$

Without a regulatory advantage, the offshore centre can obtain some revenue only if $\tau > \tau^*$; that is, if it imposes a lower tax than the home country. The rate that maximizes revenue for the offshore centre can again be calculated in the usual manner. The result is

$$[20] \quad \tau_{max} = \frac{\tau + (\alpha/i)}{2 [1 + (\alpha/i)] - [\tau + (\alpha/i)] \theta_f / (\theta_f + \theta_h)} .$$

For the case $\alpha = 0$, this collapses to

$$[20]' \quad \tau^*_{max} = \frac{\tau}{2 - \tau \theta_f / (\theta_f + \theta_h)} .$$

The revenue maximizing rate of the offshore centre is thus close to one half of the rate imposed in the home country. In contrast to the result for the home country, the revenue maximizing rate for the offshore centre is not linear in the rate chosen by the home country.

The result of (Nash) tax competition with an offshore centre can then be found by combining [18] and [20], which give the revenue maximizing rates for the two countries. To obtain a manageable solution, α was set equal to zero; however, this should not affect the nature of the results. Solving this system of two equations yields a quadratic expression for the Nash equilibrium home country tax rate:

$$[21] \quad \tau^2 - \tau\Omega[1 + (3/2)(\theta_f/i)] + \Omega^2\theta_f/i = 0,$$

where Ω is a composite parameter defined as $\Omega \equiv (1 + \theta_h/\theta_f)$.

This equation has two positive real roots and it can be shown that one root has to be smaller than one. Nash tax competition with an offshore centre therefore does not inevitably lead to zero tax rates as sometimes claimed. It can be shown that at the smaller root (which is between zero and one) the reaction curve of the offshore centre intersects the reaction curve of the home country from below. In a sequential game, the equilibrium would therefore be stable. For example, starting from a situation of zero tax rates everywhere and assuming the home country moves first, the home country would find it optimal to impose the positive tax rate given by [9]. The offshore centre would then also impose a positive tax, this would induce the home country to increase its tax and the offshore centre would follow in turn until the Nash equilibrium is reached.

It is obvious that cooperation between the two countries could increase overall welfare since, if the offshore centre were to agree to impose the same tax as the home country, the home country could raise higher tax revenues and compensate the offshore centre with a side payment for the revenue loss. Evasion costs would be eliminated, since, with the same tax rate in the home country and the offshore centre, firms and households would not incur the cost of going abroad.

5. Limitations of the Analysis and Avenues for Further Research

The purpose of this paper was to develop a simple analytical model of tax-evasion-motivated financial intermediation through offshore centres. A central idea of the framework proposed here is that this financial intermediation is not without cost. It follows that it is possible to tax interest income to some extent even with open capital markets. This seems more realistic than the usual polar assumption that either such intermediation does not exist at all or that it is totally costless.

That considerable tax-induced "round trip" capital movements exist in reality can be deduced from the fact that for most European countries gross capital movements are a large multiple of net movements, i.e. most countries have contemporaneous large in- and outflows which far exceed the net movement [see Gros, 1989]. Although certainly not all of these capital movements are tax motivated, the extent of two-way flows of capital is difficult to justify with the usual intertemporal models in which capital flows are merely the counterpart of current account deficits and might also have a portfolio diversification aspect. It should be stressed, however, that the present paper explains only the "round trip" movements; but as regards the net movement, the assumption is made that it is not affected by taxes. The ideal model would, of course, continue the traditional approach, which stresses the effects of taxes on investment and savings decisions and therefore on the current account, which drives net movements. An integration of the traditional approach with the approach used in this paper is one avenue for further research.

Another avenue for further research would be to improve the overly simplistic linear model developed in this paper. The main results of the paper should survive, as correlations, a more general specification of the switching costs, but the numerical results concerning the total tax revenue could then no longer be obtained. An addition to the model with potentially far-reaching effects would be to introduce the possibility of unlimited short selling, since this would mean that the intramarginal investor would be able to earn the same return as the investor for whom it is profitable to go to the Euromarkets. All these improvements in the analytical model should, however, not change the basic message of the paper: there is some sand in the mechanism of international financial intermediation, and it is therefore possible to tax interest income to some extent even with open capital markets.

Bibliography

GIOVANNINI, Alberto, "Reforming Capital Income Taxation in the Open Economy: Theoretical Issues." In: Horst SIEBERT (Ed.), Reforming Capital Income Taxation. Tübingen 1990, this volume.

GROS, Daniel, Capital Controls in the EMS: A Model of Incomplete Market Separation. Centre for European Policy Studies, Brussels 1989, mimeo.

LEVICH, Richard M., Ingo WALTER, "Tax-Driven Regulatory Drag: European Financial Centres in the 1990s." In: Horst SIEBERT (Ed.), Reforming Capital Income Taxation. Tübingen 1990, this volume.

PAPKE, Leslie E., International Differences in Capital Taxation and Corporate Borrowing Behaviour: Evidence from the US Withholding Tax. Boston University, School of Management, Working Paper 89-02, Boston, Mass., 1989.

RAZIN, Assaf, Efraim SADKA, International Tax Competition and Gains from Tax Harmonization. IMF Working Paper No. 37-89, Washington 1989.

—, —,"Capital Market Integration: Issues of International Taxation." In: Horst SIEBERT (Ed.), Reforming Capital Income Taxation. Tübingen 1990, this volume.

SCHLESINGER, Helmut, "Taxation and Capital Outflow — The Case of the Federal Republic of Germany." In: Horst SIEBERT (Ed.), Reforming Capital Income Taxation. Tübingen 1990, this volume.

SLEMROD, Joel, "Tax Havens, Tax Bargains and Tax Addresses: The Effect of Taxation on the Spatial Allocation of Capital." In: Horst SIEBERT (Ed.), Reforming Capital Income Taxation. Tübingen 1990, this volume.

Comment on Daniel Gros, "Tax Evasion and Offshore Centres"

Robert P. Hagemann

I enjoyed reading and thinking about this paper. It has the merits of being focused, succinct, generally straightforward and, for the most part, unencumbered by complex mathematics, although the author always provides an intuitive explanation of each demonstrated point. For someone unfamiliar with the relationship between the taxation of interest income on the one hand and the propensity to use offshore centers or tax havens on the other, the paper would be a very useful starting point.

The paper highlights a number of the implications of differential taxation of bond interest income, switching or transaction costs, and offshore activity, as well as how the home country and the tax haven can potentially benefit from some tax harmonization. While there are many model-derived implications in the paper, I retain as most essential the following:

- —To the extent that there exists a domestic/offshore interest rate differential, its size will vary with the difference in the rate of taxation of onshore and offshore bond interest income, regulatory cost differentials, and the transaction costs of households relative to those of firms. The total amount of offshore activity depends upon the total (as opposed to the relative) switching costs of households and firms. Capital market liberalization will increase offshore activity for any given tax rate differential since liberalization lowers transactions costs.
- —The government faces a Laffer-type revenue curve with respect to interest income, and the critical level at which a higher rate yields less revenue is lower in the presence of capital market liberalization. Since, for a critical level of the domestic tax rate and switching costs, there is likely to be some flow of borrowing and saving offshore, the tax haven authorities can benefit by imposing a tax on interest income earned on offshore-source financial capital, but of course at a low enough rate that all attracted intermediation is not deterred. Some fairly involved math leads to the formula that says the revenue-maximizing tax for the offshore center is close to half the rate imposed in the home country. But cooperation between the two countries, in particular if tax rates in both countries are equalized, could raise welfare.

Remark: The views expressed are the author's and do not necessarily reflect those of the OECD or its member governments.

On the surface, these and other conclusions in the paper seem reasonable and somewhat difficult to quarrel with. For instance, as stated in the paper, "even those households and firms with the highest switching costs will go to the offshore centre as taxes are raised towards 100 per cent"(p. 121). In fact, it seems to me that as marginal tax rates rise, even under the constraint imposed by the author of having to physically go to the offshore center to transact,[1] opportunities arise for offshore transaction "services" to be set up whereby households closest to the tax haven might effect the transactions on behalf of others.[2]

If we go beyond the elegant derivations of this nifty model, and ask ourselves about the realism of the assumptions, I think we may be a little less sanguine about the prospects for dealing with tax havens. For instance, I think it is important not to loose sight of the fact that a tax haven is presumably the parking lot for savings from a large number of countries. To the extent that each of these is likely to tax domestic interest income at a different *effective* marginal tax rate, bilateral harmonizations would be required, followed by selective application by the offshore center of different withholding rates applicable to foreign savers. I would imagine that this would present insurmountable difficulties.

There are a few other implicit or explicit operational assumptions that are possibly puzzling — for instance, the exogeneity of the domestic interest rate and the equality of the domestic shares of investment and saving in offshore activity. Still, I am reasonably confident that the broad conclusions of the paper are robust to relaxation of most of these assumptions.

But I am also of the conviction that the paper is incomplete. First, it seems to me that a significant limitation of the exercise is the failure to formally model the demand for, and supply of, loanable funds. This would have made explicit the significance of the elasticities of supply and demand and, hence, would have allowed for a richer assessment of the welfare costs of offshore activity. This is most evident where the author characterizes the welfare losses in terms of the direct evasion costs. Just as in the case of tax reform, where expenditure on accountants' services to reduce tax liabilities is waste and is thus part of the cost of an inefficient and inequitable tax system, switching costs are unnecessary, too. Still, the other perhaps most important cost is the deadweight loss — the true Harberger triangle — associated with the distortionary tax. And here the presence of the offshore center may *lower* social costs by forcing the onshore authorities to maintain the lowest possible marginal tax rate on capital income. This reduction in social costs will, as we know, be greater, the larger the compensated elasticity of supply of saving is

1 The constraint imposed by the author that households must personally go to the offshore center would appear to be too stringent, given the growth and sophistication of electronic banking.

2 This is a bit like the possibilities for VAT avoidance that Sinn [1989] sees as potentially arising if there remain large international differences in VAT rates. Parisians may be able to purchase a German refrigerator by simply picking up the telephone.

with respect to the after-tax rate of return. In this respect, the welfare costs derived by the author may *overstate* the true loss to society. At the same time, I am not advocating that offshore centers provide the best method for reducing any existing disincentive to save. It naturally would be preferable to attack the saving problem directly.

It seems to me that tax havens play a dual role, one which is good and one which is bad. Clearly, to the extent that economic agents move savings offshore, "cheating" occurs, undermining taxpayer morale and equity, and this lowers tax revenue and, ceteris paribus, forces other tax rates higher or reduces levels of public services. This is clearly bad, since it may have adverse welfare effects through higher distortions.

But at the same time, and this is the perspective also adopted by Grubel [1985], the mere existence of the offshore center maintains pressure on the onshore country with respect to both regulatory policies toward financial intermediation and tax policies. To the extent that the higher offshore rate of return may increase aggregate savings, savings that will flow back to the country at a later time, the country may benefit in the longer run.

This leads me to wonder why it would not be preferable to impose substantial but credible penalties on cheaters who are caught evading, while at the same time allowing countries to freely establish the level and structure of taxes that they consider optimal given their efficiency and distributional objectives. While there may be a case for some coordination of administration and enforcement of taxation in a highly integrated world, I wonder if countries with broadly different levels of public goods should really have to harmonize, particularly on capital income, since it may even be the case that capital taxes are not benefit taxes, or at least less so than other taxes. Optimal tax theory tells us that we should apply the lowest tax rate to the factor most elastic in supply, other considerations aside. Raising capital income tax rates in some countries to limit the outflow from others strikes me as resembling somewhat the policy of killing the patient to cure the disease. Why not simply increase enforcement, which, as we all know, would be less necessary in a world of low marginal tax rates.[3]

A final thought that came to me while reading the paper is the "sequence" of harmonization that should be followed: that is, should international harmonization come before any domestic harmonization? As is widely known, not all returns to savings are taxed at effectively similar rates in most countries. Interest income, with which the paper is concerned, is quite exposed to taxation when the interest is earned legally and openly. On the other hand, owner-occupied housing receives quite favorable treatment in many countries, and so the existence of tax havens may be

---

3 Lindsay [1985] presents evidence that about half of the revenue that would have been lost as a consequence of the income tax rate reductions was recouped as a result of favorable taxpayer response.

seen by some taxpayers as providing more horizontal equity. In terms of the model, I suppose I am raising a question about the true or relevant meaning of i beyond the simple bond interest rate.

This underscores my sense that the problem of the use of tax havens would simply not arise if taxation were based on consumption — coupled with progressivity measures such as inheritance taxation — rather than on income.

Bibliography

GRUBEL, Herbert G., "Towards a Theory of Free Economic Zones." Weltwirtschaftliches Archiv, Vol. 118, 1982, pp. 39-61.

LINDSAY, Laurence B., "Taxpayer Behaviour and the Distribution of the 1982 Tax Cut." NBER Working Paper 1760, Cambridge, Mass., 1985.

SINN, Hans-Werner, Tax Harmonization and Tax Competition in Europe. Paper presented at CEPR Workshop on Capital Income Taxation and European Integration, London 1989.

Jacob A. Frenkel
Assaf Razin
Steven Symansky

Simulations of Global Effects of VAT Harmonization

1. Introduction

This paper presents a simulation analysis of the dynamic effects of international VAT harmonization. Such policies form an important ingredient of the wide-ranging measures associated with the move towards the single market of Europe of 1992. In the fiscal area the European Commission has drawn up various proposals on the approximation of the rates and the harmonization of the structures of VAT.

The process of harmonization of the VAT systems started with the First Council Directive of April 1967 and has proceeded thereafter through consecutive directives. The process involved the adoption of VAT in various member countries and the continuous convergence of rates and structures among members of the community. Much of the discussions surrounding the practical implementation of the convergence of the VAT rates concerned the width of the bands within which various VAT rates should be placed, the products to which a reduced rate would be applicable and the problem of zero-rated products.[1] For 1992 the Commission envisaged a standard VAT rate ranging between 14 and 20 percent, and a reduced rate (applied to selected categories, such as foodstuffs) ranging between 4 and 9 percent. The Commission proposes to abolish the higher rate that presently exists in some member countries on certain categories of goods. In subsequent discussions an alternative proposal was considered, according to which the standard rate band would be replaced by a minimum rate applicable from January 1, 1993. Each member state would choose a rate at least equal to the minimum rate, with due regard to the budgetary implications and to the "competitive pressures" arising from the rates chosen by other neighboring states and their main trading partners. Table

Remark: We wish to thank Sijbren Cnossen for useful discussions and Ravina Malkani for efficient research assistance. This paper was written while Assaf Razin was a visiting scholar in the Research Department of the IMF.

1 Zero-rated products involve the reimbursement of taxes levied on inputs, with the result that the final good is completely untaxed.

1 provides summary information on VAT rates in the European Community. It illustrates the disparities among the various member-country VAT rates.[2]

Table 1 — VAT Rates in the European Economy, 1990

Country (year of VAT introduction)	Statutory rate			Revenue contribution as percentage of total tax revenue[a]	Revenue contribution as percentage of GDP[a]
	reduced rate	standard rate	higher rate		
	percent				
Belgium (1971)	1, 6 and 7	19	25 and 33	16.3	7.2
Denmark (1967)	0	22	–	26.9	9.8
France (1968)	5.5 and 7	18.6	25	20.9	8.7
Germany (1968)	7	14	–	13.1	3.8
Greece (1987)	3 and 6	16	36	20.9	7.8
Ireland (1972)	0, 2.2, and 10	23	–	18.9	8.0
Italy (1973)	2 and 9	18	38	31.1	4.7
Luxembourg (1970)	3 and 6	12	–	13.3	6.0
Netherlands (1969)	6	18.5	–	15.2	7.9
Portugal (1986)	8	17	30	18.8	7.7
Spain (1986)	6	12	33	16.0	5.3
United Kingdom (1973)	0	15	–	16.3	6.0
Commission proposal					
A:	4 to 9	14 to 20	abolished		
B:	4 to 9	minimum rate	abolished		

[a]1986.

Source: Cnossen, Shoup [1987, Table 2.1]; Emerson et al. [1988, Table 3.5.1]; EC [1987]; OECD [1990].

One of the central issues that needs to be addressed is the budgetary consequences of the harmonization in the VAT systems. A few member states (notably Denmark and Ireland) would suffer considerable tax revenue losses, while others (notably Spain, Luxembourg and Portugal) would see their tax revenue go up considerably. In the subsequent section, we present dynamic simulations of the consequences of international harmonization of VAT.

---

2 For a recent, broad survey of the international practice and problems in the area of VAT, see Tait [1988].

2. Simulations of VAT Harmonization with Current-Account Imbalances

In this section we use dynamic simulations to analyze the effects of revenue-neutral VAT harmonization. We use a two-country model of the world economy and presume that prior to the VAT harmonization, the two countries use very different tax systems. The home country tax revenue stems from high income tax, while the foreign country revenue stems from high VAT. The harmonization of VAT entails a rise in the home country VAT rate and an equivalent reduction in the foreign VAT rate. Our analysis allows for current-account imbalances.

To avoid the budgetary imbalances consequent on the changes in the VAT rates, we ensure revenue neutrality by assuming that the induced budgetary imbalances are corrected through changes in income-tax rates. Accordingly, in the home country, the rise in the VAT is accompanied by a reduction in income-tax rates, whereas in the foreign country the fall in the VAT rate is accompanied by a corresponding rise in income-tax rates. The narrowing of the international disparities between VATs captures the Commission's proposal of reducing the disparities in VAT rates among member countries and categories of goods. The maintenance of budgetary balance through appropriate changes in income-tax rates reflects the supposition that due to considerations involving monetary policy and debt management, member countries do not wish to drastically change their budgetary stance.

In performing the simulations, we first computed a baseline equilibrium. This equilibrium was then perturbed by the assumed VAT harmonization. The various figures presented below show the effects of the tax restructuring, measured as percentage deviations from the baseline levels. The Appendix outlines the formal simulation model.

As indicated by previous theoretical analyses, one of the key factors governing the effects of revenue-neutral tax conversions is the time pattern of the current-account position.[3] Since the current-account positions can be expressed in terms of the saving-investment gap, they reflect intercountry differences in either saving propensities, induced, for example, by differences between the subjective discount factors, δ and δ^*, or in investment patterns, induced, for example, by differences between the productivities of capital, r_k and r_k^* (variables with asterisks refer to the foreign country, those without refer to the home country). To highlight the key role played by current-account positions, we plot in Figure 1 the simulation results for cases distinguished according to the time pattern of current-account imbalances. In

3 For examples of such an analysis, see Frenkel and Razin [1987; 1989] and Frenkel et al. [1990].

Figure 1 — VAT Harmonization: 6 Percent Permanent Increase in Home Country VAT and 6 Percent Permanent Reduction in Foreign Country VAT (percentage deviations from baseline solution)

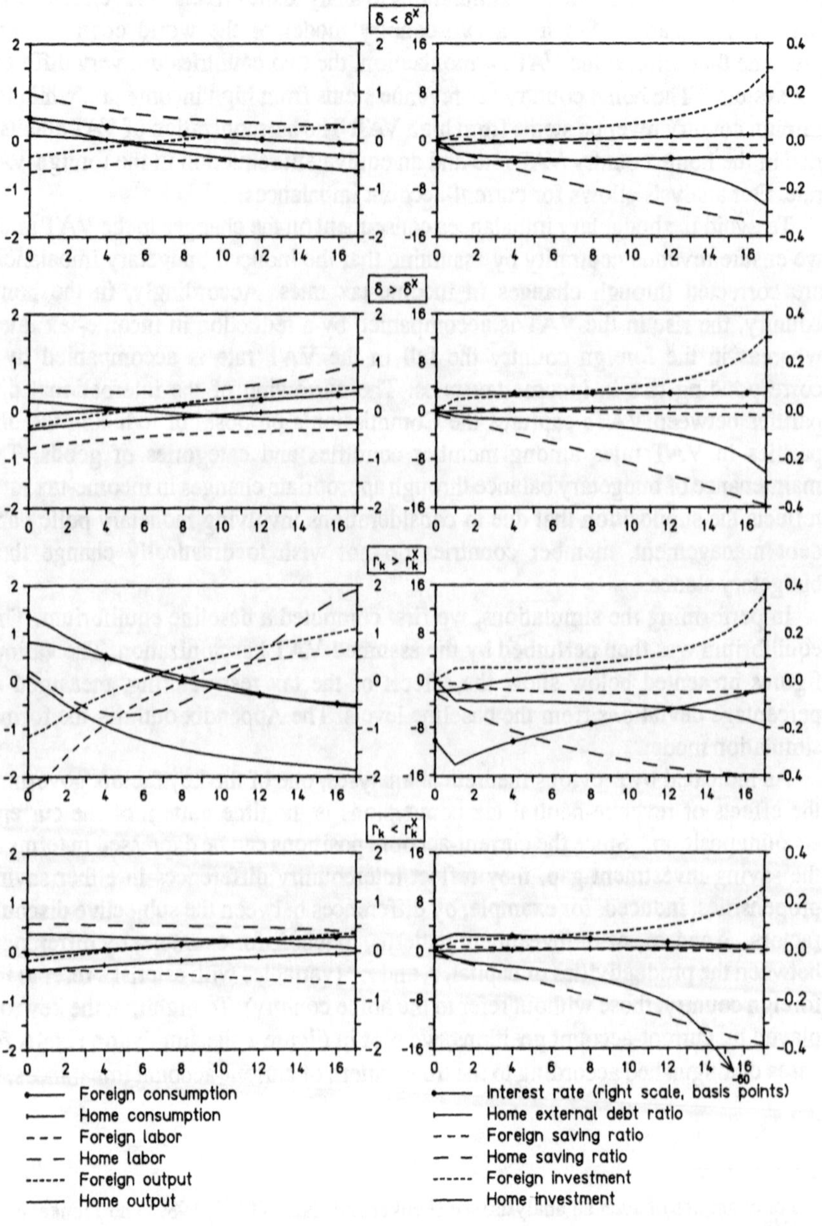

this figure we assume that the income tax used in both countries is of the cash-flow variety.[4]

We assume that the home country raises its VAT permanently by 6 percent and restores its tax revenue by lowering its cash-flow income tax rates; the foreign country (whose initial VAT rate is assumed to be high) lowers its VAT permanently by 6 percent and restores its tax revenue by raising its cash-flow income tax rates. The figure shows the paths of domestic and foreign output, labor supply, savings, investment and consumption as well as the paths of the world rate of interest and the home country's external debt consequent on the VAT harmonization. All paths are expressed as percentage deviations from the baseline (except for the rate of interest, whose deviation is expressed in basis points). The simulations reveal that the international VAT harmonization triggers a dynamic response in all the key macroeconomic variables. The specific nature of the dynamic response reflects international differences in the parameters governing saving and investment patterns.

The key features of the simulation analysis of tax harmonization underlying Figure 1 are summarized in Table 2, which also reports the welfare implications of the VAT harmonization. In order to capture the essence of the dynamic evolution of the various variables, we report the direction of changes for both the short run (SR) and the medium run (MR). The results in Table 2 demonstrate the key role played by the current-account position. Specifically, if in the early stage the home country runs a current-account deficit due to low saving or high investment (e.g., if $\delta < \delta^*$ or $r_k > r_k^*$), then the paths of domestic and foreign income-tax rates rise over time so as to maintain tax revenue, and as a result the world rate of interest falls.[5] In that case, the rates of growth of domestic and foreign consumption (g_c and g_c^*, respectively) fall, both in the short and in the medium runs.

If on the other hand the configuration of saving and investment propensities is such that the home country runs a current-account surplus in the early stage, then the dynamic effects of the VAT harmonization on these variables are reversed. Specifically, if, in the home country, saving is high or investment is low (e.g., if $\delta > \delta^*$ or $r_k < r_k^*$), then the paths of domestic and foreign income-tax rates fall, while the world rate of interest rises. In this case, the rates of growth of domestic

4 This specification of income tax is equivalent to a VAT system imposed according to the *source* (rather than *destination*) of income. We are indebted to Sijbren Cnossen for this observation. In contrast, the VAT system used in the text is based on the destination principle.

5 Intuitively, the rise in the home country VAT accompanied by an equiproportionate fall in the income tax broadens the tax base and raises tax revenue in the current period if the home country runs a current-account deficit. To restore tax revenue, the income tax rate must be lowered. The opposite changes occur in the future period in which the current-account position is in surplus, reflecting the intertemporal budget constraint. Similar considerations imply that the path of income tax abroad also steepens. As a result the tax incentives to investment decline, yielding a fall in the world rate of interest [see Frenkel, Razin, 1987, Ch. 8].

Table 2 — Effects of VAT Harmonization under Alternative Current-Account Positions (deviation from baseline)[a]

Variable	Home country current-account deficit				Home country current-account surplus			
	$\delta < \delta^*$, $r_k = r_k^*$		$\delta = \delta$, $r_k > r_k^*$		$\delta > \delta^*$, $r_k = r_k^*$		$\delta = \delta$, $r_k < r_k^*$	
	SR	MR	SR	MR	SR	MR	SR	MR
Path of τ_y	rising		rising		falling		falling	
Path of τ_y^*	rising		rising		falling		falling	
r	−	−	−	−	+	+	+	+
g_c	−	−	−	−	+	+	+	+
g_c^*	−	−	−	−	+	+	+	+
I	−	−	−	−	−	−	−	−
I^*	+	+	+	+	+	+	+	+
L	+	+	−	+	+	+	+	+
L^*	−	−	−	−	−	−	−	−
Y	+	−	−	−	+	−	+	+
Y^*	−	+	−	+	−	+	−	+
C	+	−	+	−	−	+	−	−
C^*	+	−	+	−	−	+	+	+
S	+	−	+	−	+	−	+	−
S^*	−	+	−	+	−	+	−	+
B	−	−	−	−	−	−	−	−
U	−	+	+	+	−	+	−	+
U^*	+	−	+	−	+	−	+	−

[a]The VAT harmonization obtains through a permanent percentage change in the consumption tax, τ_c (i.e., reduction in the home country together with a rise in the foreign country). Budget balance obtains through appropriate adjustments in the periodic income-tax rates, τ_y and τ_y^*. SR and MR denote, respectively, the short run and the medium run. The tax system is a cash-flow system. In general, the short run pertains to the first few periods while the medium run pertains to the remaining periods in the simulation. For the utility index, SR pertains to the discounted sum of utilities over the entire periods, except for the final one, while MR pertains to the final period utility (reflecting the entire future beyond the simulation period). The other symbols are defined as follows: δ = subjective discount rate, r_k = marginal product of capital, r = rate of interest, g_c = growth rate of consumption, I = net investment, L = labor supply, Y = income, C = consumption, S = savings, B = international borrowing, U = utility (asterisks denote the foreign country variable).

and foreign consumption rise. Thus, under the present cash-flow income-tax system, the direction of changes in the world rate of interest and in the growth rates of consumption consequent on international VAT harmonization depend exclusively on the paths of the saving-investment gap.

The lower panel of Table 2 summarizes the corresponding short- and medium-run changes in other key economic variables. As can be seen in the cases considered, the international VAT harmonization crowds out domestic investment and crowds in foreign investment independently of the current-account positions. These investment responses reflect the changes induced in the domestic and foreign tax incentives and in the world rate of interest. These changes yield two conflicting effects: the effect of the change in the world rate of interest and the opposite effect of the change in the tax wedges induced by the alteration of the time paths of income-tax rates.

The changes in the tax structure also alter the intraperiod tax incentives governing labor supply and consumption demand. These tax incentives are subject to conflicting forces, since the changes in the consumption-tax rates and the associated changes in the income-tax rates induce opposite effects on both labor supply and consumption demand. In addition to these conventional substitution mechanisms, the simulation results also reflect wealth effects on labor-supply and consumption demand induced by changes in the intertemporal terms of trade (the world rate of interest) and by changes in the excess burden associated with the distorted tax system. Finally, the time paths of labor supply and consumption demand are altered by the intertemporal substitution induced by changes in incentives governing labor supply and consumption demand. The changes in incentives arise from the change in the world rate of interest and, in the case of labor supplies, from the changes in the time paths of income taxes.

The welfare effects of term-of-trade changes depend on the magnitude of the change in the terms of trade and on the gap between purchases and sales of the good whose relative price has changed. In our intertemporal context, the terms of trade correspond to the world rate of interest, and the gap between purchases and sales corresponds to the current-account position. As illustrated by Table 2, in all cases the change in the terms of trade operates in favor of the country that raises its VAT. When the country runs a current-account deficit (i.e., when it borrows in the world economy), its intertemporal terms of trade improve since the rate of interest falls. Likewise, if the country's current-account position is running a surplus, its intertemporal terms of trade also improve since the rate of interest rises. As illustrated by the table, this improvement in the home-country welfare, induced by the changes in the world rate of interest, can be mitigated (or even offset) by the excess-burden effects of the VAT harmonization. Similar considerations apply to the welfare consequences of the reduction in VAT in the foreign economy.

A comparison between the effects of the international VAT harmonization on the domestic and the foreign economies reveals that in the two countries the levels of foreign employment, investment, output and some other key macroeconomic indicators change in opposite directions. In fact, in most cases the utility index indicates that domestic and foreign welfare move in opposite directions. This phenomenon suggests the possibility that international VAT harmonization may induce international conflicts of interest. A resolution of such conflicts may necessitate international fiscal transfers from countries that benefit from the VAT harmonization to countries that do not. The potential difficulties arising from international conflicts of interest may be augmented by internal conflicts of interest associated with redistributions of income between labor and capital in the short and medium runs.[6]

3. Simulations of VAT Harmonization with Current-Account Balances

The foregoing analysis was confined to the case in which the income taxes used to restore budgetary balance following the international VAT harmonization were of the cash-flow variety. Under such circumstances the current-account positions played the key role in determining the direction of changes in the world rate of interest and the growth rates of domestic and foreign consumption. As indicated by the simulations in Figure 1 and by the summary results in the lower panel of Table 2, the dynamic effects of the international VAT harmonization on the paths of the other key macroeconomic variables do not depend only on the current-account positions. In fact, for the cases shown in these simulations, domestic investment, foreign employment, foreign savings (in the short run), and the level of the domestic country's external debt are reduced independently of the current-account positions, while foreign investment and foreign savings (in the medium run) always rise.

In order to gain further insights into the effects of VAT harmonization under alternative income-tax systems in cases where the current-account position does not play a role, we focus in this section on an analysis of VAT harmonization in circumstances where the saving and investment propensities do not differ internationally. Accordingly, we assume in the following that $\delta = \delta^*$ and $r_k = r_k^*$; and we consider, in addition to the cash-flow income-tax system, other tax systems: labor-income tax, capital-income tax combined with saving incentives, and capital-income tax combined with investment incentives. The results of these simulations are shown in Figure 2 and are summarized in Table 3.

The multiplicity of mechanisms and channels operating on the various tax incentives results in a variety of configurations of the responses of the other key economic variables, as illustrated for the cases given in Table 3. Of special interest are the welfare effects indicated by the utility index in the simulations. As always, the welfare consequences of tax policies can be decomposed into two components. First, those arising from changes in excess burden, and second, those arising from terms of trade effects. The changes in the degree of excess burden induced by VAT harmonization depend on the elasticity of the tax base as well as on the magnitude of the existing distortion. In the cases illustrated by the simulations, we have chosen

---

6 As an example for induced changes in the functional distribution of income, consider the left-hand column of Table 2. There, the VAT harmonization raises the share of labor and lowers the share of capital income in the domestic economy for both the short and medium runs while inducing opposite redistributions in the foreign economy.

Figure 2 — VAT Harmonization: 6 Percent Permanent Increase in Home Country VAT and 6 Percent Permanent Reduction in Foreign Country VAT under Alternative Tax Systems (percentage deviations from baseline solution)

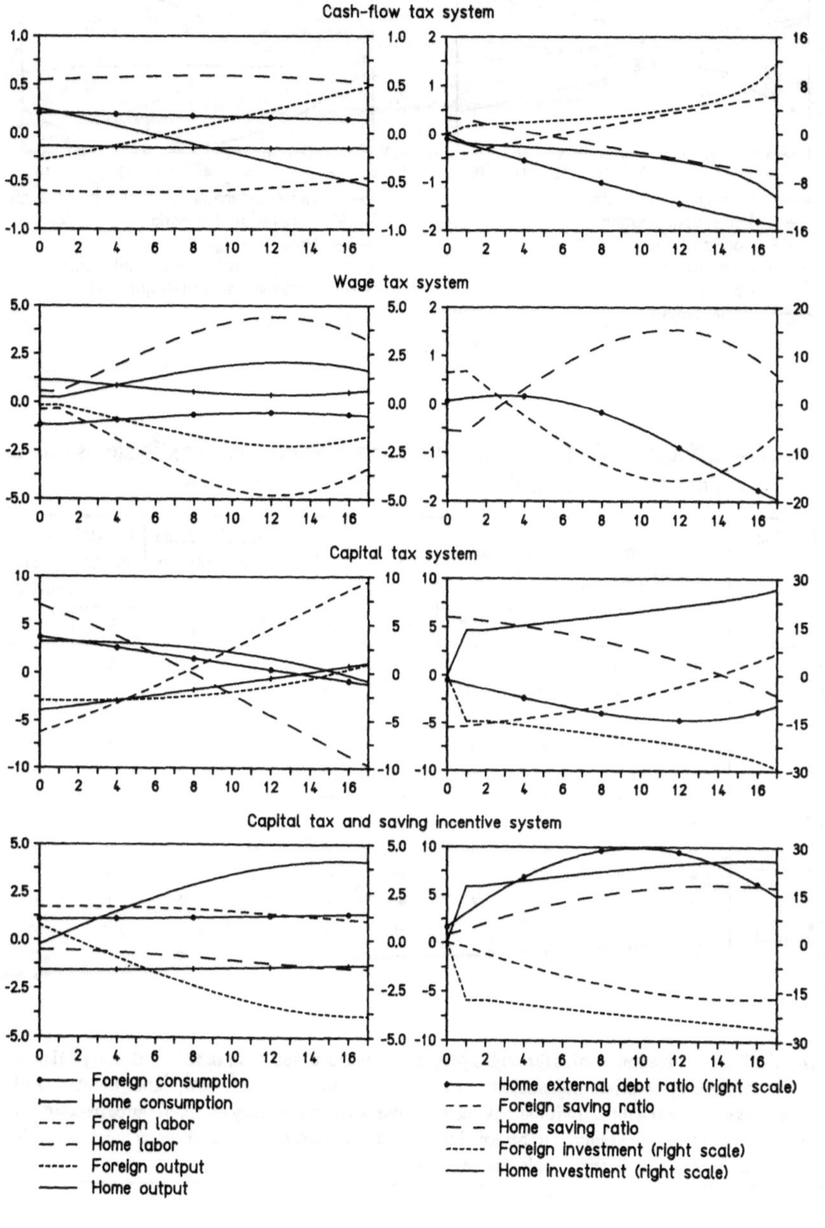

Figure 2 continued

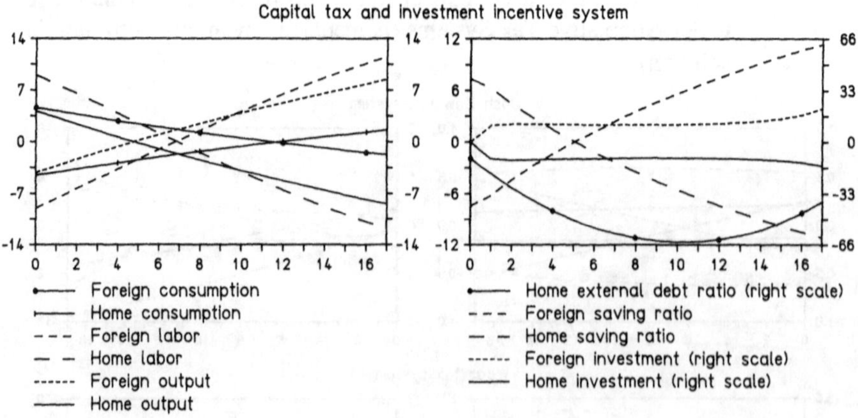

Table 3 — Effects of VAT Harmonization under Alternative Tax Systems (deviations from baseline)[a]

Variable	Cash-flow income tax		Labor-income tax		Capital-income tax		Capital-income tax and saving incentives		Capital-income tax and investment incentives	
	SR	MR	SR	MR	SR	MR	SR	MR	SR	MR
r	0	0	0	0	0	0	0	0	0	0
I	–	–	0	0	+	+	+	+	–	–
*I**	+	+	0	0	–	–	–	–	+	+
L	+	+	+	+	+	–	–	–	+	–
*L**	–	–	–	–	–	+	+	+	–	+
Y	+	–	+	+	+	–	–	+	+	–
*Y**	–	+	–	–	–	+	+	–	–	+
C	–	–	+	+	–	+	–	–	–	+
*C**	+	+	–	–	+	–	+	+	+	–
S	+	–	–	+	+	–	+	+	+	–
*S**	–	+	+	–	–	+	–	–	–	+
B	–	–	+	–	–	–	+	+	–	–
U	–	+	–	+	–	+	–	+	–	+
*U**	+	–	+	–	+	–	+	–	+	–

[a]The VAT harmonization obtains through a permanent rise in τ_c and a fall in τ_c^*. Budgetary balance obtains through appropriate adjustments in the periodic rates of cash-flow, labor-income, and capital-income taxes (with and without saving incentives). The technology and preference parameters of the two countries are assumed to be equal (so that the current-account position is balanced). SR and MR, as well as the other symbols, are defined as in Table 2.

parameters that result in relatively low investment and labor-supply elasticities, and a relatively high consumption elasticity.[7] This choice suggests that in this cash-flow income-tax system, the excess burden associated with a consumption tax is relatively high in comparison with the corresponding excess burden associated with an income tax.

The assumption that the saving and investment propensities do not differ internationally implies that the initial current-account positions are balanced. As a result, the international VAT harmonization does not alter the world rate of interest. The dynamics of adjustment in this case arise only from the effects of the tax wedges on the various incentives. These are the circumstances underlying Figure 2 and Table 3.

We first note that with a labor-income tax system, the VAT harmonization does not induce any change in the time path of domestic and foreign investment. Second, whenever the income-tax system contains an investment-incentive component, it dominates in its effect on the paths of investment. Indeed, under the cash-flow income-tax system (which obviously contains an investment-incentives component), and under a system of capital-income tax combined with investment incentives, the path of domestic investment consequent on the reduced income tax is lowered for both the short and the medium runs. The opposite occurs in the foreign country. This pattern is reversed under the income-tax systems that do not contain incentives to investment.

Third, and analogously to the foregoing reasoning, whenever the income-tax system contains a saving-incentive component (which eliminates the double taxation of savings), its effect dominates the changes in consumption. Thus, under the cash-flow income-tax system, and under a system of capital-income tax combined with saving incentives, the path of domestic consumption consequent on the VAT harmonization is lowered for both the short and the medium runs. The opposite occurs in the foreign country. This pattern is reversed under the labor-tax system.

Fourth, whenever the income-tax system contains a tax on labor income, changes in that tax dominate the effect of the VAT harmonization on employment. Thus, under the cash-flow income-tax system, and under the system of labor-income tax, the path of domestic employment consequent on the reduced income tax is raised for both the short and the medium runs. The opposite occurs in the foreign country in which income taxes rise. Finally, by inspecting Figure 2, one could infer the effects of the VAT harmonization under alternative tax systems on the growth rates of domestic and foreign output and on the path of external debt.

---

7 The intertemporal labor-supply elasticity, indicated by σ, is 0.3; the coefficient of the cost of adjustment for investment, referred to as *KADJ* in the Appendix, is 40; and the intertemporal elasticity of substitution for consumption is unitary. To examine the sensitivity of the results with respect to the values of the elasticities, we also performed a simulation with a lower cost-of-adjustment coefficient and a higher labor-supply elasticity. Under these circumstances the welfare cost of VAT diminished relatively, while the welfare cost of income taxes increased relatively.

The previous discussion of the simulations underlying Figure 1 and Table 2 indicated the potential for international conflicts of interest with respect to the implementation of VAT harmonization under the cash-flow income-tax system. An examination of Figure 2 and Table 3 suggests that the potential for such conflicts of interest is not unique to the cash-flow system. In fact, as is evident under all the tax systems considered, the direction of changes in domestic and foreign employment, output, consumption, savings and investment, consequent on the international VAT harmonization, are opposite to each other in both the short and the medium runs. The same phenomenon emerges from an examination of the utility indices of economic welfare: in all the cases considered, the domestic and foreign SR utility indices (given by the discounted sums of utilities over the entire period, except for the final one) move in opposite directions, and in general the same holds for the MR utility indices (reflecting the entire future beyond the simulation period). Furthermore, the cases considered the VAT harmonization results in a redistribution of welfare between generations. This is evident by the opposite direction of changes in the SR and MR utility indices within each country. The various simulations show that the changes in the utility indices reflect, by and large, a *redistribution* of world welfare, since the *sum* of the domestic and foreign utility indices does not change appreciably. This result underscores the notion that the resolution of international conflicts of interest in implementing the VAT harmonization may necessitate a compensation mechanism by which gainers compensate losers.

4. Concluding Remarks

One of the major developments in the world economy during the 1990s is likely to be the move towards the single market of Europe of 1992. The removal of barriers to trade and factor movements, the unification of markets, the development of new monetary arrangements, and the increased harmonization of fiscal policies and tax structures are all key factors in a process that is likely to shape the global economic system for years to come.

One of the elements of the move towards tax harmonization in the European Community involves a convergence of the various VAT systems. In this paper we have analyzed the global effects of such an international VAT harmonization. To examine the quantitative implications of international VAT harmonization, we have performed dynamic simulations. The analysis as well as the simulations demonstrate that the effects of VAT harmonization on the key macroeconomic variables (such as output, employment, investment, consumption, interest rates, the current account, and the value of external debt) are very significant. Furthermore, these effects (quantitatively and qualitatively) are not spread evenly across income groups, generations and countries. As a result, such a VAT harmonization may give rise to internal conflicts of interest within each country (arising from changes in the distribution of income among members of each generation as well as among generations) and between countries. The international differences in the incidence of the VAT harmonization arise from differences in the current-account positions (reflecting underlying differences in saving and investment propensities) as well as from differences in the tax structures. The resolution of the various conflicts of interest regarding the adoption of VAT harmonization may give rise to the development of a fiscal mechanism by which gainers compensate losers within countries as well as between countries.

5. Appendix: The Simulation Model

The model described in this appendix is used in the simulations discussed in the main text. We present below the exact computer printout of the model, which is based on the theoretical model described in Frenkel et al. [1990].

Endogenous Variables

B —home international borrowing (*–B* for the foreign country)
BP(*) —home(foreign) private-sector international borrowing
C(*) —home(foreign) private consumption
E(*) —home(foreign) private total expenditures (inclusive of leisure consumption)
INVADJ(*) —home(foreign) net investment
INV(*) —home(foreign) gross investment
K(*) —home(foreign) capital stock
L(*) —home(foreign) labor supply
P(*) —home(foreign) price index of utility-based real spending
R —rate of interest plus 1
RR —present value plus 1
RR(*) —home (foreign) tax-adjusted present value plus 1
R20(*) —home(foreign) tax-adjusted present value factor in period *T*
SAV(*) —home(foreign) savings
SURP(*) —home(foreign) cumulative government surplus
TERK(*) —home(foreign) capital stock consumed in period *T*
τ_b (*) —home(foreign) tax rate on bonds
τ_i (*) —home(foreign) tax rate on investment
τ_s (*) —home(foreign) tax rate on savings
τ_w (*) —home(foreign) tax rate on wages
U(*) —home(foreign) period utility-based total expenditure
W(*) —home(foreign) wealth

$V(*)$ —home(foreign) lifetime utility from $t = 0$ to T
$Y(*)$ —home(foreign) income

Exogenous Variables and Parameters

$a\,(*)$ —home(foreign) fraction of consumption of end-period capital stock
$\beta\,(*)$ —home(foreign) distributive parameter of consumption
$\delta\,(*)$ —home(foreign) subjective discount rate
$G(*)$ —home(foreign) government spending
$INV0(*)$ —home(foreign) investment in period 0
$KADJ(*)$ —home(foreign) adjustment parameter of the capital stock
$r_k\,(*)$ —home(foreign) marginal product of capital
$\sigma\,(*)$ —home(foreign) consumption/leisure elasticity of substitution
$\theta\,(*)$ —home(foreign) rate of depreciation of capital stock
$t_{by}\,(*)$ —home(foreign) tax policy parameter (bond and wage taxes)
$t_{iy}\,(*)$ —home(foreign) tax policy parameter (investment and capital taxes)
$t_{ky}\,(*)$ —home(foreign) tax policy parameter (wage and capital taxes)
$t_{sy}\,(*)$ —home(foreign) tax policy parameter (savings and capital taxes)
$\tau_c\,(*)$ —home(foreign) consumption tax rate
$\tau_k\,(*)$ —home(foreign) capital tax rate
$WAGE(*)$ —home(foreign) wage rate

Equations

$$[1]\; Y = WAGE \cdot L + (r_k - \theta) \cdot K$$

$$[2]\; Y^* = WAGE^* \cdot L^* + (r_k^* - \theta^*) \cdot K^*$$

$$[3]\; C = (1-\beta)^{\sigma} \cdot (1+\tau_c)^{(-\sigma)} \cdot E \,/\, [(1-\beta)^{\sigma} \cdot (1+\tau_c)^{(1-\sigma)} + \beta^{\sigma} \cdot (WAGE \cdot (1-\tau_w))^{(1-\sigma)}]$$

$$[4]\; C^* = (1-\beta)^{\sigma^*} (1+\tau_c^*)^{(-\sigma^*)} \cdot E^* \,/\, [(1-\beta^*)^{\sigma^*} \cdot (1+\tau_c^*)^{(1-\sigma^*)} + \beta^{\sigma^*} \cdot (WAGE^* \cdot (1-\tau_w^*))^{(1-\sigma^*)}]$$

$$[5]\; 1-L = \beta^{\sigma} \cdot \{WAGE \cdot (1-\tau_w)^{(-\sigma)} \cdot E \,/\, [(1-\beta)^{\sigma} \cdot (1+\tau_c)^{(1-\sigma)} + \beta^{\sigma} \cdot WAGE \cdot (1-\tau_w)]^{(1-\sigma^*)}\}$$

$$[6]\ 1-L^{*} = \beta^{\sigma *} \cdot \{WAGE^{*} \cdot (1-\tau_w^{*})^{(-\sigma *)} \cdot E^{*} / [(1-\beta^{*})^{\sigma *} \cdot (1+\tau_e^{*})^{(1-\sigma *)} + \beta^{\sigma *} \cdot WAGE^{*} \cdot (1-\tau_w^{*})]^{(1-\sigma *)}\}$$

$$[7]\ P = [(1-\beta)^{\sigma} \cdot (1+\tau_e)^{(1-\sigma)} + \beta^{\sigma} \cdot (WAGE \cdot (1-\tau_w))^{(1-\sigma)}]^{(1/(1-\sigma))}$$

$$[8]\ P^{*} = [(1-\beta^{*})^{\sigma *} \cdot (1+\tau_e^{*})^{(1-\sigma *)} + \beta^{\sigma *} \cdot (WAGE^{*} \cdot (1-\tau_w^{*}))^{(1-\sigma *)}]^{(1/(1-\sigma *))}$$

$$[9]\ 0 = \text{IF YEAR ( ) EQ 20 THEN } INVADJ - INVO \text{ ELSE } (-(1-\tau_i(-1)))/RR(-1) \cdot (1+KADJ \cdot INVADJ / K(-1)) + (1-\theta)^{(20-TIME)} \cdot (r_k - \theta + \alpha) / R20 + \sum_{I=1}^{19} \{(1-\theta)^{(I-1)} \cdot (1-\tau_k(I-1)) / RR(I-1) \cdot IDUM(I-1) \cdot (r_k - \theta) + (1-\tau_i(I-1)) \cdot KADJ/2 \cdot (INVADJ(I)/K(I-1))^2\}$$

$$[10]\ 0 = \text{IF YEAR ( ) EQ 20 THEN } INVADJ - INVO^{*} \text{ ELSE } (-(1-\tau_i^{*}(-1)))/RR^{*}(-1) \cdot (1+KADJ^{*} \cdot INVADJ^{*} / K^{*}(-1)) + (1-\theta^{*})^{(20-TIME)} \cdot (r_k^{*} - \theta^{*} + \alpha^{*}) / R20^{*} + \sum_{I=1}^{19} \{(1-\theta^{*})^{(I-1)} \cdot (1-\tau_k^{*}(I-1)) / RR^{*}(I-1) \cdot IDUM(I-1) \cdot (r_k^{*} - \theta^{*}) + (1-\tau_i^{*}(I-1)) \cdot KADJ^{*}/2 \cdot (INVADJ^{*}(I)/K^{*}(I-1))^2\}$$

$$[11]\ K = (1-\theta) \cdot K(-1) + INVADJ$$

$$[12]\ K^* = (1-\theta^*)\cdot K^*(-1) + INVADJ^*$$

$$[13]\ INV = INVADJ\cdot(1 + KADJ/2\cdot INVADJ/K(-1))$$

$$[14]\ INV^* = INVADJ^*\cdot(1 + KADJ^*/2\cdot INVADJ^*/K^*(-1))$$

$$[15]\ TERK = \text{IF YEAR ( ) LT 40 THEN 0 ELSE } a\cdot K$$

$$[16]\ TERK^* = \text{IF YEAR ( ) LT 40 THEN 0 ELSE } a^*\cdot K^*$$

$$[17]\ RR = \text{EXP}(\sum_{J=-19}^{0}\{\text{LOG}(1-\tau_b(J) + (1+\tau_e(J))\cdot(1-\tau_k(J))\cdot(R(J)-1))\})$$

$$[18]\ RR^* = \text{EXP}(\sum_{J=-19}^{0}\{\text{LOG}(1-\tau_b^*(J) + (1+\tau_e^*(J))\cdot(1-\tau_k^*(J))\cdot(R(J)-1))\})$$

$$[19]\ R20 = \text{IF YEAR ( ) EQ 20 THEN } RR(20)/(1-\tau_k(20)) \text{ ELSE } R20(-1)$$

$$[20]\ R20^* = \text{IF YEAR ( ) EQ 20 THEN } RR(20)/(1-\tau_k^*(20)) \text{ ELSE } R20^*(-1)$$

$$[21]\ U = (1-\delta)\cdot W/P/(1-\delta^{21})\cdot\delta^{TIME}\cdot RR$$

$$[22]\ U^* = (1-\delta^*)\cdot W^*/P^*/(1-\delta^{*21})\cdot\delta^{*TIME}\cdot RR^*$$

$$[23]\ E = P\cdot U$$

$$[24]\ E^* = P^*\cdot U^*$$

$$[25]\ W = \text{IF YEAR ( ) EQ 20 THEN } \sum_{J=0}^{19} \{((1-\tau_w(J)) \cdot WAGE(J) + (1-\tau_k(J)) \cdot (r_k-\theta) \cdot K(J) - (1-\tau_i(J)) \cdot INV(J+1)) / RR(J)\} + ((1-\tau_k(20)) \cdot (TERK(20) + (r_k-\theta) \cdot K(20)) + (1-\tau_w(20)) \cdot WAGE(20)) / RR(20) - (1-\tau_b + (1-\tau_k) \cdot (1+\tau_s) \cdot (R(-1)-1)) \cdot BP(-1) \text{ ELSE } W(-1)$$

$$[26]\ W^* = \text{IF YEAR ( ) EQ 20 THEN } W^* - R + 1 \text{ ELSE } W^*(-1)$$

$$[27]\ SURP = SURP(-1) \cdot R(-1) + (\tau_b \cdot (BP - BP(-1)) + \tau_c \cdot C + \tau_w \cdot L \cdot WAGE + \tau_k \cdot ((r_k-\theta) \cdot K - (R(-1)-1) \cdot BP(-1) + TERK) + \tau_s \cdot (1-\tau_k) \cdot (R(-1)-1) \cdot BP(-1) - \tau_i \cdot INV(1) - G)$$

$$[28]\ SURP^* = SURP^*(-1) \cdot R(-1) + (\tau_b^* \cdot (BP^* - BP^*(-1)) + \tau_c^* \cdot C^* + \tau_w^* \cdot L^* \cdot WAGE^* + \tau_k^* \cdot ((r_k^*-\theta^*) \cdot K^* - (R(-1)-1) \cdot BP^*(-1) + TERK^*) + \tau_s^* \cdot (1-\tau_k^*) \cdot (R(-1)-1) \cdot BP^*(-1) - \tau_i^* \cdot INV^*(1) - G^*)$$

$$[29]\ \tau_b = t_{by} \cdot \tau_w$$

$$[30]\ \tau_b^* = t_{by}^* \cdot \tau_w^*$$

$$[31]\ \tau_I = t_{iy} \cdot \tau_k$$

$$[32]\ \tau_I^* = t_{iy}^* \cdot \tau_k^*$$

$$[33]\ \tau_W = t_{ky} \cdot \tau_k$$

$$[34]\ \tau_w^* = t_{ky}^* \cdot \tau_k^*$$

$$[35]\ \tau_S = t_{sy} \cdot \tau_k / (1-\tau_k)$$

$$[36]\ \tau_s = t_{sy}^* \cdot \tau_k^*/(1-\tau_k^*)$$

$$[37]\ BP = ((1-\tau_c)\cdot C - (1-\tau_w)\cdot L + WAGE - (1-\tau_k)\cdot((r_k-\theta)\cdot K + TERK) + (1-\tau_i)\cdot INV(1) + (1-\tau_k)\cdot(1+\tau_e)\cdot(R(-1)-1)\cdot BP(-1))/(1-\tau_b) + BP(-1)$$

$$[38]\ BP^* = ((1-\tau_c^*)\cdot C^* - (1-\tau_w^*)\cdot L^* + WAGE^* - (1-\tau_k^*)\cdot((r_k^* - \theta^*)\cdot K^* + TERK^*) + (1-\tau_i^*)\cdot INV^*(1) + (1-\tau_k^*)\cdot(1+\tau_e^*)\cdot (R(-1)-1)\cdot BP^*(-1))/(1-\tau_b^*) + BP^*(-1)$$

$$[39]\ V = \sum_{I=0}^{19}\{\delta^I \cdot \mathrm{LOG}(U(I))\}$$

$$[40]\ V^* = \sum_{I=0}^{19}\{\delta^{*I} \cdot \mathrm{LOG}(U^*(I))\}$$

$$[41]\ G + G^* + C + C^* + INV(1) + INV^*(1) = Y + Y^* + TERK + TERK^*$$

$$[42]\ RR = \mathrm{EXP}(\sum_{J=-19}^{0}\{\mathrm{LOG}(R(J))\})$$

$$[43]\ B = C - Y + R(-1)\cdot B(-1) + INV(1) + G - TERK$$

Equations [1] and [2] define home and foreign country income as labor income plus the return on capital. Equations [3]–[8] are the behavioral equations derived by maximizing utility subject to the lifetime present-value budget constraint. Equation [3] is the home consumption equation, equation [5] is the leisure equation, and [7] is the price equation. They correspond to equation [7], [8], and [6] in Frenkel et al. [1990]. The foreign country equations for these three variables are [4], [6], and [8].

The home and foreign investment equations, [9] and [10], are derived by maximizing wealth, and include the rate of depreciation (θ) which is omitted from the theoretical description in Frenkel et al. [1990]. Equations [11] and [12] define the home and foreign capital stocks, equations [13] and [14] adjust investment demands for adjustment costs, and equations [15] and [16] account for the proportion of the terminal year's capital stock that is consumed.

Equations [17]–[20] are definitions of tax-adjusted discount factors that are used in other equations. Real utility based expenditures are given in equations [21] and [22] while the values in terms of the consumption good of these expenditures are defined in [23] and [24]. Home country wealth is defined by equation [25]. A similar equation could be written for foreign wealth, but by Walras' law, we have dropped this equation from the model and use the relationship to solve for the interest rate. Note that these equations solve for W_0 and R_0 in period $t = 0$ (year 20 in the computer model). However, for $t = 1$ to T, these equations set wealth to their previous values (i.e., W_0 and W_0^*) thereafter.

The next ten equations are used to describe government behavior and vary depending upon the type of scenario that we are simulating. Equations [27] and [28] define the home and foreign country's cumulated surplus as tax receipts less spending. Various values of parameters, (t_{iy} , t_{by} , etc.) are used in the simulations to capture alternative tax policies. For example, in the simulations of the cash-flow model all the t_{by} (*), t_{ky} (*)and t_{ny} (*) are set to 1. For the other tax systems, either some set of equations [29]–[36] are dropped and the other tax variables are assumed exogenous or some parameters are set to "0."

Equations [37] and [38] define the privately held home (foreign) stock of international borrowings. The definitions of lifetime utility are given in equations [39] and [40]. Note that since the model is simulated for only 20 years, the only relevant calculation for V and V^* is in the first year.

The final three equations do not have home and foreign counterparts. Equation [41] is the equilibrium condition for world output; demand for world output must equal the supply of world output. Equation [42] defines the present value factor. Finally, the stock of international borrowing in terms of the home country is defined in equation [43]. Obviously, the negative of B defines the foreign country's position.

The parameter values used in the baseline simulations are: $\beta = \beta^* = 0.4$, $\delta = \delta^* = 0.97$, $\sigma = \sigma^* = 0.3$, $r_k = r_k^* = 0.3$, and $a = a^* = 0.2$. For intercountry differences in the parameter values of the discount factor we use: ($\delta = 0.95$, $\delta^* = 0.97$) or ($\delta = 0.97$, $\delta^* = 0.95$), while for intercountry differences in the parameter values of the marginal product of capital we use: ($r_k = 0.2$, $r_k = 0.3$ $r_k = 0.3$, $r_k^* = 0.2$).

Bibliography

CNOSSEN, Sijbren, Carl S. SHOUP, "Coordination of Value-Added Taxes." In: Sijbren CNOSSEN (Ed.), Tax Coordination in the European Community. Antwerp 1987, pp. 59-84.

EMERSON, Michael, Michel AUJEAN, Michel CATINAT, Philippe GOYBET, Alexis JACQUEMIN, "The Effects of Market Barriers." The European Economy, March 1988, pp. 44-107.

EUROPEAN COMMUNITY (EC), "The Evolution of VAT Rates Applicable in the Member States of the Community." Inter-Tax, March 1987, No. 3, pp. 85-88.

FRENKEL, Jacob A., Assaf RAZIN, Fiscal Policy and the World Economy: An Intertemporal Approach. Cambridge, Mass., 1987.

—, —, "International Effects of Tax Reforms." The Economic Journal, Vol. 99, March 1989, pp. 38-59.

—, —, Steven SYMANSKY, "International Spillovers of Taxation." In: Assaf RAZIN, Joel SLEMROD (Eds.), Taxation in the Global Economy. Chicago 1990, pp. 211-261.

ORGANIZATION OF ECONOMIC COOPERATION AND DEVELOPMENT (OECD), Revenue Statistics of OECD Member Countries. Paris 1990.

TAIT, Alan A., Value Added Tax: International Practice and Problems. International Monetary Fund, Washington 1988.

III

The Harmonization Issue

Assaf Razin
Efraim Sadka

Capital Market Integration: Issues of International Taxation

1. Introduction

International capital market integration has become the subject of major theoretical and practical interest in recent times. Policymakers are becoming more and more aware of the potential benefit accruing from such integration, which allows more efficient allocation of investment and savings between the domestic and the foreign market. In particular, with the prospective comprehensive integration of capital markets in Europe in 1992, some key policy issues arise.[1] The implications of capital market integration for financial, monetary and exchange rate management policy have been widely discussed in the context of the European Monetary System (EMS); see, for instance, the survey by Micossi [1988]. However, capital market integration also has profound effects on the fiscal branch of each country separately and on the scope of tax coordination among them. These issues have not been dealt with extensively so far.[2]

One issue is the tax-induced distortions in the allocation of world savings and investment. In a world with international capital mobility, the equality between savings and investment need not hold for each country separately, but rather for world aggregate savings and investment. This separation brings out new issues in the theory and practice of taxation. In a closed economy, a tax on capital income drives just one wedge between the consumer/saver marginal intertemporal rate of substitution and the producer/investor marginal productivity of capital. In a world of open economies, there are two more types of distortions which can be caused by

1 In a recent paper Micossi [1988, p. 218] provides a succinct survey of the proposed institutional arrangements for the 1992 European integration. He writes: "It [the European integration] entails the elimination of restrictions and discriminatory regulations and administrative practices concerning: (i) the right of establishment and acquisition of participations by foreign institutions in domestic financial markets; (ii) permitted operations of foreign-controlled financial institutions; (iii) cross-border transactions in financial services. The first two items basically involve the freedom to supply services in EC national markets, the third, the freedom to move capital throughout the Community."

2 For an earlier discussion of the interaction among taxes, government consumption, and international capital flow, see Razin and Svensson [1983].

capital income taxation: (1) international differences in intertemporal marginal rates of substitution, implying an inefficient allocation of world savings across countries; (2) international differences in the marginal productivity of capital, implying that world investment is not efficiently allocated across countries.

The fundamental result of the theory of second best suggests that adding distortions to already existing ones may very well enhance efficiency and welfare. To put it differently, reducing the number of distortions in the economy may well lower well-being. Thus, even though there are gains to be derived in general from international trade, some restrictions on free trade may be called for in a distortion-ridden economy.

The opening up of an economy to international capital movements affects the size and structure of the fiscal branch of its government. Capital flows influence both the optimal structure of taxes (on domestic as well as foreign-source income) and the welfare cost of taxation. As a result, the optimal size of government (the optimal provision of public goods) and the magnitude of its redistribution (transfer) policies are affected as well.

Another issue is capital flight. There is now substantial evidence that governments encounter severe enforcement difficulties in attempting to tax foreign-source income. Dooley [1987] estimates that in the 1980-82 time period as much as $250 bill. invested by US residents may have been involved in capital flight. Tanzi [1987] reports that tax experts were concerned that lowering the US individual and corporate tax rates in the US Tax Reform Act of 1986 would induce capital drain from other countries by providing a tax advantage to investments in the US. The concerns are based on an implicit assumption that the governments of these countries cannot effectively tax their residents on their US income so as to wipe out the US tax advantage. The issue of capital flight is even more relevant for developing countries. Cumby and Levich [1987] estimate that a significant portion of the external debt in developing countries is channeled into investments abroad through overinvoicing of imports and underinvoicing of exports. Dooley [1988] estimates that capital flight from a large number of developing countries amounted to about one-third of their external debt in the time period 1977-84.

Finally, integration of capital markets brings up the issues of international tax coordination, harmonization and competition. There are two polar principles of international taxation: the residence (of the taxpayer) and the source (of income) principles. According to the first principle, residents are taxed on their world-wide income equally, regardless of whether the source of income is domestic or foreign.[3] A resident in any country must earn the same net return on his/her savings, no matter to which country he/she chooses to channel his/her savings (the rate-of-return arbitrage). If a country adopts the residence principle, taxing capital income from

[3] A credit is given against taxes paid abroad on foreign-source income in order to avoid double taxation.

all sources at the same rate, then the gross return accruing to an individual in that country must be the same, regardless of which country is the source of that return. Thus, the marginal product of capital in that country will be equal to the world return to capital. If all countries adopt the residence principle, the capital income taxation does not disturb the equality of the marginal product of capital across countries which is generated by a free movement of capital. However, if the rax rate is not the same in all countries, then the net returns accruing to savers in different countries vary and the international allocation of world savings is distorted.

According to the second principle, residents of a country are not taxed on their income from foreign sources and foreigners are taxed equally as residents on income from domestic sources. Now, suppose that all countries adopt this principle. Then a resident of country *H* will earn the same net return in country *F* as the resident of country *F* earns in country *F*. Since a resident in country *H* must earn the same net return whether he/she channeled his/her savings to country *H* or to country *F*, it follows that residents of all countries will earn the same net return. Thus, intertemporal marginal rates of substitution will be equated across countries, implying that the international allocation of world savings is efficient. However, if the tax rate is not the same in all countries, then the marginal product of capital will also not be the same in all countries. In this case the international allocation of the world stock of capital will not be efficient.

Although there are these two extreme principles of international taxation, in reality, countries adopt a mixture of the two polar principles. Accordingly, in practice, countries partially tax foreign-source income of residents and domestic-source income of nonresidents, in which case both the international allocations of world savings and of world investments are distorted.

These issues are of particular relevance for Europe 1992. In the absence of a full-fledged harmonization of the income tax systems, the creation of a single capital market in the European Community will raise the possibility of tax competition among the member countries. Also, the possibility of capital flight from the EC to low-tax countries elsewhere has strong implications for the national tax structures in the EC. These developments have renewed the interest among public finance and international finance economists in the issues of tax harmonization and coordination, tax competition, the international structure of taxation, etc.[4]

---

4 See, for instance, Alworth [1988], Bovenberg [1988], Giovannini [1988; 1989a; 1989b], Gordon [1986], Razin and Sadka [1989a; 1989b; 1990], Razin and Slemrod [1990], Sinn [1987], and Slemrod [1988].

2. Restrictions on Capital Mobility

Since there are distortionary taxes as part of real world fiscal programs, obviously the resource allocation is not Pareto-efficient: the intertemporal allocation of consumption, the leisure-consumption choice and the private/public consumption trade-offs are all distorted. Nevertheless, when the government can tax its residents on their foreign-source capital income, it should allow capital to move freely in or out of the country. That is, optimal policy [see Razin, Sadka, 1989b; 1990] requires an efficient allocation of capital between investment at home and abroad, so that the marginal product of domestic capital must be equated to the world rate of interest (net of foreign taxes). Evidently, this is an open economy variant of the aggregate efficiency theorem in optimal tax theory [see Diamond, Mirrlees, 1971; Sadka, 1977; Dixit, 1985].

Notice also that this production-efficiency result also implies that there should be no differential tax treatment of foreign and domestic sources of income. One might argue that the investment efficiency result (i.e., equating the return on capital at home to the return on capital abroad via free international capital flows) is not valid when the government is concerned about financing its debt, for opening an economy to international capital flows will raise the domestic interest rate to the world rate. In such a case, a government that is burdened by an ongoing deficit incurs a higher interest cost in financing this deficit. In fact, it loses some of its monopsony power in the domestic capital market. It can then be argued in this case that the government may not wish to allow residents to invest abroad. However, in this case it can be shown that the investment efficiency result is still valid nevertheless [see Razin, Sadka, 1989b]. This is because the government can offset the cost of losing its monopsony power by pursuing an appropriate tax policy.

Suppose now that the government cannot effectively tax income from investment abroad. In this case, if the government allows unlimited exports of capital, then capital will flow out of the country up to the point where the net return on domestic investment equals the net return on investment abroad. This means that the marginal productivity of domestic capital will exceed the world rate of interest, so that the domestic stock of capital will be too small. The mirror image of such an underinvestment in capital at home is an overinvestment in capital abroad.

Therefore, an interesting issue that arises in this context is whether it is now efficient from the societal standpoint to restrict the exports of capital, and if so, how severe should the restriction be? One may ask, for instance, whether the restriction on exports of capital should bring the domestic capital stock all the way back to a level that is even higher than the level that is necessary for equating the marginal productivity of domestic capital to the world rate of interest (i.e., whether restrictions on capital exports should induce an overinvestment in domestic capital). Furthermore, is it possible that capital exports should be altogether banned when foreign-source income cannot be effectively taxed?

One can show that when the government cannot effectively tax foreign-source income, it should put severe restrictions on capital exports and bring the marginal product of domestic capital to a level that is even below the world rate of interest. The loss in the return to the private sector on total investments (at home and abroad) due to the reallocation of capital from abroad to home is more than offset by the extra tax revenues accruing to the government from the income from the capital shifted back home [see Razin, Sadka, 1990].

Furthermore, if, under financial autarky, the marginal product of capital is sufficiently close to the world rate of interest, then a total ban on capital exports is called for. The rationale for this result is straightforward. When the marginal product of capital is close to the world rate of interest, investing abroad results in very little gain for society as a whole because this gain is equal only to the difference between the marginal product of capital and the world rate of interest (although the private sector can still gain considerably from investing abroad because the net-of-tax marginal product of capital may be considerably below the world rate of interest). However, the government loses a significant amount of tax revenues from the outflow of capital. Therefore, in this case, it is not efficient to allow exports of capital.

3. Liberalization, the Cost of Public Funds and the Size of Government

The optimal size of government, or more precisely the optimal provision of public goods, must be determined by an appropriate cost-benefit analysis. Such analysis implies that the marginal cost of public funds must be equated to the marginal utility from public goods. To find the effect of liberalization in the international capital markets on the optimal quantity of public goods, we discuss here the effect of such a liberalization on the cost of public funds in a small open economy.

In calculating the cost of public funds, one must take into account the optimal response of the structure of taxation (on incomes from all sources) to international capital market liberalization because the cost of public funds is derived from a process of a tax optimization. Therefore, we must also discuss the effect of liberalization on the structure of taxation. Of course, entangled with the structure of taxation is also the issue of the optimal size of income redistribution.

Suppose that the government can effectively tax income from capital invested abroad. In this case, a liberalization of the capital market improves welfare. Therefore, such a liberalization entails an income effect. And such an effect usually tends to increase the marginal utility of public goods. In addition, it may lower the marginal cost of public funds because the government benefits directly from the liberalization as it taxes the increased amount of income from the capital invested abroad and can therefore lower the tax burden on domestic sources. Therefore, the income effect tends to increase the provision of public goods and the size of income redistribution. On the other hand, the liberalization may change the internal terms of trade (e.g., the real wage, etc.) and affect directly the cost of producing public goods [see Razin, Sadka, 1990]. The effect of this change in the terms of trade on the cost of public funds and the size of government cannot be determined a priori and should be examined empirically.

4. Feasible International Tax Structure

Capital market integration between two large countries brings up the issue of the feasibility of their tax structures. When residents of one country invest in the other country, one must reckon with the possibility of tax arbitrage, which may undermine the feasibility of integration.

To highlight this issue, consider a two-country world with perfect capital mobility. Denote the interest rates in the home country and the foreign country by r and r^*, respectively. In principle, the home country may have three different tax rates applying to interest income:

(a) t_{RD} — the tax rate levied on domestic residents on their domestic-source income,

(b) t_{RF} — the tax rate levied on domestic residents on their foreign-source income,

(c) t_{NRD} — the tax rate levied on nonresidents on their interest income in the home country.

Correspondingly, the foreign country may have three tax rates which we denote by t_{RD}^*, t_{RF}^* and t_{NRD}^*. Furthermore, assume that these rates apply symmetrically for both interest earned and interest paid (i.e., assume full deductibility of interest expenses, including tax rebates).

A complete integration of the capital markets between the two countries (including the possibility of borrowing in one country in order to invest in the other country) requires, due to arbitrage possibilities, the fulfillment of the following conditions:

[1] $r(1 - t_{RD}) = r^*(1 - t_{NRD}^*)(1 - t_{RF})$ and

[2] $r(1 - t_{NRD})(1 - t_{RF}^*) = r^*(1 - t_{RD}^*)$.

The first condition applies to the residents of the home country and it requires that they be indifferent between investing at home or abroad. Otherwise, they can borrow an infinite amount in the low (net-of-tax) interest rate country in order to invest an infinite amount in the high (net-of-tax) interest rate country. Similarly, the second condition applies to the residents of the foreign country.

Notice that unless

$$[3] \quad (1 - t_{RD})(1 - t^*_{RD}) = (1 - t_{NRD})(1 - t^*_{RF})(1 - t^*_{NRD})(1 - t_{RF}),$$

the only solution to the linear system of equations [1]–[2] is a zero rate of interest in each country: $r = r^* = 0$. Thus, some feasibility conditions on the structures of taxes must be met in order to satisfy [3] and yield a sensible world equilibrium.

Somewhat surprisingly, the two most common polar schemes of source-based or residency-based taxation are examples of feasible tax structures even when the two countries do not adopt the same scheme. Consider first the case in which both countries adopt the source-based tax scheme. In this case, income is taxed according to its source, regardless of the residency of the taxpayer. This implies that

$$[4] \quad t_{RD} = t_{NRD},\ t^*_{RD} = t^*_{NRD},\ t_{RF} = t^*_{RF} = 0,$$

so that [3] is satisfied and we can have a world equilibrium with positive rates of interest.

Similarly, consider the case where both countries adopt the residence principle: income is taxed according to the residency of the taxpayer, regardless of its source. This implies that

$$[5] \quad t_{RD} = t_{RF},\ t^*_{RD} = t^*_{RF},\ t_{NRD} = t^*_{NRD} = 0,$$

so that, again, [3] is satisfied.

Next, consider the case in which one country adopts one tax scheme, while the other adopts another one. Suppose, for instance, that the home country adopts the residence principle, while the foreign country adopts the source principle. In this case, we have

$$[6] \quad t_{RD} = t_{RF},\ t_{NRD} = 0, \text{ and } t^*_{RD} = t^*_{NRD},\ t^*_{RF} = 0$$

and, again, [3] is satisfied.

However, if the two countries do not stick to one of the two polar schemes, then [3] need not hold and no sensible world equilibrium exists. Suppose, for instance, that each country levies the same tax rate on its residents (irrespective of the source of their income) and also on all nonresidents investing in that country. In this case, we have

$$[7] \quad t_{RD} = t_{RF} = t_{NRD}\,,\; t_{RD}^{*} = t_{RF}^{*} = t_{NRD}^{*}\,.$$

Hence, unless $(1 - t_{NRD})(1 - t_{NRD}^{*}) = 1$, which is just a sheer coincidence, condition [3] is violated.

Thus, some feasibility conditions on the tax structure are essential for a full capital market integration. Any mutually beneficial tax coordination or harmonization must satisfy the tax arbitrage condition [3].

5. Tax Competition and Tax Harmonization

International tax competition, or any fiscal policy competition for that matter, has major effects on the resource allocation across countries as well as within each country. For example, the aggregate (world-wide) level of savings as well as its cross-country composition may be distorted by such competition; similarly, the aggregate level of investment and its international allocation may become inefficient. In general, these effects on resource allocation can be decomposed into two elements. One concerns the indirect manipulation of the international terms of trade by various fiscal measures (other than explicit trade barriers such as tariffs and quotas), which is akin to the familiar "trade wars." The second element, which has received less attention in the literature, concerns the international and domestic misallocation of resources that is generated by tax competition for given terms of trade.

This section focuses on the second of these two elements, since the first one has been exhaustively studied and has become by now a textbook case. Consider therefore a stylized model in which tax competition within the group of countries that we analyze cannot affect their terms of trade. This can be accomplished by assuming that this group of countries is small relative to the rest of the world, which effectively sets the international terms of trade.

Suppose first that fiscal policies are not harmonized internationally, so that the two countries are engaged in tax competition. However, also suppose that some minimal degree of coordination between the two countries and the rest of the world prevails, so that they can effectively tax, should they wish, their residents on foreign-source income.

It can be shown that in this case no country would desire to tax foreigners on their income from capital invested in that country [see Razin, Sadka, 1989b]. Each one of the competing countries would tax its residents uniformly on their capital income from all sources, domestic as well as foreign. Thus, tax competition leads each country to adopt the residence (or world-wide) principle for the taxation of income from capital. Furthermore, there are no gains from tax harmonization.

In order to effectively implement a policy of taxing world-wide income, a considerable degree of coordination among countries is required, such as, for example, exchange of information among the tax authorities, withholding arrangements, relaxing bank secrecy laws, etc. Suppose that the competing countries can reach such coordination, which enables each to effectively tax its residents on their income from capital invested in the other country, even though they continue to engage in tax competition. However, assume now that they cannot tax the income from capital invested in the rest of the world, as they have no coordination (exchange of information, etc.) agreements with the rest of the world. This seems to be a rather interesting and realistic case, a case that captures the essence of one of the problems hindering European integration, namely, that of capital moving to low-tax countries in the rest of the world.

It can be shown in this case that the rate-of-return arbitrage condition prevents each one of the competing countries from taxing its residents on their income from capital invested in the other country, even though their tax authorities can cooperate on such things as tax withholding, etc. This may explain why the EC dropped the idea of imposing a withholding tax on capital income. Tax competition leads to an extreme situation where no tax whatsoever is imposed by any of the competing countries on capital income from any source. All of the tax burden falls on the internationally immobile factors (unskilled labor, land, etc.). Here again, it can be shown that tax harmonization among our initially competing countries will yield no gains for them.

In conclusion, there are no gains from tax harmonization among competing countries that constitute just a fraction of the world economy, regardless of whether or not they are coordinated with the rest of the world. However, the first case, in which there is some coordination with the rest of the world, is preferable to the second case, where no such coordination exists. These propositions underscore the important role of tax coordination.

Bibliography

ALWORTH, Julian S., The Finance, Investment and Taxation Decisions of Multinationals. New York 1988.

BOVENBERG, A. Lans, The International Effects of Capital Taxation: An Analytical Framework. International Monetary Fund, Washington 1988, mimeo.

CUMBY, Robert, Richard LEVICH, "On the Definition and Magnitude of Recent Capital Flight." In: Donald R. LASSARD, John WILLIAMSON (Eds.), Capital

Flight and Third World Debt. Institute for International Economics, Washington 1987.

DIAMOND, Peer A., James MIRRLEES, "Optimal Taxation and Public Production." The American Economic Review, Vol. 61, 1971, pp. 8-27 and 261-278.

DIXIT, Avinash, "Tax Policy in Open Economies." In: Alan AUERBACH, Martin FELDSTEIN (Eds.), Handbook on Public Economics, Vol. 1, Amsterdam 1985, Chapter 6, pp. 314-374.

DOOLEY, Michael P., "Comment on the Definition and Magnitude of Recent Capital Flight by Robert Cumby and Richard Levich." In: Donald R. LASSARD, John WILLIAMSON (Eds.), Capital Flight and the Third World Debt. Institute for International Economics, Washington 1987.

—, "Capital Flight, a Response to Differences in Financial Risks." IMF Staff Papers, Vol. 35, 1988, pp. 422-436.

GIOVANNINI, Alberto, International Capital Mobility and Tax Avoidance. Graduate School of Business, Columbia University, New York 1988, mimeo.

— [1989a], International Capital Mobility and Capital-Income Taxation: Theory and Policy. Graduate School of Business, Columbia University, New York 1989, mimeo.

— [1989b], "National Tax Systems vs. the European Capital Market." Economic Policy, Vol. 4, 1989, pp. 345-386.

GORDON, Roger H., "Taxation of Investment and Savings in a World Economy." The American Economic Review, Vol. 76, 1986, pp. 1087-1102.

MICOSSI, Stefano, "The Single European Market: Finance." Banca Nazionale del Lavoro Quarterly Review, Vol. 165, 1988, pp. 217-235.

RAZIN, Assaf, Lars E. O. SVENSSON, "The Current Account and the Optimal Government Debt." Journal of International Money and Finance, Vol. 2, 1983, pp. 215-224.

—, Efraim SADKA [1989a], International Tax Competition and Gains from Tax Harmonization. Foerder Institute for Economic Research, Tel-Aviv University, Working Paper No. 37-89, Ramat Aviv 1989.

—, — [1989b], Optimal Incentives to Domestic Investment in the Presence of Capital Flight. IMF Working Papers, No. 90, Washington 1989.

—, —, "Integration of the International Capital Markets: The Size of Government and Tax Coordination." In: Assaf RAZIN, Joel SLEMROD (Eds.), Taxation in the Global Economy. Chicago 1990, pp. 211-262.

SADKA, Efraim, "A Note on Producer Taxation and Public Production." Review of Economic Studies, Vol. 44, 1977, pp. 385-387.

SINN, Hans-Werner, Capital Income Taxation and Resource Allocation. Amsterdam 1987.

SLEMROD, Joel, "International Capital Mobility and the Theory of Capital Income Taxation." In: H. AARON, H. GALPER, J. PECHMAN (Eds.), Uneasy Compromise: Problems of a Hybrid Income-Consumption Tax. Brookings Institution, Washington 1988.

TANZI, Vito, "The Response of Other Industrial Countries to the U.S. Tax Reform Act." National Tax Journal, Vol. 14, 1987, pp. 339-355.

Comment on Assaf Razin and Efraim Sadka, "Capital Market Integration: Issues of International Taxation"

Stefan Sinn

If governments could effectively enforce the world-wide principle of capital income taxation vis-à-vis their residents by exchanging information (i.e., if tax coordination prevailed), which tax system for capital income would they actually choose? Would the result be different if governments did not exchange information on the foreign capital income of their respective residents (i.e., if tax competition prevailed)? In either case, can governments gain from harmonizing capital income taxes? These are the questions addressed by Assaf Razin and Efraim Sadka.[1] Their central results are (1) that if countries are not able to effectively tax their residents on capital income earned abroad, tax competition leads to a full exemption from tax for the mobile factor capital, and (2) that no gains relative to the competitive outcome can be obtained from tax harmonization, regardless of whether the world-wide principle can be enforced or not.

The basic reason why capital income is not taxed at all if the residence principle of capital income taxation cannot be enforced is portfolio arbitrage. Razin and Sadka consider the case of two small competing countries and a rest of the world which remains passive. The authors show that, in equilibrium, after-tax rates of return on capital converge to a global level which is determined by that country which levies the lowest capital income tax. But it is not necessarily true that capital income cannot be taxed at all, rather capital income cannot be taxed over and above the tax rate levied by the rest of the world on nonresidents' capital income. Both small countries will levy capital income taxes on nonresidents up to this level. All this holds true if the residence principle cannot be enforced. If, on the other hand, as Razin and Sadka show, governments always had full information on the capital income their citizens earn abroad, they could set their taxes independently of one another, irrespective of which of them adopt the residence principle. The only way residents could arbitrage to a lower tax regime would be by emigrating. Tax competition would in this case operate through the exit mechanism of feet and not through the exit mechanism of capital movements. Tax competition would not be as intense as in the absence of tax coordination.

---

1 Razin and Sadka's contribution to this conference volume differs from the paper presented at the conference. I shall concentrate on Sections 4 and 5, which were presented in an extended version at the conference. See Razin, Sadka [1989].

Razin and Sadka also report that tax harmonization does not result in gains to the countries involved. At first sight, I found this result surprising because the underlying model has very similar features to models in the policy coordination literature, where inevitably in a two-country world the noncooperative Nash outcome can be improved upon by coordination.[2] To see why this is not the case here, note first that in the standard two-country setup, policy measures in one country affect the attainment of the policy targets in the other country. If there is a negative spillover from policy-making, countries find themselves in a beggar-thy-neighbor world; with positive spillovers, the picture of a locomotive world is evoked [Canzoneri, Gray, 1985]. In Razin and Sadka's paper, such policy spillovers do not occur between the two countries because of a passive third player, the rest of the world. If both governments set their policies such that, for example, both countries wanted net capital imports, a conflict would arise in the standard two-country analysis. The outcome of such a conflict is the noncooperative Nash-equilibrium, which is Pareto-inferior to policy coordination. In the present model, however, the rest of the world accommodates whatever policies are chosen by the two countries. Specifically, one country can always offset the capital flow consequences of the other country's tax and expenditure policies by adjusting capital flows with the rest of the world. Since only net flows matter, the two countries do not affect each other and, as a consequence, there is no need for tax harmonization. This result rests of course on the assumption that the hypothetical rest of the world does indeed remain passive, but I consider it valid if the two countries, taken together, are small compared to the rest of the world. If they are not, it is not likely that the rest of the world would maintain its benign neglect.

This result can be seen from another angle. It is well known that international policy coordination may improve welfare if governments pursue a number of targets that exceed the number of instruments available to them. In Razin and Sadka's setup, there is no such shortage of policy instruments. The welfare of the representative individual depends on four variables: consumption in period 1 and in period 2, labor supply in period 2, and public consumption in period 2. The government has four instruments; namely, public consumption in period 2, the present value post-tax consumer prices of second-period consumption and labor, and the combined capital account with the second country and with the rest of the world. The use of the last instrument implies that the government is able to exactly determine the size of a subpart of its capital account (namely, its capital account balance with the rest of the world) so as to offset the capital account balance that results from the other country's fiscal policy. I wonder whether it is realistic to assume that such a fine tuning of the capital account can actually be a feasible policy option. To summarize my argument here: Sadka and Razin's result of no gains from

2 Cooper [1985] summarizes the economic literature on international policy coordination.

tax harmonization rests on the assumptions that there is a passive rest of the world willing to accept the combined capital account consequences of both countries' fiscal policies and that each country is able to effectively steer a subpart of its capital account.

Since these assumptions may not always be fulfilled in reality, I wonder whether the case for no gains from tax harmonization cannot be made stronger. Let me therefore finally comment on the concept of tax competition as it is modeled here. I think the dispute about whether or not tax competition is a good thing is fundamentally related to the concept of competition. In this paper and many others on coordination of tax policy or of economic policy in general, only the end results of competition, namely, the equilibrium conditions, are used to evaluate whether or not policy competition leads to efficient results. What is missing in my opinion is an evaluation of the welfare gains that result from the competitive process itself leading to the equilibrium results. If one views competition as a process, an additional welfare gain that is neglected in standard analyses emerges: information is created and spread about by the trial and error process of competition among policies. This point was noted early on by Eucken [1960, p. 57] and I would like to offer two historic instances where such a learning process might have been at work among competing governments: The 1970s saw a gradual convergence of inflation rates on a low level after the breakdown of Bretton Woods, and the 1980s saw a similar move towards lower tax rates. Both seem to me to illustrate that governments learn from the policy failures and successes of others. Thus, support of policy competition need not rely on the view that government behavior is best described by the Leviathan paradigm. All one needs to assume to advocate policy competition is that governments are not omniscient.

Bibliography

CANZERONI, Matthew B., Jo Anna GRAY, "Monetary Policy Games and the Consequences of Non-Cooperative Behaviour." International Economic Review, Vol. 26, 1985, pp. 547-564.

COOPER, Richard N., "Economic Interdependence and Coordination of Economic Policies." In: Ronald W. JONES, Peter B. KENEN (Eds.), Handbook of International Economics, Vol. II. Amsterdam 1985, pp. 1195-1234.

EUCKEN, Walter, Grundsätze der Wirtschaftspolitik. 3. unveränderte Aufl., Tübingen 1960.

RAZIN, Assaf, Efraim SADKA, International Tax Competition and Gains from Tax Harmonization. Foerder Institute for Economic Research, Tel-Aviv University, Working Paper No. 37-89, Ramat Aviv, October 1989.

Vito Tanzi
A. Lans Bovenberg

Is There a Need for Harmonizing Capital Income Taxes within EC Countries?

1. Introduction

Many of the EC countries are now part of the European Monetary System (EMS) arrangement, which requires them to maintain what is essentially a fixed nominal exchange rate policy vis-à-vis other member countries. Over the years, such a policy has forced the EMS countries to harmonize their monetary policies, and, as a result, the rates of inflation of the EMS countries converged significantly during the 1980s [see Tanzi, Ter-Minassian, 1987].

With similar inflation rates and free capital movements, the borrowing rates for prime borrowers in different countries (for governments, large enterprises, and financial institutions, etc.) tend to be relatively close. If trade barriers were totally eliminated and taxes that affect the movement of goods and services across EC countries were largely harmonized, then neither the pretax borrowing cost of capital nor commodity taxes and trade barriers would play much of a role in determining the location of production plants by major enterprises within the EMS area. Other factors such as distance from markets, quality of public services, labor costs, regulations, and capital and income taxes would become more important in determining the location decisions made by enterprises.

In the situation outlined above, enterprises would lose their national character and would become increasingly European. As a recent newspaper article has put it: "The mergers and acquisition movement that started to snowball in Europe three years ago has grown into an avalanche that is remaking the Continent's corporate landscape. That avalanche will likely continue to thunder as companies rush to prepare for the more competitive era that will result as the European Community snaps internal barriers by the end of 1992" [Greenhouse, 1989].

Furthermore, enterprises will become increasingly sensitive to tax factors. For example, a recent survey of 173 large UK companies polled by the Institute of Fiscal

---

Remark: The views expressed in this paper are those of the authors. They do not necessarily reflect the official positions of the International Monetary Fund. The authors would like to thank Ed Gardner for preparing several tables and George Kopits for providing helpful comments.

Studies found that almost 80 percent of these companies indicated that they are usually influenced by tax considerations when deciding where to set up a production plant [see Devereux, Pearson, 1989].

2. On the Concept of Tax Harmonization

Tax harmonization can have different meanings and can be related to different objectives. In line with the Single European Act, this paper defines tax harmonization within the European Community as a process by which the tax systems of the EC countries are aligned with each other so that tax considerations no longer influence the movements of commodities and factors of production (including portfolio capital) within the Community. This process is intended to achieve a more efficient allocation of resources by leveling the playing field across the EC countries.

It should be clear, however, that tax harmonization, per se, does not guarantee a more efficient allocation of resources within the Community than occurs in the absence of harmonization. It all depends on the characteristics of the tax systems that result after harmonization has taken place. Perhaps an analogy will help explain this point. Harmonization of monetary policy within the EMS has led Germany to largely determine monetary policy for all EMS countries. Given that German monetary policy had been consistent with a low inflation rate for many years, and that low inflation was assumed to be the predominant objective of monetary policy, it made sense to many observers that German monetary policy would become the norm for other EMS countries.

Tax harmonization, however, is far more complex. It is not obvious that any of the tax systems in the EC countries are obviously preferable to the others as the natural candidate around which to harmonize the other tax systems. The existing systems presumably reflect objectives that are given different weights by different countries. Furthermore, even if both tax rates and tax bases were harmonized, as long as tax enforcement is not equally effective across countries, one could not say that effective (as compared with statutory) harmonization has been achieved. Tax harmonization must also inevitably require some harmonization of expenditure levels and, perhaps, even of expenditure patterns, since tax expenditures may substitute for government expenditure and the pattern of government expenditure may be influenced by the level and structure of the tax systems. To increase overall economic efficiency in the Community, tax harmonization must occur around a good tax structure. Otherwise, the benefits achieved by leveling the field *across* EC countries can be offset by additional distortions within each country that are introduced by the new tax system.

Unlike the case of monetary policy, tax harmonization cannot come about by imposing the current statutory tax system of a country (even of an economically powerful one) on the others. It does not seem realistic, for example, to expect that the Community would accept the German (or the French or the British) tax system as the norm for the rest of the Community. But if this is the case, should harmonization be left to market forces, as argued by some economists and some governments? Or should a supranational body suggest or impose concerted harmonization toward desirable tax systems?

In this paper we shall restrict our discussion to a few major questions regarding the harmonization of taxes, these being questions concerning:

(a) the profits of corporations;
(b) cross-border portfolio income;
(c) interest income and expense; and
(d) income from housing investment.

The tax treatment of the activities of insurance companies, pension funds, banks, and other financial institutions are also likely to raise important issues as these activities become European rather than national. However, we shall not deal with them in this paper.

3. Corporate Income Taxation

a. Statutory Tax Rates and Tax Arbitrage

After the United Kingdom and the United States lowered their statutory rates in 1984 and 1986, respectively, most EC countries reduced their rates as well (Tables 1 and 2). Despite this "spontaneous" harmonization process, substantial differences in tax rates remain, with high rates of 50 percent or higher in Germany and Denmark and low rates of 35 percent in the Netherlands, Spain, and the United Kingdom.

Intra-EC differences in statutory corporate rates create opportunities for tax arbitrage. Although these transactions may not necessarily change real investment decisions, they affect the intra-EC distribution of tax revenue. EC countries presently rely on the separate accounting method to assign taxable profits of multinational corporations to each jurisdiction. Hence, each multinational corporation separately computes taxable profits in each jurisdiction in which it operates by using transfer prices applied to transactions between the entity subject to tax and the subsidiaries abroad. These prices should, in principle, reflect so-called arm's length prices, that is, prices for transactions between nonrelated parties. If they do not, tax administrations are authorized to adjust the taxable profit accordingly. However,

Table 1 — Selected Industrial Countries: Main Statutory Corporate Income Tax Rates (Central Government), 1977 and 1989 (percent)[a]

	1977	1989	Proposed or announced rate
EC countries			
Belgium	48.0	43.0	38.0
Denmark	37.0	50.0	35.0
France	50.0	39.0	—
West Germany[b]	56.0	56.0	50.0 (1990)
Greece	39.0[c]	35.0[c]	—
Ireland	45.0	43.0[d]	—
Italy	25.0	36.0	—
Luxembourg	40.0	36.0	—
Netherlands	48.0	35.0	—
Portugal	36.0[e]	36.5	—
Spain	36.0	35.0	—
United Kingdom	52.0	35.0	—
Selected non-EC countries			
Australia	50.0	39.0	—
Canada	46.0[f]	38.0	—
Japan[b]	40.0	42.0	37.5 (1990)
New Zealand	45.0	33.0	—
Sweden	56.0[g]	52.0	30.0 (1991)
United States	48.0	34.0	—

[a]Some countries apply lower rates to small enterprises. — [b]Rates apply to retained earnings. — [c]Rate for industrial companies quoted on the Athens Stock Exchange. — [d]A 10 percent rate applies to industrial companies until the end of the year 2000. — [e]Includes the complementary tax on retained earnings. — [f]Including basic rate of provincial tax credit (10 percent). — [g]Inclusive of municipal taxes, which were eliminated as of 1985. — Not applicable: —.

Source: Price Waterhouse [various issues]; various national sources.

tax administrators often face conceptual difficulties in determining transfer prices, especially regarding trade in specific intermediate products that are not traded on open markets. Thus, corporations may manipulate transfer prices and cost allocation of common expenses (e.g., on research and development) in order to shift taxable income from high to low tax countries. Multinational firms can also move taxable profits across borders by altering their financial structure so as to take interest deductions in high tax jurisdictions.[1]

The opportunities for these types of tax arbitrage are likely to increase in the near future. The liberalization of capital movements raises the scope for avoiding taxes through purely financial transactions. At the same time, intracompany trade should

1 Legislative remedies against "thin capitalization" (i.e., excessive interest deductions) are generally not fully effective in preventing this kind of tax avoidance. Unrelated parties can also engage in tax arbitrage if tax rates differ across countries [see, e.g., Gordon, 1986].

Table 2 — European Community: Corporate Tax Rates, 1989

	Main statutory corporate income tax rate[a]		Net worth and capital based tax rate[c]
	central government	central and local government[b]	
Belgium	43.0	43.0	0.0
Denmark	50.0	50.0	0.0
France	39.0	39.0	0.62[d]
West Germany	56.0/36.0[e]	62.0/45.0[e]	0.13/0.58[f]
Greece	35.0[g]	35.0[g]	0.0
Ireland	10.0[h]	10.0[h]	0.0
Italy	36.0	46.0	0.0
Luxembourg	37.0[i]	43.0	0.11/0.88[j]
Netherlands	35.0	35.0	0.0
Portugal	36.5	40.0	0.0
Spain	35.0	36.0[k]	0.0
United Kingdom	35.0	35.0	0.0

[a]Some countries apply lower rates to small enterprises. — [b]Net rates. — [c]Estimates of effective tax rates, excluding local property taxes on land and buildings. — [d]Taxe Professionnelle. — [e]Split rate system: first rate applies to retained earnings, second rate to distributed earnings. — [f]Gewerbesteuer and net worth tax. Rates for debt and equity financed capital. — [g]Rate for industrial companies quoted on the Athens Stock Exchange. — [h]Rate for industrial companies, to remain in effect until the end of the year 2000. The standard rate for other companies is 43 percent. — [i]Including a 2 percent surcharge (deductible) for the employment fund. — [j]Net worth tax and business capital tax. Rates for debt and equity financed capital. — [k]Includes the surcharge for the chamber of commerce.

Source: International Bureau of Fiscal Documentation [various issues]; Price Waterhouse [various issues]; and various national sources.

grow because lower intra-EC trade barriers allow corporations to increasingly separate production from national markets.[2] Moreover, products for which transfer prices are especially difficult to determine account for an expanding share of intracompany trade.[3]

The ability of multinational corporations to engage in tax arbitrage through financial transactions increases the scope for EC countries to impose adverse externalities that affect the equity, efficiency, and revenue objectives of the fiscal systems in other member countries. In particular, countries lowering their statutory corporate rate erode foreign corporate income tax bases by encouraging multinationals to shift their taxable income. This shifting of profits does not necessarily

---

2 The adoption of the EC company statute and the completion of the internal market will give impetus to the establishment of EC-wide companies that will be able to use intra-EC differences in corporate tax rates to engage in tax arbitrage.

3 Intangibles, such as brand names, marketing, and research and development, are prime examples of such products. More generally, the growing complexity of intrafirm transactions makes it increasingly difficult to devise effective administrative rules aimed at mitigating the abuses of transfer pricing.

require a change in the allocation of real investment across countries but may be brought about through purely financial transactions.

In order to avoid a serious erosion of their corporate tax bases, other countries may be forced to reduce their corporate statutory rates. This reduction affects the equity and revenue objectives of the entire income tax system because it puts downward pressure on personal income tax rates in order to reduce incentives facing taxpayers to shelter personal income in the corporate sector.[4]

The tax arbitrage transactions also harm efficiency by complicating the use of the corporate tax as a benefit tax. A country that provides more public services to capital than other countries will find it more difficult to finance these services by charging higher corporate taxes. Through tax competition, this mechanism is likely to result in either an underprovision of public services that benefit capital or the introduction of taxes that do not correspond to benefits received.

As an alternative to lowering their own tax rates, countries may impose capital controls or tighten administrative controls—including transfer price regulations or thin capitalization rules. This tends to increase the costs of complying with corporate tax provisions for EC-wide companies and may also result in double taxation.

b. Corporate Tax Systems and Real Investment Decisions

Statutory rates are imperfect indicators of how corporate taxes affect investment decisions in EC countries because major intra-EC differences remain regarding both the definition of the tax base (see Table 3) and the degree of enforcement. Another potential determinant of investment incentives in a particular source (or host) country is the treatment of cross-border capital flows by the investor's residence (or home) country. In principle, several EC countries (as residence countries) adhere to the residence principle, in accordance with which they levy tax on global corporate income from direct investments—irrespective of whether the income originates at home or abroad. However, corporate taxes in the source country are a major determinant of tax incentives to locate real capital in that country because, in practice, corporate taxes conform closely to the source principle.[5] Countries typically allow multinationals to defer taxes on the profits of foreign subsidiaries until these profits are repatriated to the home country.[6] Furthermore, residence countries typically limit the foreign tax credit to the residence country's own tax

---

4 One of the common trends of recent tax reforms has been to bring the marginal tax rate on personal income taxes more in line with the basic corporate income tax rate [see Tanzi, 1987b].

5 See also Fuente and Gardner [1990] and Bovenberg et al. [1989].

6 However, multinationals can not usually defer residence taxes on income generated by foreign branches.

Table 3 — European Community: Factors Determining the Corporate Tax Base, 1989

	Investment incentives	Loss carryover		Capital cost recovery allowances				First year convention[c]
				methods[a]		indicative or typical lifetimes[b]		
		carry-forward	carryback	machinery	buildings	machinery	buildings	
Belgium	13 percent deduction	5	0	SL, DB	SL	5.0	20.0	Full year
Denmark[d]	—	5	0	SL, DB	SL[e]	7.0	30.0	2/3 of the year
France	—	5	0	SL, DB	SL	7.0	20.0	Pro-rated[f]
West Germany	—	5	2	SL, DB	SL, DB[e]	7.0	25.0	Half year
Greece	—	3	0	SL	SL	7.0	20.0	Pro-rated[f]
Ireland	—	no limit	1	AD	SL[e]	—[g]	13.5	Full year
Italy	—	5	0	AD	AD	8.5	21.3	Pro-rated[f]
Luxembourg	12 percent credit[h]	5	0	SL, DB	SL	5.0	33.3	Half year
Netherlands	—	8	3	SL, DB	SL	10.0	33.3	Pro-rated[f]
Portugal	—	5	0	SL	SL	6.7	25.0	Full year
Spain	5 percent credit	5	0	SL, DB	SL	12.5	33.3	Pro-rated[f]
United Kingdom	—	no limit	1	DB	SL	—[i]	25.0	Full year

[a]SL = straight line; DB = declining balance; AD = accelerated depreciation. — [b]Including accelerated depreciation. — [c]Share of the year over which depreciation is allowed in the first tax year. — [d]Denmark allows depreciation to start at the time the capital is ordered or construction initiated. Also, the depreciable base is indexed to the price level. — [e]More than one rate applies over the life of the asset. — [f]Pro-rated from date of acquisition or installation. — [g]Depreciation method is declining balance with a 50 percent depreciation allowance in the first year, 25 percent thereafter. — [h]Machinery only. — [i]Declining balance method with a 25 percent rate. — Not applicable: —.

Source: International Bureau of Fiscal Documentation [various issues]; Price Waterhouse [various issues]; and various national sources.

rate on the same income. Hence, source tax rates determine the tax on international capital income if corporations are in an excess credit position.[7] Moreover, while most countries attempt to apply the residence principle to the personal taxation of portfolio investments by individuals, they typically do not credit the underlying corporate tax.

7 The US Tax Reform Act of 1986 has increased the number of US multinationals in an excess credit position because it reduced the US tax rate. This has increased the weight of EC corporate taxes in determining effective tax rates for US multinationals that invest in the EC.

Table 4 gives corporate tax wedges summarizing the effect of several aspects of the corporate tax systems—including the statutory rate, depreciation allowances, investment credits, wealth and net worth taxes—on the incentives to invest in EC countries.[8] These wedges, which have been computed by Ed Gardner and Angel de la Fuente as part of a research project carried out in the Fiscal Affairs Department of the International Monetary Fund, are defined as the difference between the cost of capital to the enterprise and the market rate of return on financial assets. The cost of capital corresponds to the marginal rate of return that the firm must earn in order to be able to pay the market rate of return (after paying corporate taxes) to a portfolio investor. Given an integrated capital market, the portfolio investor financing the investment is assumed to be an institutional investor with a nonresident status in each EC country. Accordingly, the wedges account for withholding taxes on dividends distributed to nonresidents as well as for the integration of personal and corporate taxes to the extent that the legal provisions apply to nonresidents (see Table 5). In line with the "old view" of dividend taxation, the tax treatment of dividends affects the cost of equity capital in proportion to the share of profits distributed as dividends. Moreover, it is assumed that corporate taxes do not correspond to benefits for public goods. For more details, see Fuente and Gardner [1990].

The dispersion of tax wedges across various EC countries provides an indication of the extent to which diverging corporate tax treatments can distort the allocation of real capital within the Community. To illustrate, a marginal equity-financed investment in buildings in Germany needs to yield a before-tax return that is more than 11 percent higher than that on a similar investment in Ireland in order to pay the same market return to investors.[9] Hence, overall EC output could be raised by reallocating capital from Ireland to Germany.

In recent years, tax reforms in many EC countries have aimed at leveling the domestic playing field by reducing the differential tax treatment of assets located domestically. From an EC-wide efficiency point of view, however, the playing field should be leveled not just *within* a country but also *across* EC countries in order to ensure that liberalizing international trade and capital flows will improve overall efficiency in the EC. Indeed, the theory of second best implies that removing some distortions (such as capital controls) in an economy where important tax distortions remain does not necessarily improve welfare. An efficient allocation of resources

---

8 These calculations ignore, of course, differences in enforcement. To the extent that tax evasion possibilities differ across countries, the wedges, calculated on the basis of statutory provisions, may not fully reflect reality.

9 These estimates represent an upper bound to actual intra-EC differences in effective tax wedges. In practice, corporations may partly escape intra-EC differences in tax treatment because they adjust transfer prices and financial arrangements in response to differences in tax systems. Moreover, intra-EC differences in effective tax rates may be correlated with differences in benefits from public services.

Table 4 — European Community: Company Tax Wedges by Source of Finance and Type of Asset[a]

	Buildings		Machinery	
	without	with tax base	without	with tax base
	harmonization[b]		harmonization[b]	
Debt financing				
Belgium	–1.17	–1.01	–2.72	–2.99
Denmark	–1.53	–0.70	–2.08	–2.39
France	–0.26	–0.37	–0.50	–1.93
West Germany	–0.48	–0.89	–2.36	–3.74
Greece	–0.70	–0.70	–0.62	–2.39
Ireland	–0.52	–0.16	–0.05	–0.59
Italy	–1.67	–1.04	–1.44	–3.46
Luxembourg	0.51	–0.45	–6.29	–4.80
Netherlands	0.06	–0.70	–1.17	–2.39
Portugal	–0.56	–0.85	–1.64	–2.85
Spain	–0.70	–1.31	–1.77	–3.35
United Kingdom	–0.46	–0.70	–1.25	–2.39
Equity financing				
Belgium	5.23	5.46	2.80	2.21
Denmark	4.15	5.21	2.49	2.44
France	4.15	4.05	3.20	1.44
West Germany	11.59	11.57	7.55	5.64
Greece	4.97	4.94	4.94	2.19
Ireland	0.37	0.88	0.91	0.34
Italy	6.19	8.00	6.61	3.54
Luxembourg	10.04	8.44	-0.74	1.52
Netherlands	6.41	5.21	4.02	2.44
Portugal	6.88	6.36	4.28	2.89
Spain	5.42	4.36	3.78	1.24
United Kingdom	3.97	3.58	2.30	1.02

[a]Common real interest rate (5.5 percent); inflation rate (2 percent); and rates of economic depreciation (7 percent for buildings, 15 percent for machinery). — [b]Based on an earlier draft proposal by the European Commission, as described in Kuiper [1988]. This proposal eliminates accelerated depreciation, depreciation of capital not yet in use, and indexation of the depreciable base. For tax purposes, machinery is depreciated at 25 percent (declining balance) with a switchover to straight line (10 percent). The corresponding depreciation rates for buildings are 6 percent (declining balance) and 4 percent (straight line). It allows enterprises to claim the full amount of depreciation for the first tax year—irrespective of when in the year the investment takes place. Under this scenario, country differences remain with respect to investment tax credits, degrees of integration with respect to personal taxes, and wealth and net worth taxes, besides differences in statutory tax rates.

Source: Fuente, Gardner [1990].

within the EC requires that, in the absence of externalities, *before-tax* returns are equalized across EC countries. In an integrated EC financial market, however,

Table 5 — European Community: Degree of Integration of Personal and Corporate Taxation, 1989[a]

	Statutory corporate income tax rate	Resident shareholder				Nonresident shareholder			Method of integration of personal and corporate taxes[e]
		tax discrimination variable[b]	degree of integration	top marginal personal rate on dividend income	payout rate[c]	tax discrimination variable	dividend withholding tax[d]	payout rate[c]	
	(1)	(2)	(3)	(4)	(5)	(6)	(7)	(8)	
Belgium	43.0	1.0[f]	0.57	25.0[f]	43.0	1.0	15.0	48.0	DC[f]
Denmark	50.0	1.25	0.63	57.0	27.0	1.0	15.0	43.0	DC
France[g]	39.0	1.5	0.87	57.0	37.0	1.5	15.0	74.0	DC
West Germany	56.0/ 62.0[h]	2.27	1.0/ 0.86[h]	56.0	38.0	1.25	15.0	40.0	SR + DC
Greece	35.0[i]	1.54	1.0	42.0[j]	58.0	1.54	42.0	58.0	DD
Ireland	10.0[k]	1.06	0.95	56.0	42.0	1.0	0.0	90.0	DC
Italy	36.0/ 46.0[h]	1.56	1.0/ 0.84[h]	62.0	32.0	1.0	15.0	39.0	DC
Luxembourg	37.0	1.0	0.63	59.0	26.0	1.0	15.0	54.0	C
Netherlands	35.0	1.0	0.65	72.0	18.0	1.0	15.0	55.0	C
Portugal	36.5/ 40.0[h]	1.0[k]	0.635/ 0.60[h]	25.0[l]	45.0	1.0	15.0	51.0	DC[l]
Spain	35.0	1.1	0.72	56.0	32.0	1.0	15.0	55.0	DC
United Kingdom	35.0	1.33	0.86	40.0	52.0	1.33	15.0	73.0	DC

[a]All rates in percent. The figures in the columns are calculated as following: (1) = tc; (2) = k; (3) = $[(100-tc)k]/100$; (4) = tp; (5) = $[(100-tc)k(100-tp)]/100$; (6) = $k1$; (7) = wt; (8) = $[(100-tc)k1(100-wt)]/100$. — [b]Defined as the opportunity cost of retained earnings in terms of gross dividends foregone. $k = 1$ under the classical system, $k > 1$ if personal and corporate tax systems are integrated. — [c]Corporate income tax inclusive of local taxes. — [d]Typical rate under treaty. — [e]DC = dividend credit; SR = split rate; DD = dividend deduction; C = classical. — [f]If the withholding tax on dividends is taken as a final tax, no dividend credit can be claimed. A dividend credit equal to 50 percent of net dividends can be claimed if dividend income is taxed as regular income (at a top marginal rate of 55 percent). As of 1990, the dividend credit will be eliminated and dividends will be taxed at the 25 percent withholding tax rate. — [g]The corporate income tax rate on distributed profits is higher than that on retained profits, or 39 percent in 1989, 37 percent in 1990. — [h]First number accounts for central government taxes only. Central and local government income taxes are included in the second number. — [i]Rate on industrial company quoted on the Athens Stock Exchange. — [j]Final withholding tax rate. — [k]Special rate for industrial enterprises. — [l]If the withholding tax on dividends is taken as a final tax, no dividend credit can be claimed. A 7 percent dividend credit can be claimed if dividend income is taxed as regular income (at a top marginal rate of 40 percent).

Source: International Bureau of Fiscal Documentation [various issues]; various national sources.

after-tax returns tend to converge, as investors arbitrage to ensure that their placements yield equal after-tax returns.

The efficiency costs due to differential tax treatments are likely to grow because the integration and liberalization of capital and commodity markets within the EC make locational decisions more sensitive to tax factors. When the creation of the internal market reduces trade barriers, corporations no longer have to produce in the country of sale. Instead, they can choose the location of their production and distribution centers within the EC on the basis of other factors, including the tax treatment.[10] Furthermore, the integration and liberalization of European capital markets is likely to increase the importance of market signals, and therefore tax factors affecting these signals, in determining investment decisions.

The higher sensitivity of locational decisions with respect to tax factors increases the scope for EC countries to impose adverse spillover effects on other member countries.[11] A country may harm the efficiency with which capital is allocated across the EC by reducing its tax rate on investment below, or increasing it above, the rate in other countries. If effective tax rates on capital are positive, the country lowering its effective rate below that in other countries shifts these welfare losses to other countries by lowering foreign tax revenues.[12] While marginal investments continue to earn the same after-tax return in all countries, marginal investments in the high-tax countries must yield a higher before-tax return to generate the additional tax revenue. Hence, the capital that moves to the low-tax country yields a lower before-tax return than before and the overall efficiency loss is reflected in lower foreign tax collections.

Unilateral changes in corporate taxes may also generate important macroeconomic effects on other member countries by setting in motion intra-EC capital flows. Macroeconomic implications include swings in the terms of trade and real exchange rates accompanied by resource flows between tradable and nontradable sectors.[13] These developments may adversely affect employment if rigidities in labor markets inhibit intersectoral labor mobility and prevent real wages from

---

10 These tax factors involve not only corporate but also personal taxes. Effective personal tax rates may be important for the locational decisions of corporations that are intensive in highly skilled, and thus more mobile, labor—especially after EC countries start to recognize professional degrees granted in other member countries and lift the remaining restrictions on the intra-EC movement of labor.

11 How sensitive locational decisions within the United States are with respect to cross-state differences in corporate tax rates is subject to some debate. See, e.g., Benson and Johnson [1985] and Papke and Papke [1986].

12 A country raising its tax rate above that in other countries, in contrast, generally absorbs the global welfare losses itself as domestic investment falls. A country may reduce its effective tax rate by providing investment incentives.

13 Sinn [1987], Tanzi and Bovenberg [1989], and Dooley and Isard [1989] discuss the international macroeconomic effects of capital income taxes. If nominal exchange rates are fixed, real exchange rates can change on account of international differences in inflation rates.

adjusting to changes in the value of the marginal product of labor in various sectors. Moreover, movements in real exchange rates could result in trade tensions and tempt countries to interfere with free trade and capital flows.[14] Large EC countries with market power can influence other countries also by affecting conditions on EC capital markets.

c. Is Harmonization Desirable?

This section discusses whether concerted harmonization of two major features of EC corporate tax systems, namely the tax base and the tax rate, would be desirable. It also explores several alternatives to concerted harmonization of tax rates. In this connection, it explores the factors that determine the relative desirability of tax competition (i.e., market-based harmonization) and concerted tax harmonization.

Compared to reducing statutory tax rates, manipulating the tax base is a less visible way to attract capital from other countries and to distort the intra-EC allocation of capital. Tax base harmonization would reduce the opportunities to pursue such nontransparent beggar-thy-neighbor policies.[15] Furthermore, it would decrease compliance costs for corporations operating in several EC countries. This would encourage firms to do business across intra-EC borders, thereby realizing dynamic efficiency gains and economies of scale in the internal market.[16] A more uniform tax base would also enhance the efficiency of decision making by contributing to more uniform and transparent accounting measures within the EC.[17]

Harmonizing the tax base in the presence of nonuniform statutory corporate tax rates would maintain the scope for tax arbitrage through purely financial transactions (see Section 3.a).[18] Moreover, nonuniform rates would continue to generate

---

14 A certain degree of stability in relative prices, and especially in real exchange rates, may be valued as an international public good because it tends to enhance the information content of relative prices and to contribute to a more stable international monetary system [see, e.g., Frenkel et al., 1988].

15 The European Commission is in the process of drafting a proposal to harmonize the determination of the corporate base [see Kuiper, 1988].

16 In this connection, removing tax obstacles to cooperation between firms incorporated in different EC countries, including the tax discrimination against international mergers and joint ventures, is also important.

17 Steuerle [1989] emphasizes the link between improvements in financial and tax accounting.

18 Musgrave [1987] argues in favor of a uniform-rate corporation tax on the basis of interjurisdictional equity considerations. Equal rates would also make it possible to simultaneously attain capital import and capital export neutrality. Sinn [1989] maintains, however, that harmonizing the tax base is more important than achieving more uniform statutory tax rates. Slemrod [1990], in contrast, argues in favor of giving priority to harmonizing statutory rates over the tax base. Uniform statutory rates would eliminate the opportunities for tax arbitrage through purely financial transactions without requiring countries to harmonize their tax bases, which, in any case, is difficult to enforce.

important locational distortions. In particular, Table 4 indicates that tax wedges on equity-financed investments would still diverge significantly across EC countries under a plausible base harmonization scenario.[19] Hence, tax rate harmonization should complement a more uniform tax base in order to significantly reduce locational distortions. Partial harmonization is not very effective, in part because some countries that levy relatively high statutory rates provide more generous depreciation allowances to offset the adverse incentive effects of high statutory rates.

As an alternative to tax rate harmonization, a more consistent application of the residence principle has been advocated. This would neutralize the effects of tax rate differentials on locational decisions without requiring countries to harmonize their tax rates. However, administrative complications make the residence principle difficult to implement—just as they inhibit the integration of corporate and personal taxes on retained earnings.[20] Moreover, opportunities for imposing adverse externalities by attracting the corporate tax base would remain because a residence-based corporate income tax system would provide incentives to move corporate headquarters to low-tax countries.[21] These incentives could become especially important when European integration makes it easier for corporations to change their country of residence.

It has also been suggested that some EC countries could maintain tax rates above those in other member countries if EC countries adopted a system of unitary taxation, which uses formula apportionment to allocate profits across jurisdictions, because such a system would be expected to reduce the incentives facing multinational firms to use accounting devices to shift profits between nations.[22] However,

---

19 This finding is broadly consistent with the results in Devereux and Pearson [1989].

20 Bird [1988] and Giovannini [1989] propose moving to the residence principle by eliminating deferral of corporate taxes on the retained earnings of foreign subsidiaries. Mutén [1983] describes several practical problems that are associated with the elimination of deferral. Integrating personal taxes and corporate taxes on foreign source income poses similar practical problems. Devereux and Pearson [1989] discuss the advantages and disadvantages of several residence-based corporate tax systems.

21 See, for example, Musgrave [1987] and McLure [1989]. A residence-based system of capital income taxation would also distort the international allocation of savings in the presence of international tax rate differentials. Moreover, it would require residence countries to provide unlimited credits for foreign taxes—even if this involved a rebate. This might tempt source countries to increase taxes on foreign-owned capital because higher source taxes would result in a redistribution of tax revenues in favor of the source country without affecting investment incentives.

22 See, for example, Bird [1988] and McLure [1989]. States within federal countries generally rely on a system of formula apportionment. This system does not compute taxable income in each state but instead allocates nationwide profits of a company across states on the basis of variables that can be more easily measured than income, such as sales, payroll, and assets. Formula apportionment, therefore, provides only a proxy for taxable income. In the United States, apportionment formulas differ across states, thereby introducing the possibility of double taxation. Under unitary taxation, formula apportionment is extended to affiliated entities.

different tax rates would continue to create distortions because firms would still be able to use accounting devices and to change real decisions to influence the factors that enter the formula governing the apportionment. In addition, the appropriate assessment of the factors and the definition of the apportionable unit could give rise to costly negotiations and conflicts. Moreover, the administrative complications of a system of formula apportionment would be formidable in the face of different currencies and intra-EC differences in legal and accounting frameworks.[23]

Tax structures may converge in response to market pressures (i.e., tax competition) rather than to concerted harmonization. In particular, countries facing capital flight and the erosion of their tax base due to lower foreign rates may reduce their own tax rates.[24] In this connection, it is important to distinguish between *concerted* and *market-based* harmonization. Whereas it tends to mitigate locational distortions, tax competition may drive tax rates down to suboptimal levels if countries do not take into account spillover effects [see, e.g., Giovannini, 1989].[25] Low corporate taxes affect the entire income tax system: when lower corporate taxes reduce taxes on capital income, taxes on labor income also become more difficult to implement because a large gap between taxes on capital and labor income provides incentives to classify labor income as capital income. Accordingly, fiscal systems may become less efficient than if the EC countries coordinated their capital income taxes because governments are forced either to use more distortionary taxes[26] or to reduce certain productive public expenditures. Tax competition may also frustrate equity objectives, as governments are no longer able to use fiscal policy to redistribute income from mobile factors to immobile low-income groups and as the tax burden increasingly falls on immobile labor.[27] Furthermore, unbridled tax competition may harm interjurisdictional equity by putting EC countries with a large stock of public debt

---

23 See, for example, Kopits and Mutén [1984], Mutén [1988], and OECD [1979].

24 Other examples of spontaneous coordination include the introduction of a value-added tax in many countries and a trend toward lower marginal personal income tax rates. See Tanzi [1987b].

25 This is especially important if benefit taxes cannot be implemented because of the difficulty of matching taxes with marginal benefits from public goods. More generally, Bewley [1981] has shown that tax competition leads to an optimal provision of public goods only under rather restrictive conditions. For example, public goods cannot be produced under increasing returns to scale.

26 The corporate tax plays an important role in an efficient tax system because it collects taxes on rents earned by factors that are supplied inelastically, such as old capital. Moreover, the corporate tax helps prevent tax evasion by collecting taxes on equity income at source and by preventing agents from sheltering personal income in corporations.

27 See, for example, Oates and Schwab [1988]. Sinn [1989] argues that redistribution enhances efficiency because it compensates for missing insurance markets. Hence, tax competition would be inefficient because it would prevent governments from satisfying the needs of risk-averse EC residents.

and a small resource base in a disadvantageous position. This may tempt these countries to interfere with the process of economic integration within the EC.

Some have argued that tax competition is preferable to formal harmonization by policymakers.[28] If distortions in the political process[29] keep overall tax and expenditure levels above their optimal levels, tax competition could be welcomed on the grounds that the downward pressure on domestic tax levels would offset some of the built-in pressures to raise public expenditures and would promote greater efficiency in the public sector by forcing governments to examine their expenditures more critically. Indeed, leveling the playing field is not sufficient to produce an efficient fiscal system. The level of the playing field and, more generally, the structure of the harmonized fiscal system should be appropriate.

Another drawback of explicit tax harmonization is that it may prevent countries from experimenting with tax policies that may turn out to be beneficial. In view of lengthy and costly negotiation processes, it may also inhibit timely adjustments of taxes in response to changing economic circumstances [see, e.g., Siebert, 1989]. Indeed, if the EC had coordinated corporate tax rates in the early 1980s, it might have been unable to reduce these tax rates in line with the worldwide trend toward lower rates and base broadening.

Whether one prefers tax competition over concerted tax harmonization depends to a large extent on the scope for undertaking beggar-thy-neighbor policy actions and on one's perspective of the level of public expenditure, the working of the political process, and the importance of intra-and interjurisdictional equity objectives. In some cases, the benefits of retaining national discretion to adjust tax policy in accordance with national priorities may outweigh the costs associated with inadequate coordination [see Cnossen, 1987]. As regards corporate income taxation, however, the case for some kind of concerted harmonization among EC countries seems particularly strong. As discussed above, corporate tax competition may harm overall efficiency and revenue, as well as intra- and interjurisdictional equity. It may also result in undesirable macroeconomic spillover effects that threaten the stability of EC capital markets and tempt countries to interfere with free intra-EC trade and capital movements.

Several forms of concerted corporate tax rate harmonization, which should be complemented by base harmonization, are conceivable. In analogy to its recent suggestions regarding the standard VAT rate,[30] the Commission of the European

---

28 See, for example, McLure [1986], Cnossen [1988], and HM Treasury [1988].

29 These distortions may allow bureaucrats and pressure groups to promote their own objectives at the expense of constituencies. These arguments are closely related to the public choice perspective on federalism. This approach suggests that taxes should be levied at a local rather than a central level because factor mobility imposes more adequate constraints on a government's ability to extract rents from the private sector. See, for example, Brennan and Buchanan [1983].

30 See Commission of the European Communities [1989a].

Communities could fix a minimum statutory corporate rate, while allowing EC countries to freely set their rate above that minimum. The minimum rate would set a floor for the contribution of the corporate tax to equity and revenue objectives.[31] Rate harmonization toward the minimum rate may involve substantial changes, especially for the countries currently levying high rates. In order to avoid disruptive capital flows within the Community, EC countries should coordinate their corporate tax adjustments.[32] Minimum rates may differ across EC countries because differences in public expenditures, regulations, tax enforcement, inflation, opportunities to use debt financing, as well as externalities and other market distortions may justify some differences in tax rates.

In view of the global character of capital markets, EC corporate tax policy should depend to a large extent on policy actions taken by non-EC countries. Hence, any harmonization arrangement within the EC should be flexible enough to quickly respond to developments outside the EC.

4. Taxes on Cross-Border Portfolio Income

The international integration and liberalization of capital markets complicates the collection of personal taxes on capital income earned by EC residents. Interpersonal equity, efficiency, and revenue objectives all support the residence principle, according to which residents should pay the same tax on worldwide investment income, irrespective of whether the income originates domestically or abroad. In theory, all EC countries apply the residence principle. In practice, however, the principle is difficult to enforce because it requires cooperation from other countries in the form of exchange of information and administrative assistance. Many host countries do not collect the information and, therefore, cannot pass it on to other countries. Even if host countries were to collect it, bank secrecy laws would often constitute formidable obstacles to the reporting of portfolio capital income to foreign countries. As a result, portfolio capital flows typically bear only the source country tax, which tends to be relatively low.

---

31 Political agreement on the minimum rates may be difficult to achieve; countries with small public sectors (reflecting, for example, relatively low priorities for public goods and equity objectives), low stocks of public debt, and large resource endowments may prefer lower minimum rates than other countries would favor. Any EC country can veto tax proposals. Most other issues, in contrast, are decided by majority voting. Musgrave [1983] and McLure [1983] argue that corporate taxes should be collected on a central level. Therefore, a minimum rate may be complemented by a long-term target for complete harmonization of statutory rates. Ultimately, a central EC tax authority may collect the corporate tax at a single rate under either a tax or revenue sharing arrangement.

32 This can be done by strengthening EC surveillance of corporate taxation through exchange of information and through exertion of peer pressure within the regular ECOFIN meetings.

EC countries presently rely on several methods to collect taxes on portfolio income (Table 6). Belgium, France, Italy and Portugal have adopted various forms of withholding, while Denmark, France, the Netherlands, and the United Kingdom use mandatory income reporting to tax authorities. Withholding taxes on interest and dividend payments to foreigners depend on tax treaties. Remaining capital restrictions, especially those applying to short-term capital flows, protect revenues in France, Greece, Ireland, Italy, Portugal, and Spain. The planned removal of these restrictions by mid-1990[33] is likely to make portfolio flows an increasingly important vehicle for tax evasion and avoidance. Evasion may grow further as liberalization and technological advancements enable financial institutions to provide more financial services to foreign residents.

The growing integration of EC capital markets allows source countries to pursue beggar-thy-neighbor policies by encouraging foreigners to move their savings to their jurisdictions. In particular, by either levying low withholding taxes on portfolio income earned by nonresidents or by refusing to provide information to other countries, these countries erode foreign tax bases and attract financial intermediation from other countries.[34] If domestic firms have access to offshore financial centers, potential distortions in the intra-EC allocation of real capital may be limited to the financial sector. However, changes in the pattern of financial intermediation may have international macroeconomic implications and affect the conduct of monetary policy.[35]

These beggar-thy-neighbor policies also affect both inter- and intrajurisdictional equity. Affluent countries with low levels of public debt and large immobile tax bases (such as natural resources) are able to attract financial intermediation because they can afford lower tax rates on capital income. As regards intrajurisdictional equity, wealthy tax evaders can escape residence taxes by investing their capital abroad, while immobile factors, such as unskilled labor, and taxpayers who comply with the tax law are forced to finance an increasing share of public spending.

Beggar-thy-neighbor policies may jeopardize further deregulation because they may tempt the affected countries to impose controls.[36] Alternatively, residence countries may reduce capital income tax rates to levels in other countries. This, in turn, may further increase the scope for tax arbitrage. For example, if countries

---

33 Greece, Ireland, Portugal, and Spain have been granted temporary exceptions.

34 The fiscal positions of other countries may worsen further as tax revenue from financial intermediation declines and domestic interest rates on public debt rise. The location of financial activities is also affected by international differences in so-called implicit taxes such as reserve requirements and other regulations.

35 This is illustrated by the effects of the announcement, introduction, and subsequent repeal of a withholding tax on interest income in Germany.

36 France, for example, has threatened on several occasions to maintain some capital controls if other EC countries do not cooperate in enforcing taxes on capital income earned by French residents.

Table 6 — European Community: Rates of Taxation of Portfolio Investment Income of Resident Individuals, 1989 (percent)

	Bond interest		Dividends		Top marginal rate on long-term capital gains[a]	Reporting of financial investment income	Declaration in case of succession[b]	Restricted capital movement of individuals[c]
	rate of withholding	top marginal income tax rate or withholding if final	rate of withholding	top marginal income tax rate or withholding if final				
Belgium	25.0	25.0	25.0	25.0	0.0	No	Yes	N
Denmark	0.0	57.0	30.0	57.0	0.0[d]	Yes[e]	(Yes)	N[f]
France	26.0[g]	26.0	0.0	57.0	16.0[h]	Yes	Yes	D
West Germany	0.0	56.0/ 53.0[i]	25.0	56.0/ 53.0[i]	0.0j	No	Yes	N
Greece	0.0[k]	63.0	42.0[l]	42.0	0.0	No	(Yes)	A[m]
Ireland	0.0/ 32.0[n]	56.0	0.0	56.0	30.0[o]	No	(Yes)	ST[p]
Italy	12.5	12.5	10.0	56.0/ 53.0[i]	0.0	No	(Yes)	ST[q]
Luxembourg	0.0	56.0	15.0	56.0	0.0	No	No	N
Netherlands	0.0	72.0/ 60.0[i]	25.0	72.0/ 60.0[i]	0.0	Yes	(Yes)	N
Portugal	25.0	25.0	25.0	25.0[r]	0.0	No	Yes	A[s]
Spain	0.0/ 25.0[t]	66.0	25.0	66.0	66.0	Yes	(Yes)	ST[u]
United Kingdom	0.0/ 25.0[v]	40.0	0.0	40.0	40.0[w]	Yes[x]	No	N

[a]Capital gains on ordinary financial transactions. — [b](Yes), is used if declaration is not automatic but only upon request by the tax authority. — [c]N = none; D = deposits; A = all; ST = short-term. — [d]Stocks held over 3 years and bonds. — [e]Interest only. — [f]All foreign securities must be purchased through an authorized domestic financial intermediary. — [g]Including 1 percent social security contribution. — [h]If transactions do not exceed F288,400, capital gains are exempt. — [i]Current rate and proposed rate for 1990, respectively. — [j]Assets held over 6 months. — [k]In practice most bonds are tax exempt, though some should, in principle, be subject to a withholding tax at progressive rates of income tax. — [l]The rate applies to registered and quoted shares. — [m]Except for some ECU denominated bonds. — [n]Zero rate for government bonds. — [o]The acquisition cost is indexed to the CPI, and a 2,000 pound exemption applies. — [p]Bonds with a maturity of less than two years and foreign bank deposits. — [q]All assets with a maturity of less than six months and foreign bank deposits. All foreign securities must be purchased and held through an authorized domestic financial intermediary. — [r]A dividend credit of 7 percent can be claimed if dividend income is globalized with other income. — [s]Investment funds can acquire foreign securities up to a limit. — [t]Zero rate for treasury notes. — [u]Securities and deposits with maturity of less than one year. All foreign securities must be held through an authorized domestic financial intermediary. — [v]Zero rate for certain public loans. — [w]A 5,000 pound exemption applies. Capital gains taxed on a real rather than nominal basis. — [x]Bank interest only.

Source: Conseil National du Crédit [1988]; International Bureau of Fiscal Documentation [various issues]; and various national sources.

reduce taxes on interest income earned by foreigners below that imposed on domestic residents, they increase the incentives for cross-haulings of capital, which results in excessive financial intermediation.[37] Moreover, low effective taxes on interest income lead to an excessive reliance on debt financing, which may harm the overall efficiency and stability of the financial system.[38] Lowering tax rates on capital income in response to foreign tax policies affects the entire tax structure because, in view of the difficulties in distinguishing between some types of labor income and capital income, it raises the costs of maintaining higher tax rates on labor income.

In a liberalized environment, the taxation of portfolio flows requires international cooperation in order to preserve some degree of autonomy in national tax policy and to prevent beggar-thy-neighbor policies. Cooperation may involve either more effective source taxation through withholding or disclosure of capital income to residence countries through an international exchange of information. In principle, the latter method is preferable because it would not necessitate convergence of tax rates across countries.[39] However, the administrative realities described above complicate the consistent application of the residence principle.

While coordination in this area seems especially urgent, the EC depends on cooperation from non-EC countries in order to effectively tax portfolio capital income earned by EC residents. If more effective taxation of personal capital income is confined to income originating in the EC, financial services could migrate offshore to Switzerland, Liechtenstein, or other tax haven jurisdictions. Hence, tax evaders remain able to shift the tax burden to honest taxpayers who comply with the tax law, borrowers who do not have access to offshore centers, and immobile factors. Nevertheless, agreement within the EC may play a useful role in facilitating cooperation on a global scale.[40] Just as countries coordinate trade policy under

---

37 Dooley [1988] describes how residents, who are exposed to domestic taxation, and nonresidents, who have access to explicit or implicit government guarantees not available to residents, can engage in tax arbitrage resulting in large gross capital flows.

38 Corporate taxes withhold only equity income at source.

39 See Giovannini [1989]. More effective source taxation could complement this approach by ensuring that at least some tax is paid and by encouraging recipients of capital income to identify themselves to the tax authorities. Bird [1988] prefers more effective source taxation in view of administrative difficulties. Note also that, under the residence principle, international tax rate differentials can cause investors to change their country of residence.

40 The EC Commission intends to open negotiations with nonmember countries on these issues either bilaterally or within a multilateral framework such as the OECD. See Commission of the European Communities [1989b].

GATT, they may have to lay down additional rules of conduct regarding capital income taxation in a multilateral international convention.[41]

5. Interest Incomes and Deductions

Lending and borrowing decisions, both within and across countries, can be distorted by five factors: (a) tax evasion; (b) inflation; (c) the level and progressivity of income tax rates; (d) the way interest income is taxed; and, finally, (e) the tax treatment of interest expenses. In this section, we shall ignore tax evasion and briefly examine the other factors.[42]

The rates of inflation in the EC countries participating in the exchange rate mechanism of the EMS have converged in recent years. However, if we consider all EC countries, we still observe significant differences. The current range in inflation rates varies from about 1 percent in the Netherlands to 13 percent in Greece and Portugal. Personal income tax rates also continue to differ significantly in spite of recent or announced reductions. The top marginal rate, for example, ranges from around 40 percent to around 60 percent. The treatment of interest income is more uniform, although in some countries, for example, in Italy, final withholding taxes may be imposed on interest incomes (see Table 6). These taxes may be levied at lower rates than the income taxes on other income. However, they are imposed on gross interest incomes, i.e., without the benefit of deductions or personal exemptions.

EC countries continue to differ considerably in their tax treatment of interest deductions, especially with respect to interest paid on mortgage loans (Table 7). Together with significant differences in the personal tax treatment of imputed rental incomes (Table 8) and of capital gains on the sale of properties, they create a situation whereby, as obstacles to capital movements are removed, financial capital moves on the basis of tax rather than fundamental economic considerations.

Take for example a country with (a) a relatively high marginal tax rate on personal income and liberal deductibility of interest payments, (b) a lenient treatment of (imputed) rental income, and (c) low or no taxes on capital gains on the sale of properties. These factors create strong incentives to invest in housing—especially if some inflation still prevails. Table 9 illustrates this. Using a real

---

41 Countries that sign such a convention may have to subject countries that fail either to provide information or levy a minimum withholding tax to sanctions. Host countries could reduce withholding taxes only if income recipients presented proof that they had reported their income to a residence country that had signed the convention. Coordination in this area could go hand in hand with enhanced coordination in the area of regulation of international capital markets.

42 Detailed discussions of these aspects can be found in Tanzi [1987a; 1987c].

Table 7 — European Community: The Tax Treatment of Interest Expenses, 1985[a]

	Interest on loans for				
	investment or business purposes	home purchases or improvements		consumer purchases	Other purposes
		principal residence	secondary residence		
Belgium	TAFD	TAPD(0)	TAPD(0)	ND	ND
Denmark	TAFD	TAFD	TAFD	TAFD	TAFD
France	TAFD(B)	TCFD(C)	ND	ND	ND
West Germany	TAFD	TAFD	ND	ND	ND
Greece	TAFD	TAFD	ND	ND	ND
Ireland	TAFD(B)	TAFD(C)	ND	ND	ND(1)
Italy	ND	TAFD(C)	TAFD(C)	ND	ND
Luxembourg	TAFD	TAPD	TAPD	TAFD	TAFD(C)
Netherlands	TAFD	TAFD	TAFD	TAFD	TAFD
Portugal	ND	TAFD	TAFD	ND	ND
Spain	TAFD	TAFD	TAFD	ND	TAFD
United Kingdom	TAFD(B)	TAFD(C)	ND	ND	ND(1)

(a) TAFD = tax allowance fully deductible (i.e., tax allowance equivalent to the total amount of expenses); TAFD(B) = tax allowance fully deductible for interest on loans for business purposes only; TAPD = tax allowance partially deductible (i.e., tax allowance up to specified percentage of expenses); TCFD = tax credit fully deductible; ND = not deductible (or creditable); (C) = subject to a ceiling or maximum; (0) = fully deductible but only against associated income; (1) = except for certain limited classes of loans.

Source: OECD [1987].

(before-tax) rate of interest of 4 percent, it calculates the real after-tax borrowing rate on the basis of various assumptions about the inflation rate and the statutory marginal tax rate at which interest payments can be deducted from taxable income. On the basis of fairly realistic assumptions, the real after-tax cost of borrowing for high-income taxpayers can range from a positive 4 percent to a negative 4 percent.

Since a growing share of the EC population will be able to freely choose the place of residence, at least upon retirement, these tax incentives may also influence decisions on where people retire. Hence, if taxes are not to play a role in capital (and population) movements, some harmonization of the tax treatment of interest deductions and owner-occupied housing would seem necessary.

Table 8 — European Community: Imputed Rent on Owner-Occupied Housing under Personal Income Tax System, 1987

	Imputed rent included in taxable income	Valuation base[a]	Assessed rental rate (percent)
Belgium	Yes	cadastral value	4.0
Denmark	Yes	assessed value under net wealth tax	2.5 to 7.5
France	No	—	—
West Germany[b]	Yes	assessed value under net wealth tax	1.4
Greece	Yes	assessed value	4.0
Ireland	No	—	—
Italy	Yes	cadastral value	—
Luxembourg	Yes	—	—
Netherlands	Yes	market value (60 percent)	1.3
Portugal	Yes	market value	—
Spain	Yes	value under wealth tax	3.0
United Kingdom	No	—	—

[a]Repair and maintenance costs are generally deductible. — [b]Tax on imputed rent was removed in 1988.

Source: Based on unpublished information.

Table 9 — Real Borrowing Rates (percent)

Inflation rates	Marginal tax rates						
	0	10	20	30	40	50	60
0	4.0	3.6	3.2	2.8	2.4	2.0	1.6
1	4.0	3.5	3.0	2.5	2.0	1.5	1.0
2	4.0	3.4	2.8	2.2	1.6	1.0	0.4
3	4.0	3.3	2.6	1.9	1.2	0.5	–0.2
4	4.0	3.2	2.4	1.6	0.8	—	–0.8
5	4.0	3.1	2.2	1.3	0.4	–0.5	–1.4
6	4.0	3.0	2.0	1.0	—	–1.0	–2.0
7	4.0	2.9	1.8	0.7	–0.4	–1.5	–2.6
8	4.0	2.8	1.6	0.4	–0.8	–2.0	–3.2
9	4.0	2.7	1.4	0.1	–1.2	–2.5	–3.8
10	4.0	2.6	1.2	–0.2	–1.6	–3.0	–4.4

Not applicable : —.

Source: Calculations by authors based on methodology discussed in Tanzi [1987a].

6. Conclusions

Is harmonization desirable for capital income taxes? Given the reality of a single market with unrestrained capital movements and free movement of goods and services, the answer to the question is a qualified yes.

For without harmonization of capital income taxes, there would be several disadvantages:

- —The allocation of capital across countries would be inefficient because the rate of return to capital across countries would tend to be equalized *after* and not *before* taxes. In view of substantial differences in tax wedges across countries, the potential welfare losses associated with the inefficient allocation of capital could be significant.
- —Unilateral fiscal actions, for example, reducing the corporate income tax or changing the tax treatment of interest income or expense, could have major adverse effects on other EC countries. In fact, countries might increasingly use the tax system as an instrument to take advantage of other countries because other policy instruments (such as more capital restrictions, trade restrictions, or an independent monetary policy) would no longer be available. Such developments might lead to retaliation, a weakening of the Community, and an underprovision of some public services.
- —Countries may use the tax system to impose their political views in the economic sphere on others. More conservative governments may force tax and expenditure reductions or less progressive taxation in the EC as a whole. For example, a country that sharply decreases the rate of the corporate income tax would force similar reductions on others, which, in turn, would most likely lead to lower marginal tax rates on personal incomes. Countries with high public expenditures might also be forced to reduce these expenditures below the levels preferred by their electorates.
- —Unilateral changes might bring about potentially disruptive capital movements that would affect real exchange rates and, therefore, make the pursuit of fixed nominal exchange rates more difficult.

Is (capital income) tax competition desirable? The answer depends to a large extent on political views. If one prefers smaller government, or if one believes that the political process incorporates a bias toward higher taxes and public spending, one would welcome tax competition because it would tend to reduce tax levels and, one hopes, public spending. Furthermore, those who believe that taxes should not be imposed on capital incomes (and many economists today share this view) may also favor tax competition.

Tax competition, however, does place an element of compulsion on other countries, especially on those that attach a high priority to equity and revenue objectives. Countries that prefer a high level of public services may also be adversely affected as benefit taxes become more difficult to implement. Tax competition may also lead to less stable tax systems because of changes of government in major countries. For example, a change to a Labor government in the United Kingdom would force other countries to adjust to a different UK tax policy. Tax changes are costly and, when they affect many countries, should not be left totally to the discretion of a government.

Thus, given the reality of a unified market with (relatively) fixed exchange rates and free movement of capital and goods, some form of harmonization of taxes, and especially of taxes on capital income, seems desirable. However, it does not follow that *any* form of harmonization is desirable. In fact, harmonizing tax systems around an inefficient structure could be worse than no harmonization at all. As regards capital income taxation, harmonization could start with an agreement on the tax base. EC countries could then agree on at least a minimum statutory rate. These harmonization agreements could be reassessed at fixed intervals.

Bibliography

BENSON, Bruce L., Ronald N. JOHNSON, "Capital Formation and Interstate Competition." In: Dwight R. LEE (Ed.), Taxation and the Deficit Economy: Fiscal Policy and Capital Formation in the United States. Pacific Research Institute for Public Policy, San Francisco 1985, pp. 407-436.

BEWLEY, Truman F., "A Critique of Tiebout's Theory of Local Public Expenditures." Econometrica, Vol. 49, 1981, pp. 713-740.

BIRD, Richard M., "Shaping a New International Tax Order." Bulletin for International Fiscal Documentation, Vol. 42, 1988, pp. 292-299.

BOVENBERG, A. Lans, Krister ANDERSSON, Kenji ARAMAKI, Sheetal K. CHAND, "Tax Incentives and International Capital Flows: The Case of the United States and Japan." IMF Working Paper, WP/89/5, Washington, January 1989.

BRENNAN, Geoffrey, James BUCHANAN, "Normative Tax Theory for a Federal Polity: Some Public Choice Preliminaries." In: Charles E. McLure, Jr. (Ed.), Tax Assignment in Federal Countries. Australian National University, Center for Research on Federal Financial Relations, Canberra, 1983, pp. 52-65.

CNOSSEN, Sijbren, "Tax Structure Developments." In: Sijbren CNOSSEN (Ed.), Tax Coordination in the European Community. Deventer 1987, pp. 19-55.

—, "More Tax Competition in the European Community?" Paper presented at 44th Congress of the International Institute of Public Finance, Istanbul, August 1988.

COMMISSION OF THE EUROPEAN COMMUNITY [1989a], "Tax Measures to be Adopted by the Community in Connection with the Liberalization of Capital Movements." COM(89) 60/3/Revision final, Brussels, 12 May 1989.

— [1989b], "Completion of the Internal Market and Approximation of Indirect Taxes." COM(89) 260, Brussels, 18 May 1989.

CONSEIL NATIONAL DU CREDIT, La fiscalité de l'épargne dans le cadre du marché intérieur européen. Paris, June 1988.

DEVEREUX, Michael, Mark PEARSON, Corporate Tax Harmonization and Economic Efficiency. Institute for Fiscal Studies Report Series No. 35, London, October 1989.

DOOLEY, Michael P., "Capital Flight: A Response to Differences in Financial Risks." IMF Staff Papers, Vol. 35, 1988, pp. 422-436.

—, Peter ISARD, Fiscal Policy, Locational Decisions, and Exchange Rates. IMF Working Paper, WP/89/49, Washington, June 1989.

FRENKEL, Jacob A., Morris GOLDSTEIN, Paul R. MASSON, International Coordination of Economic Policies: Scope, Methods, and Effects. IMF Working Paper, WP/88/53, Washington, June 1988.

FUENTE, Angel de la, Edward GARDNER, Corporate Income Tax Harmonization and Capital Allocation in the European Community. IMF Working Paper, Washington, 1990 (forthcoming).

GIOVANNINI, Alberto, "National Tax Systems vs. the European Capital Market." Economic Policy, Vol. 4, 1989, pp. 345-386 .

GORDON, Roger H., "Taxation of Investment and Savings in a World Economy." The American Economic Review, Vol. 76, 1986, pp. 1087-1102.

GREENHOUSE, Steven, "Europe's Buyout Bulge." New York Times, Sunday, 5 November 1989, Section 3, p. 1.

HM TREASURY, Taxation in the Single Market: A Market-Based Approach. London, September 1988.

INTERNATIONAL BUREAU OF FISCAL DOCUMENTATION, European Taxation. Amsterdam, loose-leaf collection, various editions.

KOPITS, George, Leif MUTEN, "The Relevance of the Unitary Approach for Developing Countries." In: Charles E. McLURE, Jr. (Ed.), The State Corporation Income Tax. Stanford 1984.

KUIPER, Willem, "EC Commission Proposes a Directive on the Harmonization of Rules for the Determination of Taxable Profits of Enterprises." European Taxation, Vol. 28, 1988, pp. 319-329.

McLURE, Charles E., Jr., "Assignment of Corporate Income Taxes in a Federal System." In: Charles E. McLURE, Jr. (Ed.), Tax Assignment in Federal Countries. The Australian National University, Centre for Research on Federal Financial Relations, Canberra 1983, pp. 101-124.

—, "Tax Competition: Is What's Good for the Private Goose also Good for the Public Gander?" National Tax Journal, Vol. 39, 1986, pp. 341-348.

—, "Economic Integration and European Taxation of Corporate Income Taxation at Source: Some Lessons from the U.S. Experience." European Taxation, Vol. 29, 1989, pp. 243-250.

MUSGRAVE, Peggy B., "Interjurisdictional Coordination of Taxes on Capital Income." In: Sijbren CNOSSEN (Ed.), Tax Coordination in the European Community, Deventer 1987, pp. 197-225.

MUSGRAVE, Richard A., "Who Should Tax, Where, and What?". In: Charles E. McLURE, Jr. (Ed.), Tax Assignment in Federal Countries. The Australian National University, Centre for Research on Federal Financial Relations, Canberra 1983, pp. 2-19.

MUTEN, Leif, "Some Topical Issues Concerning International Double Taxation." In: Sijbren CNOSSEN (Ed.), Comparative Tax Studies: Essays in Honor of Richard Goode. Amsterdam 1983, pp. 417-442.

—, "A New International Tax Order?" Bulletin for International Fiscal Documentation, Vol. 42, 1988, pp. 471-472.

OATES, Wallace E., Robert M. SCHWAB, The Allocative and Distributive Implications of Local Fiscal Competition. University of Maryland Working Paper, College Park, Maryland, June 1988.

ORGANIZATION FOR ECONOMIC COOPERATION AND DEVELOPMENT (OECD), Transfer Pricing and Multinational Enterprises. Paris 1979.

—, Taxation in Developed Countries. Paris 1987.

PAPKE, James A., Leslie E. PAPKE, "Measuring Differential State-Local Tax Liabilities and Their Implications for Business Investment Location." National Tax Journal, Vol. 39, 1986, pp. 357-366.

PRICE WATERHOUSE, Corporate Taxes: A Worldwide Summary. New York, various issues.

SIEBERT, Horst, "The Harmonization Issue in Europe: Prior Agreement or a Competitive Process?" In: Horst SIEBERT (Ed.), The Completion of the Internal Market. Symposium 1989. Tübingen 1990, pp. 53-75.

SINN, Hans-Werner, The Policy of Tax-cut-cum-base-broadening: Implications for International Capital Movements. Paper presented at 43rd Congress of the International Institute of Public Finance, Paris, August 1987.

—, Tax Harmonization and Tax Competition in Europe. Invited paper presented at the Fourth Annual Congress of the European Economic Association, Augsburg, September 1989.

SLEMROD, Joel, "Tax Principles in an International Economy." In: Michael J. BOSKIN and Charles E. McLURE, Jr. (Eds.), World Tax Reform. International Center for Economic Growth, San Francisco 1990, pp. 11-23.

STEUERLE, Eugene, Capital Income and the Future of the Income Tax. Paper presented at International Seminar in Public Economics on the Future of Personal Income Taxation, Erasmus University, Rotterdam, January 1989.

TANZI, Vito [1987a], Income Taxes, Interest Rate Parity, and the Allocation of International Savings in Industrial Countries. IMF Working Paper, WP/87/53, Washington, August 1987, published in: Antonio PISTONE (Ed.), Tax Policy and Economy. Padova 1987, pp. 113-132.

— [1987b], "The Response of Other Industrial Countries to the U.S. Tax Reform Act." National Tax Journal, Vol. 40, 1987, pp. 339-355.

— [1987c], "The Tax Treatment of Interest Incomes and Expenses in Industrial Countries: A Discussion of Recent Changes." In: Frederick D. STOCKER (Ed.), Proceedings of the 80th Annual Conference 1987. National Tax Association—Tax Institute of America, Pittsburg, November 8-11, 1987, pp. 128-136.

—, A. Lans BOVENBERG, "Economic Interdependence and the International Implications of Supply-Side Policies." In: Gerhard FELS, George M. von FURSTENBERG (Eds.), A Supply-Side Agenda for Germany. New York 1989, pp. 153-180.

—, Teresa TER-MINASSIAN, "The European Monetary System and Fiscal Policies." In: Sijbren CNOSSEN (Ed.), Tax Coordination in the European Community, Deventer 1987, pp. 337-357.

Comment on Vito Tanzi and A. Lans Bovenberg, "Is There a Need for Harmonizing Capital Income Taxes within EC Countries?"

Pascal Salin

The paper by Tanzi and Bovenberg gives a comprehensive account of the present taxation of capital income in the EC countries and of the arguments in favor or against tax harmonization, their own inclination being rather in favor of some harmonization. The paper is well informed and well balanced, maybe too much so in my opinion. As regards myself, I shall take a less balanced view and I shall explain why I am firmly against any harmonization of capital income taxes.[1]

I have used this general view to express my opposition to a common monetary policy or tax harmonization, especially VAT harmonization. See, for instance, Salin [1980; 1984].

The debate on tax harmonization is too frequently restricted to the consideration of apparent tax rates, although it is essential to consider the existence of tax-shifts and the use of public resources in order to analyze any tax system (Section 1). Moreover, there are some confusions between the claim in favor of tax harmonization and the desirable suppression of (national) tax distortions (Section 2). Finally, I stress the role of the "political market" in designing tax systems (Section 3).

1. The Equalization of After-Tax Returns

According to Tanzi and Bovenberg, without harmonization of capital income taxes, "the allocation of capital across countries would . . . tend to be equalized *after* and not *before* taxes" (p. 193), and this allocation would be inefficient because fewer investments would take place in the high-rate countries if capital were mobile, in spite of higher before-tax returns. Although one must agree that there is equalization of *after-tax* returns, it does not follow that the allocation of capital is inefficient when there is tax diversity. In fact, one cannot evaluate this situation without taking

---

1 More generally, I am against any harmonization policy within the EC. As I have expressed on several occasions, the argument in favor of harmonization usually rests on a wrong definition of a common market and a confusion between competition — which allows market integration — and the harmonization of the conditions of production. A common market implies competition, it does not imply the harmonization of the conditions of production. When there is freedom of entry to a market, different producers can compete, although they are in different environments and subject to different conditions of production.

the structure of public expenditures, as well as possible tax-shifts, into consideration.

a. Provision of Specific Public Services to Capital

We may assume, first, that a government provides services to capital (for instance, safety or communication services), so that a capital income tax is a sort of user tax. Thus, it may happen that taxes on capital income are low in country *A*, but firms must pay to use roads, to educate their staff, to get security services, etc. In country *B*, there is public provision of these services, but taxes are high. When choosing where to locate their activities, owners of capital take these bundles of benefits and taxes into consideration, and not only specific taxes.

In this sense, there is an international equalization of returns which does not correspond to what is usually called an "optimal allocation" (from the point of view of an external observer who is assumed to have a perfect knowledge of all costs and benefits), but to some subjective optimum. Whenever there is competition, individuals can choose the specific bundles of goods and bads which they prefer, such that there is equalization of *their own* marginal utilities over all the different possible places of location. This means that allocative optimality cannot be measured.

Thus, the diversity of capital income taxes may only be the counterpart of the diversity in the services given by various governments to capital owners. To be sure, governments sell complex goods and it is difficult to evaluate to what extent these goods constitute benefits for capital owners. However, given that information is so poor, there is no a priori reason to believe that an administrative process of harmonization would imply convergence to a situation in which there would be a better correspondence between taxes and benefits. It may also be stressed that, if capital income taxes are considered to be payments for specific services given to capital owners, it would be better justified to have a tax on the total activity of the firm and/or a tax on capital than a tax on profits, such as the corporate income tax. Therefore, it would be more important to replace or to suppress some of the present taxes than to harmonize their rates.

Thus, our provisional conclusion is that there is *no need for harmonization*. The sole comparison of taxes and tax rates between countries does not give significant information on the factors of investment choices and possible "distortions" in capital allocation.

b. Transfer Policies

Let us assume now that public expenditures benefit mainly citizens and contribute to their general welfare (public goods) or to their specific needs (distribution policy) and that a capital income tax cannot be analyzed as a user charge. According to the usual view — broadly adopted by Tanzi and Bovenberg — there is a risk of capital flight and a need for harmonization in order to obtain a better allocation of capital and a "fair" distribution of the burden of taxation.

In an integrated market in which capital and commodities are mobile, there is normally an after-tax equalization of returns, as well as an equalization of commodity prices. This means that, if the rate of a capital income tax, such as the corporate income tax, is ever raised in a country, commodity prices and after-tax rates of return being determined from outside, the burden of the tax is shifted to the less mobile factors, for instance, to wage-earners. Thus, they pay the tax indirectly in the form of lower returns, instead of paying it more explicitly, for instance, in the form of an income tax or a VAT. Under certain conditions, a corporate income tax, an income tax or a VAT are equivalent ways to tax production factors. The actual after-tax return of a production factor depends on its relative international mobility.

In any case, there is no more reason to harmonize capital income taxes than there is to harmonize income taxes or VAT rates. Moreover, the diversity of rates for the corporate income tax — or any capital income tax — does not create a distortion in the allocation of capital insofar as the burden of taxation is shifted to other factors of production. Once more we do not know exactly to what extent various factors of production are mobile and to what extent tax shifts do occur. However, this lack of information is not a justification for harmonization, quite the contrary.

c. Place of Taxation

This raises the problem of the place of taxation, which is touched upon by Tanzi and Bovenberg. As an example, let us take the case in which all taxes serve to finance distributive activities. As is underlined by Tanzi and Bovenberg, it would not be fair that some citizens avoid paying the tax by evading towards other countries. However, if the only aim of public expenditures and taxes were to determine changes in income distribution, the taxation system ought to be designed so that *individuals* would have to pay for other individuals. Therefore, any justification for taxes such as corporate income taxes or interest income taxes disappears: it is meaningless to ask capital or capital income to pay for the welfare of some individuals, since neither of these are endowed with will and mind. If public policy aims at distribution, one ought not to tax specific *activities* but to tax *individuals*. The very reason for what appears to be tax evasion is that the tax structure does not correspond precisely to the assumed role of the state. One does not correct this built-in error by harmonizing taxes. In fact, such a tax system exists because it is easier for politicians to tax activities and firms than to tax individuals: the tax is less visible and less burdensome. It makes tax illusion possible.

d. Tax Harmonization or Tax Reform?

More generally, the tax structure in a country ought to correspond to the expenditure structure. For instance, the ratio of "personal taxation" to "activity taxation" ought to correspond to the ratio between distribution expenditures and allocation expenditures. To make it simple, if, for instance, in country *A*, one half of expenditures were supposed to be made for distribution reasons and one half to produce safety services for capital, a personal tax (lump-sum tax or income tax) ought to represent one half of total taxes, and a capital tax the other half. In such a case, there would not be any reason for capital flight. The personal tax would allow the distribution policy between individuals located in a given country, whereas the capital income tax would correspond to a user charge. In other words, insofar as distribution were the target of public policy, citizens would have to contribute as citizens and not as possible owners of capital.

If such a correspondence between expenditures and taxes did exist in European tax systems — different countries being characterized by different mixes of distribution and allocation policies — the sole harmonization of capital income taxes would introduce distortions between the expenditure side and the revenue side. As we do not know to what extent the structure of taxation in the present EC countries does correspond to the structure of expenditures, no general plea in favor of harmonization can be justified. And, if we ever had reasons to believe that the structure of expenditures and the structure of taxation do not correspond, the solution would not be harmonization, but tax reform in each country.

The fact that investors declare in surveys that taxes influence their decisions — as is stressed by Tanzi and Bovenberg (p. 172) — does not prove anything. Investors certainly take taxes into consideration, as they do wages and all other production costs. However, they do not know what these costs would be under different tax systems, since changes in tax rates or in tax structures would be shifted to these costs in an unknown way. (Wages, for instance, are not the same when public expenditures are financed by a VAT, an income tax or a corporate tax.)

2. Distortions in Tax Systems

Arguments in favor of harmonization implicitly assume that existing tax systems are "optimal," so that an increase in the mobility of capital — due, for instance, to the suppression of former exchange controls — would cause undesirable capital flows if tax rates were not "harmonized."

However, existing tax systems are not optimal and they include a lot of "distortions," for instance, specific taxes or specific rates to be paid for some specific activities or specific forms of savings. The corporate income tax, which I have already mentioned, is one example of this. Quite often, there is also an overtaxation of savings through the income tax, insofar as that part of an income which is consumed is taxed only once, whereas the saved part gives birth to future returns that may enter into the definition of future incomes and be taxed as such. This distortion in the respective taxation of consumption and savings is greater, the more progressive the income tax is. Just because people do not generally know that income tax is a tax on savings, they do not claim that income tax rates have to be harmonized. The usual discussion about harmonization focuses on appearances — for instance, the diversity of corporate income taxes, although after-tax returns may be equalized by the market — and not on important, but less visible "distortions," for instance, those which may exist in all countries between consumption and savings (which does not mean, anyhow, that these "distortions" ought to be harmonized).

For the time being, most European tax systems are overtaxing savings and capital. Therefore, the "average" tax structure ought not to be the norm towards which all national systems should converge. The only valid criterion for tax reform is a better tax structure in each country.

Many of the taxes that Tanzi and Bovenberg discuss as candidates for harmonization are not justified because they introduce specific distortions. This is the case, for instance, with the corporate income taxes when there are no equivalent tax credits for the payment of the income tax, with the income tax and with the double taxation of savings, etc. The taxes would have to be modified or suppressed, for internal reasons, *with or without* the present process of European integration. But one does not suppress distortions by harmonizing them. If a tax is stupid, it is no less stupid because it is generalized and harmonized.

In fact, the plea in favor of harmonization stems mainly from authorities who, for a long time, have been able to tax captive sources of revenues (due to exchange controls and other similar policy measures) and who fear that the process of liberalization in Europe will suppress this situation of "tax slavery." In order to maintain at least part of their power to spoliate captive resources, they try to convince other countries to implement tax structures similar to their own.[2]

The problem I am discussing is much similar to that of protection. As it has long been demonstrated, there is no justification for protection, and it is a costly way of levying taxes. When protection is suppressed, the state looses tax revenues, and there is a reshuffling of trade flows that could be labelled a "commodity flight," to

2 From this point of view, a footnote in Tanzi and Bovenberg's paper is quite characteristic. According to them, "The corporate tax plays an important role in an efficient tax system because it collects taxes on rents earned by factors that are supplied inelastically, such as old capital" (footnote 37). This sentence stresses quite clearly that old capital cannot escape taxation — it is an enslaved source of taxation — and that the tax system has to exploit such a situation. However, the use of the term "efficient" is completely misleading: it is easy for the state to extort resources from a captive source, but this does not mean that it is fair or efficient for the taxpayers.

use a term parallel to that of "capital flight." However, the citizens benefit from these changes in trade flows and tax systems (even if one assumes that a fairer and more "efficient" tax replaces the former customs duties, so that total public revenues are unchanged). Similarly, the liberalization of capital flows implies a possible loss of revenues for the state and a gain for citizens, since they can obtain higher returns on their savings.

It is generally possible to find ways to diminish or to suppress distortions. Thus, a general expenditure tax would be a way to suppress the double taxation of savings that results from taxing income.[3] Meanwhile it would solve the problem of tax evasion: in such a case, it would not matter for a government whether savings were invested in the home country or abroad, since there would be an incentive for the taxpayer to declare the savings which are invested abroad. Savers would not be penalized for looking for the best allocation of their resources.

Other papers in the present volume (for instance, those by Cnossen or Razin and Sadka) stress not only that tax diversity is defensible, but also that, in such a case, some tax coordination is necessary (for instance, as regards the exchange of information between national tax administrations). But I believe that tax coordination only appears necessary in tax systems which are not optimal. The fewer distortions there are in a tax system, the less necessary tax coordination is. Thus, the replacement of an income tax by a general expenditure tax would suppress the double taxation of savings and would make the exchange of information between tax administrations useless, since people would have an incentive to declare their investments abroad. Whenever a tax system is not "optimal" (from the point of view of citizens), individuals try to evade taxes and the authorities are compelled to take measures to thwart evasion. In such a second-best world, tax coordination may appear desirable. But it would be preferable to improve the tax system.

According to Cnossen (in the same volume), if we want tax diversity — which he considers acceptable — we need some degree of tax coordination, but it is difficult to determine exactly the extent of this coordination. To me, the answer is quite clear: the optimal degree of tax coordination is zero. As Hayek has frequently emphasized, "competition is a coordination process." This concept might also be applied to tax problems: tax competition is the best way to "coordinate" tax systems. Instead of "coordinating" second-best tax systems via centralized and badly informed processes, it is better to obtain a gradual improvement of all tax systems via competition and the information it brings.

Tax decisions always have to be evaluated according to their own merits and not in comparison with what exists in other countries. Individual producers do not consider the "do-as-your-neighbor" criterion to be a valid criterion for decisions. In a competitive setting, they adopt their own criteria and they try to do better than

---

3 I develop arguments in favor of a general expenditure tax in my book [Salin, 1985].

others. Why should this "do-as-your-neighbor" criterion become justified and allow allocative efficiency and social justice when applied to public decisions? *Therefore, there is no need for tax harmonization, but there is a need for better tax systems.*

3. The Working of the Political Market

The need for improved tax systems is not unknown to Tanzi and Bovenberg, since, according to them, harmonization ought to be in the direction of a "good tax structure" (p. 172). But politicians — those who decide tax rates — do not aim at attaining "good taxes." What they aim at is to extract the highest possible resources from the taxpayers at the least visible cost. They do not know the problems of tax incidence, and they have no incentive to adopt good tax structures.

Therefore, there is no hope that a coordinated process of harmonization between people who do not aim at good tax structures at the national level could bring about a good harmonized tax structure. The process of harmonization or coordination is, in reality, decided by a collusion of people who, more or less, aim at a bad tax structure. Would it not be preferable to make it possible for citizens who, in a given country, benefit from a relatively better tax structure to keep their relative advantage (i.e., their relatively lower level of spoliation)? Spoliation is always spoliation: harmonized spoliation by cooperative actions — i.e., by means of a cartel — is still spoliation.

No one is inclined to behave "correctly" on all occasions, unless he is pushed by his own interests. Competition is the best way to constrain people so that their decisions benefit others. Authorities must also be constrained to improve the tax system, either by constitutional rules (preventing, for instance, tax discrimination or the overtaxation of savings) or by competition. When there is tax competition and a bad tax system is adopted, then tax bases vanish. In this sense, one cannot say that there is a *risk* of capital flow diversion to countries with lower taxes. It is an *opportunity* for the owners of capital. Governments have "tax slaves" and they want to keep them. As capital is more mobile than labor, governments are more concerned by capital flights than they are by brain drain.

4. Conclusion

I certainly belong to the category of people who believe in a spontaneous process of harmonization caused by tax competition. But competition does not imply that all tax systems would converge towards a unique model. There can be different desired mixes of public expenditures and taxes, and there can be different equivalent tax structures (since different taxes can be different ways of collecting resources from the same individuals).

Tanzi and Bovenberg are mainly concerned with ways of preventing tax evasion. Contrary to them, I am in favor of what is *called* tax evasion, insofar as it allows individuals to escape from spoliating and discriminatory tax systems. I understand Tanzi and Bovenberg's concern. However, I cannot accept that they call it "allocative efficiency."

Bibliography

SALIN, Pascal, European Monetary Unity: For Whose Benefit? Ipswich 1980.

— (Ed.), Currency Competition and Monetary Union. The Hague 1984.

—, L'arbitraire fiscal. Paris 1985.

—, The Case Against Tax Harmonization. Report prepared for the Conference on "Global Disequilibrium," McGill University, Montreal, 17-19 May 1989 (forthcoming).

HAYEK, Friedrich August von, Law Legislation and Liberty, Vol. 2, The Mirage of Social Justice. London 1976.

Comment on Vito Tanzi and A. Lans Bovenberg, "Is There a Need for Harmonizing Capital Income Taxes within EC Countries"

Horst Siebert

Locational competition in a Tiebout world is an important aspect of tax competition. We cannot analyze tax competition and neglect the provision of public goods. The discussion so far has ignored the expenditure side of government taxation. I agree with Sijbren Cnossen that this is a crucial point, since the locational decision of firms is influenced by the public goods supplied as well as by the taxes paid. Indeed, there might very well be a willingness to pay for high quality public goods.

Tax competition or institutional competition has to be analyzed in a broader framework that includes the supply of public goods. Such a broader model of institutional competition contains the following elements. The government provides public goods such as the transportation infrastructure (roads, ports, airports), the communications infrastructure (telephone system), basic research and the educational system. In an even broader context, other public goods or even merit goods may be considered, for instance, museums and other forms of cultural infrastructure. These public goods are specific to a country. They are an argument in the production function; they may also be an argument in the utility function of a national policymaker.[1]

Public goods are financed by taxes, for instance, corporate income tax and other taxes, such as payroll taxes. Some factors of production are mobile, such as capital, technical knowledge in the form of blueprints, and very highly skilled managerial labor. Other factors of production are immobile, such as land, most forms of labor, and environmental endowment.

Taxes, among other things, determine the rates of return on the mobile and the immobile factors of production; they influence the attractiveness of a country. But taxes are not the whole story. Public goods also influence the attractiveness of a country. Locational competition is a competition of the immobile factors for the mobile factor. In locational competition, both tax rates and the provision of public goods play a role.

High corporate taxes drive away private capital, but the provision of public goods may ease production or attract qualified people; thus, public goods will attract

---

1 See $v(G)$ in Giovannini's [1989] equation [1], and G^H in Razin and Sadka's [1989] equation [1], where public goods enter directly in the utility function $U=U(C) + V(G)$. Alternatively, public goods may enter the production function of firms or the macroeconomic production function, such that $U=U(C)$, with $C=f(Y)$ and $Y=h(G)$.

capital. When public goods are an argument in the production function or in the utility function, tax competition does not lead to zero taxation. When public goods are provided, firms are willing to pay taxes. There is a balance between the burden and the benefit of taxation. This calculation of benefit taxation is relevant when the beneficiary of a public good and its payer are identical. Things become more complicated if the user and the payer are not identical, for instance, when the transportation infrastructure is financed by general taxes.

In a Tiebout world [Tiebout, 1956], the users of a public good are willing to pay for such a good. The Tiebout model shows that in a nation consisting of a large number of communities, each with its own mix of local public goods and local taxation and with costless mobility, the optimal level of local public goods will be provided, and the nation's residents will locate in an efficient manner. The driving force in the model is the mobility of production factors. Although the original Tiebout model is not always explicit in its claims, and although its empirical verification causes problems,[2] the intuitive appeal of the model is clear: it can be easily generalized to a world with a large number of countries. Here, the result of perfect mobility of factors is also an optimal provision of public goods.[3]

In a Tiebout world, competing with public goods and their financing does not create a problem. Each country chooses its optimal supply of public goods and the corresponding method of financing. When the taxation becomes excessive, capital goes elsewhere, and taxation is corrected. When the supply of public goods is too small, capital leaves the country as well.[4]

This paradigm can easily be applied to environmental quality. In the absence of spillover effects, there is no need for the harmonization of environmental policies [Long, Siebert, 1989; Siebert, 1989]. It seems to me that the paradigm of policy competition is more useful than the strategic trade literature, in which it is maintained that countries compete with export subsidies [Brander, Spencer, 1985].

Most immobile production factors supplied by governments are not public goods, but *clubgoods*, which can in principle be financed with user charges. Therefore, policy competition in the provision of public goods and in taxes has an important institutional aspect. This is the issue of fiscal equivalence [Olson, 1969], i.e., the problem of finding the correct institutional arrangement of financing a spatially limited public good. Apparently, this institutional setting cannot be taken as given. The communications infrastructure, for instance, the telephone services, may be privatized; then we no longer have an issue of policy competition. Immobile private goods, like communications services, imply nationally differentiated prices. This may also hold for other public goods that can be interpreted as clubgoods, such

2 See, e.g., Oates [1969] for an empirical test, and Edel and Sclar [1974] for criticism.

3 Note that the mobility of factors *itself* should not generate externalities.

4 Note that in the Tiebout world, people can also move and vote with their feet.

as roads and airports. They can all be financed by user charges. Thus, one can envisage an institutional arrangement in which user charges finance roads, ports, airports and other "public" goods. For instance, roads may be financed by imposing a mileage tax on cars for using the roads and an emissions tax on cars for polluting the environment. For such a scenario, the issue of tax competition vanishes; it has become a matter of differentiated prices for immobile private goods. And different prices for immobile factors of endowment are a regular part of trade theory.

Bibliography

BRANDER, James A., Barbara J. SPENCER, "Export Subsidies and International Market Share Rivalry." Journal of International Economics, Vol.16, 1985, pp. 83-100.

EDEL, Matthew, Elliot SCLAR, "Taxes, Spending and Property Values: Supply Adjustment in a Tiebout-Oates Model." Journal of Political Economy, Vol. 82, 1974, pp. 941-954.

GIOVANNINI, Alberto, "Reforming Capital Income Taxation in the Open Economy: Theoretical Issues." In: Horst SIEBERT (Ed.), Reforming Capital Income Taxation. Tübingen 1990, this volume.

LONG, Ngo Van, Horst SIEBERT, Institutional Competition versus Ex-Ante Harmonization: The Case of Environmental Policy. Kiel Institute of World Economics, Kiel Working Papers, 396, October 1989.

OLSON, Mancur, "The Principle of 'Fiscal Equivalence': The Division of Responsibilities among Different Levels of Government." The American Economic Review, Papers and Proceedings, Vol. 59, 1969, pp. 479-487.

OATES, Wallace E., "The Effects of Property Taxes and Local Public Spending on Property Values: An Empirical Study of Tax Capitalization and the Tiebout Hypothesis." Journal of Political Economy, Vol. 77, 1969, pp. 957-971.

RAZIN, Assaf, Efraim SADKA, International Tax Competition and Gains from Tax Harmonisation. Foerderer Institute for Economic Research, Tel-Aviv University, Working Paper No. 37-89, Ramat Aviv, October 1989.

SIEBERT, Horst, Europe '92. Environmental Policy in an Integrated Market. Kiel Institute of World Economics, Kiel Working Papers, 365, March 1989.

TIEBOUT, Charles M., "A Pure Theory of Local Expenditures." Journal of Political Economy, Vol. 64, 1956, pp. 416-424.

Sijbren Cnossen

On the Direction of Tax Harmonization in the European Community

1. Introduction

Tax harmonization may be compared with cartelization. Cartelization is a process whereby independent industrial enterprises form a syndicate to secure a monopoly in a specific world market. As a result, a higher price is "extorted" from other producers and consumers than would be possible under competitive conditions. Equally, tax harmonization may be described as a process whereby governments of independent nation-states conclude agreements on the level and the structure of their tax systems: the type of tax that will be levied, the basis of assessment that will be employed, and the rates that will be applied. It is then possible that the tax burden is raised to a higher level than would have been the case without the agreement.

Although every comparison can be faulted to some extent, it cannot be denied that tax harmonization looks surprisingly like cartelization. Yet, thus far, tax harmonization, unlike "smelly" cartelization, has had an aura of great respectability. It is ardently propagated by the Commission of the European Communities, which believes that the approximation and equalization of the taxes on products and profits in the various member states is a necessary condition for the formation of a single, integrated market in which competition and economies of scale will promote greater prosperity.

The opposite of tax harmonization is tax competition.[1] Proponents of the theory of public choice who support tax competition liken governments to market place participants competing for scarce resources. In the proponents' view, tax competition is a virtue, as it restrains the unbridled growth of the public sector and promotes efficiency in the use of government finances. In short, competition in the private and the public sector are two cuts from the same cloth. Support for this position can be gathered from an increasing number of studies which show that, at the margin,

---

Remark : I am indebted to A. Lans Bovenberg for his stimulating comments on an earlier draft of this paper.

1 For a flavor of the issues in respect of product taxes, see Siebert [1989].

a high tax burden significantly slows down saving and investment, and hence economic growth.

Tax harmonization and tax competition may be viewed as polar cases of tax coordination which, particularly in the context of the European Community (EC), may be described as a process aimed at removing the tax obstacles to the formation of a common market, such that the member states retain maximum flexibility in arranging their own tax system. Tax coordination permits tax diversity, which seems to accord better with the principal objectives of the Community than tax harmonization interpreted, as is usually done, as tax uniformity, or than tax competition, which, per force, would also lead to the convergence of the various tax systems.

Against this background, the following section of this paper discusses the principles that should govern the coordination of the taxes that are levied by the Community's member states. Next, the main achievements in the field of tax harmonization since the Community was established in 1958 are sketched. Then, some arguments for the preferability of tax diversity to tax uniformity are reviewed. There may even be some reasons why a dose of tax competition among member states might do no harm. Following this, the starting points and contours of the minimum level of tax coordination that seems desirable are sketched. The paper ends with some concluding thoughts.

2. Principles of Tax Coordination

An important rule of "good" tax conduct that the member states of the EC should adhere to is that their tax systems should have as few cross-border effects as possible. Taxes whose incidence is on the residents of other member states should not be allowed. Basically, tax burden export should be prohibited. Without this rule competition would be distorted and retaliatory measures might be taken, which would make the envisaged cooperation a negative sum game.[2]

Import and export duties are the most obvious examples of tax burden export. Imposed on imports, they decrease the price that the foreign producer receives; imposed on exports, they increase the price that the foreign consumer or producer has to pay. In a common market, therefore, such duties should simply be forbidden. Tax burden export, however, may also occur in respect of sales taxes and excises (hereafter referred to as indirect taxes) if the tax incorporated in the price of exports

2 For a fascinating exposition of the tax principles that should govern the relationships between independent countries and the states of a federation, as well as the appropriate tax assignment rules in each situation, see Musgrave [1983]. This book has a number of interesting contributions on the fiscal system in federal countries, such as the United States, Canada, Germany, Switzerland and Australia, which are of interest in shaping the thinking on these issues in the European Community.

is not rebated, or if the tax on imports is higher than the tax on similar, domestically produced goods and services. For these reasons, indirect taxes in a common market should be so designed that "border tax adjustments" can be effected precisely, fully, and without delay. In other words, taxes on goods and services should be applied according to the destination principle: only the member states where the product is finally consumed or used should be allowed to levy them.[3]

The importance of full border tax adjustments on the basis of the destination principle deserves some emphasis. The basic rationale is that a destination-based tax, which is added to price, will not affect intra-community trade because such a tax does not change the relative prices faced by the consumer or the producer in the importing member state. As a result, taxes on goods and services will not influence the choice of a manufacturing location.[4] The law of comparative advantage then continues to hold because every member state will carry on producing those goods which it can produce cheaper than other member states. As a result, all member states will enjoy a higher real income than would be possible if, on account of the tax (and not because of increasing cost conditions), they had also produced goods and services that could have been made cheaper elsewhere.

Of course, the prohibition on tax burden export is also applicable to taxes on income and profits (hereafter referred to as direct taxes). As is well known, the primary entitlement to these taxes may be assigned to either (a) the member state in which the recipient of the income or the profits lives or resides (domicile principle), or (b) the member state in which the income or the profits accrue (source principle). These principles are not each other's alternative, but in practice they coexist. Generally, the domicile principle is applied in respect of the income from portfolio investments (dividends, interest), while the source principle is applied in respect of the income from direct investments (holdings, permanent establishments) of, for instance, corporations. The domicile principle fits a personal, progressive, global income tax. The source approach is perhaps more appropriate under a separate corporation tax whose international effects are as neutral as possible.

---

3 The alternative would be to base the indirect taxes on the origin principle, under which exports are taxed and imports are exempted. Assuming full exchange rate and domestic price flexibility, the equivalence theorem shows that the trade effects of the origin principle are identical to those of the destination principle. That the theorem does not hold in the real world is argued in Cnossen [1983]. Initially, the European Commission, to be able to remove border controls, wanted to levy the indirect taxes on the basis of the origin principle, but since 1985 it has dropped the idea.

4 This is a basic criterion of the Treaty of Rome. Nonuniform, destination-based taxes, of course, will affect the level and structure of Community trade. Thus, indirect taxes on goods that are mainly imported should restrain the demand for those goods, even if such goods are not taxed at a higher rate than other domestically made products. If the objective is to preclude all changes in the terms of trade, then the taxes should either be abolished or fully harmonized. Finally, it should be emphasized that the argument abstracts from interstate distortions of consumer preferences that are caused by divergent indirect taxes. Here the focus is on locational neutrality.

If priority were given to the domicile principle, tax burden export would not occur if the source state did not levy any tax (not a very realistic assumption) or if the domicile state extended a full tax credit (including a refund if necessary) for a similar tax levied on income or profits in the source state. If, on the other hand, the source principle were given priority, tax burden export could only be avoided if the source state taxed the income or profits of its nonresident investors on the same footing as would have been the case if the income or profits had been taxed by the domicile state (also not a very realistic assumption) or if the domicile state again extended a tax credit for the tax paid in the source state. It will be clear that in the feasible cases the domicile state plays a crucial role in preventing tax burden export. Only this state has the possibility of achieving capital-export neutrality.[5] However, whether it is also actually able to do so is doubtful, considering the degree of administrative integration that is required.

The prohibition on tax burden export cannot deal with the existing levies on natural resources (e.g., natural gas) that are charged to domestic as well as foreign users and the proceeds of which flow into the treasury of the source country. To rationalize these levies, recourse must be taken to the broader, more legally shaded, nondiscrimination principle that, just like the locational neutrality criterion, plays an important role in the Treaty of Rome.[6] The nondiscrimination principle is of even greater importance for direct taxes, because it prescribes that the source state cannot tax the profits of foreign investors higher than the profits of investors who have their domicile in the source state itself.[7] However, allocative efficiency will still be affected if the effective rates of corporation tax in particular are not equalized among the various member states.

An important difference between the coordination of indirect taxes, on the one hand, and direct taxes, on the other hand, is that the former can be effected unilaterally if border controls exist. For the coordination of direct taxes, however, a Community-wide exchange of tax information is required, certainly if residents are to be taxed on the basis of the sum of their domestic and foreign income. Even the source concept, which exempts foreign direct investment income, does not obviate the need for an exchange of information, because it would still be possible to manipulate the profits accruing in the domicile state through the use of transfer prices that are not determined in accordance with the arm's length principle. Strikingly, information on such prices is not required in respect of the border tax

---

5 As in the case of product taxes, however, nonuniform, domicile-based taxes should still affect the level and structure of the allocation of capital in the Community through their effect on asset prices.

6 Application of the nondiscrimination principle to natural resource taxes means that the additional revenues result in a non-optimal increase in the size of the public sector in the source state. For a good treatment of this, see Mieszkowski [1983].

7 For a useful treatment of this, see Raad [1986].

adjustments for the value-added tax (except in the case of imports by end-users), because the tax credit mechanism ensures that any underpayment of the import tax is corrected at the first inland stage.

A number of additional complications will arise in a common market that increasingly acquires the characteristics of a domestic market. If border controls are eliminated along with internal borders, then border tax adjustments will have to be effected in a different manner, at least if the destination principle is to be maintained. The increased mobility of people and capital also implies that taxpayers who are assessed on their world income by reference to the domicile principle will pack their bags more readily and move to a milder tax climate. Emigration of people and capital will be difficult to restrain in a community which has been created precisely for the purpose of promoting the mobility of factors of production.

3. What Has Been Achieved?[8]

As set out in Article 3, the Treaty of Rome aims at the creation of a common market free of restrictions on the movement of goods; the abolition of obstacles to the free movement of people, services and capital; and the institution of a system ensuring that competition is not distorted. This is quite a mouthful which boils down to the principle that competition should be the allocating mechanism in the Community. Tax coordination is then its corollary insofar as it aims at ensuring that tax-induced distortions of competitive conditions do not occur.[9]

The road towards a common market runs by way of a customs union in which the duties levied on imports and exports between member states are abolished and a common tariff is established with respect to third countries. This process was completed in 1968.[10] Additionally, Article 3 of the Treaty requires the abolition of

8 For a detailed review, see Cnossen [1987]. For a useful review of the issues, see also Sørensen [1989].

9 According to the European Commission, tax harmonization should proceed in three stages. In the first stage, agreement should be reached on the type of tax that the member states should adopt (e.g., a value-added tax instead of a cumulative turnover tax). Following this, differences in the basis of assessment (e.g., the taxable value for the value-added tax or taxable profits for the corporation tax) should be eliminated. Finally, an approximation of the rates should be pursued. Initially (see the harmonization program launched in 1967), the ambitions of the Commission extended to almost all taxes. However, after it appeared that many ideas were not, or were not yet, feasible, the harmonization endeavors were confined to the turnover tax, the excises, the corporation tax, the withholding taxes on dividends and interest, and some capital duties.

10 It should be noted that various member states have tried to collect some revenues at borders through various duties and charges for licenses, statistical purposes, health controls, etc. However, the European Court of Justice has sternly forbidden these levies. In cases of doubt, the Court decided in favor of the imported product, which, it ruled, should not be taxed higher than was commensurate with the lowest rate applicable to a similar domestic product.

quantitative restrictions "and of all other measures having equivalent effect." Article 36 contains a tall exception, however, by permitting restrictions on the movement of goods, "justified on grounds of public morality, public policy or public security; the protection of health and life of humans, animals or plants. . . ." In fact, this article, more than any other provision, is the rationale for the maintenance of internal customs posts that, of course, have no place in a real common market. With respect to health (and the environment), the Commission, according to its 1985 White Paper, wants to promulgate minimum regulations, but otherwise adopt as guiding principle that if a product is lawfully manufactured in one of the member states it is deemed to be so manufactured in the other member states.[11]

The Commission's most notable feat in the area of tax coordination is the introduction of a nearly uniform value-added tax. Under the old cumulative turnover tax, which was levied in 5 out of the 6 original member states, the required border tax adjustments could not be determined precisely, because it was not known how much tax had been levied in previous stages (in case of rebates at export) or how much tax should be levied on imports to impose the same burden as borne by similar domestic products. As is well known, the value-added tax does not have this shortcoming: the tax to be rebated is stated on purchase invoices and the tax credit mechanism ensures that any over- or underpayment at import is corrected at the first taxable inland stage. Therefore, the value-added tax does not affect the intra-Community movement of goods and services. The adoption of this tax is presently one of the conditions for Community membership. It should be noted that the Sixth Directive substantially harmonized the basis of assessment. Only the rate structures still diverge fairly widely.

Although the value-added tax does not distort intra-Community trade, border tax adjustments are still required. In principle, unless, as in the Benelux, a deferred payment scheme is in effect under which the first inland stage accounts for the import value-added tax, these adjustments, as the concept implies, have to be made at the border. Customs officers collect the value-added tax payable on imports and refund the tax on exports. Therefore, if customs controls are removed from internal borders in 1992, an alternative arrangement must be found for the adjustments.

In its White Paper, the Commission has proposed to shift the border tax adjustments to the taxpayers' account books. Exports will then be taxed, but the import state will obtain a refund from the export state for the tax remitted by exporters (and charged to customers/importers), which, in turn, equals the tax credit claimed by importers (and paid to suppliers/exporters). With respect to these

---

11 Often more important are the differences in product specifications, which impede the establishment of a common market because they contribute to the continuation of national monopolistic situations. The Commission has proposed a large number of laudable measures to eliminate these kinds of barriers, which economically are similar to import duties.

demands, a multilateral clearing mechanism will be created.[12] Thus, the destination principle is maintained for registered traders, but border controls have become redundant and as far as the value-added tax is concerned, the barriers can be removed.[13] Furthermore, in 1987, the Commission proposed to adopt a dual rate structure with a rate band of 4-9 percent for essential products and 14-20 percent for all other goods and services. Subsequently, the Commission confined the recommendations in respect of the VAT-rates to a minimum standard rate of 15 percent.

So far as the harmonization of the value-added taxes has proceeded, little has been achieved with respect to the "major" excises on wine, beer, spirits, tobacco manufactures and mineral oils. But for the harmonization of the bases of assessment for tobacco products (and to some extent the rate structure), hardly any approximation of the excises has occurred. Inflation has greatly reduced the real value of the specific excise duties on alcoholic beverages and mineral oils (often mitigating the effect of increases in oil prices). This de facto approximation of the excises may be viewed as a form of tax harmonization.

Furthermore, the European Court of Justice has stopped some of the most blatant forms of excise discrimination. France and Italy, for instance, used to levy much higher excises on distilled spirits made of grain, such as gin, whisky and wodka, than on spirits made of wine, such as cognac, armagnac and calvados. Because the grain distillates were imported, the excise structures favored domestic products, although there was no open discrimination on the basis of origin. The Court held that the beverages should be taxed equally. In similar cases, Denmark, Ireland and the United Kingdom were called to order.

In its White Paper, the Commission proposes to harmonize the bases of assessment and the rates of the various excises, although it does not elaborate. Also, the Commission wants to devise a common system for the tax-free, in-bond transportation of excisable goods until they are released from bond in one of the member states. As under the value-added tax, border tax adjustments would be shifted inland. Enforcement, however, will be much more difficult and the excises may prove to be a greater stumbling block to the removal of physical barriers than the value-added tax. In its 1989 amendments, the Commission limits the proposed changes to the adoption of minimum rates.

---

12 This system was anticipated in Cnossen [1983]. In the meantime, however, the Schengen countries (Belgium, France, Germany, Luxemburg, the Netherlands) have agreed to introduce the deferred payment scheme. In the end, this may well carry the day, too, in the other member states.

13 Some believe that the destination principle will thus be abolished. This is emphatically not the case: instead of settling the tax on exported products directly with his own tax administration (by applying the zero rate), the exporter settles the tax indirectly through the importer in the importing member state in conjunction with the tax clearance procedure between the respective tax administrations.

Aside from the capital duties, which are hardly worth mentioning, very little harmonization has been achieved in the area of direct taxes. In 1975, the Commission produced a draft directive in which it was proposed to adopt an imputation system for corporation tax. The rates for the corporation tax were to be in the range of 45-55 percent and shareholders were to receive a tax credit of 45-55 percent of the net dividend against their income tax. Member states were to extend this tax credit to shareholders in other member states and bear its cost by means of a clearinghouse. Furthermore, it was proposed to harmonize the dividend withholding tax at 25 percent. The directive stranded in the European Parliament, however, which argued that it made little sense to harmonize the rates and the treatment of distributed profits as long as, possibly large, differences existed in the determination of taxable profits. With respect to the latter subject, a draft directive is presently circulating in the Community.

The Commission, initially supported by a number of heavy-weight advisory committees, has always interpreted the provisions on tax in the Treaty of Rome as a mandate to pursue more or less complete equalization of the various taxes in the member states. In its own words: "The level of taxes influences a wide range of factors, including the structure of consumption and hence of production, company profitability, the location of investment projects and, generally speaking, the conditions of competition. With the prospect before us of a thrust of economic integration, these various factors must not artificially be influenced by differences in tax burdens. Eventually, therefore, closer alignment of these burdens will be necessary" [Commission of the European Communities, 1980, p. 8]. But is this really the case? Even though taxes affect real factors, is this sufficient cause to equalize them?

4. Why Tax Diversity?

A fundamental premise which, it may be surmised, underlies the creation of the European Community is that by strengthening the whole, better safeguards can be created for preserving the integrity of the constituent parts. In light of this, the crucial question with regard to tax coordination is not, it appears, how the various taxes can be equalized as soon as possible, but, on the contrary, how much diversity can be permitted without interfering with the establishment of a common market and further down the road a monetary and economic union. Various arguments, largely philosophical *and* practical in nature, can be advanced to support the view that far-reaching tax harmonization is neither necessary nor desirable.

First, tax harmonization cannot be considered of such importance in itself that the objective should be to find that average of existing practices on which the member states can be induced to agree. Certainly, no contribution would be made to the Community's welfare if inequitable and distortionary tax structures of some member states were imposed on other member states. More fundamentally, tax harmonization, like tax reform, must proceed from widely agreed-upon criteria and objectives relating to revenue, equity, efficiency, and administrative feasibility. In contrast to the view of the Commission, tax convergence, therefore, should proceed by reference to a mutual point of arrival instead of by different points of departure [see Kay, Keen, 1987, p. 85]. In other words, it is not the process and the fact of harmonization that are significant, but rather the end on which the Community ultimately harmonizes its taxes. If this end cannot be clearly articulated, let alone agreed upon, then, in analogy to the medical "nihil nocere" rule, it is far better to leave things as they are.

Second, taxes that appear identical on paper may diverge widely in practice. The Danish value-added tax, for instance, which is scrupulously administered, is worlds apart from the Italian value-added tax, which, reportedly, is widely evaded.[14] Differences in effective enforcement of statutorily identical taxes are likely to affect entrepreneurial behavior and consumer preferences. Even if the basis of assessment is the same (in this case as laid down in the Sixth Directive) and even if the rates were equalized, there might still be large differences in economic effect. Another example is the corporation tax. Even if the provisions with respect to the determination of taxable profits were harmonized and even if the same rate were applied, the number and the nature of the taxable persons subject to this tax, and hence its impact, would still differ considerably between, say, Germany, where incorporation is the exception and, say, the Netherlands, where it has become the rule.

Third, differences in the level and the composition of expenditures should also be taken into account in assessing the impact of governments' intervention in the functioning of the Common Market. More specifically, diverse patterns of tax-induced incentives and disincentives may be offset or accentuated by non-neutralities on the expenditure side of the budgets of the member states. To mention an obvious example, protectionist import duties may take the form of free services or subsidies to industry rather than taxes collected at borders. More broadly, subsidies, procurement policies, and administrative rules and regulations pervasively influence the behavior of the market participants in every member state. The point is that in the final analysis it is net burdens and benefits that matter in evaluating the distortionary effect of government interventions. A priori there is no reason to assume that tax harmonization per se will improve resource allocation or, more narrowly formulated, competitive conditions.

Fourth, if as envisaged in the Treaty of Rome, the Common Market evolves into a monetary and economic union, the member states will have to give up control over monetary and exchange rate policy, in addition to the earlier surrender of the

[14] See Pedone [1981, p. 35], who calculates that on average some 40 percent of potential value-added tax revenues is evaded in Italy.

control over tariffs and trade policy. To keep as much room as possible for independent social and economic policies in the individual member states, the weight on tax and expenditure instruments for short-term stabilization and long-term structural adjustments will then increase. This context does not permit undue constraints on the tax systems of the member states nor, by extension, on their expenditure budgets. Indeed, it may well be that an inventive and constructive view on the autonomous use of these instruments would pave the way for the establishment of a monetary and economic union.

Fifth, actual tax practices in federal countries such as the United States, Canada and Switzerland show that subnational tax systems can differ widely from one another, yet this does not seem incompatible with the functioning of the domestic market. In the United States, for example, 43 out of 50 states have their own personal income tax, 45 states have a corporation tax, and 45 states plus the District of Columbia have their own sales tax. All of these taxes on income, profits, and sales are levied on widely varying tax bases and at widely varying rates.[15] Yet, no one would want to assert that the United States does not have one domestic market. Similar differences are found in Canada and Switzerland.

Sixth, tax harmonization, broadly viewed, does not take account of differences in preferences for one tax over another in the various member states reflecting differences in economic and social structures, different perceptions on the role of taxation, differences in the acceptability and feasibility of various taxes and, perhaps more fundamentally, differences in preferences for public sector size among the member states.

Last but not least, the Community is but an instrument for achieving a better and fuller life for its citizens; it cannot be considered a goal in itself. Diversity to accommodate differences in preferences is an important economic and cultural commodity. Diversity may entail economic and administrative costs, but these should be acceptable particularly if those whose interests are being served pay the price. Perhaps an analogy can be made to the Commission's laudable approach to the removal of the various technical barriers: lawful manufacture in one of the member states implies lawful manufacture in all other member states. It is this thrust of moving away from the concept of uniformity towards that of mutual recognition and equivalence that should also determine the direction of the tax coordination process.

---

15 See Bird [1989]. It should be noted that tax competition with respect to the corporation tax is mitigated, because taxable profits are ascertained on the basis of the "unitary system," in which the base is allocated to the various states according to the "Massachusetts formula": a key comprising sales per state, the payroll, and the value of the company's assets in each state. Furthermore, some interstate differences may be ironed out through the federal corporation tax. However, even if these factors are taken into account, substantial differences between the states remain and they continue to lure investors with tax concessions.

5. Towards Tax Competition?

The case for as much tax diversity as is commensurate with the establishment of a common market may perhaps be stretched a bit further. If competition promotes the efficient allocation of resources in the private sector (the basic tenant of the Treaty of Rome and the Commission's 1985 White Paper), is there not a presumption that interstate tax competition would do the same with respect to the public sectors in the member states [McLure, 1986]? Tax harmonization, understood as uniformity of tax bases and tax rates, may throw the baby out with the bath water, because ever-revenue-hungry governments would use it as a vehicle for maintaining, and possibly raising, the prevailing high levels of taxation.

Revenue levels in the Community's member states, primarily comprising tax receipts and social security contributions, have reached daunting heights. On average, they rose from some 20 percent of gross domestic product (GDP) in the 1920s to 30 percent in the late 1950s and, the trend continues, to nearly 45 percent in 1989, hardly 30 years later. This is the average of the tax levels in Germany, France, Britain, and Italy: four member states which together account for 80 percent of the Community's combined gross product. The tax burden is higher still in the small member states: on average, 51 percent in the Netherlands, Belgium, Denmark, Ireland, and Luxembourg. In sharp contrast is the much lower figure for the United States and Japan where the revenue intake of the government is only 31 percent of GDP.

The causes of the relatively sharp increase in the tax burdens in the Community vis-à-vis the United States and Japan will not be discussed [see Cnossen, 1988]. But it should be noted that the high burdens may jeopardize the Community's competitive trading position in the world.[16] High tax burdens widen the wedge between the social and the private rate of return on economic activities. They impose burdens over and above the amount of revenue that is raised (in the literature on tax these costs are referred to as "excess burdens" or "deadweight losses"). Labor and capital are diverted from highly taxed to lightly taxed activities: from work to leisure, do-it-yourself jobs and barter; from occupations with fully taxable monetary rewards to occupations with a higher nontaxable content (usually of the in-kind type) of the gross remuneration or with more opportunities to reduce the taxable income through deductible costs; from conventional forms of saving (which, as is well known, are taxed twice under the income tax) to consumption or (qualitatively different) forms of institutional saving; and from assets with high taxable returns (plant and capital equipment) to assets with no or low taxable returns (houses, yachts). Also, the widening of the difference between the gross and the net-of-tax

---

16 For an argument that the composition of the tax burden rather than the total burden matters, see Sinn, in this volume.

returns will reduce the domestic mobility of labor and capital and will make emigration and capital flight more attractive.

These substitution effects, which induce people to do things they would not have done in the absence of the tax, are an economic waste. In the tax literature, it is generally assumed that their magnitude increases with the square of the effective marginal tax rate. The empirical evidence on tax-induced forms of economic waste is scarce, but on the basis of in-house and other research, the Organisation for Economic Cooperation and Development (OECD) [1987, p. 353] notes that "the overall effects of taxation both on labour supply and on efficiency could be large enough to affect economic performance measurably." On balance, the OECD concludes that "estimates suggest that $1 raised through taxes may, at the margin, reduce national income by 10 to 15 cents and possibly considerably more, depending on the tax measures used, while the net overall cost of present tax systems could be in the order of 3 to 5 percent of GNP." Moreover, in addition to the detrimental economic effects, there are harmful consequences for the social fabric of society (tax evasion, the underground economy) the long-term effects of which should not be underestimated.

Finally, proponents of tax competition point out that tax harmonization, i.e., tax equalization, might mean that the governments of the member states have to be less concerned about where and how to get the money to finance their expenditures, or how to spend such money as wisely and efficiently as possible. It is then conceivable that politicians and bureaucrats will continue to further their own agenda rather than the interests of their constituents or the welfare of the Community at large. Tax harmonization may mean that there will be less pressure to create a leaner and more efficient public sector. Subsidies for pressure groups may be given priority over outlays for infrastructure, environmental protection and other government services that are essential for the private sector and the consumer.

6. Starting Points for Tax Coordination

Even though a good case can be made for tax diversity and even though a dose of tax competition might do no harm, there remains the question as to how much tax harmonization is minimally required or desirable. The political answer to this question depends mainly on the way in which the expenditures of the Commission (or, say, a supranational government) are financed. Three choices are conceivable: (a) "contributions" voted annually by the member states; (b) "own resources" of the Community, i.e., taxes levied and collected by the member states, with the proceeds being transferred in whole or in part to the Community; and (c) the

Community's own "tax jurisdiction." So far, only contributions and own resources have been in the picture.[17]

If the ultimate objective is to create a taxing jurisdiction for the Community, then harmonization of the taxes designated therefor may be a useful halfway station. The way in which the common expenditures are financed, however, is not dependent on the constitutional form that will ultimately be chosen for the Community. Even if the Community were to aim for, say, a confederal system of government with its own, if limited, duties and responsibilities, then it is still quite conceivable that its tasks could be financed in the same manner as is currently the case with respect to the EC-budget. Moreover, even if harmonization were required, it would still be possible to leave the taxes involved under the management of the member states.

On the assumption that the member states should keep as much tax sovereignty as possible, the issue of tax coordination is determined mainly by economic and administrative considerations. The main condition that member states should adhere to in arranging their tax system is, as indicated above, that they should not usurp the tax base of other member states. Every member state should stick to its own tax base. If it wants to impose a higher tax rate thereon than other member states, then this should be permitted, provided that the member state itself carries the burden of that action, for instance, in the form of cross-border shopping, capital flight, or emigration. To prevent unbridled tax competition, it may be necessary to agree on some minimum arrangements for the coordination of some taxes.

The maintenance of as much tax sovereignty as possible is promoted by leaving those taxes with the member states whose bases are characterized by little intra-Community mobility. The immovable property tax is probably the best example; not surprisingly, it is one of the most appropriate local taxes. Because consumer purchases cannot be shifted over great distances without increasing their cost, differentiated sales taxes, as indicated by the experience in the United States and Canada, can also coexist without great difficulties in a common market.[18] The same applies to taxes on labor income, present and past (wage taxes, but also social security premiums, particularly if withheld at source). Such taxes can be tied to the domicile of the employer, the pension fund, or the employee. All in all, this is a fairly formidable tax arsenal for most member states. In addition, the administration of user charges, e.g., charges related to motoring, should not be hampered by the

17 At present, all import duties collected on dutiable items imported from third countries are remitted to the Community, as well as the proceeds of the levies on agricultural products and a 1.4 percent levy on a uniformly determined value-added tax base.

18 Provided that the member state that wants to levy a higher-than-average rate of tax is large enough to minimize cross-border shopping. Luxembourg is not in that position and has made a virtue of necessity by usurping part of the tax base of neighboring member states through low-rate indirect taxes. This should be allowed to some extent in a common market, I believe. As the large member states will exploit their relatively strong position, it is difficult to fault small member states for exploiting their own administrative weakness.

abolition of internal borders, particularly not if they can be linked to a registration obligation that coincides with the domicile of the taxpayer.

The other side of the picture is that non-benefit-based taxes that are levied from a mobile base would have to be closely approximated or transferred to the Community. In particular, this applies to taxes on capital income and corporate profits (see Tanzi and Bovenberg, this volume), as well as to the excises. If it is considered desirable on ability-to-pay grounds or for income redistribution purposes to tax income from capital comprehensively and progressively, then a liberalized capital market requires either a far-reaching exchange of tax information or a much closer taxation of corporations and capital income on the basis of the source principle. Administratively, it appears that the latter alternative is easier to effect than the former approach.

7. How Much Tax Harmonization?

What does this all mean for the member states on the way to 1992, when internal borders will be abolished, and beyond, when the Community moves toward a monetary and economic union? Which changes in their tax systems are necessary and which are desirable? Before an attempt is made to answer these questions, it is essential to emphasize what the abolition of internal borders implies.

In terms of taxation, 1992 means that the customs house with all the red tape and delay that it entails will disappear from internal borders. From that date, there will be no systematic registration at borders of the movement of goods and services between member states. Of course, it is possible, as suggested by the British, to abolish the physical barriers at the borders only partially. Also, it is conceivable that the barriers themselves will be removed, but that the customs' activities will move to one or another electronic (nether) world. However, such solutions are at variance with the idea of a common market that has all of the characteristics of a domestic market. The objective of the removal of internal customs is precisely to cut off any possibility of reinstating those borders for national purposes, at the penalty of being excised from the Community.

Internal borders cannot be eliminated without improving the coordination of controls at external borders. This has the attention of Brussels, but regrettably the Commission's White Paper does not contain any proposals in this respect. In addition to taxing duties (import duties, value-added taxes, excises), customs personnel at external borders are charged with the control of persons, drugs and fire arms, and the observation of health and safety regulations. The formation of a common market should not leave any doubt in any of the member states whether or not another member state has properly admitted some person or good. The cooperation of national customs at external frontiers, therefore, should be intensified. Perhaps it is not too early to think about establishing a common customs service.

As explained above, the intention is to shift border tax adjustments for the value-added tax to taxpayers' books of account in conjunction with the intra-Community clearance of VAT-claims. This mechanism will probably function somewhat more easily if the number of rates in each of the member states is limited to two, as the Commission has proposed, and if the coverage of the goods and services subject to the lower rate is streamlined.

It is not clear, however, why the various rates should be approximated. After all, even under the proposed arrangement, all goods and services that are shipped from one member state to another member state through taxable trading channels will ultimately always be taxed at the rate of the member state where the product is finally used or consumed. This can also be achieved for out-of-state purchases by governments and exempt entities by requiring them to file a return for tax purposes. Only purchases by consumers in other member states will have to be taxed according to the origin principle. It is then possible that some diversion of sales in border areas will occur, but it remains to be seen whether there will be much change vis-à-vis the present situation. The generous VAT-exemption at the import stage and the practically unhindered passage through internal borders suggest that this will not be the case.

It has been pointed out that the clearing system exhibits asymmetric interests as regards each member state's role as a tax-credit debtor, on the one hand, and as a creditor, on the other hand [see Lee et al., 1988]. Although correct, the requirement of a loyal interstate exchange of information is also pertinent to the deferred payment system. How can the actual exportation of a commodity be verified in a common market other than through a check at the point of destination? Moreover, it is of interest to note that the verification of transfer prices for corporation tax purposes in cooperation with the country of destination of the exported goods has never existed. Yet, each member state continues to impose the tax on the basis of the "separate accounting" principle, although a thorough cross-border check of transfer prices is essential for doing so.

To meet a number of objections, it would be important if the Commission were to be charged with the responsibility of verifying the claims that the member states will present to each other (of course, the countervalue of each claim would already have been received by the debtor state — through its exporters — from the importers in the creditor state). To avoid the red tape involved with the operation of the clearinghouse mechanism, claims could also be cleared on the basis of trade statistics (which would not anymore be collated at borders), instead of information culled from VAT-returns. Economically, this should not meet with any objections because direct intergovernmental clearing does not affect the destination principle. The Commission is currently exploring the feasibility of this avenue.

As alluded to above, the elimination of border controls with respect to the excises is much more difficult to bring about. The tobacco excise, for instance, amounts to some 70 percent of the retail price: which means that strict supervision is required to prevent fraud. Furthermore, close approximation is necessary if excisable goods are not to be sold at low rates through outlets in Luxembourg. Approximation should not be too difficult regarding the level of the taxes on tobacco (which excepting Denmark vary only from 67-75 percent), but would be more problematic with respect to the structure of the rates: the ratio of the specific element to the ad valorem element of the tobacco excise varies from 5-55 percent. The excises on alcoholic beverages and mineral oils have moved closer together in the past 30 years, but are still far from being harmonized. Some differentiation at the retail level should be possible (among other means, through the use of banderoles or seals), but generally closer approximation is desirable. It should be noted, however, that uniform rates are in no way the rule among, say, subordinate units of government in the United States and Canada.

Close approximation would certainly be necessary with respect to effluent levies in respect of cross-border pollution. As is well known, effluent levies are imposed on producers for the negative externalities caused by their products or production processes. Therefore, these levies should be incorporated in prices regardless of where the end-use of the taxable products occurs. In other words, effluent levies should be imposed on the basis of the origin principle: there should be no rebate at export. Here, tax competition might work at cross-purposes with the objective of a clean environment. The ease with which environmental damage crosses borders emphasizes the importance of a centralized authority to contain the damage.

Finally, there is the corporation tax. Controls on capital movements will be completely dismantled by 1990, leaving direct investment flows open to the non-neutralities of differences in the effective tax rates of what is essentially a source-based tax. The competitive pressure to reduce the rates further might increase. Moreover, as trade and industry are further integrated, it will become increasingly difficult and probably largely impossible to determine the taxable profits separately for each company in every member state on the basis of "separate accounting." For neutrality purposes and to prevent unbridled tax competition, it might then be desirable to introduce uniform, equal-rate, in rem taxes on corporate profits. The desired degree of integration with the individual income tax would then be a matter which might be left to the individual member states to decide.

Three comments may be made about the Commission's endeavors to harmonize the basis of assessment for the corporation tax. First, the harmonization of the type of corporation tax can be viewed as an issue separate from the harmonization of the basis of assessment. How much corporation tax shareholders should be able to credit against their income tax is an issue that does not affect the computation of taxable profits. In this respect, the European Parliament was wide of the mark. Second, harmonization of the profit concept will not lead to the same effective tax rates (even if nominal rates are the same) if the basis of assessment is not indexed for inflation (as long as monetary policies are not harmonized). Third, it will not be possible, as the Commission proposes, to tax all enterprises that make up an annual balance sheet and a profit and loss account according to some harmonized profit concept. In the case of corporations, profits are a return to equity. However, in the case of partnerships and proprietorships, profits are a combination of labor income and capital income. In practice, these elements cannot be separated. Moreover, for tax purposes, labor income can accrue in the form of profits from enterprise, but also as proceeds from employment. The possibilities for shifting these labels differ substantially from one member state to another. It is not possible therefore to lump all profits from enterprise together.

8. Concluding Thoughts

I end with an attempt to put the previous considerations in a somewhat broader perspective. Selective tax harmonization is desirable to reduce trade, locational change, capital movement and labor distortions. Generally, however, a strong case can be made for maintaining as much tax diversity as is commensurate with the establishment of a common market. Even some tax competition might do no harm. Since the European Council wishes to create a more favorable environment for stimulating enterprise, competition and trade, it is necessary to keep a close watch on the high level of the tax burden in the Community, which may erode the Community's competitive position vis-à-vis the United States and Japan. Diversity of tax and expenditure systems may also be conducive to the preservation of national identities and cultural values.

The most important contribution taxation can make to the establishment of an integrated market is the abolition of border controls. As Shoup [1969, p. 641] noted already some twenty years ago: "The mere psychological gain from complete absence of border control within a common market can scarcely be overrated; it creates a spirit of unity, an expansiveness of outlook, that is a good, if not close, substitute for political unity." By far the best way to remove the border controls for the value-added tax is to shift border tax adjustments to books of account in conjunction with the establishment of a tax credit clearing mechanism. The coordination of the excises on smoking, drinking and driving deserves more thought. Perhaps, it would be better if some excises were levied and collected for the Commission, possibly by a Community customs service that should also guard the external frontiers. This is certainly the case with respect to effluent levies.

Finally, a case can be made for the approximation of the various corporation taxes. Otherwise, these taxes might be lost in the wheels of unbridled tax competition. This also applies to other taxes on capital income. Although the efficiency case for taxing capital appears to be weak, there are strong equity grounds for not saddling labor with nearly the whole tax burden. Why? Because, as Shannon [1986, p. 340] has put it succinctly in a somewhat different context: "It is not in the long range interest of those who favor the maintenance of a competitive environment to let the winners win too much and the losers lose too much."

Bibliography

BIRD, Richard M., "Tax Harmonization in Federations and Common Markets." In: Manfred NEUMANN, Karl W. ROSKAMP (Eds.), Public Finance and Performance of Enterprises. Detroit, forthcoming.

CNOSSEN, Sijbren, "Harmonization of Indirect Taxes in the EEC." In: Charles E. McLURE, Jr. (Ed.), Tax Assignment in Federal Countries. Canberra 1983, pp. 150-168.

—, "Tax Structure Developments." In: Sijbren CNOSSEN (Ed.), Tax Coordination in the European Community. Deventer 1987, pp. 19-55.

—, "Day of Reckoning Approaches for the European Community." In: Herbert STEIN (Ed.), Tax Policy in the Twenty-First Century. New York 1988, pp. 125-147.

COMMISSION OF THE EUROPEAN COMMUNITIES, Report on the Scope for Convergence of Tax Systems in the European Community. Bulletin of the European Communities, Supplement 1/8a, 1980.

KAY, John, Michael KEEN, "Alcohol and Tobacco Taxes: Criteria for Harmonisation." In: Sijbren CNOSSEN (Ed.), Tax Coordination in the European Community. Deventer 1987, pp. 85-111.

LEE, Catherine, Mark PEARSON, Stephen SMITH, Fiscal Harmonisation: An Analysis of the European Commission's Proposals. Institute for Fiscal Studies, IFS Report Series, No. 28, London 1988.

McLURE, Charles E., Jr., "Is What's Good for the Private Goose, Also Good for the Public Gander?" National Tax Journal, Vol. 39/3, 1986, pp. 341-348.

MIESZKOWSKI, Peter, "Energy Policy, Taxation of Natural Resources, and Fiscal Federalism." In: Charles E. McLURE, Jr. (Ed.), Tax Assignment in Federal Countries. Canberrra 1983, pp. 129-145.

MUSGRAVE, Richard A., "Who Should Tax, Where, and What?" In: Charles E. McLURE, Jr. (Ed.), Tax Assignment in Federal Countries. Canberra 1983, pp. 2-19.

ORGANIZATION FOR ECONOMIC COOPERATION AND DEVELOPMENT (OECD), Structural Adjustment and Economic Performance. Paris 1987.

PEDONE, Antonio, "Italy." In: Henry J. AARON (Ed.), The Value Added Tax: Lessons from Europe. Washington 1981, pp. 31-42.

RAAD, Cornelis van, Non-discrimination in International Tax Law. Deventer 1986.

SHANNON, John, "Interstate Tax Competition — The Need for a New Look." National Tax Journal, No. 39, 1986, pp. 339-340.

SHOUP, Carl S., Public Finance. Chicago 1969.

SIEBERT, Horst, "The Harmonization Issue in Europe: Prior Agreement or a Competitive Process?" In: Horst SIEBERT (Ed.), The Completion of the Internal Market. Symposium 1989, Tübingen 1990, pp. 53-75.

SINN, Hans-Werner, "Can Direct and Indirect Taxes Be Added for International Comparisons of Competitiveness?" In: Horst SIEBERT (Ed.), Reforming Capital Income Taxation. Tübingen 1990, this volume.

SØRENSEN, Peter Birch, Tax Harmonization in the European Community: Problems and Prospects. University of Copenhagen, Working Paper, October 1989.

TANZI, Vito, A. Lans BOVENBERG, "Is There a Need for Harmonization of Capital Income Taxes Within EC Countries?" In: Horst SIEBERT (Ed.), Reforming Capital Income Taxation. Tübingen 1990, this volume.

IV

Restructuring Capital Income Taxation

John Odling-Smee
David Lawton

Reforming Capital Income Taxation: The UK Experience

1. Introduction

By the end of the 1970s, the tax burden in the UK had risen to nearly 34 per cent of GDP. It rose further in the early 1980s to a peak of over 39 per cent as public sector borrowing was reduced, before falling as public expenditure declined in relation to GDP. There was widespread concern about the damage that the high level of taxation was doing to the performance of markets, and particularly the effects on incentives.

Apart from reducing the level of taxation, the main objectives of tax policy in the 1980s have been to improve incentives, strengthen market mechanisms and allow markets to work more freely. This paper concentrates on reforms to capital income taxation. But tax reform has gone much wider than taxes on capital income to cover, for example, the improvement of incentives and the reward of effort in labour markets.

This paper begins with a brief description of the basic UK approach to taxing capital income, concentrating on the broad principles rather than the fine details. It then outlines the main tax changes which have been implemented in the last decade. The following section picks out the common themes running through all these changes. It summarises the objectives and comments on some of the effects on the economy. Finally, the paper addresses the lessons which can be drawn from the UK experience, in the light of what economic theory tells us about optimal tax systems, and of the need to cope with the second-best situations of the real world.

Remark: The authors are grateful for helpful comments from colleagues in HM Treasury and the Inland Revenue. The views expressed are the authors' own and not necessarily those of the Treasury.

2. The UK Approach to Taxing Capital Income

a. Saving by Sector

Unlike in many countries, the personal sector in the UK is a less important source of savings than the company sector (Table 1). In the last three or four years, personal saving has declined quite sharply, although this fall has been largely offset by higher saving by the company and government sectors.

Table 1 — National Savings by Sector (per cent of GDP)[a]

	Personal	Company	Government	National
1960-64	5.8	8.3	3.7	17.9
1965-69	6.0	6.8	6.6	19.4
1970-74	6.0	7.6	5.7	19.3
1975-79	7.1	8.7	1.7	17.5
1980-84	7.8	8.2	1.4	17.4
1985	6.2	10.8	1.0	18.1
1986	5.3	10.9	1.0	17.2
1987	4.0	12.1	1.2	17.3
1988	2.8	11.6	2.9	17.3

[a]Excluding stock appreciation, but before providing for depreciation.

Source: CSO [1990].

b. Basic Principles of Tax Treatment

For income and capital gains originating in the UK, and passing to an individual UK resident, the basic principles of taxation are simple. Investment income reaching the hands of the individual saver is charged to income tax in the same way as employment income. Broadly speaking, this is on a receipts basis. The annual personal allowance of tax-free income can be set against income from all sources (with an exception, until 1990, for married women with investment income), and any income above the allowance is charged at the saver's marginal income tax rate.

In the same way that tax on employment income is deducted by employers via the Pay-As-You-Earn (PAYE) system, so for administrative simplicity tax on many forms of investment income is also accounted for at source. Important examples of this type are dividend income and interest from bank and building society deposits. In the case of dividends, the shareholder receives from the company a dividend which carries with it a tax credit. The tax credit discharges liability to basic rate tax. Non-taxpayers can claim the tax credit from the Inland Revenue. Higher rate liability is settled separately with Inland Revenue.

In the case of interest, the banks and building societies account for tax on interest at a fixed composite rate. Non-taxpayers are unable to obtain repayments, and to reflect this the composite rate tax (CRT) rate is set to yield the same amount of tax as would be payable if savers paid at their marginal rate (excluding higher rate liability which is charged separately). It thus stands slightly below the basic rate.

Capital gains reaching the hands of the individual saver are added to other income and taxed at marginal income tax rates. Full allowance is made for inflation, so that only real gains are taxed (and pre-1982 gains are exempt). The tax is levied only when gains are realised, and not as they accrue. Income and realised gains are not fully assimilated, however, since gains are adjusted for inflation whereas interest income is not, and there is a separate annual exemption of tax-free gains to eliminate a large number of small gains from assessment.

Two important exceptions to this pattern of income tax treatment are owner-occupied housing and private pensions. Here more favourable treatment is given in order to pursue the wider objectives of social policy and to encourage prudent planning for the future. The returns to housing (both the imputed income and, for the principal residence, capital gains) are untaxed, and the interest payments on the loan taken out to purchase the house are tax-deductible (up to a limit). The contributions to a pension fund also attract tax relief, and the build up of income within the fund is tax-free. Pension payments are taxed as income (although part can be commuted into a tax-free lump sum). (The tax regime for the life assurance industry is also unique, and is described in more detail below.)

The company sector has its income and capital gains, after deducting costs including interest payments, taxed at the corporation tax (CT) rate of 35 per cent. An indexation allowance is given for capital gains. Retained earnings are taxed at the full CT rate, but distributions are partly deductible under the partial imputation system.[1] Companies with taxable profits of less than £150,000 pay tax at the small companies rate of 25 per cent.

---

1 Company profits are subject to corporation tax (CT), but that part of profit which is distributed — as dividends — is also subject to income tax in the hands of the investor. To reduce the impact of this "double-taxation" of dividends, the UK operates a partial imputation system. When a dividend is paid, a company pays advance corporation tax (ACT) at a rate of 25 per 75 of dividend. The final corporation tax payment, made after netting off ACT, is called mainstream corporation tax (MCT). Shareholders receive their dividends, along with a tax credit which discharges their liability to basic rate income tax. If shareholders are non-taxpayers (e.g. pension funds), they can claim the tax credit from Inland Revenue. Higher-rate taxpayers offset the credit against their total tax liability, and pay over the difference.
To illustrate this suppose a company has profits of £231. Corporation tax at 35 per cent is some £81, leaving post-tax profits of £150. The company intends to retain half its post-tax profits (£75) and distribute the remainder (£75). It will pay ACT of £25, leaving some £56 MCT. The shareholder receives a dividend of £75, and because of the tax credit of £25, a basic rate taxpayer has no further liability. If the shareholder is a non-taxpayer, he is entitled to claim the tax credit and so receives £100. If, on the other hand, the shareholder pays tax at the higher rate of 40 per cent, his total tax liability is £40. As he has a tax credit of £25, he owes the Inland Revenue a further £15.

The individual saver can invest directly in shares. Or he may choose to invest via a collective investment vehicle such as a unit or investment trust or, even more indirectly, via pension funds or life assurance. Unit and investment trusts enjoy some advantages over direct investment such as tax relief for management expenses, and tax-free roll-up of capital gains. Pension fund income is not subject to tax. Where tax is withheld at source, or credits are given, the Inland Revenue arranges repayment back to the fund.

The tax treatment of life assurance is complex. Broadly speaking, for basic life assurance business, the tax is charged on the investment income and realised gains of the fund, less the expenses of management. Premium relief on new policies was abolished in 1984 and further reforms were made in the 1989 Budget.

The general principle for taxing overseas income is that it is taxed on a residence basis. In other words, the UK recipient is liable for UK tax on that income in the same way as if it were UK income. Credit may be given for part or all of any tax already paid in the country of origin. Under a system of double taxation agreements negotiated bilaterally between the UK and other countries, the other country may make repayments of tax.

c. Personal Sector Asset Holdings

The composition of the assets held by the personal sector, including funds held in life assurance and pension funds, is shown in Table 2. The distribution has changed markedly over the past 30 years or so. The proportions of total assets held as owner-occupied housing and in pension funds, the assets which the tax system treats most favourably, have gone up. Those of assets which are taxed more heavily have

Table 2 —Personal Sector Assets[a] (per cent of total, end year)

	1957	1967	1979	1987
Housing[b]	19.3	29.0	50.3	41.0
Notes, coins and deposits	24.2	23.2	19.6	16.3
National savings	12.1	5.9	2.4	2.6
Gilts and marketable debt	11.5	4.5	2.2	2.0
Shares & unit trusts	19.1	21.2	8.1	10.7
Life assurance	8.9	16.2	8.4	11.7
Pensions	4.9		9.0	15.6
Total	100.0	100.0	100.0	100.0

[a]Excludes consumer durables, physical assets other than housing, overseas assets, and miscellaneous financial assets. In 1987, the assets included accounted for around 80 per cent of personal sector assets. — [b]Net of loans for house purchase.

Source: CSO [1989]; HM Treasury [internal estimates].

tended to decline. Tax is, however, far from being the only influence on this pattern of saving. For example, social trends and the effects of rent controls have encouraged the growth of owner-occupation, and the portfolio composition is affected by changes in relative asset prices. Moreover, in competitive financial markets, we would expect pre-tax returns to adjust so that the post-tax returns of close substitutes will tend to be equalised. So while tax considerations have no doubt influenced the composition of the portfolio, they do not account for all the changes.

d. Scale of Capital Income Taxation

Capital income taxation amounted to 7 per cent of GDP in 1988, almost 20 per cent of all taxes and contributions (Table 3).[2] It had risen from 5 per cent of GDP in 1978, a sharper rise than for taxation as a whole. The rise in capital income taxation relative to GDP between 1978 and 1988 was roughly balanced by a fall in other taxes on income (essentially employment income). There were also increases in other expenditure taxes and social security contributions relative to GDP in the early 1980s.

Table 3 — Capital Income Taxation and Total Taxation (per cent of GDP)

	1978	1983	1988
Capital income taxation			
Personal sector income taxation[a]	2.5	2.4	2.9
Corporate sector income taxation[b]	1.9	3.4	2.7
Other taxes on capital income[c]	0.7	0.9	1.5
Total	5.0	6.6	7.1
Other taxes on income	9.2	8.6	7.6
Other taxes on expenditure	13.3	15.9	15.7
Social security contributions	6.0	6.8	6.8
Total taxes and contributions	33.5	38.0	37.2

[a]Excluding capital gains tax. — [b]Net of tax credits on dividends, etc., paid to the personal sector (to avoid double counting with the personal sector, for which capital income taxation is defined before deducting tax credits). — [c]Mainly capital gains tax, inheritance tax and stamp duties (see Table 5).

Source: CSO [1989].

Capital income taxation comprises the taxation of personal and corporate income from capital, and other taxes, mainly capital gains tax, inheritance tax and stamp duties (on asset turnover). By national accounting convention, personal sector income from capital includes income from self-employment, imputed rent from owner-occupation, and interest and dividend income from life assurance and

2 This includes all tax paid on income from self-employment, which includes a labour as well as a capital element.

pension funds, as well as the interest and dividend receipts of households. Imputed rent is exempt from tax, most interest payments by the household sector are deductible from income for tax purposes, and tax relief is given on employees' contributions to pension funds. As a result, that part of household income from self-employment, interest, dividends and rent which is subject to income tax is well under half of the total (Table 4). There was a rise in taxable household sector income

Table 4 — Household Sector Income from Capital (bill. £; per cent of GDP in parentheses)

	1978		1988	
Income from self-employment[a]	11.3		36.6	
Rent, dividends and interest receipts	6.2		28.5	
Less imputed rent of owner-occupied dwellings	5.4		15.5	
Less total interest paid	4.2		21.6	
Less employees' contributions to pension schemes	2.0		6.1	
Total: approximate tax base[b]	6.0	(3.6)	21.9	(4.7)

[a]After deducting interest payments, capital consumption and stock appreciation. — [b]This is only an approximate estimate of the tax base because it does not take proper account of, for example, capital allowances offsettable against trading income and interest payments which do not qualify for tax relief.

Source: CSO [1989].

Table 5 — Other Taxes on Capital Income[a] (bill. £; per cent of GDP in parentheses)

	1978		1988	
Tax payments				
Capital gains tax	0.4		3.7	
Inheritance tax[b]	0.4		1.1	
Stamp duties	0.4		2.3	
Total[c]	1.2	(0.7)	7.1	(1.5)
Cost of main reliefs and exemption				
Capital gains exempt amount and gains accrued but unrealised at death	–		1	
Capital gains on main residence	1		9	
Inheritance tax : transfers to spouse and other reliefs[d]	–		1	
Stamp duty : exemptions of govt. stocks	1		2	

[a]Includes payments by both personal and corporate sectors. — [b]Includes capital transfer tax. — [c]Includes development land tax. — [d]Excludes cost of threshold.

Source: CSO [1989]; Board of Inland Revenue [1978; 1979; 1988; 1989].

from capital between 1978 and 1988 relative to GDP. Tax paid on total personal sector income from capital (i.e. including life assurance and pension funds) rose by less, partly because of the reduction in income tax rates.

The reasons for the rise in corporate sector taxation of income from capital between 1978 and 1988 are discussed later. Other taxes on capital income are shown in Table 5. There was a rise in tax payments relative to GDP between 1978 and 1988, mainly reflecting the increase in capital gains and asset turnover. Tax rates actually fell over the period. There are numerous reliefs and exemptions from these taxes, the most important being that for capital gains on the main residence. The cost of the main reliefs and exemptions shown in the table exceeds tax actually collected.

3. Tax Reform since 1979

The tax system as described above represents a considerable change on that which was in force at the end of the 1970s, with the major reforms being made in the 1979, 1984 and 1988 Budgets. This section briefly outlines what the main reforms affecting the returns to saving and investment have been.

a. Personal Taxes

Investment income of individuals is charged to income tax. Since 1979, the basic rate of income tax has been reduced from 33 to 25 per cent, and the maximum rate on earned income has gone down from 83 to 40 per cent. The investment income surcharge of 15 per cent, which was an additional tax applied to investment income above a separate threshold (taking the top marginal rate to 98 per cent) was first reduced, and then, in 1984, abolished, at an estimated full year cost of £360 mill. (At its peak, the surcharge was paid by nearly 1 million out of 21 million personal income tax units.) Personal allowances have been raised in successive budgets and now stand some 25 per cent higher in real terms than in 1979.

Capital gains tax has been reformed. Previously, tax was charged on the full nominal gain made on an investment at the flat rate of 30 per cent. Since 1982, indexation relief has been given to capital gains (with modifications in 1985) before the gains are charged to tax. In 1988, the base for capital gains tax was brought forward to 1982 (effectively exempting pre-1982 gains), and the tax rates were aligned with income tax rates. Real gains (above an exempt amount) are now added to other income and charged at marginal income tax rates. Company gains are likewise now indexed and charged at the corporation tax rate.

The composite rate tax arrangements for building society interest were extended to bank deposits in 1984 to even up tax treatment and to simplify administration.

b. Company Taxes

Business taxation underwent a major restructuring in 1984. The pre-1984 system essentially combined a high rate of corporation tax with high first year capital allowances (i.e. accelerated depreciation provisions) for some, but not all, investment. The reforms retained the same overall structure of company taxation (the imputation system, with full interest deductibility), but reduced the rate of corporation tax from 52 to 35 per cent and replaced the 100 per cent first-year allowances with smaller allowances spread over a number of years. The tax relief given for the increase in the value of a business' stocks (i.e. inventories) was also abolished. The rate of tax charged on small companies was brought down to the basic rate of income tax. These measures, taken as a package, were expected to be broadly revenue-neutral over the transition period.

Development land tax, a charge on development value realised either through the sale of land or the commencement of a project, was abolished in 1985.

c. Inheritance Tax

The taxation of transfers between generations has also been reformed. The tax on most lifetime gifts has been abolished. Capital transfer tax has been renamed inheritance tax, and made less onerous; the threshold has more than doubled in real terms since 1979 and fourteen tax bands, with a top rate of 75 per cent, have been progressively simplified, and eventually collapsed into a single rate of 40 per cent. Only 24,500 estates will be paying tax in 1989-90, compared with 38,000 in 1978-79, although real personal sector wealth has risen both absolutely and in relation to income.

d. Institutional Saving

The regime for private pensions has been made much more flexible. The rules for occupational (defined benefit) schemes have been simplified, so that companies are now free to pay their employees whatever pension they like, but a new limit has been set on tax privileges by restricting them to pensions paid out on earnings of £60,000 per year or less. The effect of this ceiling will take some time to build up, as it applies only to new schemes set up from 14 March 1989, and to new members joining existing schemes from 1 June 1989. Employees remaining within existing schemes will be unaffected. Other changes to occupational schemes include improvement of early leavers' rights, allowing membership to be voluntary, and enabling employees to make additional freestanding contributions. In 1983 (the latest year for which figures are available) there were 11 million employees in occupational schemes, and a further 5 million people receiving pensions from such schemes.

A further far-reaching reform in the 1986 Social Security Act enabled money purchase schemes to be used for contracting out of SERPS (the state earnings-related pension scheme; there is also a state flat-rate pension). These schemes can be run by employers on behalf of their employees or sold directly to individuals by financial institutions (in this case, they are known as personal pensions). The Act also extended to these new schemes the tax privileges of occupational schemes, and offered an additional rebate, over and above the basic contracted-out rebate, to those newly contracting out. This special incentive lasts until 1992-93. Already, over 3 million people have taken out personal pensions, and some 11,000 new contracted-out employers' schemes have been established.

The 1989 Budget announced significant changes to the tax regime for life assurance in order to reduce the distortions of the old system and to align the tax treatment more closely with that of other forms of saving. From 1 January 1990, life assurance companies' pensions and general annuity businesses will be taxed separately. Relief for the expenses of acquiring new life assurance business will be spread over seven years (rather than allowing an immediate write-off as previously). To partially offset these changes, the rate of tax charged on the income and capital gains attributable to policy holders will be reduced to 25 per cent. The immediate yield will be reduced by the carry-forward of unrelieved expenses from past years, but over the longer term, the measures are expected to yield about £250 mill. per year.

e. Other Tax Reliefs

In a number of areas, tax reliefs have been restricted. Relief on mortgage interest has been subject to a ceiling on the capital sum since 1974. The ceiling was raised by £5,000 to £30,000 in 1983, but has subsequently remained fixed, and has applied on a residence rather than an individual basis since 1988. Relief on loans for home improvements has been abolished. As a consequence, the proportion of the mortgage stock attracting relief has fallen from 91 per cent in 1983-84 to an estimated 75 per cent in 1989-90. Life assurance premium relief was ended for new policies in 1984 and the rate of relief for existing policies has been steadily reduced from 17 to 12 per cent. The use of forestry as a tax shelter has been ended by taking woodlands out of the income tax system altogether. Capital gains tax relief on gifts has also been ended.

f. Other Measures

Marketable loans (i.e. bonds) were taken outside capital gains taxation in a two stage process in 1984 and 1985, to prevent their being used to generate indexation losses.

Stamp duty on transactions in land and buildings has been reduced from 2 to 1 per cent on purchases above a £30,000 threshold. For transactions in shares, the rate was cut further to 0.5 per cent in 1986 and the base was extended to some previously exempt transactions such as takeovers. Two other minor transaction taxes, life assurance policy duty and capital duty on new equity issues have been abolished.

Several other measures have been taken to encourage wider share ownership. Personal Equity Plans (PEP), introduced in 1986 and subsequently expanded, allow savers to earn tax-free returns from investment in equities up to an annual investment limit of £4,800, and over £600,000 plans have so far been taken out. Tax reliefs for employee share schemes and employee share ownership plans have also been made more generous.

A Business Expansion Scheme (BES) has been established to encourage venture capital investment in smaller businesses. It aims to facilitate the supply of equity by offering tax relief to individuals investing in unquoted companies (subject to a limit of £500,000 per company per year). In 1988, the scheme was extended to companies investing in private rented housing. The estimated cost in 1988-89 of all these reliefs for PEPs, share schemes and BES is £300 mill.

4. Objectives and Effects of Tax Reforms

At first glance, these measures appear to be rather diverse. Some taxes have been completely reformed and others have been abolished. New schemes have been introduced and many of the remaining taxes have had their rates restructured. Despite this diversity, five major common themes and objectives underlying the changes can be distinguished:

- —lower marginal rates,
- —reduction in tax reliefs,
- —a simpler tax structure and system,
- —greater neutrality,
- —the promotion of flexible markets.

a. Lower Marginal Rates

Lower marginal rates are the key to improving incentives and rewarding enterprise. As Table 6 shows, the marginal rates of income tax, corporation tax, stamp duty, and inheritance tax have all been significantly reduced.

Table 6 — Marginal Tax Rates (per cent)

	1978-79	1988-89
Income tax		
Basic rate	33.0	25.0
Highest rate	83.0	40.0
Investment income		
Surcharge	15.0	abolished
Corporation tax	52.0	35.0
Inheritance tax		
Highest rate	75.0	40.0
Stamp duty		
Property and land[a]	2.0	1.0
Shares	2.0	0.5

[a]On purchases over £30,000.

Source: Board of Inland Revenue [1979; 1989].

Marginal rates for many married savers will be further reduced by independent taxation. From April 1990, all taxpayers — male or female, married or single — will be entitled to the same personal allowance to be set against income of all kinds. In addition, there will be a married couples allowance, to go to the husband in the first instance, but with any unused amount being transferable to the wife. Over 2 million wives will be able to use their allowance against unearned income which is currently taxed at the husband's marginal rate.

b. Reduction in Tax Reliefs

At the same time as marginal rates have been brought down, the tax base has been widened by the scaling back of reliefs. In the company sector, stock relief and 100 per cent first-year allowances have been abolished. In the personal sector, limits have been set, and tightened, on the tax privileges available for pensions, life assurance and owner-occupied housing. (Despite this, the absolute value of the latter relief has risen rapidly, mainly because of the sharp increase in house prices and the rise in interest rates.) The extent to which the beneficial income of company cars is undertaxed has been reduced. Forestry has been taken out of the tax system altogether, and a number of other minor reliefs have been reduced. Of course, with lower tax rates, there is both less need for tax reliefs (or shelters) and less benefit to be obtained from them.

c. Simpler Tax System

Lower marginal rates and the reduction of tax reliefs have allowed a much simpler tax system to take shape — simpler for the taxpayer and simpler for the Inland Revenue. As Figure 1 shows, there are now only two rates of income tax (25 and 40 per cent) in contrast to 11 in 1979. Systems have been introduced to give relief at source for mortgage interest and life assurance premiums. The composite rate scheme has been extended to bank deposits. By making significant strides towards simplification, it has become less worthwhile to avoid or evade tax. Avoidance and evasion bring the system into disrepute and involve an expensive diversion of resources.

Figure 1 — Marginal Income Tax Rates, 1978-79 and 1989-90 (married man, with income in 1989-90 prices)

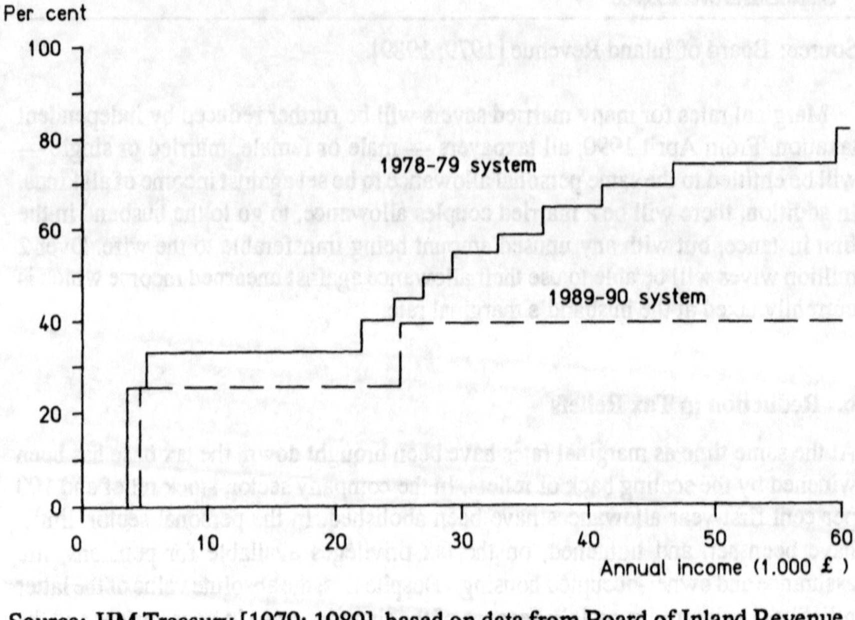

Source: HM Treasury [1979; 1989], based on data from Board of Inland Revenue.

d. Greater Neutrality

The tax system has been pushed towards greater neutrality. Saving and investment decisions are being more strongly influenced by the underlying return or profitability rather than being dominated by tax considerations. One useful indicator of this is the "tax wedge", the difference between pre- and post-tax returns. Such wedges can be calculated in a number of different ways depending on the assumptions about inflation and rates of return. Nevertheless they do give an idea of the relative degree of privilege enjoyed by different investments.

At the household level, the reduction in income tax rates, the greater alignment of capital gains and income, the reduction in inflation and the other measures outlined above have combined to narrow the spread of tax wedges considerably. Figure 2 illustrates this diagrammatically, using the concept of the degree of fiscal privilege defined by John Hills [1984][3] and assuming a constant 3 per cent pre-tax real rate of return on all assets. Much of the narrowing of the dispersion is attributable to the reduction in inflation rather than to tax reform and it has widened again somewhat with the recent upturn in inflation. But overall, the picture is clear: owner-occupied housing, life assurance, and pensions have all become less privileged; other media, equities and deposits, for example, are now receiving more favourable tax treatment.

This move towards a "level playing field" for personal sector savers has gone hand in hand with other policies which have encouraged greater deregulation and innovation in financial markets. Together, these changes have reduced the segmentation of markets, helping to promote fairer competition between different saving media and more efficient capital markets.

A similar move towards greater neutrality has also occurred in the company sector. The pre-1984 system combined a high corporation tax (CT) rate with a narrow base and effectively provided subsidies for investment in plant and machinery, and industrial buildings. The high CT rate also magnified the distortions in the choice between different forms of finance, giving favourable treatment to debt finance in particular. Investment with negative pre-tax rates of return could be made profitable by the tax system, especially where financed by borrowing, thus giving a particular bias to capital intensive projects in the manufacturing sector. The quantity of investment may have been increased, but it was at the expense of quality.

Table 7 shows the extent to which the pre-1984 tax system distorted the incentives to investment by comparing the real pre-tax return needed to earn a 5 per cent real return after corporation tax (but before personal taxes) for different types of investment. These calculations are for a full tax-paying company and assume a 10 per cent nominal post-tax return, an inflation rate of 5 per cent and the 1984

---

3 The degree of fiscal privilege (DFP) is the investor's marginal income tax rate less the effective tax rate (where the latter is defined as the tax paid as a proportion of the real pre-tax return). A DFP of 0 thus represents income tax treatment.

Figure 2 — Fiscal Privilege: 1978/79 and 1988/89 (actual inflation)

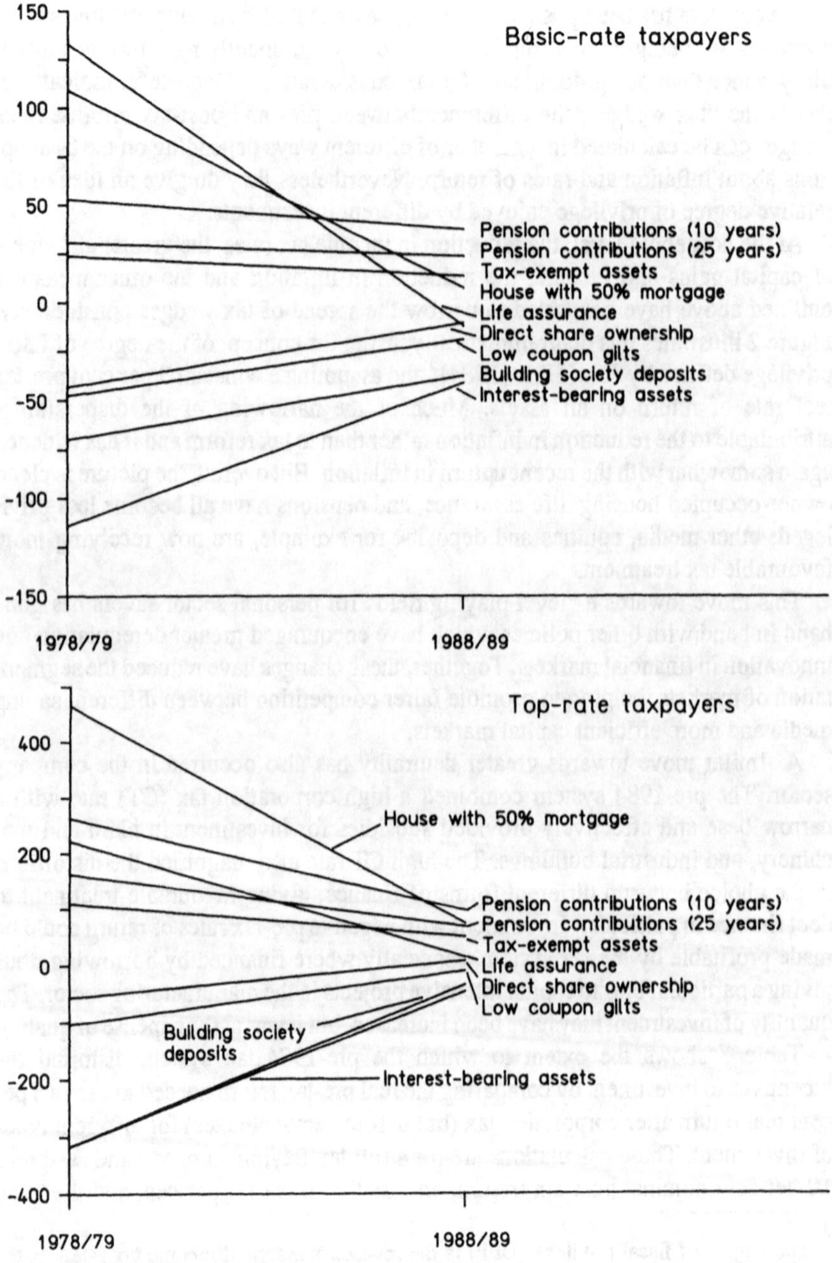

Source: Saunders, Webb [1988]; reproduced with permission.

Table 7 — Pre-Tax Returns Needed to Earn Normal Post-Tax[a]

	Debt finance	Equity finance	Retained profit finance
Pre-1984 regime[b]			
Plant and machinery	–0.2	2.0	5.0
Industrial buildings	–0.1	2.2	5.5
Commercial buildings	3.2	7.7	13.9
Post-reform regime[b]			
Plant and machinery	2.5	3.1	6.7
Industrial buildings	2.8	3.4	7.8
Commercial buildings	4.1	4.8	9.5

[a]After corporation tax, but before personal income tax. — [b]Inflation rate.

Source: House of Commons [1984].

imputation rate of 30 per cent. The same calculations for the reformed system under the same assumptions show that the wide dispersion of pre-tax returns became much narrower afterwards. (Note that a pre-tax return of less than 5 per cent does not necessarily imply a subsidy, since personal taxes also need to be taken into account.)

For example, under the pre-1984 regime, because allowances were much more generous than true economic depreciation, debt-financed investment in plant and machinery could earn a negative pre-CT return but still yield a 5 per cent real return post tax. Investment in commercial buildings financed by equity on the other hand required a pre-tax return of nearly 8 per cent to earn the same 5 per cent post-tax. After the reforms, the corresponding required pre-tax returns were 2 per cent and nearly 5 per cent respectively.

The choice between different forms of finance depends not only on corporation tax, but also on the tax treatment of returns in the hands of the investor. Table 8 shows the spread of total tax wedges (defined here as the difference between the pre-tax rate of return as calculated in Table 7, and the final post-tax return to the investor) for the illustrative case of a basic rate taxpayer.[4] It compares the tax wedges under the pre-1984 company and personal tax rates with those under the rates in force in 1989. Again, the wide range of wedges has been narrowed as a result of the reforms, and subsidies (i.e. a negative wedge) eliminated.

Taken together, these reforms should encourage a more productive use of capital. First, those projects which, despite having a negative pre-tax return, could turn in a profit simply because of favourable tax treatment, ought now to be eliminated. Second, the general assessment made in 1984 was that the reforms raised the marginal cost of capital somewhat, although because of information and index

4 Table 7 uses an illustrative equilibrium cost of capital of 5 per cent to calculate the required pre-tax return. Investors thus receive a real return of 5 per cent before tax. The total tax wedge is then the difference between the pre-tax return and the post-personal tax return in the hands of the investor.

number problems, there are considerable difficulties in weighting up the illustrative figures shown in Tables 7 and 8 to produce aggregate figures. On average, investment will at the margin have to earn a higher rate of return, pre-tax, than before, and the substitution of labour for capital will be encouraged.

Table 8 — Total Tax Wedge for Basic Rate Taxpayer

	Debt finance	Equity finance	Retained profit finance[a]
Pre-1984 regime[b]			
Plant and machinery	–2.2	0.0	1.5
Industrial buildings	–2.1	0.2	2.0
Commercial buildings	1.2	5.7	10.4
Post-1988 regime[c]			
Plant and machinery	0.0	1.2	3.0
Industrial buildings	0.3	1.7	4.1
Commercial buildings	1.6	3.1	5.8

[a]Assuming retained profits are capitalised one-for-one into share prices; and no allowance made for the benefit of deferral until realisation, or for the capital gains tax exemption. These assumptions almost certainly imply that these figures overstate the effective tax wedge. — [b]Inflation rate 5 per cent, imputation rate 30 per cent. — [c]Inflation rate 5 per cent, imputation rate 25 per cent.

Source: Author's own estimates.

e. Promoting Flexible Markets

Finally, many of the measures have been aimed at promoting flexible markets in order to help improve the performance of the economy. In general, this is probably best served by a move to fiscal neutrality, and the progress that has been made in that direction has already been outlined. But some measures have opened up markets in other ways.

For example, choice in the pensions market has been greatly increased: there is a wider range of schemes, a wider range of pension providers and a wider range of contribution rates. This has been achieved by allowing membership in employers' occupational schemes to be voluntary, by improving early leavers' rights, by extending the privileges of occupational schemes to money purchase schemes and by freeing companies to pay whatever pension they like. This can only be for the good of individual welfare, for competition in the pensions industry and for labour mobility.

Efficiency in the stock market has been raised by the abolition of capital duty on new equity issues and the reduction in the rate of stamp duty, which have markedly lessened the tax on transactions. Full indexation of the capital gains tax (CGT) and the bringing forward of the base to 1982 have reduced the tendency for investors holding assets with large pre-1982 gains to be "locked-in". In 1988-89, the volume of stock market turnover was up by over half on 1985-86.

In addition, there has been a place for some carefully considered tax incentives, to promote more flexible markets. For example, the Business Expansion Scheme has been set up to encourage the flow of new capital into risk-taking small businesses. And several measures have been implemented to encourage wider share ownership — PEPs, employee share schemes and employee share ownership plans.

f. Effects of Reform on the UK Economy

Attempts to draw conclusions about the effects of these tax reforms on the economy must be subject to considerable qualifications. The performance of the UK economy has improved significantly during the 1980s. Since 1980, real GDP growth has averaged about 2 per cent a year, as has labour productivity growth. Investment has grown at 4 per cent a year. Tax reform has undoubtedly contributed to this improvement, but it has not been the only factor at work. It is not possible to compare actual performance with a counter-factual which controls for exogenous changes in non-tax variables.

Tax reform may have contributed to the sharp growth of capital income and hence capital income tax receipts. As Table 3 illustrates, the taxation of capital income rose relative to GDP over the 1980s. This partly reflects the fact that the share of GDP accounted for by income from employment fell from 67 per cent in 1978 to 63 per cent in 1988, implying a corresponding shift towards capital income and income from self-employment. There was also a rise in capital gains and in asset turnover. These economic developments may in turn owe something to the greater average reduction in tax rates on capital income than on labour income, although this is impossible to prove. One can, however, assert with more confidence that the reduction in tax reliefs and in the incentive to avoid tax on capital income may have helped to hold up effective tax rates relative to statutory tax rates.

It is interesting to look in more detail at the rise in taxable income and tax payments in the case of companies. When corporation tax (CT) was reformed in 1984, it was expected that in the long run, CT payments would fall as a result of the reduction in the CT rate. In fact, company profitability has recovered significantly during the 1980s (Figure 3), and this has contributed to the buoyancy of corporate tax revenues. Despite the increase in the marginal cost of capital, company investment has continued to show strong growth — since 1980, UK total fixed investment has grown faster than in any other EC country.

The tax burden is now spread much more equitably between companies and across industries. In 1983, 34 per cent of a sample of 400 firms were tax-exhausted

Figure 3 — Real Rates of Return for Industrial and Commercial Companies (per cent)

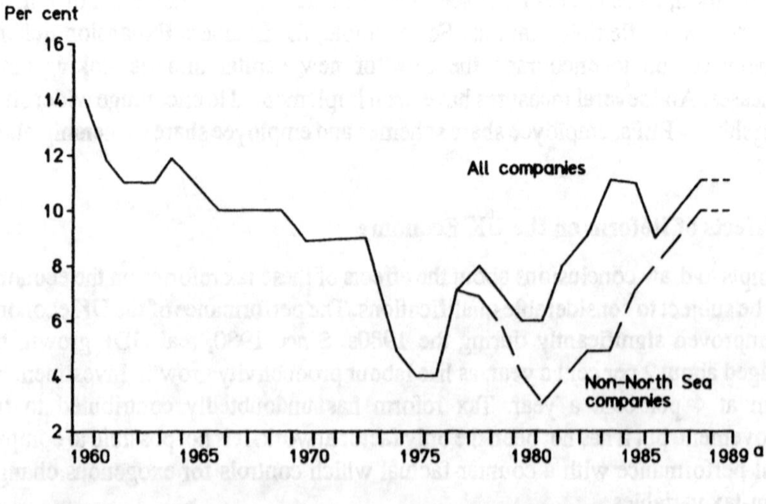

a Forecast for 1989.

Source: HM Treasury [1989].

[Devereux, 1987].[5] The recovery in company profitability has reduced this overhang of tax losses, and the abolition of stock relief and first year allowances has prevented any further build-up. About 35 per cent more companies are now paying corporation tax.

Companies are also paying out more of their increased profit as dividends —again, the fall in the proportion of tax-exhausted companies may be a factor here, since a tax-exhausted company does not benefit from partial imputation as it has no taxable profit to offset ACT against. The payout ratio showed another step change in 1988. Following the 1988 capital gains tax reforms, the bias for higher rate taxpayers in favour of receiving returns in the form of capital gains rather than income has been reduced. So companies may have been induced to increase dividends relative to retentions (although, of course, important institutional players in the market, such as pension funds, are exempt from CGT and so would not directly benefit from a switch in returns from gains to income).

5 A tax-exhausted company is defined as one having negative taxable profit, after deducting capital allowances, stock relief, net interest payments and losses carried forward, but before allowing for ACT and double taxation relief.

5. Lessons from the UK Experience

This section sets the changes which the UK has made during the 1980s in the context of what economic theory tells us about optimal tax systems, interpreted in the light of the complexities of the real world. In doing so, it aims to highlight the practical lessons which can be drawn for the taxation of capital income from UK experience.

a. Possible Goals of Tax Reform

One possible overall goal of tax reform might be to align the tax base with one of the two benchmark tax systems of economic theory — the comprehensive income tax (CIT) or the expenditure tax (ET). Both have their advocates, but neither is without theoretical flaws. Under a CIT, all forms of income would be taxed equally, whether earned or unearned, whether in cash, in kind, dividends, capital gains or imputed returns. This would, in principle, be fairer in terms of horizontal equity, and would equalise the tax treatment of different forms of capital income. But there would be substantial administrative problems in operating a CIT; for example, institutional income would have to be unbundled and attributed to individuals, income in kind would have to be taxed, as would capital gains as they accrued. Allowance would need to be made for inflation in the taxation of interest income as well as capital gains.

The expenditure tax differs from a comprehensive income tax by completely exempting saving from tax. It therefore avoids some of the difficult valuation problems associated with a CIT. By exempting all capital income from tax, it would produce neutrality between different forms of saving, by not taxing any of them. An ET would probably require higher marginal rates than an income tax to yield the same total revenue because of the narrower tax base, and there is a danger that these higher rates would harm work incentives more than an income tax. The tax base could be widened by taxing gifts and bequests at marginal rates, for which a wealth tax might be a suitable proxy. This case would correspond to a tax on lifetime income.

One argument often advanced in favour of the ET is that it would remove the double taxation of saving inherent in an income tax system which is said to impart a downward bias to aggregate saving. There are a number of reasons in practice for being rather cautious about such a conclusion. First, the effective burden of tax may not in practice fall entirely on the saver if competitive pressures mean that relatively heavily taxed assets have to offer a higher pre-tax return. Second, holdings of some assets are likely to be insensitive to the returns on them, which may dampen the impact on total saving of income taxation. Third, the effects of the rate of return on saving is, a priori, ambiguous anyway due to the familiar opposite pulls of the income and substitution effects. Finally, even if saving is depressed to some degree, the tax system also tends to reduce the levels of investment and employment. This raises the very difficult issue of what is the optimal balance of distortions, given that in practice some distortions are inevitable if any tax revenue is to be raised.

b. The Nature of the UK Tax System

The UK system contains both expenditure and income tax elements. Tax reform in the 1980s has not been concerned with moving towards one or the other of these benchmarks. The expenditure tax was explicitly rejected by the then Chancellor of the Exchequer in his 1984 Budget speech when he noted that "even if a root-and-branch change of this kind were desirable, it would, I believe, be wholly impractical and unrealistic". In the same year, he set the seal on this in reforming company taxation, not along the lines of a cash-flow corporation tax, which would dovetail with the ET, but along the lines of the existing system. Both the corporate and personal income tax bases have been broadened.

But, on the other hand, nor has the UK gone down the CIT route. Owner-occupied housing and private pensions are still (effectively) more privileged than they would be even under an ET. And new measures, such as PEPs and personal pensions, which allow savers more favourable tax treatment than they would receive under a CIT have been introduced.

In view of the importance of owner-occupied housing and private pensions in the personal sector portfolio (Table 2), the average tax treatment of the return to saving in the UK is probably closer to the ET than to the CIT, suggesting that the choice between consumption and saving in aggregate may not be badly distorted by the current tax system. It seems probable though that the *marginal* tax rate on additional saving and investment will be somewhat higher, since access to the more tax-privileged forms of saving is limited by ceilings for mortgage interest relief and pension contribution relief, and because these assets are relatively illiquid, lumpy investments or subject to long-term contracts.

c. Efficiency

The main objective of the UK reforms has been to raise economic efficiency. An inefficient tax system imposes substantial deadweight costs, including administrative and compliance costs as well as the costs arising from distorted behaviour. The reduction in marginal tax rates and the broadening of the tax base have reduced distortions and hence increased efficiency.

A related principle is that arbitrary discrimination should be avoided. There *have* been significant moves towards neutrality, but tax treatment has by no means been completely equalised. Contrary to what many commentators suggest, it is not clear that the *net* efficiency gains from a shift to complete neutrality would be worth the effort. But avoidance of arbitrary discrimination really amounts to equal treatment for close substitutes. This has guided the pension reforms, the extension of the composite rate arrangements to bank deposits, and the alterations in the CGT treatment of gilts and company bonds.

By simplifying the system, administrative and compliance costs have been reduced. A recent study notes that ongoing compliance costs are minimised if a tax is as simple as possible, with a single rate, minimum borderlines, minimum reliefs and exemptions and a convenient form of threshold [Sandford et al., 1989]. These general guidelines are consistent with the thrust of UK policy over the past decade — charging fewer taxes, at fewer and lower rates, on a broader base.

There are dynamic as well as static benefits to be gained from improved efficiency. Lower marginal rates, for example, sharpen incentives, which over the longer term will increase the willingness to take risks, increase investment in knowledge and skills and so on. A simpler system with lower marginal rates also reduces the incentives to avoid or evade tax, which is particularly important in the case of capital income taxation. More transactions are likely to be made through the market where prices can do their allocative work.

d. Conclusion

The reforms made to the taxation of capital income in the UK have entailed lower marginal rates, a reduction in tax reliefs, a simpler tax structure and system, greater neutrality, and the promotion of more flexible markets. The lesson to be drawn from the UK experience is that substantial and worthwhile improvements to efficiency are possible, without commitment to a pristine but impracticable theoretical ideal.

The reforms implemented in the UK have been mirrored around the world. A recent OECD survey summarised the position thus: "Tax reform features prominently in the structural adjustment programmes of OECD governments. The common broad objectives have been efficiency, equity, simplicity and ensuring an adequate flow of revenues. . . . Progress has been substantial in reducing distortions that impair economic efficiency, especially those associated with high marginal tax rates and special tax concessions" [OECD, 1989, p. 17].

Bibliography

BOARD OF INLAND REVENUE, Inland Revenue Statistics. HMSO, London, various issues.

CENTRAL STASTICAL OFFICE (CSO), United Kingdom National Accounts. London 1989.

—, Economic Trends Annual Supplement. HMSO, London 1990.

DEVEREUX, Michael, "Taxation and the Cost of Capital: The UK Experience". Oxford Review of Economic Policy, Vol. 3, 1987, No. 4, pp. XVII-XXXII.

HILLS, John, Savings and Fiscal Privilege. Institute for Fiscal Studies, Report Series No. 9, London 1984.

HOUSE OF COMMONS, Fourth Report from the Treasury and Civil Service Committee, Session 1983-84: The 1984 Budget. HMSO, London 1984.

ORGANISATION FOR ECONOMIC CO-OPERATION AND DEVELOPMENT (OECD), Surveillance of Structural Policies. Report by the Economic Policy Committee. Paris 1989.

SANDFORD, Cedric, Peter HARDWICK, Michael GODWIN, Administrative and Compliance Costs of Taxation. Fiscal Publications, Bath 1989.

SAUNDERS, Michael, Steven WEBB, "Fiscal Privilege and Financial Assets: Some Distributional Effects". Fiscal Studies, Vol. 9, November 1988, No. 4, pp. 51-69.

HM TREASURY, Autumn Statement 1989. HMSO, London 1989.

Comment on John Odling-Smee and David Lawton, "Reforming Capital Income Taxation: The UK Experience"

Hans-Georg Petersen

The present paper very ably summarizes the UK tax reforms since 1979. For the evaluation, the authors use the existing stock of knowledge about the effect of taxation on the supply of effort, especially the impacts on capital income and capital formation. The argument is rather pragmatic, starting with the hypothesis that high marginal tax rates are harmful for the incentives within market economies [see, for example, Seldon, 1984]. A major concern is the importance of neutrality for the capital income tax system.

The same concern is often put forward in papers that are much more theoretically oriented and that use neoclassical models (at best, general equilibrium models) to derive results that could be used to aid tax policy. But in looking at models that are very sophisticated in a formal sense, one should not disregard the problem that all the marginal or equilibrium conditions are not usually met in reality. Without doubt, the results of comparing different capital income tax schemes with the help of neoclassical models are of great importance; but to obtain definite policy directives from these results requires that the existing distortions should be evaluated and taken into consideration. In practice, as the authors note, this might often be impossible.

This dilemma might have led the authors to opt for policy relevance instead of formal elegance. And the relevance of the paper is undisputed. The discussant has not been confronted with the UK tax system for more than ten years; since then some fundamental changes have taken place. With British understatement, the authors mention that the tax reforms have contributed to the improvement in the performance of the UK economy as well as to greater neutrality. This is surely true, but compared to the tax reforms in the Federal Republic of Germany during the last decade, these substantial changes should be called revolutionary.

It is impossible to comment on all the details of these reforms; therefore, I will concentrate on the major changes. The authors define capital income in a broad sense, so that the impact of capital income taxation is analyzed from the point of view of the company sector as well as the household sector. Under the Schanz-Haig-Simons concept of the "comprehensive income tax base," the taxable base of capital income within the income, corporation, and capital gains taxes covers:

—dividends from corporations,
—interest payments from bank and building society deposits,

—realized capital gains (adjusted for inflation),
—pension payments (contributions to pension funds are tax free).

Without going into detail, following the reforms of the 1980s, the most important UK exception to this treatment seems to be owner-occupied housing (see Odling-Smee and Lawton, this volume, p. 233). A similar situation obtains in the FRG, with the difference that in the UK interest payments on the loans on houses are tax-deductible. Compared to the FRG [see, for example, Petersen, 1986; 1988], the UK tax base is more broadly defined,[1] although the theoretical comprehensive income tax base is not fully achieved because of some pragmatic solutions due to practical pressures. However, the treatment of capital income in the UK seems to be much more neutral than in the German income and corporation tax system, which discriminates between different productive assets.

A major result of the UK reforms is that since 1988 the capital gains tax (which does not exist in the FRG) has been integrated into (or perhaps better, harmonized with) the income and corporation tax. But major changes have also been made to the structure of the tax rates. The highly progressive income tax schedule — which formerly had marginal rates up to 83 percent, and up to 98 percent including the abolished investment income surcharge (see Odling-Smee and Lawton, this volume, p. 237) — was replaced by a two-bracket income tax schedule with a basic marginal rate of 25 percent and the higher rate of 40 percent [for further details, see Sutherland, 1990, p. 309]; since 1979, the highest marginal rate has been more than halved — compared to the reduction in the FRG marginal rate from 56 to 53 percent in 1990, the Thatcher administration has executed a real turnaround in tax policy.

Beyond this, the double-taxation of dividends has been substantially reduced; the system is organized differently from the system in the FRG, but it seems to yield the same results (see Odling-Smee and Lawton, this volume, footnote 1). Presently, the highest marginal rate in the direct tax system (including the inheritance tax) in the UK is 40 percent. The rate for the corporation tax has been reduced from 52 to 35 percent, but the 100 percent first year allowances have been replaced by smaller allowances spread over several years.

The broadening of the tax base and the reduction in marginal rates were accompanied by a real simplification of the British tax system. The view of mainstream economics is that such reforms would have a strong impact on economic activities, especially the supply of effort (labor supply, saving and investment behavior, etc.). The authors have only some rough assumptions about the impact

1 In the FRG, interest receipts from banks and government bonds belong in principle to the taxable base; but because these receipts are not liable to the withholding tax (as in the case of dividends from corporations), the majority of interest receipts are not reported to the fisc, thus leading to tax evasion. Realized capital gains are mainly tax free, and so are pension payments because of the existing exemptions for pensioners. Therefore, the loopholes in the German income tax base seem to be much larger than those in the UK [see Petersen, 1986].

on the labor supply, but this aspect of the tax reform, as interesting and important it might be, is beyond the scope of this paper. As for the impact on national saving, the authors obviously present Table 1, but unfortunately no interpretations are given in the paper. If one compares the development of the savings ratios in the UK and the FRG since 1980, one sees that the savings ratios in the company sector have increased, but more strongly in the FRG than in the UK; the personal saving ratio in the FRG has remained broadly constant, whereas in the UK this ratio has decreased strongly. The increase in the corporation saving ratio in the FRG could be partly due to a strong increase in firms' profits, and the rise in the UK ratio could perhaps partly reflect the impact of the tax reforms — but there might be a lot of other important factors, besides tax, that need to be taken into consideration.

An effect which seems to be more obvious can be seen in Table 2, which shows the pattern of asset-holding in the personal sector. In 1979, the ratio of housing assets to total personal sector assets was 50.3 percent, a pretty high rate! Let us take housing as an example of a typical durable good. In their first edition, Kay and King [1978, p. 55] present an interesting analysis of the incentives that the former British tax system gave to holding such durables: "If investment in shares, in bank deposits, or in investment property is very heavily taxed, it is not surprising that many rich people buy large houses, or several houses, valuable pictures and furniture, cars, hobby farms, and so on. Such purchases yield no taxable income; their main return is the pleasure they give to the owner, his family, and his friends. . . . if they generate capital gains, these are lightly taxed, and then only if they are actually sold."

One should only add that the speculative profits from holding such assets were taxed at the formerly low rate of the capital gains tax, which could be completely avoided if the sale took place within the shadow economy. Therefore, Kay and King [1978, p. 51] were perfectly right in stating: "The pressure to avoid tax becomes so strong that virtually any avoidance scheme becomes worth-while, and no aspect of the activity in question is of any importance other than its tax implications."

In view of these opinions, it is obvious that the UK tax reforms have had some opportunity costs: trade in objets d'art and antique furniture will become less profitable, and perhaps the sales of auctioneers will be reduced; but at the same time the profitability of productive assets has been substantially increased — a fact which Bracewell-Milnes [1981] regrets [see Petersen, 1983]. In 1987 — the year before the fundamental tax reform of 1988 — the ratio of housing assets (as proxy for the assets in nonproductive areas) declined to 41.0 percent — perhaps as a consequence of the tax changes in 1979 and 1984. The future will show whether the 1988 reform has further improved the incentives to invest in productive assets.

Petersen [1988, Vol. II] has suggested which reforms were necessary for the German direct tax system. Comparing the UK reforms with his blueprint, only the full adjustment of the basic allowances and the income brackets within the income tax schedule are missing, as well as some measures to allow tax rates to be averaged over several years. And the effects of the UK tax reforms reinforce the discussant's assumption that a substantial reduction in marginal tax rates is more important than replacing existing and introducing new taxes. The very first results of this paper are certain proof, but a lot of empirical work still has to be done.

But there are also some minor shortcomings which impair the understanding of this paper. For the structure of the argument, it would have been better to describe the elements of the reform before their effects were analyzed, thus putting some empirical material (for instance, Tables 1 and 2), together with a fuller discussion, at the end of the paper. And there are some open questions that perhaps could have been answered by the authors:

- —Why are the interest payments for government bonds not subject to the composite rate tax (CRT)?
- —To what extent has the double-taxation of dividends been reduced?
- —Do they have any views or presuppositions about the extent of tax avoidance, tax evasion, and tax flight under the current direct tax regime?
- —Are the incentives to save and invest substantially improved?
- —What reforms to direct taxation still need to be made in their opinion?
- —Do the authors (since all my remarks have been made with regard to the principle of economic efficiency) have any information about the distributive effects?

I think we all agree that the answers could only be subjective ones. But in my opinion, the British experience is also of great importance for our tax policy. Hence, reducing marginal tax rates for capital income yielded an increasing proportion of capital income revenue to total tax revenue (see Table 3), and the impact of the 1988 reform is still to come. In a paper for the Kiel Week Conference 1979, I analyzed the possibility of Laffer curve effects for the total tax revenue with respect to the macroeconomic tax rate [see Petersen, 1981; 1984]. At that time this hypothesis had to be rejected. Although I was right in the short run, I must confess that I was wrong in the long run. Looking at the British experience with tax reforms, it might become possible to verify such effects, at least for certain kinds of income. One should be aware that such effects are not only due to the reduced scale of tax avoidance and tax evasion, but also to the progress made in the direction of a comprehensive tax base.

However, in the history of taxation the British tax system has more than once been a model for German economists as well as tax politicians. In the postwar period this changed. But today again, we should admire the courage of the UK tax reformers and use their example as a yardstick for our future tax policy.

Bibliography

BRACEWELL-MILNES, Barry, The Taxation of Industry. Fiscal Barriers to the Creation of Wealth. London 1981.

KAY, John A., Mervyn A. KING, The British Tax System. Oxford 1978 (3. Ed. 1983).

PETERSEN, Hans-Georg, "Taxes, Tax System and Economic Growth." In: Herbert GIERSCH (Ed.), Towards an Explanation of Economic Growth. Symposium 1980. Tübingen 1981, pp. 313-247.

—, "Book Review on Bracewell-Milnes." Finanzarchiv, N.F., Vol. 43, 1983, pp. 507-508.

—, "Impact of the Tax System. Federal Republic of Germany." In: Walter BLOCK, Michael WALKER (Eds.), Taxation: An International Perspective. Vancouver, B.C., 1984, pp. 283-329.

—, "Steuer- und Sozialreform, aber wie?" Wirtschaftsdienst, Vol. 66, 1986, pp. 599-607.

—, Finanzwissenschaft, Vol. I, II. Stuttgart 1988.

SELDON, Arthur, "Taxation in the United Kingdom." In: Walter BLOCK, Michael WALKER (Eds.), Taxation: An International Perspective. Vancouver, B.C., 1984, pp. 157-213.

SUTHERLAND, Holly, "Simulation Model of the UK Tax and Benefit Model." In: Johann K. BRUNNER, Hans-Georg PETERSEN (Eds.), Prospects and Limits of Simulation Models in Tax and Transfer Policy. New York 1990.

Dieter Schneider

Capital Income Taxation in the Federal Republic of Germany — An Assessment from an Efficiency Perspective

1. The Entrepreneurial Approach to Efficiency

Efficiency in the usual sense of production efficiency is related to models of tax neutrality in investment and/or in capital costs. This *neutrality approach to efficiency* is an implication of the assumed existence of an equilibrium in perfect and complete capital markets. But in such an equilibrium the observable consequences of taxation (the liquidity problems of tax payment, the activities necessary to raise taxes, such as filing a tax return or accounting) are defined away, and the fact that corporations as taxpayers are decision units that are separate from their owners is disregarded.

The neutrality approach to efficiency does not inform about the direction of the path to be followed to erect a state of equilibrium starting from an observable disequilibrium, where entrepreneurs invest because of positive expected capital values in the majority of the expected future states of the world. This path is not marked out by tax legislation, and is only deduced as a mathematical necessity for a zero point of competition (the equilibrium itself). It is well known that the dynamic process of erecting a state of equilibrium requires mathematical conditions completely different from those which are used to prove the existence of an equilibrium.

In such a dynamic context, it is especially doubtful whether intertemporal allocative efficiency creates a real problem. In a world with uncertainty in entrepreneurial planning and asymmetric information between competitors on the demand side and supply side, one can forget that ex ante plan coordination (if it exists) leads to a realized unique market interest rate that equals the marginal rate of return of capital in firms, and allows households to save or finance their consumption corresponding to their subjective rates of time preference. If it is true that one cannot know today what one will know in the future [Popper, 1950/51, pp. 118f.], then one plans in such a way that one cannot plan anything (i.e., there will be ex post surprises), and all equilibrium theory is reduced to a juggling act with more or less hazy notions describing the hopes for plan coordination. But this plan coordination as it relates to intertemporal allocative efficiency is extremely improbable for three reasons:

- —Most corporations are independent decision makers that are separate from households. Group decisions in corporations can practically never end in a unique time preference in consumption; the well-known problems of social welfare functions appear here, too.
- —The central bank policy and the creation of money by banks give no reason for the marginal productivity of real capital to equal the time preference of household consumption.
- —The variety of financial markets cannot be augmented by all real-capital markets in such a way that a competitive equilibrium interest rate exists. The implied consequence is that in such an equilibrium, money (outside a numéraire) has to vanish.

Contrary to the neutrality approach, the ***entrepreneurial approach to efficiency*** focuses on the influence taxes have on entrepreneurs' decisions, especially corporate investment decisions, when uncertainty and asymmetric information exist between entrepreneurs or investing corporations and their shareholders and bondholders, and especially between these agents in capital markets and the state, which regulates financial markets by commercial and tax legislation.

An entrepreneurial approach to efficiency does not result in any formalized concept of allocative efficiency. Rather, it wants to achieve efficiency in the sense of maintaining the ability to compete. This approach to such a kind of efficiency looks for tax rules that minimize tax arbitrage as well as distortions in the ranking of individual investment decisions, but it does not imply that there results a tendency to any equilibrium point. The entrepreneurial approach to efficiency has to show from the outset how the reality of taxation interferes with entrepreneurial actions in competition, and how taxation distorts the emergence of a spontaneous order (if such an order exists).

Mainstream equilibrium thinking in public finance, with its tinsel of so-called hypotheses about effective incidence, generally ignores

- —that any investigation of effective incidence assumes a knowledge of formal incidence (i.e., the tax burden of each and every taxpayer); and
- —that, up to now, the knowledge of formal incidence is very incomplete, since there are deficiencies in the measurement methodology as well as in the badly arranged details of the tax laws.

Therefore, an assessment of capital income taxation in Germany has to focus first on the tax burden borne by the taxpayer. By discussing how German tax law changes entrepreneurial decisions concerning investment and finance, and how it distorts market allocation processes by providing incentives for tax arbitrages, this writer hopes to expand the limited knowledge about formal incidence to some extent. Of course, my assessment of German capital income taxation from an efficiency perspective is restricted to this small progress in our knowledge concerning formal incidence.

2. The Incomplete Knowledge of Capital Income Tax Burden

a. Nominal and Effective Tax Burden of the Taxpayer

Assuming that entrepreneurial decisions are rational, the *changes* in all tax payments between capital using alternatives, i.e., the marginal tax burden, are especially relevant. Here, value-added taxes and excise taxes have to be taken into account, as well as taxes based on property or on income; subsidies have to be deducted.

As concerns formal incidence we have to separate two meanings of tax burden. *First*, the nominal tax burden relates tax payments to income as defined by current tax legislation. Discriminations and privileges in the tax base are ignored. Restricting this nominal approach to profit taxation, the top rate of retained profits in corporations is determined in Germany by adding the business profits tax rate (Gewerbeertragsteuer) and the corporation tax rate (Körperschaftsteuer). More specifically, the business profits tax rate is determined by multiplying the local collection rate (Hebesatz), 480 percent in the case of Frankfurt (1988), by the basic rate (Steuermeßzahl), 5 percent, and dividing the product by itself plus one: (480% x 5%)/(1 + 480% x 5%) = 19.35%. Adding this value to the corporation tax rate of 50 percent (1990), applied to the difference between profits and business profits tax, results in a total tax burden of 59.7 percent. If we choose for the business profits tax the average local collection rate of 359 percent (1988), the total burden amounts to 57.6 percent.

The marginal tax burden for a sole proprietorship (including church tax, which amounts to 9 percent of income tax and which is deductible from the income tax) differs between 0 percent and 63.8 percent (the latter rate is applied to salaries above DM 120,000 annual income for unmarried individuals and DM 240,000 for married couples).

Second, the effective tax burden is defined as tax payments divided by a theoretical (neutral) tax base in which the discriminations and privileges of the actual tax base are no longer included. The marginal nominal tax burden and the marginal effective tax burden are equal only in a model with investment neutrality in the tax base.

For an example of the differences between the nominal and the effective tax burden, look at the abolishment (outside of Berlin) of the regional investment subsidy (Investitionszulage) in the German tax reform of 1990. An investment may be used for eight years, yielding a 10 percent internal rate of return. The net cash receipts may diminish in such a way that for this rate of return the earliest tax depreciation for machines (beginning at 30 percent, declining balance method, later combined with the straight-line method) equals economic depreciation. Further, the following is assumed (before 1990): a tax-free investment subsidy of 8.75 percent, which inflows one year after investment, a 56 percent corporation tax rate, and a 360 percent local collection rate for the business profits tax. The cut in the corporation tax rate from 56 to 50 percent in 1990 will not compensate for the abolishment of the investment tax subsidy. To equalize the after-tax rate of return before 1990 and later, a reduction to the minimal income tax rate of 19 percent would be necessary in the case of a reinvestment in subsidized assets, or 44 percent in the case of nonsubsidized reinvestments [Schneider, 1989b, pp. 295f.].

If we regard only firms as taxpayers, a corporate tax wedge is calculated. This is the first step for calculating the tax burden of a saver who has made a profit-linked financing arrangement with a corporation (tax wedge across the capital market). Legally permissible tax evasions, like shareholders' loans instead of equity financing, have to be taken into consideration.

b. The Restricted Empirical Content of International Comparisons of Tax Burdens

The international competitiveness of corporations is influenced by intersectoral distortions caused by taxation. Unsolved problems in international comparisons of tax burdens hinder valid assessments of efficiency distortions. The three common methods of comparing international tax burdens disclose the following main defects:

- Comparing tax rates and tax bases given by law does not provide reliable information. Only the combination of all regulations for tax bases (including loss offset), subsidies, and tariffs can lead to a measurement of the effective tax burden.
- Simulating tax assessments of "typical" corporations [OECD, 1985; Leibfritz, Meurer, 1985; DIW, 1989] only pretends empirical content. First, up to now, such a simulation does not determine marginal effective tax rates, but, at best, average effective tax rates. Second, the empirical assumptions are pretty often based on mistakes, because economists in economic research institutes are not always able to read balance sheets correctly, so that they misinterpret the

modest informational content presented there [for example, see Schneider against DIW, 1989a].

— In calculating marginal effective tax rates, King and Fullerton [1984] and others try to construct tax wedges across the capital market. For this reasonable aim, they combine unrealistic equilibrium conditions with only a limited selection of the casuistic details in the tax laws. Therefore, marginal effective tax rates on investment can only be taken for *paradigms* of how tax law *may* influence profitability. Thus, for Germany, the calculation of marginal effective tax rates given by King and Fullerton needs correcting (Table 1).

Table 1 — Marginal Tax Rates for the Federal Republic of Germany (percent)

	Marginal effective tax rate	Marginal nominal tax rate for profits (corporate wedge)
Original figure	–59 to + 102	up to 65
Corrected for 1980[a]	–20 to + 102	
Calculated for 1990 (3 % inflation assumed)	–35 to + 70[b]	up to 60

[a]The subsidies on investments and the business profits tax are calculated incorrectly in King and Fullerton; other assumptions in question have not been changed. — [b]The reduction from 102 to70 percent is caused mainly by the general legal acceptance by tax law beginning in 1990 of the LIFO method (last-in, first-out method of inventory valuation).

Source: King, Fullerton [1984, pp. 318-320]; own calculations.

Calculations of the range of marginal effective tax rates in the main industrial countries are not available for 1990. The reduction of tax rates after 1980 in the US, UK, Japan, France, etc., does not allow the conclusion that the range of marginal effective tax rates in all these countries has been reduced. First, a reduction of tax rates shortens the "after tax value" of deductible expenses, though it increases the profit after tax. Second, the tax bases have often been changed together with the reduction of tax rates.

A reduced range of marginal effective tax rates could be interpreted as a sign of smaller distortions in intersectoral efficiency. In my opinion, however, conclusions like this are not allowable because of the narrow equilibrium assumptions and the limited transformation of tax law into marginal effective tax rates. The following tries to point out more carefully the variability of the tax burden for capital income caused by German tax law.

3. The Burden for Capital Income from Corporate Investment in Germany

a. Excess Burden Caused by Value-Added Tax and Excise Taxes

There are differing views concerning the efficiency effects of so-called indirect taxes. It is wrong that a value-added tax and excise taxes do not influence the efficiency of capital allocation:

— A value-added tax realized "purely," i.e., without special political regulations, lowers the profits of investment in a firm if the firm faces a downward sloping demand curve that does not shift in a profit compensating manner because of treasury expenditures resulting from the value-added tax yield. A value-added tax is mainly profit independent, because all labor costs increase the value added. Therefore, substituting a higher value-added tax for a lower profit tax reduces the risk-taking of risk-averse entrepreneurs. This happens if we assume the same tax yield for a riskless investment that has the same expected pretax utility as a risky one [Schneider, 1989b, pp. 413f.]. Furthermore, we find distortions caused by the political regulations in the value-added tax law. Actually, there are 11 different VAT rates in Germany, and a lot of special regulations in the tax base, all of which distort the demand between the different business branches. Only one important circumstance of corporate investment needs to be illustrated here: Since 1980, advance payments exceeding DM 10,000 have been declared liable to the value-added tax by Article 10, Section 2 of the Sixth EC-Directive. This has been of little consequence for the value-added tax yield because the advance payments have been paid almost only by firms that could reduce their value-added tax liability by the value-added tax they have paid to their suppliers. Nevertheless, the German treasury expected an additional yield of DM 6 bill. in 1980 (1990: about DM 8 bill.). The reason is that the paying firms have to include the value-added tax on the asset side of the balance sheet without being permitted to charge the profit and loss account. One percent more in the value-added tax implies about DM 600 mill. additional yield in profit taxes.

— Quantification of the excess burden caused by excise taxes is only possible in the case of the single firm that is taxed. An ecologic tax system, recently becoming popular, together with higher excise taxes on pollutive production factors or production engineering, will surely diminish efficiency. Whether environmental pollution will be restricted to a desirable extent is uncertain and the consequences for distribution are still ambiguous because an increase in prices will hit the poor harder than the rich.

—The composition of the German tax yield according to source is as follows: the value-added tax accounts for 25 percent of the total yield; the excise taxes account for 11 percent; taxes on property for 4 percent; the business profits tax for 6 percent; the corporation tax, assessed income tax (partly paid by entrepreneurs) and the withholding tax on dividends account for 15 percent; the wage tax for 34 percent; and other taxes for the remaining 5 percent. The proportion of direct tax yields to total yields is higher in Germany than in most of the other industrial countries. If we accept that indirect taxes imply an excess burden, the German tax system would be less inefficient than that of other industrial countries. For this reason, it seems to be misguided advice when German economic advisory committees recommend increasing indirect taxes in order to decrease direct taxes. At least this seems to be what some politicians imply by maintaining that while the ideal relationship (in percent) of direct taxes to indirect taxes is 50:50, the relationship in reality is unfortunately 59:41 [Breuel, 1988, p. 10]. In this case, precedence has obviously been given to a relationship that would appear to be ideal, rather than to one that is based on economic reasoning.

b. Excess Burden Caused by Taxes Based on Property

Approximately three-fifths of the DM 5 bill. wealth tax yield is paid by firms. The wealth tax rate amounts to 0.6 percent for 75 percent of the tax value of corporate property financed by equity, and to 0.5 percent for other property. The wealth tax payment is not deductible from taxable income.

Across the capital market we find a double wealth tax burden: a corporation pays wealth tax, and the shareholder also pays it on the taxable value of his shares. If the shareholders are not wealth taxable (which often is the case because of tax exemptions and the shareholder's lacking tax ethic), the wealth tax burden, t_w, is given by $t_w = w(1-p)/(1-n)$, with w = wealth tax payment, p = marginal income and church tax rate of the saver, n = marginal nominal tax rate of business profits tax and corporation tax (or income tax for the sole proprietorship). Therefore, if 480 percent is assumed as the local collection rate, the decreases in personal after-tax income caused by DM 1 of wealth tax amounted in 1989 to DM 1.11-2.81 for the shareholder and DM 1.00-2.96 for the sole proprietor. In 1990 the decrease will amount to DM 1.11-2.48 and 1.00-2.76, respectively.

Business capital tax (Gewerbekapitalsteuer) is 0.2 percent times the local collection rate of 480 percent times 75 percent of the taxable value of equity-financed property, the product of which is subjected to several corrections (e.g., one-half of the debts that are not of a short-term nature are added). The yield from the business capital tax will amount to around DM 5 bill. in 1989. The business capital tax is deducted from taxable profit, so that there is a net tax burden of around DM 2 bill. Local land tax will not be taken into account.

The smaller the corporation's rate of return is, the more the wealth tax and the business capital tax raise the tax burden on corporate profits. This is the reason why in some studies branches with poor profitability demonstrate high tax burdens on profit (e.g., 77.7 percent in the textile industry, calculated by DIW [1989, p. 110]). These calculations reveal measurement errors: to include taxes based on property in a tax burden on profits only makes sense for the assumed rate of return and only for the set of additional assumptions concerning the relationship of taxable profits to the taxable value of property.

As taxes based on property have to be paid even in years with losses, they hinder risk-taking by risk-averse entrepreneurs (with only a few exceptions in a Bernoulli-Pratt/Arrow-framework). Compared internationally, Germany's tax burden on property has a relatively high bias towards inefficiency.

c. Tax Privileges and Tax Discriminations Caused by Tax Accounting in General

In an income tax system (including costs of capital in the tax base), the cash flow is a neutral tax base if and only if depreciation and pension reserves, financing payments, costs of capital reinvestments and personal consumption have been excluded. Numerous tax distortions result from differences between this narrow concept of cash flow and accrual accounting. The differences lead to important tax privileges as well as to tax discriminations.

Tax privileges result from cash receipts in the year(s) before tax payment or from tax deductibility in the year(s) before cash expenses. In particular, they result from:

- advance payments for deliveries in the following years;
- accruals and deferred income, e.g., prepayments of rent;
- tax-free income, e.g., from investment subsidies in Berlin, and revenues from foreign investments, which are tax free because of double taxation treaties;
- deductions for inventories that will be paid for in the future;
- anticipation of losses by using the accounting principle "costs or market, whichever is lower," which makes these anticipated losses partly tax deductible;
- accrued liability for pending transactions;
- tax-free capital gains or tax-free reserves for many years in the case of forced sales of land or other investments.

Tax discriminations result analogously from tax payments in the year(s) before cash receipts or from cash expenses before tax deductibility. For example, they result from:

—sales with delay of payments (accounts receivable become higher),
—costs of construction in progress and the manufacturing of products, to the extent that they are higher than payments made in the same year,
—nondeductible expenses like wealth tax, monetary fines, sanctions against cartel agreements, fringe benefits and half of the supervisory board fee.

Most of these privileges or discriminations are of a revolving nature and compensate each other to a different degree from year to year. Up to now, in calculations of marginal effective tax rates, these effects have been left out of consideration.

d. Depreciation

An international comparison of tax laws concerning rates of depreciation shows that German building depreciation seems to be advantageous, depreciations on other goods, however, are not. Besides the very restricted informational content gained by comparing depreciation rates (2.b), depreciation on plants amounts to more than 10 percent of all costs for only a few branches of business, and normally the maintenance expenses of fixed assets that will be charged immediately are at least of that value. Therefore, economists generally overestimate the importance of depreciation regulations for investment policy.

In income tax systems that tax interest, an increase in the profitability of investment will occur only if tax depreciation is higher than economic depreciation. This means, in the case of profitable investments, it must be allowed to deduct more than the investment outlay (i.e., the value of earnings). Only if net cash receipts during the time of investment, the rate of inflation, the rates of interest, and tax rates were the same in all countries, would a higher depreciation rate assure an increase in after-tax profitability.

As long as interest is part of the tax base, tax depreciation regulations can only accidently coincide with economic depreciation. Even a change to full depreciation during the time of investment could be distorting. Regarding uncertainty in planning, immediate depreciation may hinder entrepreneurial risk-taking in many circumstances [Schneider, 1989b, pp. 416-421]. Furthermore, cash-flow taxation induces a maximization of internal finance, with the consequence of minimizing the market allocation of risky capital (the main function of a market economy).

Whether depreciation for tax purposes supports risk-taking depends on:

—expectations concerning the flow of net cash receipts between more or less risky investments in time;
—tax depreciation and accrual of maintenance expenses;

— expectations concerning the structure of interest and the risk of interest rate changes, which results in a hypothetical interest rate used by the risk-taker to calculate capital value and economic depreciation;
— the decision rule under uncertainty. If the Bernoulli-principle is used, it is not sufficient to know the kind of Pratt-Arrow risk aversion, but generally the individual utility function has to be known. Furthermore, the Bernoulli-principle is empirically questionable for individual decisions. In the case of group decisions it cannot be used at all, and important investment decisions are always group decisions.

Therefore, if we understand efficiency as defined by an entrepreneurial approach (maintaining the ability to compete), no tax depreciation regulation (immediate depreciation included) seems to be unambiguously preferable. The distortions caused by depreciation regulations might be reduced by substituting depreciation against an investment subsidy.

e. Pension Reserves

In Germany business pensions for employees are generally financed by pension reserves. Pension reserves not subject to tax now amount to DM 200-220 bill. By law (§ 16 BetrAVG), employees are entitled to a cost-of-living adjustment every three years, but employers are not allowed to anticipate this when calculating pension reserves. Thus, in order to derive the total liability of the firms, an additional amount of DM 20-50 bill. (according to conservative estimates and depending on the method of calculation), must be added to the above DM 200-220 bill.

However, a 6 percent interest rate is assumed when calculating the annuities for the pension reserves (4 percent in Berlin before 1990, 5 percent after 1990), whereas there is a minimum profit requirement to pay interest on long-term debt-financing (which is actually near 9 percent, including half of the business profits and business capital tax burden). In this 6 percent (or 5 percent) interest rate, we find a distortion in competition at the expense of debt-financing in the capital market.

Out of this difference in interest rates arises a special leverage effect in cases of high internal rates of return, making possible an overamortization of future pension payments. But there also exist cases where the tax regulations for pension funds (§ 6a EStG) result in tax discrimination, compared with tax neutral internal financing by means of pension reserves [see Schneider, 1989b, pp. 581f.].

This leverage effect of pension reserves has not been taken into account in determining marginal effective tax rates. It lowers the marginal effective tax rates in big corporations remarkably and distorts efficiency especially between big, profitable corporations and smaller firms with little opportunity to finance internally by means of pension reserves.

4. Tax Burden for Capital Market Income in Germany

a. Nominal Tax Burden of Dividends in Public Corporations

The nominal tax rate for profits distributed to domestic stockholders equals the business profits tax rate for the corporation plus the personal marginal income tax rate plus loss of interest because of the imputation system. This is because the corporation tax rate of 36 percent in cases of distribution and a 25 percent withholding tax on dividends (100 percent – 36 percent) will not be deducted from income tax payment before the following year.

The nominal burden for domestic stockholders differs between 15.25 percent (business profits tax only, if a local collection rate of 360 percent is supposed) and 62 percent (including 53 percent income tax rate, as well as church tax).

Usually it cannot be recommended for corporations traded at the stock exchange to distribute profits and subsequently perform equity financing. Profit retention is advantageous for a sole proprietor whose income is around DM 99,000, if the decision to distribute and take back profits, or to self-finance, does not influence the market price of stocks.

b. Nominal Tax Burden of Profits in Closely Held Corporations

Because of the imputation system, shareholders in closely held corporations can avail themselves of interperiodical progression levelling. The shareholder's tendency towards consumption does not oppose this progression levelling, as he regularly receives (for his services as a manager) a salary or income out of rent and debt-financing agreements between the corporation and the shareholders. This is a special way to reduce the business profits tax.

The shareholders in closely held corporations can get substantial tax reliefs from capital gains taxation if they sell a large interest in, or an independent division of, their corporation. After six months, capital gains derived from selling less than 25 percent of the corporation's shares are tax free for private persons.

From 1990 onwards, profits of up to DM 30 mill. will be taxed, after exemptions are taken, at half of the average tax rate if this limit is exceeded. This capital gains taxation, together with regional subsidies in Berlin, leads to the scandalous situation in which shares may earn important after-tax profits for their holders, although bankruptcy was planned from the beginning. Other forms of tax arbitrage result from special contracts for buildings or apartments. In the last decades this tax-induced "gray" capital market has been one of the most criticized inefficiencies in German capital income taxation.

c. Distortions of Neutrality Caused by the Taxation of Interest

In Germany interest income is not reported to the treasury by banks. It is not allowed to include interest income in the bank's tax audit (§ 30a AO). This is one reason for tax evasion on interest income. In cases of inheritance, banks are required to report to the treasury the assets which belonged to the estate of the late person. From this report, the treasury can calculate approximately how much interest should be declared in the income tax return. A random test conducted by the General Accounting Office (Bundesrechnungshof) in 1984/85 for 827 cases of inheritance showed that only 3.7 to 47.7 percent (on average, one-fourth) of interest income had actually been taxed [see Tipke, 1989, p. 157].

Insofar as interest income is declared (in order to deduct interest payments), violations of neutrality happen if bonds with discounts, especially zero bonds or bonds with attached warrants, are bought by taxpayers that are not obliged to keep account books. Neutrality of interest taxation demands the calculation of economic profit for each financial asset (even cash-flow taxation could only make part of economic profit in interest income tax free, which would considerably reduce the alleged easiness of cash-flow taxation).

For non-bookkeeping taxpayers, debt discount becomes taxable at the moment of disposal or redemption of zero bonds. This leads to three effects of taxation:

- —tax deferral, in contrast to an annual interest-bearing bond without discount,
- —progression evasion, if the discount income is transferred to the pension period,
- —progression compensation, as the disposal can be transferred to years with smaller taxable income.

For closely held corporations, the following tax arbitrages emerge. Instead of the corporation taking over an annual interest-bearing bank loan, the shareholders incur debts and pass them by means of zero bonds to the corporation. The interest payments of shareholders to banks lower the shareholders' taxable income. The corporation's profits decline annually because of the depreciation of the debt discount. In contrast to this, shareholders' earnings from zero bonds are taxed at the time of redemption or disposal; thus, the earnings therefrom are taxed in a progression evasive or compensative manner.

5. The Need for Reforming Capital Income Taxation

German tax law offers a nearly unsanctioned way for households to evade taxes on interest income. In an income tax system, this is untenable for efficiency and equity reasons. German tax law offers numerous possibilities for legal tax avoidance or deferrals, especially through contracts between closely held corporations and shareholders. The legal possibilities permit far-reaching progression levelling, too. Anyone who maintains that constant effective tax rates result in better efficiency than progression rates has to recognize that this "efficiency gain" by means of progression levelling implies unfair treatment of employees or civil servants.

Concerning the tax base, we find a great deal of tax-induced internal financing that has not yet been factored into the marginal effective tax rates. This is one reason for the restricted capital allocation across the market. Supporters of a competitive system will insist that this internal financing constitutes a loss in entrepreneurial efficiency that cannot be quantified.

Proposals to reform capital income taxation have to take into account our restricted knowledge concerning the nominal tax burden caused by capital income taxation and our lack of knowledge concerning the effective incidence. Insofar as it is possible to make assessments, the following order in reforming capital income taxation in Germany seems to be justified:

(a) To cleanse the Augean stables of German tax law means, first, cutting inefficient and unfair taxes, e.g., the tax on equity financing by corporations (Gesellschaftsteuer), the stock exchange transaction tax, and the wealth tax. Second, it seems necessary to wipe away those tax bases that spread the range of marginal effective tax rates and distort the equity of taxation (assessed valuation of real property and business capital, 5 methods of determining income, as well as business profits tax). Third, privileges for pressure groups (special tax-free earnings for farmers, exemptions for nonprofit institutions like labor unions) have to be abolished.

(b) The entrepreneurial approach to efficiency demands improvements in risk-taking concerning innovations and investments by abandoning the wealth tax and the business capital tax, as well as paying interest on carryback and carryforward losses or other means approaching a full loss offset.

(c) To get rid of distortions in tax burden as far as financing by capital market is concerned: equity financing should not be taxed more heavily than debt financing, whereby it is necessary to replace the business tax with a tax that does not discriminate against investments in firms. This could be realized by introducing a local surcharge on income tax (including wage tax) and corporation tax. The revenue would be divided between the community of work and the community of residence.

(d) To match marginal effective with marginal nominal tax rates, internal financing, apart from depreciation (3.d), should be reformed, e.g., a full loss offset instead of accrued liability, a "net cash-receipt" tax base instead of accrual accounting for inventory. The distortions induced by pension reserves can be reduced by adding the increase in pension reserves to taxable salary and increasing the discount rate to near the market rate for long-term debts.

(e) Finally, and only if there is room to reduce tax revenue, the tax rates for income and corporation profits should be lowered. Here are four reasons against lowering the income and corporate tax rates:

— As long as we have a business profits and a business capital tax, cutting the rates for income and corporation tax favors well-paid functionaries of all kinds (politicians, managers and civil servants) more than entrepreneurs, as after cutting the rates for income and corporation tax, the business tax leads to a higher burden. In the case of the top income tax rate, the cut would amount to one-fifth at a local collection rate of 480 percent and one-sixth at a local collection rate of 360 percent.

— A cut in tax rates has a twofold effect on internal financing: an improvement in self-financing through income retention, and a decline in tax-induced internal financing through accrued liability or depreciation.

— A cut in tax rates can hinder risk-taking. Even for the simple case of uncertainty that today can be scientifically reconstructed, the influence a cut in tax rate has on risk-taking is ambiguous. Even if the model conditions are linked closer to reality, the lack of clearness about whether risk-taking decreases or increases still prevails.

— It is a common thesis that cutting top tax rates and introducing linear progression would increase risk-taking as well as the tendency to be innovative. But no proof of this thesis has ever been provided. The opposite thesis is more than 250 years old. It was put forward by Gottfried Leibnitz, David Hume, and especially the cameral scientist von Justi, who maintained in 1766 that "duties which are too low support laziness." This statement may be wrong for today's entrepreneurs and managers, but why should the contrary be right?

Bibliography

BREUEL, Birgit, "Steuerreform aus Landessicht." In: Steuerreform — Steuergerechtigkeit. Universität Osnabrück, Institut für Finanzierung und Steuerrecht, 1988, H. 1, pp. 7-15.

DEUTSCHES INSTITUT FÜR WIRTSCHAFTSFORSCHUNG (DIW), Die Besteuerung der Unternehmensgewinne — Sieben Industrieländer im Vergleich. Berlin 1989.

JUSTI, Johann Heinrich Gottlob von, System des Finanzwesens. Halle 1766 (reprint Aalen 1969).

KING, Mervyn A., Don FULLERTON (Eds.), The Taxation of Income from Capital. Chicago 1984.

LEIBFRITZ, Willi, Cornelia MEURER, Steuerliche Investitionsförderung im internationalen Vergleich. Berlin 1985.

ORGANIZATION OF ECONOMIC COOPERATION AND DEVELOPMENT (OECD) (Ed.), Two Reports by the Committee on Fiscal Affairs on Quantitative Aspects of Corporate Taxation. Paris 1985.

POPPER, Karl R., "Indeterminism in Quantum Physics and in Classical Physics." The British Journal for the Philosophy of Science, Vol. 1, 1950/51, pp. 117-133, 173-195.

SACHVERSTÄNDIGENRAT ZUR BEGUTACHTUNG DER GESAMTWIRTSCHAFTLICHEN ENTWICKLUNG, Arbeitsplätze im Wettbewerb. Jahresgutachten 1988/89. Stuttgart 1988.

SCHNEIDER, Dieter [1989a], "Eine neue Milchmädchenrechnung zur Steuerbelastung der Unternehmensgewinne." Handelsblatt, 11./12. August 1989, p. 5.

— [1989b], Investition, Finanzierung und Besteuerung. 6. Aufl., Wiesbaden 1989.

TIPKE, Klaus, "Die rechtliche Misere der Zinsbesteuerung." Betriebs-Berater, Vol. 44, 1989, pp. 157-159.

Comment on Dieter Schneider, "Capital Income Taxation in the Federal Republic of Germany — An Assessment from an Efficiency Perspective"

Manfred Rose

My expositions are directed more at adding some arguments concerning the efficiency picture of our capital income tax system than at commenting on Schneider's specific assessments. Nevertheless, some of his theses or criticisms that seem to be rather doubtful will not be left undiscussed. In the first part of the following expositions, I would like to make some comments on Schneider's efficiency concept. The second part is directed at working out some efficiency effects on which Schneider did not focus. In the third part I will comment on Schneider's general assessment of the well-known proposal to raise the value-added tax rates in order to compensate for the loss in tax revenue caused by lower profit tax rates and thereby to generate a higher proportion of indirect tax yields in Germany.

1. On the Efficiency Criterion

Held [1872] wrote in his monograph on taxing income that an assessment of a single tax cannot be worked out appropriately without basic principles at which the whole tax system should be aimed. Thus, generally speaking, the first question in this context is whether the tax we intend to assess fits into a good tax system where "good" means "according to the basic principles." Accepting the efficiency view as an approach for deriving guidelines for reforming the current tax system, one should not forget that this is a framework at the secondary stage. But before applying efficiency criteria, we first have to specify the primary functions of taxation. Following the traditional dogmas, the main function of taxes is to raise money in order to finance government expenditures. Wagner [1890] emphasized the importance of the social policy function of taxation that guides the modern fiscal system of income redistribution. Furthermore, we have learned from Lerner [1951] that the economic function of taxes is directed at demand management in order to help government to allocate the disposable resources of an economy between the private and the public sectors without simultaneously producing inflation and/or unemployment. Last but not least, taxes are also an essential component of the set of all the instruments that a democratic political system needs to work out well, i.e., taxes also have — as Wicksell [1896] pointed out — a general political function. It is one of the sad facts of life that politicians and the people from the tax administration usually accept only the fiscal (financing) function of taxation and neglect the importance of the other main functions that should guide good tax systems.

One must now distinguish between the aforementioned tax functions and the principles of taxation, like, for example, the principle of a fair and efficient way of taxing. These principles are applied in order to evaluate different kinds of taxes and different ways of assessing taxes with respect to fulfilling tax functions.

Thus, we can speak of a *(functionally) efficient* tax system if it is impossible to reach a higher degree of realization of all tax functions at the condition of the tax burdens given. Dually, a tax system is *efficient with respect to minimizing tax burdens* if it is impossible to reach the actual degree of realization of each of these functions with fewer tax burdens. The burden-minimizing criterion of efficiency confronts us with the question as to which real tax burdens result from levying specific taxes or from a total tax system. When assessing the efficiency of a tax system with respect to the involved burdens, we have to pay special attention to very specific phenomena of resource wasting, well-known as dead-weight losses of taxation.

In order to discuss taxes from an efficiency point of view, one needs a reference system, which can never be a complete description of the real world and a reference point at the same time. Thus, one can choose an isolated pure agent basis, a partial market equilibrium platform or a system approach. The system approach implies taking into account the phenomenon of the economic interdependency of all agents and outcomes. Schneider rejects this rather comprehensive view of efficiency. He prefers to restrict the tax efficiency analysis to the isolated world of a single economic decision unit, i.e., to the entrepreneurial view of how capital income taxes may produce privileges or discriminations with respect to the ranking of investment and financing alternatives. This may be justified for a lot of reasons, but it remains unclear why a tax system that is inefficient with respect to one agent should also be inefficient with respect to the whole economy. Thus, I cannot see what Schneider bears in mind when he attacks system-oriented assessments of capital income taxes.

Furthermore, I would like to point out that his discussion of marginal effective tax rates as indicators of losses in efficiency is totally superfluous in view of his rejection of a system approach and a Pareto-optimal reference point. What counts here is the fact — and this should not be interpreted as revealing my concerned preference — that unequal effective tax rates result in unequal before-tax rates of return, which implies that the allocation of capital is not Pareto-optimal. But this can only be deduced by taking system effects into account.

2. Taxing Profits from an Efficiency Point of View

Now let me turn to some of the kinds of inefficiencies that are effected by the present capital income tax system and that Schneider does not mention or does not stress in spite of their importance. The aspects of efficiency that I would like to discuss are more theoretically oriented and thus directed more at assessing whether business profits taxes (Gewerbeertragsteuer) can be justified with regard to the tax functions that guide good tax systems.

To begin with, it is necessary to realize where and in which form the incidence of capital income taxes levied on firms usually appears.

a. The Incidence and Real Burden of Profit Taxes — Some Basic Insights

The process that begins with the tax payments of firms and ends with the final incidence is still a matter of theoretical and empirical research. However, one fundamental truth concerning this topic is quite obvious and should be kept in mind when evaluating tax systems. The fact is that the final burden of every tax usually takes on the shape of a personal sacrifice in consumption. Consequently, private households are the carriers of the burden that the current tax system continuously generates. That individuals are forced by way of personal taxes to renounce consumption is quite obvious from this statement. With business taxes, especially in the case of taxing profits that are used as equity funds to finance real investment, the forced renunciation of the consumption of private goods is not immediately recognizable. If this kind of taxation, on the one hand, is neutral with respect to investment, a reduction in private consumption will arise from shifting the taxes forward to the consumers via higher prices of consumption goods. If business profits taxes, on the other hand, cannot be shifted partly or totally and if this leads to a reduction in private investment and in the real capital stock, fewer consumption possibilities will be available in the future.

Summing up, the real burden of the German business income taxes occurs at the household level in the form of utility losses from reduced consumption. But the information as to the distribution of these burdens is extremely limited and I do not believe we have a very good chance of gaining significant insight into it.

b. Some Kinds of Inefficiency that Are Effected by Profit Taxes

I do not claim that the following list of arguments is complete. Thus, for example, the whole spectrum of arguments concerning the allocation of capital will be left out here.

Functional Aspects

The realization that real tax burdens always represent sacrifices in consumption obtains a special meaning from the viewpoint of target-oriented tax policy. In principle, it holds good for all target-instrument problems that the target effectiveness of instrument application should be as direct as possible. Looked at in this way, a rational, good tax system should be characterized by the closest possible relation between the form of assessing a tax, the tax effect aimed at and the effective tax incidence.

The recognition that business profits taxes do effect losses in private consumption, but not in a direct and controllable way, gives the impression that these instruments are not very useful to the government as instruments for handling its basic reallocation task or generating the desired distribution of tax burdens. To bring about the desired reallocation, private consumer demands must be pushed from the market in order to withdraw resources for private use and to make room for public demands. Furthermore, when generating the desired distribution of private consumption, the demands of the more wealthy households need to be reduced in order to make consumption possible for the poor. By taxing capital income, which serves the purpose of financing investment, this job can hardly be done efficiently. The reason is perfectly obvious from the aforesaid. Thus, business income taxes, especially taxes on retained profits, are inefficient instruments with respect to achieving the government's reallocation and redistribution targets in a clear-cut manner. The best way to abolish this inefficiency is to abolish these taxes and to establish a consumption-oriented tax system in which the formal tax incidence, the effective tax burden and the (allocative and distributive) fiscal policy target objects are nearly identical.

Further, efficiency arguments against the existing taxation of income from capital can be put forward with regard to the political function of taxes. In our current capital income tax system, the suffering consumer in general is unaware that his or her tax burden lies well above his or her tax payment contribution. In particular, consumers have no information whatsoever as to what part they bear of those taxes that they do not pay themselves. Fiscal burden illusion exists particularly with respect to the corporation income tax, the personal income tax on profits retained in personally held companies and the business tax (Gewerbesteuer). Therefore, German consumers are — like consumers in other countries — not adequately provided with the information they need to evaluate the net advantages of being provided with public goods and services. For our democratic society, this doubtlessly implies inefficiency with respect to the political voting system, which is based on the idea of perfectly informed voters.

Utility Aspects

The shifting forward of the capital income taxes paid by firms results in new levels of nearly all consumer prices. Thereby, uncontrolled excess burdens may arise for each consumer group. But there is not the slightest possibility of adjusting this effective tax incidence even roughly according to those principles that were developed for optimal commodity taxation in order to minimize dead-weight losses.

If capital taxes paid by firms are not shifted forward and therefore must be borne by the shareholders, the well-known distortion of intertemporal decisions of households with respect to consumption will arise. This negative efficiency effect in the utility space was recently stressed again by Wenger [1988]. Focusing on the statutory rates of all taxes in Germany that reduce the rate of return of an equity-financed asset invested by a corporation, he calculated that the formal incidence with respect to the present value of DM 1.00 spent on future consumption can amount to 827 percent. This calculation was based on a reasonable time span of thirty years between the working phase and the retirement phase.[1] It is to be assessed with respect to the rule of optimal taxation in an intertemporal setting calling for higher taxes on consumption in present working phases rather than on consumption in future retirement. These findings obviously contradict Schneider, who states that "it is especially doubtful whether intertemporal allocative efficiency creates a real problem" (p. 259).

Aspects of Competition

Even if we are right in assuming that the business sector as a whole is successful in shifting forward the profits tax with the aid of additional government expenditure and demand, this is not necesarily true for each single firm. I agree with Schneider that comparable cases also arise from levying our value-added tax, which — one should not forget — is a business tax. Consequently, incomplete shifting may result in a financial burden for the firms concerned and thereby result in a lower rate of investment. Because this effect may be quite different for firms in the same branch of business, competitive disadvantages will arise. Big firms usually have no difficulty in switching to more debt financing. As everybody knows, such options are much more restricted for the small and medium-sized firms. Thus, profit taxation may not only reduce the rate of growth of our economy, but also stimulate the process of concentration.

---

1 The formal incidence (I_f) was calculated according to the following formula:

$I_f = 100 \left(\frac{1}{1+r_a}\right)^{30} / \left(\frac{1}{1+r_b}\right)^{30}$, where r_b is the rate of return before tax and r_a is the rate of return after tax. For more details, see Wenger [1988].

One specific discrimination with respect to capital income taxes is especially worrying German export firms. In realizing a full shifting, they depend primarily not only on a rate-/base-equivalent business profits tax system abroad, but also on the foreign government's demand for goods and services, bringing about the necessary level of prices on the markets for export goods. Some economists believe that such differences in the financial burden of business profits taxes may be compensated by a corresponding adjustment of the exchange rate. But my impression is that these market forces do not work very efficiently. On the other hand, looking at our surplus on current account, German export firms seem to be extraordinarily competitive on foreign markets. The problem which actually exists is that the international capital income tax differentials may induce German firms to move new investment activities to countries with lower tax rates or with better shifting conditions and to deter foreign companies from investing in Germany.

Altogether, this implies additional welfare losses for our consumers and must be seen as a severe inefficiency.

3. Should We Vote for Higher Indirect Consumption Taxes in Order to Finance Lower Profit Taxes?

One obvious consequence of the inefficiencies of the German capital income tax system as elaborated above and in Schneider's paper would be to cut the tax rates concerned and to increase the rates of the value-added tax at the same time in order to keep tax revenue constant.

Schneider is right in pointing out that such a tax reform would not phase out all the distortions discussed above: different firms would face different VAT rates and different possibilities for shifting the VAT to the consumers. This would result in discrimination against those firms that face the highest tax rates and the most unfavorable conditions for shifting. This situation is not very different from the situation with our present business profits taxes — as far as firms producing for domestic markets are concerned. But contrary to the case of the business profits taxes, the export firms would not be discriminated against in relation to their competitors on the international markets.

Enlarging our perspective from Schneider's entrepreneurial view of efficiency to the system-wide view common in the theory of public finance, we have to observe the fundamental principle of the theory of the second best. From this principle it follows that the differentiation of the VAT rates that appears to be a disadvantage from the entrepreneurial view of efficiency can even be a necessary condition for a second-best optimum of the whole economy. For example, it could be efficient to levy a higher tax rate on those goods which are more complementary to leisure than others. Therefore, a uniform VAT rate on all consumption goods would be less efficient than our present system.

Summing up, a transition from the business profits tax to the VAT might be justified on efficiency grounds. But from my point of view, a consumption-oriented revision of the bases of our total system of direct taxation is a much better alternative for abolishing or at least reducing the distortions in the German capital income tax system.

Bibliography

HELD, Adolf, Die Einkommensteuer. Finanzwissenschaftliche Studien zur Reform der direkten Steuern in Deutschland. Bonn 1872.

LERNER, Abba, Economics of Employment. New York 1951.

WAGNER, Adolph, Finanzwissenschaft, II. Teil: Theorie der Besteuerung. Leipzig 1890.

WENGER, Ekkard, "Besteuerung und Kapitalbildung als intertemporales Optimierungsproblem." In: Herbert HAX, Werner KERN, Hans-Horst SCHRÖDER (Hrsg.), Zeitaspekte in betriebswirtschaftlicher Theorie und Praxis. Stuttgart 1988, pp. 279-295.

WICKSELL, Knut, Finanztheoretische Untersuchungen nebst Darstellung und Kritik des Steuerwesens. Jena 1896.

Alfred Boss

Reform of Capital Income Taxation in the Federal Republic of Germany — Policy Options

1. The Problem

Tax reform is a major economic policy issue in the Federal Republic of Germany. Having already adjusted the personal income tax in three steps [Presse- und Informationsamt der Bundesregierung, 1988], the government announced a reform of company taxation during the next period of administration (starting at the end of 1990). There are some substantial defects in the German system of capital income taxation; a relatively low rate of economic growth in the 1980s and persistently high net capital outflows are seen as an indication of this. Possibly, the detrimental effects have increased because several other industrialized countries enacted significant tax cuts and/or tax reform measures during the eighties [Pechman, 1988].

The purpose of this paper is to summarize the major defects in the German system of capital income taxation and to discuss some of the policy options available. These relate to structural tax reform measures that are not necessarily combined with cuts in government expenditures. However, options to cut the level of taxes and expenditures should be given priority because the degree of subsidization is high in the German economy: overall subsidies amounted to DM 128 bill. (6 percent of gross national product) in 1988 [Klodt, Schmidt et al., 1989].

2. Defects in the System of Capital Income Taxation from an Efficiency Perspective

Measuring the defects in a tax system is possible only if measurement criteria are established. The criteria underlying this paper are:

- —neutrality, e.g., with respect to the consumption-saving decision, the kind of financing investment expenditures, the type of investment goods purchased or the choice of the legal status of the firm (corporation versus unincorporated firm),
- —neutrality in the case of inflation,

— the share of investment risks the government bears, and
— the administrative burden.

Thus, liquidity effects of tax policy are neglected; this implies that the analysis abstracts from capital market restrictions. Equity considerations are set aside, too.

An important defect in the German tax system is that it leads to the non-neutrality of the individual's choice between present and future consumption. Because of the dominance of the income tax instead of a consumption tax, savings are discriminated against. The opposite could be considered to be necessary to correct a distortion in the intertemporal allocation of capital.

There are some economic arguments in favor of subsidizing savings [Sinn, 1987b; 1989]. First, a case can be made for some subsidization of savings because of the incomplete guarantee of property rights as concerns material resources (e.g., loss of property as a result of changes in the economic order) or because of positive utility externalities of private savings that are not taken account of in private savings decisions [Marglin, 1963; Sen, 1961]. However, it is not quite clear what the empirical relevance of the argument is. If it is relevant, government interference will not necessarily increase efficiency; government failure instead of market failure might result. Second, as labor supply is variable, second-best considerations according to optimal taxation theory may lead to the conclusion that present consumption should be taxed at a higher rate than future consumption in order to have a kind of substitute for a tax on leisure that cannot be implemented directly. The plausible assumption behind this is that leisure and present consumption are in a stronger complementarity relationship than leisure and future consumption [Sinn, 1987a].

One argument in favor of promoting investment (and/or savings) maintains that tax policy has to compensate the negative effects of wage (wage structure) rigidities on employment. However, following such a line of reasoning would mean taking away the unions' and the employers' associations' responsibility for providing full employment; the responsibilities for the achievement of macro-targets would be blurred. An inefficient assignment of economic policy tools to economic policy targets would be the result.

The arguments in favor of subsidizing savings may be assessed as not convincing. However, discrimination against savings is a major defect in the German system of capital income taxation.

Apart from the basic non-neutrality of overall savings, there are other reasons for the inefficiency in the system of capital income taxation in the Federal Republic of Germany.

First, various forms of savings are exempted from the income tax base (e.g., exemptions for life insurance premiums). Second, investment in inventory is taxed higher than other investment, especially investment in nonresidential construction. Investment in specific regions or for specific purposes is treated preferentially (e.g., by granting tax credits). Third, given the increasing marginal income tax rates, favoring real assets (e.g., by using the realization principle for capital gains taxation or by allowing accelerated cost recovery) and thus discriminating against financial assets results in portfolio specialization [Sievert et al., 1989]. High-income earners see incentives to hold real capital, low-income earners are driven into financial assets. The problem is aggravated because discriminating against financial assets means favoring negative financial assets, i.e., liabilities.

Fourth, equity financing of real capital formation is punished, e.g., by the specific business capital tax (Gewerbekapitalsteuer). Fifth, corporations are generally discriminated against. The specific reasons for both of these defects are as follows [Sievert et al., 1989]: Debt financing of investment is cheaper for the unincorporated firm than financing by issuing equity because the specific taxes on business profits and capital (business profits tax + business capital tax = business tax) need only be paid on part of the debt and on part of the interest on debt. For the unincorporated firm there is tax neutrality between financing by issuing new shares and financing investment expenditures by retaining profits. Comparisons of the legal status of firms show that financing investment expenditures by retaining profits is taxed higher in corporations than in unincorporated firms. This is due to the (additional) tax on corporate property and to the incomplete integration of the corporation and the individual income taxes (i.e., to the deferred shareholder's tax credit for the corporate income tax on retained profits). In the case of debt financing, corporate marginal investment is taxed less than noncorporate marginal investment. If three kinds of financing and two types of the legal status of a firm are compared, debt financing by corporations is taxed at the lowest rate, while corporate financing using retained profits is taxed at the highest rate.

Sixth, "income," e.g., nominal (realized) capital gains, is taxed even if it results from inflation and thus does not indicate a change in real income. A point related to this is bracket creep, i.e., the increase in marginal tax rates as a result of inflation; bracket creep, of course, is a problem for wage income taxation, too.

Finally, the government only imperfectly shares the risk of investors. This is due to the effects of the progressive tax rate structure in the case of fluctuating income and to the restricted (though recently improved) possibilities of carrying losses forward. This point is also related to the tax treatment of profits from innovation [Schumpeter, 1918].

3. Policy Options for Reforming Capital Income Taxation

a. General Comments on the Target of Reform Measures

Any reform measures should aim at abolishing the defects described. This means that the system should gradually approach a consumption tax (possibly a net value-added tax) dominated system.

There are three ways to reduce or even to totally avoid the taxation of capital formation. These are:

- — the exemption of savings from the income tax base,
- — the exclusion of investment expenditures from the (individual or corporation) income tax base, and
- — the exemption of capital income from the tax base.

If capital income were taxed less and if total tax revenues were not to change, other taxes (e.g., the net value-added tax) would have to be raised despite the fact that a partial self-financing of structural reform measures (via higher growth rates of real income) could be expected. However, reform proposals have generally included expenditure cuts as well as tax cuts — apart from structural tax reform measures. Some of the options available are described and assessed in this section.

b. Corrections on the Side of Savers

Abolition of the Company Tax (Gesellschaftsteuer) and the Stock Exchange Transactions Tax (Börsenumsatzsteuer)

The company tax (the tax on new equity of corporations) is an impediment to their issuing shares. It should be abolished because of its discriminating effects (on the different kinds of financing investment as well as on the kind of the legal status chosen by firms). The stock exchange transactions tax has discriminating effects, too.

Both taxes are to be abolished as of 1991 according to an announcement the government made in early November 1989.

Taxation of Consumption instead of Income

Taxing consumption instead of income would mean the end of punishing capital formation; it would eliminate the distortions between different kinds of savings and it would result in less administrative difficulties: problems in measuring depreciation allowances, capital gains, etc., would not occur any longer (for a proposal of taxing consumption in Germany, see Mitschke [1985]; for a US perspective, see Bradford [1986]). Finally, a consumption tax can be viewed as a convincing solution from an equity point of view, too. However, politically there seems to be no chance for a switch from the income-tax-dominated system to a consumption tax system in the Federal Republic of Germany.

c. Corrections on the Side of Investors

Reducing taxes on the formation of real capital means that the resident's investment abroad is discriminated against, whereas — contrary to measures reducing taxes on savings — domestic investment financed by foreigners is fostered. Favoring domestic investment is beneficial from a single nation's perspective; a precondition for this could be the levying of some kind of withholding tax on dividends flowing abroad. At first glance, a misallocation of the world capital stock might result. However, if other countries pursue the same policy, general tax incentives for domestic investment may be adequate from a world welfare perspective, too [Sievert et al., 1989].

Reduction of Taxes on Capital Stock

The abolition of the business capital tax (Gewerbekapitalsteuer) is one of the reform measures that is recommended most often. The tax is a kind of supertax that cannot be found in other countries (except in Luxemburg). For investment projects to be profitable, a marginal productivity of capital above the market rate of interest is required. Thus, the tax discriminates against real capital formation.

The same is true for the general property tax (Vermögensteuer) on business capital. The tax rules even mean double taxation of the corporate sector's business property. The property concerned is taxed at the personal level as well as at the corporate level. Issuing equity is discriminated against; the choice of the economically optimal legal status of a firm is impeded.

Different measures for avoiding double taxation are possible: One solution is to abolish the corporate property tax. Another option is to introduce an imputation (integration) system comparable to the system used in corporate income taxation. A strong point in favor of abolishing the corporate property tax is that no additional prescriptions would be necessary to prevent foreigners from being discriminated against.

Indexation of Depreciation Allowances, Changes in Inventory, Capital Gains and Interest Paid and Received

Indexing the tax system means legislating a formula that automatically removes the influence of inflation on real tax liabilities. Tax indexing is favorable not only because distortions are avoided, but also because automatic tax increases and additional public expenditures as a result of this cannot occur. Indeed, incentives for legislators to pursue inflationary policies would be removed by indexing capital income taxes.

Indexing means not only restructuring the income tax rates, i.e., avoiding bracket creep (as is the case in France, the UK, the United States, etc.), but also eliminating any mismeasurement of income as a consequence of inflation. This relates to prescriptions concerning depreciation allowances, capital gains, inventory (LIFO accounting) and interest income. As to the depreciation allowances, it is possible to allow firms an immediate deduction equal to the present value of the depreciation deductions to which they would be entitled if there were no inflation [Auerbach, Jorgenson, 1980].

Improving Depreciation Rules and Tax Credits

Apart from indexation, other measures for alleviating the depreciation of real assets have been proposed: shorter periods of depreciation, interest on depreciation allowances that cannot be used because of current losses, and depreciation allowances of more than 100 percent or anticipated allowances (favoring uninvested retained profits). Tax credits or tax-free grants are another means of not discriminating against investment. All these measures — though imperfect — are also substitutes for adjusting depreciation allowances in line with the inflation rate.

d. Corrections in the Taxation of Capital Income

Apart from introducing measures relating to the tax treatment of savings and/or investment, there are other options for reforming capital income taxation. Some considerations follow.

Reduction of the Marginal Income Tax Rates

The main issue — in an economic perspective, not in the political debate in the Federal Republic of Germany — is reducing the top rate of the individual income tax. Of course, this can be done together with or without a broadening of the tax base. Reducing the high marginal tax rates (which reached a maximum of 56 percent up to 1989, and which will reach a maximum of 53 percent as of 1990) would probably increase savings. In addition, entrepreneurial activities would become more attractive because the negative effects in the case of uneven income flows would be reduced. The effects of non-indexation of the income tax (e.g., bracket creep) would become less severe. Finally, the corporate income tax rate for undistributed profits could be reduced without creating new distortions with respect to the choice of the legal status of the firm.

A significant reduction of the high marginal tax rates or even the abolishment of the system of (directly) increasing marginal tax rates would be opposed by many groups in the population despite the fact that there is no (economic) justification for having progressively structured tax rates [Hayek, 1983].

Full Integration of the Personal Income Tax and the Corporate Income Tax

The German income tax system is already characterized by a relatively high degree of integration of the individual and the corporate income tax (as a result of a reform in 1976). Nevertheless, integration could be completed by attributing not only distributed profits but also undistributed profits to the shareholders and by taxing total profits at the individual income tax rates.

Cash Flow Taxes

The motivation for a cash flow tax is to apply the principles of a consumption (or expenditure) tax to the corporate sector. Different systems are possible.

The basic principle of the R base (real base) tax is to levy a tax on the net cash flow to the company resulting from its real economic activities [Meade Committee, 1978; King, 1986; Bradford, 1986]. The (tax-inclusive) base is the difference between the receipts from sales of goods and services and the purchases of all goods and services required in the production process (including investment in real capital). Double-entry bookkeeping implies that the tax base is identical to the (tax-exclusive) difference between dividends paid to shareholders and issues of new shares minus real profits from transactions in financial assets (other than equities).

Mainly, the R base tax is characterized by

- —immediate expensing of all investment expenditures (100 percent first-year depreciation allowances),
- —identical tax rates for retained and distributed profits,
- —no deduction of interest paid by corporations (and other firms),
- —no taxation of capital income at the saver's level (otherwise retained profits would be favored).

The same rules would be necessary for unincorporated firms [Sievert et al., 1989]. In addition, the imputed "wage" income of the entrepreneur(s) of such firms would have to be subtracted from the tax base. This "wage" income would be hit — as wage incomes paid by corporations — by the consumption (or expenditure) tax. Negative tax payments or similar arrangements (e.g., tax reserve certificates [Meade Committee, 1978], interest-bearing carryforward of losses) would be necessary in order to have a symmetrical treatment of profits and losses.

The R+F (real plus financial) base tax (the base including expenditures and revenues associated with financial transactions) or S (share items) base tax [Meade Committee, 1978; King, 1986] is neutral with respect to the intertemporal allocation of capital and the kind of financing investment [Sinn, 1985]. Its base is net payments to shareholders. A practical problem with such a tax is avoiding tax evasion that results from paying overly high (untaxed) interest income to shareholders giving loans to the company.

The treatment of overseas investment and profits remitted from abroad would raise some problems if a cash flow corporation tax were introduced. With such a tax the government is a partner in the firm's equity. Thus, there is no obvious reason to grant credit for foreign taxes paid. If, nevertheless, a credit on foreign taxes were granted, the government would not receive the total share in the return on the investment in the firm's activities overseas.

If a cash flow tax were to be introduced, some arrangements for a period of transition would be necessary [King, 1986]. These relate to depreciation allowances not yet subtracted and to "losses" that are expected to be offset against future profits according to the "old" tax system.

A substitute for a cash flow tax of the R or S type was proposed by Sinn [1985]. Contrary to the R base tax, firms should be allowed, according to this proposal, to deduct interest payments — as is the case with an income tax. Interest income, however, would have to be taxed at the receiver's level by the rate used at the firm's level (rate for retained profits). The elements of the proposal are immediate expensing of investment expenditures, identical tax rates for retained profits and the interest income of households (e.g., by applying a flat rate to capital income or by using the rate of the representative shareholder) and a tax on distributed profits.

The advantage of realizing the proposal was believed to be that it was not politically radical. However, the history of the German withholding tax on interest income (Schlesinger, this volume) shows that a precondition for the reform package to be effective, namely, taxing capital income including interest income, can hardly be fulfilled. An international aspect is important, too. It would be advantageous or even necessary to use the source principle when taxing interest income of foreigners; otherwise, income is transferred to foreign countries if the interest rate in relation to the real before-tax rate of return to equity capital rises as a consequence of introducing the new system. However, as concerns interest income, most international double taxation treaties are based on the residence principle of taxation. If the treaties could be changed in the direction of taxing interest income at the source, the Sinn proposal would become more attractive [Sievert et al., 1989].

Using cash flow taxes would mean simplicity of taxation as well as intertemporal and intersectoral efficiency. The measurement of economic income would be removed from the concern of the tax authorities. The calculation of the economic depreciation of an asset and the measurement of realized (and/or unrealized) capital gains would not be necessary; any measures that are required to index the tax system for inflation and that are difficult to implement in practice would be superfluous, too.

Tax Preferences for Undistributed Profits

A preferential tax treatment of undistributed profits has been called for by some of the German employers' associations. However, this would impede the optimal allocation of capital among firms; new firms would be discriminated against. Savings, not necessarily investment in real capital, would be favored. Nevertheless, there are some foreign countries that have decided upon such a measure (e.g., France).

e. Special Issue: Reforming Municipal Taxes

Reforming capital income taxation in the Federal Republic of Germany raises questions as to the revenue-sharing between the federal government, the states (Länder) and the local governments (municipalities). Currently, most of the revenues from the business tax (Gewerbesteuer), which causes inefficiency in several respects, flow to municipalities. These revenues amounted to 43 percent of their total tax revenues in 1988. Reducing the business tax would create distributional problems within the public sector. These problems as well as the allocative aspects concerned cannot be dealt with in this paper. However, any solution should be based on considerations of fiscal federalism. The British solution, the introduction of a community charge (poll tax), is an answer to the question of how to finance parts of the expenditures of municipalities. A local net value-added tax as recommended by some advisory committees [Sachverständigenrat, 1989; Wissenschaftlicher Beirat, 1982] can be taken into consideration, too.

f. Risk-Taking, Entrepreneurial Activities and Taxes

From a risk-theoretical point of view, taxes on business property are detrimental. They reduce the expected net return on investment expenditures without reducing the risk, i.e., the variance of the expected net returns; taxes on business property have to be paid even in the case of losses. The government does not share the investment risk, as is the case with taxes on profits (and losses). This leads to the conclusion that business property taxes should be reduced. However, this is only part of the story. Leaving these taxes unchanged and cutting taxes on profits means that successful entrepreneurs — compared to the less successful ones, i.e., those with fewer profits — would be punished less. And these entrepreneurs may be the ones who bear (and succeed in overcoming) risks that can be influenced by their own entrepreneurial decisions. Risk, i.e., the probability distribution of the outcome of economic decisions, is not necessarily given; the entrepreneur may react to changes in the economic environment [Sievert et al., 1989]. Low profit tax rates are favorable as concerns the entrepreneur's efforts. Thus, any considerations of risk effects in a comprehensive sense do not lead to clear-cut conclusions as to the question of whether capital taxes or profit taxes are worse.

4. Two Examples for Reform Packages

a. The Underlying Reasoning

If it were certain that the level of government expenditures is economically optimal, tax reform would not have to result in tax cuts. However, a large part of public expenditures in the Federal Republic of Germany (DM 80 bill. or 3.8 percent of gross national product in 1988) are subsidies. These expenditures should be cut in order to increase (static) efficiency and competition [Klodt, Schmidt et al., 1989]. This would give a great deal of scope for cutting taxes, especially capital income taxes.

All of the reform measures should be steps towards the realization of a system dominated by a consumption tax, possibly the net value-added tax. Actually, there should be tax rate reductions only. Distortions because of exemptions or tax preferences (loopholes) granted by the income tax would become automatically smaller. This would be all the more so, the longer the process of gradually reducing the (capital income and business property) rates continued.

Along these lines, there are of course different options as to the amount of expenditures and tax reductions. Two tax packages are presented below. They include the abolition of the tax on bills of exchange (Wechselsteuer), the company tax and the stock exchange transaction tax. In 1989, the receipts from these taxes were about DM 1.7 bill. or 0.3 percent of the total tax revenues in that year. However, the abolition of these taxes probably would not mean that there would be losses in tax revenues — at least in the medium run.

b. The Radical Solution

If subsidies in the form of government expenditures were reduced, there would be a great deal of room for cutting taxes. As an example, it would be possible — as of 1991 — to reduce these subsidies by 50 percent (DM 40 bill. or about 2 percent of gross national product) and to cut taxes by the same amount.

In detail, the top rate of the individual income tax and the corporation income tax rate could be reduced to 36 percent. This is a rate in the neighborhood of the rates in other countries. As it is the prevailing rate for the distributed profits of corporations, the need for complementary measures for dividends flowing abroad would be less than in the case of a rate of, e.g., 38 or 35 percent. In addition, the property tax for corporations and the business capital tax could be abolished. This would mean — in a static sense — tax revenue losses for the public sector in the range of about DM 4 bill.

Deciding upon such a reform package would reduce many distortions. All the defects described above would become less severe. The effective marginal tax rates on investment would fall (for simulations of the effects of some measures, see Sievert et al. [1989]). Nevertheless, the income tax rates would have to be reduced further until such time as some kind of consumption tax system (not necessarily supplemented by a personal property tax) emerged. However, the political opposition to tax reform along these lines would be strong, mainly because of distributional or equity considerations.

c. A Significant Improvement

An influential advisory committee to the federal government, the "Sachverständigenrat zur Begutachtung der gesamtwirtschaftlichen Entwicklung," proposed a different reform package in November 1989 [Sachverständigenrat, 1989, Sec. 345-346). It is more in line with prevalent public opinion. It seems to aim at a comprehensive income tax with reduced tax rates. Such a system would leave no space for a property tax. Thus, the general property tax as well as the business capital tax are to be abolished. The latter, together with the business profits tax, are to be replaced by a local net value-added tax for municipalities. The top rate of the individual income tax and the corporation income tax rate are to be identical at a rate of 48 percent or somewhat less. The company tax and the stock exchange transactions tax are to be abolished, too. All these measures would mean a tax cut of DM 13 bill. The tax package would amount to DM 16 bill. if the income tax rates were reduced to 46 instead of 48 percent.

5. Concluding Remarks

Recently, tax policy in other countries has made increasingly apparent that there are some defects in the German tax system, and this has become a powerful argument for reforming capital income taxation. Given tax cuts and/or tax reform measures abroad and given a high degree of capital mobility, comparable tax reform measures at home are recommended by many advisory committees. Otherwise, it is felt that the future real incomes of residents will be lower than in the no-change case, because more domestic or foreign capital would be attracted by foreign countries.

Capital income tax reform measures along the lines discussed would induce more capital inflow into the Federal Republic of Germany and less capital outflow. This would probably lead to reform decisions abroad, just as the tax reform movement in Germany is driven by tax reform activities abroad. If tax competition arose in such a way, it would be a favorable outcome for the world as a whole. It would not justify any harmonization measures within the EC or even the Western world.

Bibliography

AUERBACH, Alan J., Dale W. JORGENSON, "Inflation-proof Depreciation of Assets." Harvard Business Review, Vol. 58, 1980, pp. 113-118.

BRADFORD, David F., Untangling the Income Tax. Cambridge, Mass., 1986.

HAYEK, Friedrich August von, Die Verfassung der Freiheit. 2. Aufl., Tübingen 1983.

KING, Mervyn, The Cash Flow Corporate Income Tax. NBER Working Paper, 1993, Cambridge, Mass., 1986, pp. 377-398.

KLODT, Henning, Klaus-Dieter SCHMIDT et al., Weltwirtschaftlicher Strukturwandel und Standortwettbewerb. Kieler Studien, 228, Tübingen 1989.

MARGLIN, Stephen A., "The Social Rate of Discount and the Optimal Rate of Investment." Quarterly Journal of Economics, Vol. 77, 1963, pp. 95-111.

MEADE COMMITTEE, The Structure and Reform of Direct Taxation. London 1978.

MITSCHKE, Joachim, Steuer- und Transferordnung aus einem Guß. Baden-Baden 1985.

PECHMAN, Joseph A. (Ed.), World Tax Reform. A Progress Report. Washington 1988.

PRESSE- UND INFORMATIONSAMT DER BUNDESREGIERUNG, Aktuelle Beiträge zur Wirtschafts- und Finanzpolitik, Nr. 45/1988 vom 8. Juli 1988. Bonn 1988.

SACHVERSTÄNDIGENRAT ZUR BEGUTACHTUNG DER GESAMTWIRTSCHAFTLICHEN ENTWICKLUNG, Jahresgutachten 1989/90. Bonn, November 1989.

SCHLESINGER, Helmut, "Capital Outflow and Taxation — The Case of the Federal Republic of Germany." In: Horst SIEBERT (Ed.), Reforming Capital Income Taxation. Tübingen 1990, this volume.

SCHUMPETER, Joseph A., Die Krise des Steuerstaats. Graz 1918.

SEN, Amartya K., "On Optimising the Rate of Saving." Economic Journal, Vol. 71, 1961, pp. 479-495.

SIEVERT, Olaf, Hermann NAUST, Dieter JOCHUM, Michael PEGLOW, Thorolf GLUMANN, Steuern und Investitionen, Teile 1 und 2. Frankfurt 1989.

SINN, Hans-Werner, Kapitaleinkommensbesteuerung. Tübingen 1985.

— [1987a], "Alternativen zur Einkommensteuer." In: ARBEITSGEMEINSCHAFT DEUTSCHER WIRTSCHAFTSWISSENSCHAFTLICHER FORSCHUNGSINSTITUTE e.V. (Ed.), Steuersystem und wirtschaftliche Entwicklung. Berlin 1987, pp. 11-50.

— [1987b], Capital Income Taxation and Resource Allocation. Amsterdam 1987.

—, "Neue Wege der Unternehmensbesteuerung: Eine Replik." Wirtschaftdienst, H. 3, 1989, pp. 159-164.

WISSENSCHAFTLICHER BEIRAT BEIM BUNDESMINISTERIUM DER FINANZEN, Gutachten zur Reform der Gemeindesteuern. Schriftenreihe des Bundesministeriums der Finanzen, H. 31, Bonn 1982.

Comment on Alfred Boss, "Reform of Capital Income Taxation in the Federal Republic of Germany — Policy Options"

Julian S. Alworth

The paper by Boss is timely. The effects of capital income taxation on savings and investment decisions have become a much more pressing issue in Germany than in the past. The tax burden on corporations is perceived as being high in comparison to other European countries, at least on paper, while the recent experience with the withholding tax suggests that a significant share of savings manages to escape tax.

My comments will be divided into three parts:

(1) a description of the basic features of the German tax treatment of capital income;
(2) an evaluation of the proposals put forth by the author;
(3) a short outline of possible suggestions for other measures.

1. The Taxation of Savings and Investment: An Overview

a. Personal Tax Treatment of Savings

The personal income tax in Germany applies to the return on all forms of savings and is quite progressive, reaching a maximum of 56 per cent, a rate comparable to that in most other continental European countries, though somewhat higher than in the United States and the United Kingdom.

There are, however, several factors which attenuate the impact of the personal tax system on the return to savings. Firstly, there are incentives to saving in the form of deductions against taxable income for life insurance premiums and deposits with building and loan associations. In addition, savings through company-linked pension funds and interest accruals thereon are exempt from personal income tax. Secondly, there is a widespread perception that the taxation on the return of a number of financial investments is evaded, and the experience with the announcement and brief reintroduction of the withholding tax bears witness to this perception. Thirdly, there are no major incentives to borrow under the personal

---

Remark: The views expressed in this commentary are personal and do not necessarily reflect those of the BIS.

income tax, such as tax deductibility provisions on consumer loans, and there are limitations on the amount of interest payments on mortgage loans that can be deducted from the personal income tax. Finally, there is no capital gains tax on securities held for more than six months.

At the same time, there is a personal net wealth tax (0.5 per cent) levied on the difference between the value of assets and liabilities (less certain deductions). Because of the deductibility of debt, households have an incentive to borrow against their real assets. All the same, underdeclaring the value of financial assets in order to avoid both the wealth tax and personal income tax appears to be widespread.[1]

b. Corporation Tax

The tax treatment of companies appears to be onerous in comparison to other countries. In spite of this year's decline from 56 to 50 per cent, the rate of corporation tax is at least ten percentage points higher than that prevailing in other European countries.[2] With the exception of investment in buildings, depreciation allowances are also somewhat less generous. However, there are two aspects of the financing pattern of German companies which make taxation and its potential effect on corporate investments less burdensome than it appears on paper. Firstly, the separation of banking and industry is less pronounced than elsewhere, which has resulted in firms having a higher debt-equity ratio (and hence higher interest rate deductions) than in other countries (at least up to the early 1980s). Secondly, accruals to pension funds are invested directly in the company to which they are attached and this cash represents a cheap source of finance for firms. A further incentive for debt finance comes from the corporate wealth tax, which is levied on the same basis as the personal wealth tax.

2. Evaluation of the Tax System

Having summarised these provisions,[3] I am left in an unfortunate position since there is very little empirical research on the effect of these provisions on personal savings behaviour and corporate investment. The empirical quantification of the various distortions has not been carried out and the paper by Boss provides no indication of the magnitude of potential problems.

---

1 The valuation of real assets is significantly below market prices.

2 If local taxes are included, the discrepancy is even more significant.

3 Local taxes on both profits and wealth operate essentially as surcharges on taxes levied at the formal level.

My brief summary suggests a very different evaluation of the tax system than that provided by Boss. Firstly, the tax system appears to incorporate a wide number of expenditure tax elements in a haphazard manner which is reminiscent of that which existed at the beginning of the 1980s in other countries, particularly the United Kingdom and the United States. Under these circumstances and in the absence of better information, it is difficult to argue that the German tax system leads to major intertemporal distortions. Secondly, if account is taken of the corporate and personal wealth tax as well as the underdeclaration of interest on certain forms of saving, there appears to be a considerable incentive for debt finance by firms. This incentive is compounded by the close relationship between banks and industry, and by the corporate pension fund system. Thirdly, incentives are targeted to some extent to domestic companies through the pension funds system. Finally, in contrast to debt instruments, the return on equity, whether in the form of retained earnings or new share issues, is taxed quite heavily.

3. The Reform Proposals

In view of these considerations and of the already high level of savings in Germany, it is difficult to argue that changes in the tax system should be directed at *promoting* savings. The prime objective of reform should be to level the playing field amongst the various types of savings and sources of finance. This could naturally be achieved by moving to some form of expenditure tax. Such a reform, however, would place Germany sharply at variance with the rest of the European Community and would be potentially disruptive for international capital flows as argued by the Meade Committee Report.

The more modest proposal of the Sachverständigenrat to scrap the wealth tax at the personal and corporate level (or alternatively to reform it so as to eliminate the deductibility of debt and lower the rate of tax) would eliminate one of the most significant differences between Germany and other countries. Some of the lost revenue could be recovered by taxing financial savings, especially through the enforcement of existing provisions, but also by reforming the tax treatment of pensions. With regard to companies, the corporate tax base should be widened by reducing depreciation provisions that favour investment in buildings, and at the same time, tax rates should be lowered to levels prevailing in the other European Community countries.

List of Contributors

Dr. Julian S. Alworth	Bank for International Settlements, Basel
Dr. Alfred Boss	Institut für Weltwirtschaft, Kiel
Dr. A. Lans Bovenberg	Ministry of Economic Affairs, The Hague
Prof. Dr. Sijbren Cnossen	Erasmus Universiteit Rotterdam
Prof. Dr. Jacob A. Frenkel	International Monetary Fund, Washington
Prof. Dr. Alberto Giovannini	National Bureau of Economic Research, Cambridge, Mass.; Columbia University, New York
Dr. Daniel Gros	Centre for European Policy Studies, Brussels
Dr. Robert P. Hagemann	Organization for Economic Cooperation and Development, Paris
Prof. Dr. Wolfgang Kitterer	Christian-Albrechts-Universität Kiel
Mr. David Lawton	HM Treasury, London
Prof. Dr. Harmen Lehment	Institut für Weltwirtschaft, Kiel
Prof. Dr. Richard M. Levich	New York University
Prof. Dr. Manfred Neumann	Friedrich-Alexander-Universität Erlangen-Nürnberg
Mr. John Odling-Smee	HM Treasury, London
Prof. Dr. Hans-Georg Petersen	Justus Liebig-Universität Gießen
Prof. Dr. Assaf Razin	Tel Aviv University; International Monetary Fund, Washington
Prof. Dr. Manfred Rose	Universität Heidelberg
Prof. Dr. Efraim Sadka	Tel Aviv University
Prof. Dr. Pascal Salin	Université de Paris-Dauphine, Paris

Prof. Dr. Drs. h.c. Helmut Schlesinger	Deutsche Bundesbank, Frankfurt am Main
Prof. Dr. Dieter Schneider	Ruhr-Universität Bochum
Prof. Dr. Christian Seidl	Christian-Albrechts-Universität Kiel
Prof. Dr. Horst Siebert	Institut für Weltwirtschaft, Kiel
Prof. Dr. Hans-Werner Sinn	Universität München; National Bureau of Economic Research, Cambridge, Mass.
Dipl.-Volksw. Stefan Sinn	Institut für Weltwirtschaft, Kiel
Prof. Dr. Joel Slemrod	University of Michigan, Ann Arbor
Dr. Steven Symansky	International Monetary Fund, Washington
Dr. Vito Tanzi	International Monetary Fund, Washington
Prof. Dr. Ingo Walter	New York University

Kieler Studien

Institut für Weltwirtschaft an der Universität Kiel

Herausgegeben von Horst Siebert
Schriftleitung: Hubertus Müller-Groeling

220. Henning Klodt et al., Forschungspolitik unter EG-Kontrolle. 1988. X, 141 S. Broschiert *DM* 47,—. Leinen *DM* 67,—.

221. Bernhard Fischer, Peter Nunnenkamp et al., Capital-Intensive Industries in Newly Industrializing Countries: The Case of the Brazilian Automobile and Steel Industries. 1988. XVII, 325 S. Broschiert *DM* 74,—. Leinen *DM* 94,—.

222. Heike Göbel, Rolf J. Langhammer, Frank D. Weiss, Wachstum im asiatisch-pazifischen Raum. Implikationen für die internationale Arbeitsteilung. 1988. XII, 199 S. Broschiert *DM* 64,—. Leinen *DM* 84,—.

223. Federico Foders, Rüdiger Wolfrum et al., Meereswirtschaft in Europa. Rechtliche und ökonomische Rahmenbedingungen für deutsche Unternehmen. 1989. XIV, 317 S. Broschiert *DM* 88,—. Leinen *DM* 108,—.

224. Konrad Lammers, Regionalförderung und Schiffbausubventionen in der Bundesrepublik. 1989. XI, 207 S. Broschiert *DM* 79,—. Leinen *DM* 99,—.

225. Uwe Corsepius, Kapitalmarktreform in Entwicklungsländern. Eine Analyse am Beispiel Perus. 1989. XIII, 212 S. Broschiert *DM* 79,—. Leinen *DM* 99,—.

226. Adrian Bothe, Die Gemeindeausgaben in der Bundesrepublik. Ein nachfrageorientierter Erklärungsansatz. 1989. IX, 154 S. Broschiert *DM* 63,—. Leinen *DM* 83,—.

227. Torsten Amelung, Die Politische Ökonomie der Importsubstitution und der Handelsliberalisierung. Das Beispiel Türkei. 1989. XIV, 259 S. Broschiert *DM* 78,—. Leinen *DM* 98,—.

228. Henning Klodt, Klaus-Dieter Schmidt et al., Weltwirtschaftlicher Strukturwandel und Standortwettbewerb. Die deutsche Wirtschaft auf dem Prüfstand. 1989. XVI, 219 S. Broschiert *DM* 69,—. Leinen *DM* 89,—.

229. Uwe Corsepius, Peter Nunnenkamp, Rainer Schweickert, Debt versus Equity Finance in Developing Countries: An Empirical Analysis of the Agent-Principal Model of International Capital Transfers. 1989. XI, 128 S. Broschiert *DM* 52,—. Leinen *DM* 72,—.

230. Erich Gundlach, Joachim Scheide, Stefan Sinn, Die Entwicklung nationaler Auslandsvermögenspositionen. Konsequenzen für die Wirtschaftspolitik. 1990. X, 137 S. Broschiert *DM* 55,—. Leinen *DM* 78,—.

231. Matthias Lücke, Traditional Labour-Intensive Industries in Newly Industrializing Countries: The Case of Brazil. 1990. XV, 214 S. Broschiert *DM* 62,—. Leinen *DM* 85,—.

232. Rolf J. Langhammer, Ulrich Hiemenz, Regional Integration among Developing Countries: Opportunities, Obstacles and Options. 1990. IX, 102 S. Broschiert *DM* 49,—.

J.C.B. Mohr (Paul Siebeck) Tübingen

Postfach 2040, D-7400 Tübingen
ISSN 0340 - 6989

Institut für Weltwirtschaft an der Universität Kiel

Symposien- und Konferenzbände

Herausgegeben von Horst Siebert

Emerging Technologies: Consequences for Economic Growth, Structural Change, and Employment
Symposium 1981
Tübingen 1982. VI, 480 S. Broschiert *DM* 98,—. Leinen *DM* 123,—.

Reassessing the Role of Government in the Mixed Economy
Symposium 1982
Tübingen 1983. VIII, 292 S. Broschiert *DM* 72,—. Leinen *DM* 92,—.

New Opportunities for Entrepreneurship
Symposium 1983
Tübingen 1984. VI, 266 S. Broschiert *DM* 62,—. Leinen *DM* 84,—.

The International Debt Problem - Lessons for the Future
Symposium 1985
Tübingen 1986. VI, 193 S. Broschiert *DM* 49,—. Leinen *DM* 69,—.

Free Trade in the World Economy: Towards an Opening of Markets
Symposium 1986
Tübingen 1987. VI, 624 S. Broschiert *DM* 90,—. Leinen *DM* 110,—.

Macro and Micro Policies for More Growth and Employment
Symposium 1987
Tübingen 1988. VII, 369 S. Broschiert *DM* 70,—. Leinen *DM* 90,—.

Services in World Economic Growth
Symposium 1988
Tübingen 1989. VII, 275 S. Broschiert *DM* 66,—. Leinen *DM* 86,—.

The Completion of the Internal Market
Symposium 1989
Tübingen 1990. VII, 387 S. Broschiert *DM* 82,—. Leinen *DM* 107,—.

Reforming Capital Income Taxation
Tübingen 1990. IX, 298 S. Broschiert *DM* 65,—. Leinen *DM* 85,—.

J.C.B. Mohr (Paul Siebeck) Tübingen

For Product Safety Concerns and Information please contact our EU representative GPSR@taylorandfrancis.com
Taylor & Francis Verlag GmbH, Kaufingerstraße 24, 80331 München, Germany

www.ingramcontent.com/pod-product-compliance
Lightning Source LLC
LaVergne TN
LVHW011115300926
849160LV00008B/394
* 9 7 8 0 3 6 7 3 0 0 8 4 5 *